Tempo: Life, Work and Leisure

HOUGHTON MIFFLIN COMPANY · BOSTON

Atlanta · Dallas · Geneva, Illinois · Hopewell, New Jersey

Palo Alto · London

Tempo: Life, Work and Leisure

D. W. CUMMINGS · JOHN HERUM

Central Washington State College

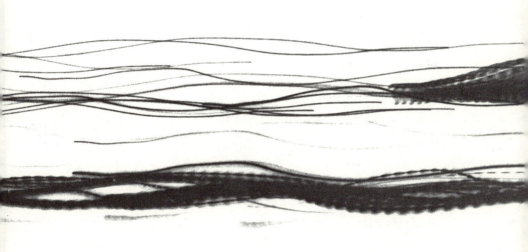

Printed in the U.S.A.

Library of Congress Catalog Card Number: 73-14018

ISBN: 0-395-17839-8

To students everywhere, all of whom must find work

Contents

Preface

Tempo is intended primarily for Freshman English courses. It uses the topics of work, play, and leisure as ways into the academic world of the arts and sciences. It presents selections, often from unlikely sources, that treat familiar practical concerns with the same humane seriousness that has traditionally been reserved for solely academic topics. Rather than starting with the grand themes and ultimate issues and asking students to apply them to daily experience, *Tempo* tries to demonstrate how those themes and issues are implicit in familiar daily concerns and how behind these concerns the ultimate issues remain the eternal ones — like truth and beauty and justice.

Tempo offers a wide range of voices and points of view—those of the novelist, the poet, the philosopher, the psychologist, the photographer, the businessman, the economist, the worker, and it raises contemporary issues such as racism, sexism, schooling, and futurism. But it focuses these voices and issues on what seem to be the recurrent questions for the student: What can I do now? What can I do with the time I have? For the rest of my life? In part, these are questions of time and pacing—questions of tempo. Rather than ignore such questions, *Tempo* starts with them. It starts with the way students question where they're at and where they're going and how they feel and should feel about what they're doing.

The diversity of material, the mixture of abstract and concrete—of formal and informal prose, fiction, poetry, dialogue, and graphics—is not merely for the sake of variety. For students to write well they must gain control over their own voices and points of view. To do this they must get some sense of the variety available to them. They must also learn to look longer at a question than they normally do. The diversity of treatment should help with this long look. The varied activities supporting each selection should help students continue to think, talk, and finally write about their own questions. Not only do the activities encourage them to look closely and analytically at the reading selections themselves, but they also encourage them to examine their own feelings and experiences and help them to analyze the language they already have for talking about the questions raised in the selections. Drawing on some recent work in semantic analysis and values clarification, these activities lead students to connect the material of their own lives with the literary material of the book. Together with the short interfaces between selections, they help students see the implicit interrelatedness of the issues in the book.

Tempo's diversity of materials also offers different points of beginning and emphasis for Freshman English courses. Those emphasizing a decidedly humanistic, philosophical questioning might want to begin with Part 5, "Work and Leisure," and use the questions of spiritual values treated there to center the problems treated elsewhere in the book. Those courses emphasizing more sociological questions might want to begin with Part 2, "The Trouble with Work and the Need for Change," and center the other sections of the book on it. Those courses emphasizing work experience or vocational questions might begin with Part 3, "The Kinds of Jobs," which deals with the ways and problems of finding a satisfying job, and emphasize how all of the other questions in the book can be seen as radiating out from the fit between the worker and his job.

Acknowledgments

Many people helped in different ways to make our work on this text less laborious and at times even playful. Among our colleagues here at Central Washington State College are Keith Rinehart, Tony Canedo, Richard Johnson, David Burt, and Elwyn Odell. David and Elwyn's support started some years back when they organized the symposia that gave us the background we needed to start the work; David also let us use one of his written statements. Among students who helped are Curtis Torp and Leslie Barnhart. Among colleagues elsewhere are the helpfully candid reviewers: Harold Magnuson of the University of Wisconsin, Jack Bateman of Kellogg Community College, Phil Giffin of Yuba City College, and James Nagel of Northeastern University. Anthologists cannot exist without librarians. We thank the staff of the Ellensburg Public Library, and Marie Anshutz and Victor Marx of our college library. The superb secretarial work of Sylvia Uusitalo and Patti Owen made everything easier. And finally we thank Carol and Jackie. They know why.

To the Student

Tempo is meant to be used in classes where writing is expected, and good writing always demands firm control over one's point of view and speaking voice. *Tempo* will help you as a writer find a position from which to look at concerns that will be important throughout your life. The prefaces—or more accurately, the interfaces—linking the selections, as well as the activities and questions that support the selections, are all meant to help you identify and clarify your roles in the often contending worlds of work, play, and leisure.

The readings themselves are grouped around central concerns—concerns about jobs you are preparing to take and about the fun you want to have, and concerns about how you will make enough money and how you will spend the money and yourself. For each area of concern *Tempo* invites you to move among and around a varied set of articulate voices with varied points of view. In each section some voices are deeply involved and talking back to others, while some remain distant, cool, and abstract. But all ask you to listen and respond with sympathy and understanding as you work out your own point of view.

All the sections and their concerns are inevitably linked—not just because an abstraction called Society might force the linking, but also because each of us must participate in jobs and play, work and leisure. Each of us is a crucial link among these various concerns. Each of us is the one who is in the office or out at the stadium, the one working around the house or the one worrying out what kinds of things are really valuable. Our sense of society and how we affect it— that is, our sense of responsibility—matures as we discover how each of the roles we play links to another. As these links become clearer, our stance towards society becomes stronger and more coherent—and more capable, therefore, of being expressed in writing so others can share our sense of how we intend to work and play.

Many people can find themselves in their jobs—and like what they find. Part 1 of *Tempo* examines the satisfactions that work promises and that some jobs provide, satisfactions that ultimately come from the need to create and the need to love. But many people labor at jobs that have little to do with creating or loving, jobs that do not and cannot help them express their own humanity. While they might have been led to expect that a job can help them become more human, become more of what they can be, many people find that their jobs simply do not match those expectations. Part 2 deals with troubles such people have and with the needs for change. Since many jobs are dull, even dehumanizing and downright trivial, it is crucial to try to choose a job that is adequate and satisfying for you. This is the subject of Part 3, which argues that choosing a job wisely depends upon certain kinds of knowledge—knowledge of the range of jobs available and knowledge of oneself.

Part 4 examines people's curious need for play and play's role in any satisfying expression of one's humanity. Play is the spirit that encourages the creative, the venturesome, the exuberant. The spirit of play is not opposed to the spirit of work, for even the most tedious work can be played with. Play leavens work. Still, in spite of everything, no matter how carefully you may choose, no matter how imaginatively playful you may be, there are still jobs that do not satisfy and cannot be made to satisfy, but that, for one reason or another, must still be done. If a person has such a job, he may be able to center his social self off the job. There is work off the job that is worth his doing and there are leisure activities that can engage his mind and body creatively. The time spent away from the job may be the only time a person has to find out who he is. What people do with that time off and what it can mean to them is the theme of Part 5.

Finally, though, there remains a great problem beyond finding one's stance or finding even one's self—at play, at work, or at leisure. All three activities make up a complex system of restless human energies, and in a world like ours, crowded and with the future rushing in on us faster and faster, some people have come to doubt that we will be able even to maintain that system. Part 6 discusses briefly the problem posed for us by the need to find a stance toward our future, the need to balance the system so that we can direct a constant and steady flow of human energies toward the release of human talents.

Tempo: Life, Work and Leisure

The Needs For Work

Work starts with the need to create order out of the chaos of impressions. The deepest sources of pleasure in work lie in the sense of creating order around and within oneself. As the sociologist Peter Berger has said, "To work is to mime creation itself." That work is creative is the first of the two major themes of this section.

Pleasure in work starts in infancy. So do its frustrations. An infant demands and he receives. Wonderful! He demands again and doesn't receive. Not so wonderful. There comes a point when the milk won't come to him and he must fetch it for himself. To do so, he learns to order himself, to order his own body, finally even to order his demands and expectations. He gains a sense of what something is only by bringing order to it or seeing order in it. He learns what water or fire is by learning to order it. He learns what his self is in a similar fashion. The power that is the self is learned and expressed because of external demands—those stubborn doors that refuse to open, those stubborn others who shield and support even as they refuse to be coerced.

One of the ironies of life is that one's sense of self is in great part a gift of others. People learn to value what they do because others value it. They learn to value themselves because others do. They learn how to open doors and control fires because others show them—and help them. As the French philosopher Yves Simon observes in his book *Work, Society and Culture*: "The worker must forever deal with the given realities, whose resistance he often can overcome only through most strenuous effort. It is for these reasons that the worker finds himself permanently in a situation which calls for help, divisions of labor, association."

Thus Simon lays out the second major theme of this section: People need the help of others. Work can be an important source of the feeling of sociality and community—and finally, of love: "The great advantage of work," says Simon, "is that it promotes precisely such feelings and not only among a chosen few but practically among the whole of mankind." Thus we arrive at the two points of focus for any attempt to understand the satisfactions of work: creativity and love.

It puzzled us. We were in Italy, shopping at the cooperative grocery in the small, old town of Fiesole. Relying on the habits of American shopping, we had been buying milk in the largest cartons, but we noticed that we were paying considerably more for the milk that way. The cheapest way to buy milk was to buy the smallest portions. It turned out that that was the cheapest way to buy a lot of things. It all seemed backwards to us, and we asked the manager of the cooperative about it. He gently pointed out that according to the American way, those who could only afford the smallest portion would be paying the highest prices. His way, he was certain, was much better. We thought about it. It made some sense, but we were unconvinced. Surely there was a flaw in his economics somewhere. We began to argue. And pretty soon we found ourselves in the role of Mr. E. L. Winthrop.

ASSEMBLY LINE

B. Traven

Mr. E. L. Winthrop of New York was on vacation in the Republic of Mexico. It wasn't long before he realized that this strange and really wild country had not yet been fully and satisfactorily explored by Rotarians and Lions, who are forever conscious of their glorious mission on earth. Therefore, he considered it his duty as a good American citizen to do his part in correcting this oversight.

In search for opportunities to indulge in his new avocation, he left the beaten track and ventured into regions not especially mentioned, and hence not recommended, by travel agents to foreign tourists. So it happened that one day he found himself in a little, quaint Indian village somewhere in the State of Oaxaca.

Walking along the dusty main street of this pueblecito, which knew nothing of pavements, drainage, plumbing, or of any means of artificial light save candles or pine splinters, he met with an Indian squatting on the earthen-floor front porch of a palm hut, a so-called jacalito.

The Indian was busy making little baskets from bast and from all kinds of fibers gathered by him in the immense tropical bush which surrounded the village on all sides. The material used had not only been well prepared for its purpose but was also richly colored with dyes that the basket-maker himself extracted from various native plants, barks, roots and from certain insects by a process known only to him and the members of his family.

His principal business, however, was not producing baskets. He was a peasant who lived on what the small property he possessed—less than fifteen acres of not too fertile soil—would yield, after much sweat and labor and after constantly worrying over the most wanted and best suited distribution of rain, sunshine, and wind and the changing balance of birds and insects beneficial or harmful to his crops. Baskets he made when there was nothing else for him to do in the fields, because he was unable to dawdle. After all, the sale of his baskets, though to a rather limited degree only, added to the small income he received from his little farm.

In spite of being by profession just a plain peasant, it was clearly seen from the small baskets he made that at heart he was an artist, a true and accomplished artist. Each basket looked as if covered all over with the most beautiful sometimes fantastic ornaments, flowers, butterflies, birds, squirrels, antelope, tigers, and a score of other animals of the wilds. Yet, the most amazing thing was that these decorations, all of them symphonies of color, were not painted on the baskets but were instead actually part of the baskets themselves. Bast and fibers dyed in dozens of different colors were so cleverly—one must actually say intrinsically—interwoven that those attractive designs appeared on the inner part of the basket as well as on the outside. Not by painting but by weaving were those highly artistic effects achieved. This performance he accomplished without ever looking at any sketch or pattern. While working on a basket these designs came to light as if by magic, and as long as a basket was not entirely finished one could not perceive what in this case or that the decoration would be like.

People in the market town who bought these baskets would use them for sewing baskets or to decorate tables with or window sills, or to hold little things to keep them from lying around. Women put their jewelry in them or flowers or little dolls. There were in fact a hundred and two ways they might serve certain purposes in a household or in a lady's own room.

Whenever the Indian had finished about twenty of the baskets he took them to town on market day. Sometimes he would already be on his way shortly after midnight because he owned only a burro to ride on, and if the burro had gone astray the day before, as happened frequently, he would have to walk the whole way to town and back again.

At the market he had to pay twenty centavos in taxes to sell his wares. Each basket cost him between twenty and thirty hours of constant work, not counting the time spent gathering bast and fibers, preparing them, making dyes and coloring the bast. All this meant extra time and work. The price he asked for each basket was fifty centavos, the equivalent of about four cents. It seldom happened, however, that a buyer paid outright the full fifty centavos asked—or four reales as the Indian called that money. The prospective buyer started bargaining, telling the Indian that he ought to be ashamed to ask such a sinful price. "Why, the whole dirty thing is nothing but ordinary petate straw which you find in heaps wherever you may look for it; the jungle is packed full of it," the buyer would argue. "Such a little basket, what's it good for anyhow? If I paid you, you thief, ten centavitos for it you should be grateful and kiss my hand. Well, it's your lucky day, I'll be generous this time, I'll pay you twenty, yet not one green centavo more. Take it or run along."

So he sold finally for twenty-five centavos, but then the buyer would say,

"Now, what do you think of that? I've got only twenty centavos change on me. What can we do about that? If you can change me a twenty-peso bill, all right, you shall have your twenty-five fierros." Of course, the Indian could not change a twenty-peso bill and so the basket went for twenty centavos.

He had little if any knowledge of the outside world or he would have known that what happened to him was happening every hour of every day to every artist all over the world. That knowledge would perhaps have made him very proud, because he would have realized that he belonged to the little army which is the salt of the earth and which keeps culture, urbanity and beauty for their own sake from passing away.

Often it was not possible for him to sell all the baskets he had brought to market, for people here as elsewhere in the world preferred things made by the millions and each so much like the other that you were unable, even with the help of a magnifying glass, to tell which was which and where was the difference between two of the same kind.

Yet he, this craftsman, had in his life made several hundreds of those exquisite baskets, but so far no two of them had he ever turned out alike in design. Each was an individual piece of art and as different from the other as was a Murillo from a Velásquez.

Naturally he did not want to take those baskets which he could not sell at the market place home with him again if he could help it. In such a case he went peddling his products from door to door where he was treated partly as a beggar and partly as a vagrant apparently looking for an opportunity to steal, and he frequently had to swallow all sorts of insults and nasty remarks.

Then, after a long run, perhaps a woman would finally stop him, take one of the baskets and offer him ten centavos, which price through talks and talks would perhaps go up to fifteen or even to twenty. Nevertheless, in many instances he would actually get no more than just ten centavos, and the buyer, usually a woman, would grasp that little marvel and right before his eyes throw it carelessly upon the nearest table as if to say, "Well, I take that piece of nonsense only for charity's sake. I know my money is wasted. But then, after all, I'm a Christian and I can't see a poor Indian die of hunger since he has come such a long way from his village." This would remind her of something better and she would hold him and say, "Where are you at home anyway, Indito? What's your pueblo? So, from Huehuetonoc? Now, listen here, Indito, can't you bring me next Saturday two or three turkeys from Huehuetonoc? But they must be heavy and fat and very, very cheap or I won't even touch them. If I wish to pay the regular price I don't need you to bring them. Understand? Hop along, now, Indito."

The Indian squatted on the earthen floor in the portico of his hut, attended to his work and showed no special interest in the curiosity of Mr. Winthrop watching him. He acted almost as if he ignored the presence of the American altogether.

"How much that little basket, friend?" Mr. Winthrop asked when he felt that he at least had to say something as not to appear idiotic.

"Fifty centavitos, patroncito, my good little lordy, four reales," the Indian answered politely.

"All right, sold," Mr. Winthrop blurted out in a tone and with a wide gesture as if he had bought a whole railroad. And examining his buy he added, "I know already who I'll give that pretty little thing to. She'll kiss me for it, sure. Wonder what she'll use it for?"

He had expected to hear a price of three or even four pesos. The moment he realized that he had judged the value six times too high, he saw right away what great business possibilities this miserable Indian village might offer to a dynamic promoter like himself. Without further delay he started exploring those possibilities. "Suppose, my good friend, I buy ten of these little baskets of yours which, as I might as well admit right here and now, have practically no real use whatsoever. Well, as I was saying, if I buy ten, how much would you then charge me apiece?"

The Indian hesitated for a few seconds as if making calculations. Finally he said, "If you buy ten I can let you have them for forty-five centavos each, señorito gentleman."

"All right, amigo. And now, let's suppose I buy from you straight away one hundred of these absolutely useless baskets, how much will cost me each?"

The Indian, never fully looking up to the American standing before him and hardly taking his eyes off his work, said politely and without the slightest trace of enthusiasm in his voice, "In such a case I might not be quite unwilling to sell each for forty centavitos."

Mr. Winthrop bought sixteen baskets, which was all the Indian had in stock.

After three weeks' stay in the Republic, Mr. Winthrop was convinced that he knew this country perfectly, that he had seen everything and knew all about the inhabitants, their character and their way of life, and that there was nothing left for him to explore. So he returned to good old Nooyorg and felt happy to be once more in a civilized country, as he expressed it to himself.

One day going out for lunch he passed a confectioner's and, looking at the display in the window, he suddenly remembered the little baskets he had bought in that faraway Indian village.

He hurried home and took all the baskets he still had left to one of the best-known candy-makers in the city.

"I can offer you here," Mr. Winthrop said to the confectioner, "one of the most artistic and at the same time the most original of boxes, if you wish to call them that. These little baskets would be just right for the most expensive chocolates meant for elegant and high-priced gifts. Just have a good look at them, sir, and let me listen."

The confectioner examined the baskets and found them extraordinarily well suited for a certain line in his business. Never before had there been anything like them for originality, prettiness and good taste. He, however, avoided most carefully showing any sign of enthusiasm, for which there would be time enough once he knew the price and whether he could get a whole load exclusively.

He shrugged his shoulders and said, "Well, I don't know. If you asked me I'd say it isn't quite what I'm after. However, we might give it a try. It depends, of course, on the price. In our business the package mustn't cost more than what's in it."

"Do I hear an offer?" Mr. Winthrop asked.

"Why don't you tell me in round figures how much you want for them? I'm not good in guessing."

"Well, I'll tell you, Mr. Kemple: since I'm the smart guy who discovered these baskets and since I'm the only Jack who knows where to lay his hands on more, I'm selling to the highest bidder, on an exclusive basis, of course. I'm positive you can see it my way, Mr. Kemple."

"Quite so, and may the best man win," the confectioner said. "I'll talk the matter over with my partners. See me tomorrow same time, please, and I'll let you know how far we might be willing to go."

Next day when both gentlemen met again Mr. Kemple said: "Now, to be frank with you, I know art on seeing it, no getting around that. And these baskets are little works of art, they surely are. However, we are no art dealers, you realize that of course. We've no other use for these pretty little things except as fancy packing for our French pralines made by us. We can't pay for them what we might pay considering them pieces of art. After all to us they're only wrappings. Fine wrappings, perhaps, but nevertheless wrappings. You'll see it our way I hope, Mr.——oh yes, Mr. Winthrop. So, here is our offer, take it or leave it: a dollar and a quarter apiece and not one cent more."

Mr. Winthrop made a gesture as if he had been struck over the head.

The confectioner, misunderstanding this involuntary gesture of Mr. Winthrop, added quickly, "All right, all right, no reason to get excited, no reason at all. Perhaps we can do a trifle better. Let's say one-fifty."

"Make it one-seventy-five," Mr. Winthrop snapped, swallowing his breath while wiping his forehead.

"Sold. One-seventy-five apiece free at port of New York. We pay the customs and you pay the shipping. Right?"

"Sold," Mr. Winthrop said also and the deal was closed.

"There is, of course, one condition," the confectioner explained just when Mr. Winthrop was to leave. "One or two hundred won't do for us. It wouldn't pay the trouble and the advertising. I won't consider less than ten thousand, or one thousand dozens if that sounds better in your ears. And they must come in no less than twelve different patterns well assorted. How about that?"

"I can make it sixty different patterns or designs."

"So much the better. And you're sure you can deliver ten thousand let's say early October?"

"Absolutely," Mr. Winthrop avowed and signed the contract.

Practically all the way back to Mexico, Mr. Winthrop had a notebook in his left hand and a pencil in his right and he was writing figures, long rows of them, to find out exactly how much richer he would be when this business had been put through.

"Now, let's sum up the whole goddamn thing," he muttered to himself.

"Damn it, where is that cursed pencil again? I had it right between my fingers. Ah, there it is. Ten thousand he ordered. Well, well, there we got a clean-cut profit of fifteen thousand four hundred and forty genuine dollars. Sweet smackers. Fifteen grand right into papa's pocket. Come to think of it, that Republic isn't so backward after all."

"Buenas tardes, mi amigo, how are you?" he greeted the Indian whom he found squatting in the porch of his jacalito as if he had never moved from his place since Mr. Winthrop had left for New York.

The Indian rose, took off his hat, bowed politely and said in his soft voice, "Be welcome, patroncito. Thank you, I feel fine, thank you. Muy buenas tardes. This house and all I have is at your kind disposal." He bowed once more, moved his right hand in a gesture of greeting and sat down again. But he excused himself for doing so by saying, "Perdoneme, patroncito, I have to take advantage of the daylight, soon it will be night."

"I've got big business for you, my friend," Mr. Winthrop began.

"Good to hear that, señor."

Mr. Winthrop said to himself, "Now, he'll jump up and go wild when he learns what I've got for him." And aloud he said: Do you think you can make me one thousand of these little baskets?"

"Why not, patroncito? If I can make sixteen, I can make one thousand also."

"That's right, my good man. Can you also make five thousand?"

"Of course, señor. I can make five thousand if I can make one thousand."

"Good. Now, if I should ask you to make me ten thousand, what would you say? And what would be the price of each? You can make ten thousand, can't you?"

"Of course, I can, señor. I can make as many as you wish. You see, I am an expert in this sort of work. No one else in the whole state can make them the way I do."

"That's what I thought and that's exactly why I came to you."

"Thank you for the honor, patroncito."

"Suppose I order you to make me ten thousand of these baskets, how much time do you think you would need to deliver them?"

The Indian, without interrupting his work, cocked his head to one side and then to the other as if he were counting the days or weeks it would cost him to make all these baskets.

After a few minutes he said in a slow voice, "It will take a good long time to make so many baskets, patroncito. You see, the bast and the fibers must be very dry before they can be used properly. Then all during the time they are slowly drying, they must be worked and handled in a very special way so that while drying they won't lose their softness and their flexibility and their natural brilliance. Even when dry they must look fresh. They must never lose their natural properties or they will look just as lifeless and dull as straw. Then while they are drying up I got to get the plants and roots and barks and insects from which I brew the dyes. That takes much time also, believe me. The plants must be gathered when the moon is just right or they won't give the right color. The insects I pick from the plants must also be gathered at the right time and under the right conditions or else they produce no rich colors and are just like dust. But, of course, jefecito, I can make as many of these canastitas as you wish, even as many as three dozens if you want them. Only give me time."

"Three dozens? Three dozens?" Mr. Winthrop yelled, and threw up both arms in desperation. "Three dozens!" he repeated as if he had to say it many times in his own voice so as to understand the real meaning of it, because for a while he thought that he was dreaming. He had expected the Indian to go crazy on hearing that he was to sell ten thousand of his baskets without having to peddle them from door to door and be treated like a dog with a skin disease.

So the American took up the question of price again, by which he hoped to activate the Indian's ambition. "You told me that if I take one hundred baskets you will let me have them for forty centavos apiece. Is that right, my friend?"

"Quite right, jefecito."

"Now," Mr. Winthrop took a deep breath, "now, then, if I ask you to make me one thousand, that is, ten times one hundred baskets, how much will they cost me, each basket?"

That figure was too high for the Indian to grasp. He became slightly confused and for the first time since Mr. Winthrop had arrived he interrupted his work and tried to think it out. Several times he shook his head and looked vaguely around as if for help. Finally he said, "Excuse me, jefecito, little chief, that is by far too much for me to count. Tomorrow, if you will do me the honor, come and see me again and I think I shall have my answer ready for you, patroncito."

When on the next morning Mr. Winthrop came to the hut he found the Indian as usual squatting on the floor under the overhanging palm roof working at his baskets.

"Have you got the price for ten thousand?" he asked the Indian the very moment he saw him, without taking the trouble to say "Good Morning!"

"Si, patroncito, I have the price ready. You may believe me when I say it has cost me much labor and worry to find out the exact price, because, you see, I do not wish to cheat you out of your honest money."

"Skip that, amigo. Come out with the salad. What's the price?" Mr. Winthrop asked nervously.

"The price is well calculated now without any mistake on my side. If I got to make one thousand canastitas each will be three pesos. If I must make five thousand, each will cost nine pesos. And if I have to make ten thousand, in such a case I can't make them for less than fifteen pesos each." Immediately he returned to his work as if he were afraid of losing too much time with such idle talk.

Mr. Winthrop thought that perhaps it was his faulty knowledge of this foreign language that had played a trick on him.

"Did I hear you say fifteen pesos each if I eventually would buy ten thousand?"

"That's exactly and without any mistake what I've said, patroncito," the Indian answered in his soft courteous voice.

"But now, see here, my good man, you can't do this to me. I'm your friend and I want to help you get on your feet."

"Yes, patroncito, I know this and I don't doubt any of your words."

"Now, let's be patient and talk this over quietly as man to man. Didn't you tell me that if I would buy one hundred you would sell each for forty centavos?"

"Si, jefecito, that's what I said. If you buy one hundred you can have them for forty centavos apiece, provided that I have one hundred, which I don't."

"Yes, yes, I see that." Mr. Winthrop felt as if he would go insane any minute now. "Yes, so you said. Only what I can't comprehend is why you cannot sell at the same price if you make me ten thousand. I certainly don't wish to chisel on the price. I am not that kind. Only, well, let's see now, if you can sell for forty centavos at all, be it for twenty or fifty or a hundred, I can't quite get the idea why the price has to jump that high if I buy more than a hundred."

"Bueno, patroncito, what is there so difficult to understand? It's all very simple. One thousand canastitas cost me a hundred times more work than a dozen. Ten thousand cost me so much time and labor that I could never finish them, not even in a hundred years. For a thousand canastitas I need more bast than for a hundred, and I need more little red beetles and more plants and roots and bark for the dyes. It isn't that you just can walk into the bush and pick all the things you need at your heart's desire. One root with the true violet blue may cost me four or five days until I can find one in the jungle. And have you thought how much time it costs and how much hard work to prepare the bast and fibers? What is more, if I must make so many baskets, who then will look after my corn and my beans and my goats and chase for me occasionally a rabbit for meat on Sunday? If I have no corn, then I have no tortillas to eat, and if I grow no beans, where do I get my frijoles from?"

"But since you'll get so much money from me for your baskets you can buy all the corn and beans in the world and more than you need."

"That's what you think, senorito, little lordy. But you see, it is only the corn I grow myself that I am sure of. Of the corn which others may or may not grow, I cannot be sure to feast upon."

"Haven't you got some relatives here in this village who might help you to make baskets for me?" Mr. Winthrop asked hopefully.

"Practically the whole village is related to me somehow or other. Fact is, I got lots of close relatives in this here place."

"Why then can't they cultivate your fields and look after your goats while you make baskets for me? Not only this, they might gather for you the fibers and the colors in the bush and lend you a hand here and there in preparing the material you need for the baskets."

"They might, patroncito, yes, they might. Possible. But then you see who would take care of their fields and cattle if they work for me? And if they help me with the baskets it turns out the same. No one would any longer work his fields properly. In such a case corn and beans would get up so high in price that none of us could buy any and we all would starve to death. Besides, as the price of everything would rise and rise higher still how could I make baskets at forty centavos apiece? A pinch of salt or one green chili would set me back more than I'd collect for one single basket. Now you'll understand, highly estimated caballero and jefecito, why I can't make the baskets any cheaper than fifteen pesos each if I got to make that many."

Mr. Winthrop was hard-boiled, no wonder considering the city he came from. He refused to give up the more than fifteen thousand dollars which at that moment seemed to slip through his fingers like nothing. Being really desperate now, he talked and bargained with the Indian for almost two full hours, trying to make him understand how rich he, the Indian, would become if he would take this greatest opportunity of his life.

The Indian never ceased working on his baskets while he explained his points of view.

"You know, my good man," Mr. Winthrop said, "such a wonderful chance might never again knock on your door, do you realize that? Let me explain to you in ice-cold figures what fortune you might miss if you leave me flat on this deal."

He tore out leaf after leaf from his notebook, covered each with figures and still more figures, and while doing so told the peasant he would be the richest man in the whole district.

The Indian without answering watched with a genuine expression of awe as Mr. Winthrop wrote down these long figures, executing complicated multiplications and divisions and subtractions so rapidly that it seemed to him the greatest miracle he had ever seen.

The American, noting this growing interest in the Indian, misjudged the real significance of it. "There you are, my friend," he said. "That's exactly how rich you're going to be. You'll have a bankroll of exactly four thousand pesos. And to show you that I'm a real friend of yours, I'll throw in a bonus. I'll make it a round five thousand pesos, and all in silver."

The Indian, however, had not for one moment thought of four thousand pesos. Such an amount of money had no meaning to him. He had been interested solely in Mr. Winthrop's ability to write figures so rapidly.

"So, what do you say now? Is it a deal or is it? Say yes and you'll get your advance this very minute."

"As I have explained before, patroncito, the price is fifteen pesos each."

"But, my good man," Mr. Winthrop shouted at the poor Indian in utter despair, "where have you been all this time? On the moon or where? You are still at the same price as before."

"Yes, I know that, jefecito, my little chief," the Indian answered, entirely unconcerned. "It must be the same price because I cannot make any other one. Besides, señor, there's still another thing which perhaps you don't know. You see, my good lordy and caballero, I've to make these canastitas my own way and with my song in them and with bits of my soul woven into them. If I were to make them in great numbers there would no longer be my soul in each, or my songs. Each would look like the other with no difference whatever and such a thing would slowly eat up my heart. Each has to be another song which I hear in the morning when the sun rises and when the birds begin to chirp and the butterflies come and sit down on my baskets so that I may see a new beauty, because, you see, the butterflies like my baskets and the pretty colors on them, that's why they come and sit down, and I can make my canastitas after them. And now, señor jefecito, if you will kindly excuse me, I have wasted much time already, although it was a pleasure and a great honor to hear the talk of such a distinguished caballero like you. But I'm afraid I've to attend to my work now, for day after tomorrow is market day in town and I got to take my baskets there. Thank you, senor, for your visit. Adiós."

And in this way it happened that American garbage cans escaped the fate of being turned into receptacles for empty, torn, and crumpled little multicolored canastitas into which an Indian of Mexico had woven dreams of his soul, throbs of his heart: his unsung poems.

FURTHER THOUGHTS

1. What does Traven's modern parable suggest about the need for creativity in one's work and the obligations of sociality and love?
2. What can a city-dweller in the city center do to achieve anything like the freedom of the Mexican basket-weaver with his less than fifteen acres and the corn he can be sure of? What about a person living in the suburbs?
3. What is the real difference between a factory-made article with its trademark stamped on it and a handmade artifact with its maker's mark scratched on it?

The little play that follows is really a kind of shaggy-dog story—about money, which may be the shaggiest dog of all. But in any case, it is certainly true that most people take jobs to make money. And making money is something the students in this play have some ideas about.

MAKING MONEY

William Saroyan

> *Making Money* is one of twenty-one short plays in a group entitled *Twenty-one Very Short Plays*. It is number fourteen as a matter of fact, and one of my favorites. That's why it's here. I find it funny, but I must remark that a number of very good editors don't agree. Well,

that's what makes great literature, as we say. Six or seven friends telling one another in print that each of them is the greatest going—and *voila,* eminence, or should one say mincemeat? Let the reader decide—I say this is a very funny play. If you find it funny, too, please tell somebody, because I never knew anybody yet who didn't want to know about a piece of funny writing. What I mean is everybody likes something that makes him laugh. (It was written in 1956, I think.)

TEACHER: Now, at this school, which is not unlike a Sunday School, we are to learn how to make money. Why do we wish to make money?

BOY: Because we need money.

TEACHER: What do we need money *for*?

GIRL: For food and rent and clothes and stuff.

TEACHER: What kind of money do we need?

BOY: United States.

TEACHER: Here, then, for each of you to examine is five dollars of United States money. What is it made out of?

GIRL: Some kind of paper.

TEACHER: Whose picture is on it?

BOY: Lincoln.

TEACHER: What is the picture on the reverse side?

GIRL: Lincoln Memorial.

TEACHER: In order to make five dollars, what must we do?

BOY: Make another piece of paper look exactly like this piece.

TEACHER: How can we do this?

GIRL: By some kind of complicated printing and photoengraving.

TEACHER: Which is?

BOY: Hard to do.

TEACHER: Which also is?

GIRL: Against the law.

TEACHER: Illegal, we say. Legal with il before it means not legal. In order to have one hundred dollars worth of money how many of these pieces of paper must we make?

BOY: Twenty.

TEACHER: A thousand dollars?

GIRL: Two hundred.

TEACHER: If we wanted a hundred thousand dollars, how many of these pieces of paper would we need to make?

BOY: A hundred times two hundred, whatever that is.

TEACHER: A great many pieces of this piece of paper. In order to have five million dollars we would need to make one million of these pieces of paper. How little is five million dollars?

GIRL: Five million dollars isn't a little, but it is less than the number of dollars many American families have.

TEACHER: Can you name some of these families?

BOY: Ford, Rockefeller, Kennedy.

TEACHER: How did these families *get* five million dollars? Twenty-five million? A hundred and twenty-five million?

GIRL: They made the money.

TEACHER: And what are we here to learn to do?

BOY: To make money.

TEACHER: How much money?

BOY: Five million dollars. A million for me, a million for her, a million for you, a million for him, a million for her.

TEACHER: A million apiece.

GIRL: Tax free.

BOY: Illegal.

GIRL: But neat.

TEACHER: Our figures are based upon units of five. There are other units. Name several.

BOY: Ten. Twenty. Fifty. One hundred.

TEACHER: Ten, twenty, fifty, one hundred? One moment, please. I believe I have an idea. Can anyone guess what the idea is?

GIRL: Let's not make fives, let's make hundreds.

TEACHER: Precisely. Using less paper we shall have more money. Some for my father, some for my mother. If we make a million of these hundreds we will have a hundred million, or twenty times as much as five million. Will that make us happy?

BOY: Yes.

TEACHER: I am delighted about having gotten the idea because it means so much more money for so many more of us. So let me hear it.

EVERYBODY: Yaaaaay.

TEACHER: Again. Louder.

EVERYBODY: Yaaaaaaaaay.

TEACHER: It's terribly thrilling, I must say. In addition to my father and my mother, I am sure I shall want to give a million each to my son, my daughter, my son-in-law, my daughter-in-law, and something for the poor.

BOY: I've got some people I want to give a million to, also, and something for Alexander.

GIRL: A million each to my father, my mother, my grandfather, my grandmother. Margaret, and something for World Peace.

TEACHER: This is indeed a great thrill.

EVERYBODY: Yaaaaaay.

BOY: Teacher?

TEACHER: Yes, my boy?

BOY: Isn't there a piece of paper for one *thousand* dollars?

EVERYBODY: Yaaaaaaay.

TEACHER: Just a minute, everybody. If there *is* such a piece of paper, and if we make a million of that—

GIRL: There *is* such a piece. I saw it on television.

TEACHER: A thousand million dollars, children?

EVERYBODY: Yaaaaay.

TEACHER: It fairly staggers the imagination.

CHILDREN: Yaaaaay

TEACHER: There will be a million apiece to give to—I'll give a million to Miss Leatherbridge.

EVERYBODY: Yaaaaay.

TEACHER: That is our first lesson, then, children. I want to sit down now and brood about this.

EVERYBODY: Yaaaaaay.

TEACHER: The management of great wealth is a great responsibility.

EVERYBODY: Yaaaay.

TEACHER: Schools, hospitals, mental institutions.

EVERYBODY: Yaaaay.

TEACHER: Go home now, then, and let me sit here and brood.

EVERYBODY: Yaaaaaay. (They go)

TEACHER: I'd like a small island. Not Cuba necessarily. But a nice island with a nice population. The children—well, to them it's a game. Still, the boy *did* think of the one-thousand principle. An ice cream soda for the others, and two for him. That will be ample. Too much money for the poor spoils them. A thousand million for me I think will just about do it.

(Softly)

Yaaaaaay.

FURTHER THOUGHTS

1. It is probably not a secret any more, but money, paper money, is nothing but and only a promise. If you have a bit of that paper on you, take it out and read it. You can grow your own corn and make your own candles, but can you really make your own money? How would you go about making money that actually worked?

2. When can real money be a token of love, a token of creativity?

3. Saroyan's little play suggests an ambiguity in the word *make*. Are you really creating something when you "make money"? Isn't there a similar ambiguity in the word *spend*? Is the money you "spend" really used up, exhausted? Check the meanings and the etymology of *spend* (and *spent*) in a good dictionary.

When we want to talk about things, we have to use words, but words don't label so much the things of the world as label what we expect of them. We expect things to do what we think their labels promise. So in our world people are labeled *cops, executives,* and *mothers.* Each label is a packet of expectations. Sometimes the labels and their promises fit exactly; sometimes we have to juggle a bit. And sometimes we have to force a situation so that the promise comes true for us. (Labels and expectations are the substance of "self-fulfilling prophecies.")

Sometimes we know the labels we give each other don't fit at all; we know they project expectations that stifle or trap the labeled person. But we go ahead and use the label anyhow, perhaps to put someone down, out of fear, knowing all along that we are fighting to bolster a shaky self-image. We seem to need scapegoats. What is worse, if the social pressure is strong enough we can make our scapegoats feel guilty. But the subject of the next selection rejects that guilt.

FINDING MY OLD SELF IN A LARGER WORLD

Eileen Diaz

Eileen Diaz is presently a coordinator for a community action program. She has worked in community social services since her marriage; before her marriage she combined social work with free-lance writing. Born in Italy and the child of immigrants, she graduated from college in the late 1940s. She has three school-age children and has worked since the youngest was two.

When I was a child my mother often told me of her only memory of her own mother. I had listened with a nebulous dread creeping over me as she described a vision of her mother going to work, passing out of a wrought iron gate in front of their home, as though the scene had been a prelude to her coming untimely death. My mother and father had emigrated from Italy and their memories were interwoven with a great nostalgia and a sense of loss. When my mother went out to work during the depression, although it was for a few months, I wonder if I relived this sadness which my mother's experience had made a part of me. If so, I have no memory of it, but thinking of it re-creates for me my own feelings when the expenses of a growing family and my own need to be back in the world of ideas and action outside of the family circle, combined to make me a working mother. Memories drift back of my youngest son, then about two, sobbing at the door, begging me not to leave, of disturbing fantasies of possible injuries, physical and psychological, which could occur that filled my mind traveling to and from work. I remember my horror when the children told me that one babysitter had chased them around the apartment and had playfully stuck pins in them when they had misbehaved. She also had put them all in the bathtub, herself included, for a community bath fun-time.

My adjustment to leaving the children and resolving my guilt feelings because I was, on one level, relieved to be away from the endless routine of child care and house cleaning, took time. Although being a mother was a joy and fulfillment, as time passed I realized that I needed some other interest. My communication with an adult world had been very limited and I went back to work with almost as much relish as others might go to a social evening.

In all this slush of feelings, separation, guilt, and anxiety, there emerged the clear intellectual evaluation with which I assured myself that I was doing the right thing; and strangely enough, this sustained me until I did manage to conquer most of my negative feelings. True, I often came home an exhausted, uninterested, harassed, screeching ugly, but I also felt a deepening appreciation for the children and on weekends tried even harder to compensate by special excursions, and wanted very much to be with them. We had fun and I felt like a more interesting person to have around. There was also more money with which to do things. A working mother feels the pressure put on her concerning her duty to her children. As a mother she is expected to devote herself to her children's well-being. If she goes out to work to help herself, provide a greater measure of the necessities of life for the family, and to help the children on their way to independence, she is still thought of by some as less of a good mother. This is based on the assumption that the good mother is one who is constantly on her children's trail and sharing every possible moment of living with them. Depending on the family income, where the family lives, and the cultural environment, this varies, but often there is a certain amount of disfavor for the mother who does not have direct care of her children as a full-time job.

Substitute mothers are hard to find. I think my greatest success was with my 79-year-old father who "retired" to care for his house and garden and was glad to be helpful by babysitting. He played baseball with them (the boys ran the bases for him) and he became "grandpa" to a variety of neighborhood children. This was a delightful arrangement until the trip into Manhattan became too tiresome for him and I reached the fortuitous point in life when I was able to arrange my hours of work to coincide with the children's time in school. One of the ways we can respond to the needs of working mothers is to provide jobs for women with school-age children for the hours that they are in school, or if not, to provide suitable day care and after school programs. The public day-care centers in New York City are run by the Department of Social Services (Welfare) and have endless waiting lists. Any "intact" family where there is income is almost automatically excluded because priority is given to women on public assistance or who would be if they could not work. The private nurseries are expensive and sparse. These services are for a limited age group although there are some facilities for older children after school. Suitable babysitters are not easy to find, and are much more expensive if you expect them to take care of the children in your own home. A new plan has been devised for women on public assistance or in a family with low income in which certain homes are licensed so that the mother may care for a specified number of children. The mothers whose children are cared for can enter training courses or work. The plan has many deficiencies from the point of view of providing the children with the most beneficial environment while the mother is at work.

One of my problems in returning to work was the onset of fatigue and the lack of energy I experienced often as I tried to cope with family responsibilities after an eight-hour work day. I had a series of jobs which taxed my strength, with anti-poverty community action programs, a settlement house, and a pilot youth program. My duties varied from group work with teenagers in a ghetto area "coffee-house" experiment to running a health services program. I organized action committees, coordinated voter-registration drives, developed a cultural arts program, supervised employment counselors, worked with elementary school children in group recreation programs, and for a time ran a housing clinic. Working in one poverty area and living in East Harlem exposed me to many challenging and exhausting situations. Helping in emergencies such as fires and acute illnesses were all part of a day's work. The frustration of being able to do relatively little in the face of problems such as deteriorated housing, rats preying on children, and the all too familiar list of hard core agonies of our cities, was an occupational hazard. These experiences also gave me an enriching involvement in the lives of people outside of the immediate family which gave my life a new dimension and brought me back to the work which had been so important to me before marriage. I had spent years working in East Harlem since college days when I started to teach catechism in an old Catholic church which was a converted bathhouse, and returned later with a friend to open a store front children's center. Later we moved into the neighborhood to extend our work. My association with the Catholic Worker movement left its mark on my conscience so that when years later I returned to work, I was happy to be a part of the struggle for social and economic justice. Although my motivation now is not religious and I do work as well to earn money, I feel more at ease with myself because of this involvement.

To compare the plus values of working to the minus is difficult. Looking back to the days I worked full-time I remember the nights I came home tired and served a thrown together meal. I remember talks with the children when I listed all the advantages of my working and heard them agree that having money to spend on things they wanted and activities was worth the sacrifices. I was developing an apologia entitled "Mother Should Work." There was the fear that my working reflected on their father's image as breadwinner, aggravated by his problems with seasonal employment and relatively low wages, and the subtle and not so subtle obstacles in his path as a first generation Puerto Rican immigrant. Some resentments arose and were not entirely resolved. He was raised in a culture where men's work is clearly defined and they expect the woman's role in the family to continue smoothly whether or not she is working. Although he was never opposed to my working and the economic advantages were clear, his occasional dissatisfactions were indications that it wasn't the best of all possible arrangements under which we were living. I had no help with the housework and meals so I was never in the mood for any criticism. My dependence on him lessened and in a way my individuality and personality were strengthened by my life outside the home. I felt livelier and more like "my old self" in that my life was not as constrained by immovable limitations. I think our relationship actually improved.

The role of women in marriage and in society is undergoing change. In our everyday lives many of us are redefining the family. Women want the freedom to make full use of their talents as persons as well as mothers. They want to participate fully in all fields of human effort and creativity. This may not necessitate as much a change in the role of women as it means removing barriers to their becoming adult in the greater society as well as within the family. When I think about the past years of combining work and home, I feel a sense of satisfaction at having overcome some family problems by going out to work. The new problems which arose I resolved reasonably well. My children are proud of me and the responsibilities I have at work. They learned to reach out to other people without ceasing to be close to me, have many interests, and positive attitudes toward school and recreation. Disclaiming objectivity, I think they are great. I found many of the fears about harmful effects to marriage, children, and home were exaggerated by my own insecurity about going back to work. The advantages I had being a college graduate and having had work experience helped. It was not difficult for me to find work. After finding work I had the benefit of working with people who put human values first and did not put undue pressure on me concerning time off for serious illnesses at home, arrangements of work schedules, coming in late on days when one of the children was in a class play or needed a special visit to the doctor. These are considerations not all workers share. Factory workers forced to work overtime and otherwise pressured by employers are at a disadvantage. The rule is, "You want to work—pay the price." Often working mothers break down under the strain, especially those who have to tune themselves to a power sewing machine or busy switchboard, work which may be depersonalized, done in an atmosphere which is punitive and demanding. The question of work, and its relation to the person, is one which has been studied and discussed but the knowledge gained has not been applied to our economic system. Man is still made for work and not work for man. Much of our effort is wasted while work which is needed is left undone, such as the rebuilding of slums, extending health care, and revitalizing our schools.

Women need to organize their political and moral strength behind a more realistic use of the work force of both sexes. We need to rebel against meaningless work, against work which is destructive to the building of world peace, dehumanizing work, and see to it that whatever power we have is exerted towards our personal good and the common good. We must reject any economic system based on war and dependent on war for its health.

Employment for women is being encouraged if they are recipients of public funds. There is a growing rancor being expressed towards dependent mothers and an eagerness to get them off the welfare rolls and into the labor market. Although this may eventually benefit the women involved, one would hope that the original purposes of the aid, the protection of the children, should be considered, as well as the woman's capability of handling two jobs at once, and her own evaluation of where her best interest and that of her children lies. At times it seems that the fundamental ethical value that a person has a right to life and what is needed to maintain life as a dignified free individual has been lost. One of the reasons for these fatherless homes is the system which does not provide wages at the level needed to maintain families and which is run with an underclass of minority groups who, if employed, are doing the menial, clean-up, back-breaking, dead-end jobs, and an inferior educational system which makes further advancement impossible without years of remediation or extensive training. If there were more emphasis placed on creating meaningful, well-paying jobs for men, especially the urban and rural poor and minority groups who have faced institutionalized discrimination in employment for decades, many of the resultant social ills would be cured. Work for women is important in that in the present reality for many individuals and families, it is a step out of poverty. It is also important as a creative outlet. Society benefits from the talent and skills of working women. Making it easier for women who do work to satisfy their children's needs, escape the deadly effects of overwork and emotional strain, is a goal we should set for ourselves. Increasing the number of day-care services, after school programs, and making more part-time jobs available are ways of helping. From my own experience, I prefer nursery school care for the preschool group. Children under two are best cared for by their mothers unless there is serious financial or emotional need, and no other way to resolve the problem. Since each woman is different it must be an individual decision. I experienced a lessening of anxiety as my own children grew older. My children, now ten, nine, and six, experienced more visible insecurity at younger ages although I did not work when they were infants, except when the first child was about one and my husband was in the hospital. I worked for about three months and was overwhelmed when my son became seriously ill with measles. Rushing from work, to baby, to hospital, I became completely drained. As soon as my husband was back at work I stopped. I didn't work again until my third child was about two. This conflict of duties is most acute when the children are sick. If they are seriously ill, there is no question, I stay home. If the serious symptoms disappear and I am reasonably sure there is no danger I go to work without much anxiety but there is no denying that often when the situation is unclear, I feel insecure as to what decision is best. Fortunately, their health is good and it's the usual run of viruses or childhood diseases that occur. Then there are those playground accidents. My six-year-old son cut his hand tumbling in the playground while I was at work. He had to have seven stitches in his hand. When I got home he was very upset and I joined him. You can't help but think that if you were there you could have prevented it. Sometimes the accidents happen in front of you and in the home, but worry about the safety of children is very much a problem for mothers who work. I have a neighbor who works near home and who is terrified when she hears a fire engine. I remember when I first started working an old rhyme kept running through my head,

> "Ladybug, ladybug, fly away home,
> Your house is on fire, and your children will burn."

Is this neurotic or realistic? A little of both I think. In neighborhoods like ours, fires are commonplace. In the apartment we lived in before we moved to a housing project there was a series of small fires started by defective wiring. Mothers are instinctively protective and these worries are very real. My son was lost for a few hours at Rockaway Beach one summer while on a day-camp trip. I waited tensely until I got word that he was safe at the police station where he was found by relieved counselors. Incidents like these happen whether or not you are at home but a mother at work feels more anxious about such things. Children also carefully compare their lives to their friends' and one of mine asked me why I couldn't stay home all day like their mother. Interestingly, when their close friends' mother got a job they came to regard mothers' working as a state of normalcy and progressed to bragging about it.

When I first thought of going back to work it was with a lack of confidence in my ability. The thought of getting through a work day and coming home to do most of the things that kept me busy at home all day was frightening. With some encouragement, I aimed high, pulled myself together and found a temporary, well-paying job with which to experiment. When I began to work at a permanent job I realized I would have to accept certain hardships but they were tempered by an enjoyment of my work and the good things which grew out of it. Battling fatigue and illness at times, I learned to be more confident about my ability to find suitable work and arrange my schedule so that much of the strain was eliminated. I am convinced that mothers who work should not settle into a 35- to 40-hour-a-week work schedule unless they are very energetic types and should do their best to avoid urban rush hours and otherwise conserve themselves. We are a long way from making this possible for the majority of women with children, especially in low-income families where there is a corresponding low educational level, lack of work experience, work skills, and often language skills. These are the families which need immediate plans for more part-time paid remediation classes and job training with opportunities for professional training as well. More important than this is that we resolve the problem of male youth and adults who are now unemployed or underemployed and who have little hope of ever earning enough to support a family in all its basic needs. This is our first priority in the area of work. It calls for radical changes in the attitudes and wills of government and industry as to their responsibilities.

FURTHER THOUGHTS

1. Part of Eileen Diaz's triumph was overcoming guilt feelings after she became a working mother. "In our everyday lives many of us are redefining the family," writes Mrs. Diaz. How was *she* redefining the family? How was she redefining the role of mother? of father? of child? At what point in your life did you change enough to redefine what your father meant? or your mother?
2. How are the themes of love and creativity expressed in Mrs. Diaz's story?

The following selection is from the novel *Up the Sandbox!* In the book the heroine watches her children playing, and while watching she daydreams. In her fantasies she becomes a Wonder Woman, performing great feats, and has exotic loves in faraway places. But as the novel progresses, she discovers she has the strength to accept a more modest, but perhaps harder, heroism—that of coping day by day with herself and those she loves.

FROM
UP THE SANDBOX!

Anne Richardson Roiphe

I push the carriage into the park; my dress is stained with perspiration. The heat muffles the street sounds and the green leaves and the grass seem so pleasant, I am glad to be here in the park. There are other mothers in the playground. It's still early and many benches are free. A child runs to the concrete fountain and by leaning with all his weight against a metal button embedded in the grainy cement produces a trickle of cool water that bubbles erratically above the metal spout. He gets his shirt all wet trying to position his mouth correctly and finally gets down, walks to his mother's side. She talks to the mother on the bench next to her about a badminton club in Brooklyn where she and her husband happily release their accumulated aggressions. I look around at the pull toys, the hoop and the roller skates that lie just beneath the bench next to mine. They have in themselves, these objects of commercial greed, mass-produced wonder and childhood lust, a curious beauty in the shade beneath the bench, like shells on the shore, emptied of their inner life.

I pick up my baby and hold him on my lap. He looks up at my face, his fingers exploring my mouth, digging at my nose. What stays on, what comes off—I can see him wondering. I could starve him—or leave him behind me, dropping him on the cement, crying in the park till the police come and assign him some nameless future. But he has nothing to fear because despite an angry thought or two, we are connected deeply and permanently. And with each feeding, each soothing, each moment we live together, I grow into him. My spirit oozes out, I feel myself contracting and him expanding, and the ties between us solidify. And I am almost his possession. Elizabeth's, too. My selfish purposes are also served, as the children make for me a universe, with a design and a rhythm and a function. And instead of being, as I was before I conceived a child, a bit of dark matter orbiting aimlessly, brooding on my own molecular disintegration, I am now a proper part of ordinary society.

I think of Paul in the library now, probably in one of the study cubicles, with its desk piled with documents on the Spanish Civil War. He said he was looking for testimony, reports from the original members of the Abraham Lincoln Brigade. I know the way his hair hangs across his face when he reads, the way he chews on his fingernails and screws up his eyes when he detects dishonesty or distortion in his text. I wish somehow I could be with him—the days seem so long when he's absorbed that way—as if I didn't matter, as if the children were peripheral noise, and if his scholarship and theories were food sufficient. And then I get sad, because nothing I have ever read or done, nothing I will ever learn or speculate about, can replace being near him. I would put anything down to go for a short walk with him. There is a terrible inequality of love in that, and I am so reduced. I am like the heroine bound and gagged by the villain, lying on the railroad tracks, waiting for her rescuer. He comes, releases her, kissing the tears away. Only he leaves, this hero with many interests, and the villain returns, and the scene must be repeated over and over. The metaphor is melodramatic. Actually, Paul and I exist in a more ordinary way. We live, not like explorers, not like Lewis and Clark charting the wilds of the northwest; more like land surveyors blocking out lots for a new housing project or a county shopping center. The possibilities for raw adventure under such circumstances are limited.

Two students walk by, peering between the playground bars. They still feel about public events as if they could mold them like the clay that used to yield beneath their fingers in art classes in elementary school afternoon programs. They go to the barricades, hair flying, jaws set, to reform a system whose basic injustices are beyond reach, hidden and perpetual. They list grievances of representation, scholarships, draft, university alliances with military matters, and they shake the ground on which they stamp their feet, and their catcalls are reported in the press, and the drama around here is great. And above them and below them, the web stays. The fabric vibrates like a trampoline, bouncing us in somersaults we execute with more or less grace. And the same words are said by different people over and over. The students move on to look at other interesting sights in the park.

If I were younger, I would join the student revolutionaries. If Paul were just a few years younger, he would have had his head bashed in on the principle of student power. As it is, Elizabeth needs a daily bath and other things, and the baby must have what the books call consistent mothering or his small soul will warp and bend in strange directions, and he might decide it's not worth growing and reverse the process, curl himself in fetal position and look only inward, refusing food until life itself is extinguished. And so with my hands, when I touch him and wipe the cereal from his face and the b.m. from his bottom, I make life again each day, like Penelope weaving a shroud, never to be complete till Ulysses returns. I wonder, if I were Penelope, if I should not have smuggled myself aboard the ship originally headed for Troy. Or if perhaps, even now, I should not accept the hot kisses of some impatient suitor who would rape me in the hills and carry me off to a different city where the language itself would be unknown to me.

I'm no Penelope, no romantic heroine or creature of historical importance. I'm just Margaret Reynolds, wife and mother, not yet thirty . . . too old for an identity crisis and yet not past the age of uncertainty. . . .

I'm now almost four weeks late—and I don't menstruate that irregularly. I flow blood easily and my periodicity is splendid, and I am always absurdly proud as well as a little shocked by this monthly performance. Of course, sometimes a cold, an upset stomach, a trip, nervous excitement, may delay the shedding of one wall for another, but four weeks is extreme. Possibly I am pregnant. At the thought, as I say the words to myself, as I write them down, my heart starts to pound. I feel a flush of pleasure and a ridiculous sense of exhilaration—but why? Things are hard enough. There are dishes and diapers and needs sufficient in my home to keep me buried for all the years that even the wildest masochist could desire. But the thought does not disappear, and it does not, despite reason, bring anxiety. X and Y, XX, XY, inside of me, right now as I write, an embryo, a fetus, finally a person. Who needs another person? No matter how talented, beautiful and gifted, the world needs fewer people, more breathing space, more food. My baby is otiose, a social inconvenience. I run to my little boy, interrupting his mouthing of old ice cream wrapper. I hug him. I won't love him less, I'll love him more. I start to plan. We can put Peter in with Elizabeth, and the baby in Peter's room, and I can borrow another crib from Louise, my friend in the building, and it will hardly cost anything at all. Perhaps I should go to the doctor to be sure. Perhaps I should first take a urine specimen to the laboratory on 114th. They'll call Dr. Z. and within six hours I can know. Oh rabbit, friend of mine—enlarge your little nipples, show symptoms of pregnancy, please.

I sit in the sun of my own anticipation for a while. Then another thought destroys my peace. X and Y, XY or XX or maybe XYZ. Mutations do happen: intrauterine second-month development of fangs, green skin, scales. Third intrauterine month, gills, longer fangs, pop eyes, hair on hands, nails sharp, in fact claws, a monster growing in me—a comic book terror building strength from

my blood system, and suddenly tearing with its pointed fangs at my uterus, like the chicken at its shell, and shattering my stomach wall open and bleeding; it would leap on to the bed, the embodiment of all that is vicious and ugly within me—the demon that causes bad fantasies personified as my baby. The child that eats up your guts on its way out to the world is not an impossible monster. But what a nightmare I am having. I am sure this third meeting of egg and sperm is developing normal-splendid. A beautiful creature with perhaps a mathematical gift. I've always admired people who can play with abstractions, moving them around in their heads like so many mosaic tiles, building portraits of mental designs so beyond my concrete imagination. My baby can be so many things hidden, recessed in the gene pattern that Paul and I keep secret in our cellular structure. ... A great-grandfather's violin-playing may result in my child's extraordinary musicality, or a grandmother of Paul's whose legs I have been told attracted all the attention at the church socials may result in a movie star three generations later, and what I really want, what I'm after, is an extension, a selfish extension of my being into more life than I can contain in one—singular—body. I want to expand myself not merely in time, but in space, out toward other connections, to be a multiple person, to experience as much as possible. Now I am allowing myself to be sentimental. Motherhood is always a greedy affair and eventually a suckling-off of the suckler—and it never works out the way it's planned. There's always a fighting and a pull. A mother and offspring on each end of a wishbone, a tugging till victory—the child's, of course: he takes the larger part, gets his wish and runs.

I take Peter smiling at me—his baby hands still exploring my mouth, my nose, pulling at me in rough play. He's dirty all over and triumphant with his new physical skills. I am now the all-powerful, all-necessary center to his narrow universe. I am his servant, his provider, his lover, his goddess, irrational like Jehovah, and yet tender like the Virgin Mary. Sometime in the not so distant future, I will be his enemy. He will flee and I will chase him. Where have you been? You must be home by twelve. No, you may not do that. No, you cannot have money for that. And then it will be like other kinds of love affairs, alternating layers of bitterness and nostalgia—and eventually a minor boredom. "Oh yes, remind me to send my mother a birthday card." And I will worship him, and even should he prove a disaster, I will carry mementoes and pictures, keep all his school reports and athletic awards. And at the end it will all be burned as rubbish when someone sorts through my private effects looking for stock market certificates and things like that that old ladies are always stashing away in hat boxes. But it doesn't matter about the end—the process is so important. (He pulls at my sandal as if to unbuckle the leather strap.) Like a medieval jousting session, the rituals that cover the fierce combat of mother-child love are magnificent, and I enter the battle joyfully, though it stretch ahead for years, because it's the only arena to really test my mettle, to shape my reputation, to give me a self whose colors I will wear with pride.

Elizabeth has come to me with a demand that I push her on the swing. I am tired of doing things. I want to stay in my own thoughts, but she's beginning to whine, sensing my withdrawal, and I will have to go, since discipline in one's work means subjugating whims and impulses, self, to higher plans. I will be disciplined, get up from this bench and go to the swings, my feet passing through the steam rising from the cement. I am a guru, an Indian yogi. I can sit on a bed of nails and walk through fire, because I can concentrate on God and exclude all other sensations. No, I cannot concentrate on God. I find when I try I only brood about myself. Elizabeth, I am coming to the swings. Tomorrow first thing I will take a urine specimen to the laboratory. Will Dr. Z. be surprised to hear from me again?

I push Elizabeth on the swing and she kicks her feet in pleasure. Her small brown sandals are scuffed and in need of a polishing they will never get. I'm perspiring from the activity and there are wet dark circles under the armholes of my cotton dress. I think of Elizabeth lying on a bed some many years from now, a boy, a man, awkwardly spreading her legs apart, touching her, and she, not knowing how to stop, how to prevent the vacuum of time from sucking her up, will lie passive and be consumed, and as I think of the heat and sensation of her body rolling on the sheets, in sex, in labor, in illness and in death, I feel a great exhaustion, a fatigue of certain defeat—that's all that can possibly come of the days I spend in the park expecting secretly the playground concrete to crack and wild orchids to push their way up to the sunlight, and lizards to dash between the slide and the swing, and nature to change back to an Eden before the apple, where Paul and I can live without erosion in perpetual beauty.

I know that we have been condemned to a simple life of increasing compromises. I know that minor hatreds and petty resentments will come more and more between us. Paul, Elizabeth, Peter, the new baby and I will grow closer and closer in memories of days that promised more than they gave and love that offers everything and then like a mirage disappears as we get closer. But what else can I do but listen to myself as I prepare chicken in wine sauce for the friends we will have to dinner tomorrow night, read Elizabeth a book about Raggedy Ann and how she got her candy heart that says "I love you" sewed right into the middle of her chest—what else can I do but tell Paul that I have not given up all hope for a revolution that will not be corrupt . . . a barricade can still be erected behind which saints may stand? I must believe evolution is not complete. I'll take Peter to the five and dime and buy him a stuffed elephant like the one he wanted to take from the carriage parked next to ours.

FURTHER THOUGHTS

1. Do the roles projected for wife and mother in the selection from *Up the Sandbox!* contradict those projected in Eileen Diaz's story? If so, what are the specific differences? What are the similarities between the two roles?
2. Some people have argued that women should be paid a regular wage for the

work they do as housewives and mothers—with fringe benefits like paid vacations and retirement plans. What do you think of that suggestion?

3. Should men be paid for the work they do as husband and father—working around the house or spending time with the children? Further, should husbands be paid in some way for making money for the family?

One label that is rich in set expectations is *cop*. There is a big difference between saying, "Here comes Mr. Galvin" and "Here comes the cop." The next two selections ask you to examine the label *cop*, from more than one point of view. As you read, consider how the images presented in these two selections agree or disagree with your own image of a cop. How does each image account for creativity and love in one's job?

THE RABBIT FIGHTS FOR HIS LIFE
THE LEOPARD EATS LUNCH

C. K. Williams

for Harvey Finkle

What if the revolution comes and I'm in it and my job
is to murder a child accidentally
or afterwards to get rid of the policemen?
I had a milkshake last week with a policeman
we talked about his payraise it eats shit
he told me what if I have that one? SAVAGE
the baby was easy
the baby went up in thin air
I remembered in Dostoevsky where they talked
about whether it would all be worth the death of one child
and you decided yes or no according to your character
my character
is how he got back in his car
like a tired businessman and listened to the radio
for a few minutes
and waved
is having to lug him everywhere

I go because I can't take him to his wife crying like this
the children have learned to throw their arms around you
without meaning it to kiss you without feeling it
to know there is something marvelous
and not pay attention
in order to say any of this at all to you
I have made myself up like somebody
in a novel
in order not
to go out of my mind I make it I can only do two things
hold you
bury you

THE COP

Kenneth Lasson

Galvin pauses outside Precinct House Number One and lights the first of twenty-five Pall Malls that he'll smoke today. He is back on the job after a vacation of two weeks, one of which he spent working overtime with the police. During the others he lay in the sun with his family at the tiny summer cottage he owns on the south shore of Cape Cod. Now back in the hazy heat of the city, he passes through the tinted glass doors of the station house, grunting preoccupied hellos to either side. He has things to think about, and he doesn't have to steel himself for another eight hours on his feet in the bowels of a congested metropolis. He learned early how to swallow tedium and hard work.

He lights up a second butt and, coughing a smoker's cough, brings up phlegm that has been in his throat all night. He has had a mild case of bronchitis ever since his childhood, spent in an unheated flat in Roxbury.

"I grew up in a semighetto, what is now mostly the black section of Boston, with my three brothers and two sisters. We lived in a cold-water tenement. I guess my father earned a decent salary considering it was during the Depression, but we never saw the money. He had his problems—drank too much, lost his check on the horses. He wasn't home that much so my mother had to keep us straight."

Roxbury has been the springboard for all of Boston's immigrant minority groups, from the Irish to the Puerto Ricans. Today the 'Berry is Boston's Harlem and Watts and South Side Chicago. It stretches from suburban Mattapan, where Black-Jewish relations have reached another boiling point, through Boston's South End, to the Combat Zone, where Terrance Galvin directs traffic. Tensions in the Combat Zone are always volatile, even when there is no July heat. The newspapers use words like boiling point and volatile, but Galvin doesn't have to read the papers to know what it's like in the streets.

"When I first came on the force you didn't have the problems we have now. You never had a riot of any large proportions, you had better contacts with people. But today the policeman's job is getting more complicated. He's dragged into almost every situation—race relations, community relations, everything. He seems to be the whipping boy for campus unrest. There was never any campus rebellion before, you never had Watts or the Harlem riots. Today you have different problems, and people try to blame it on the policeman.

"It all started with the goddamn war. It's draining us, and it's giving the radicals food to pounce on. You end that war and 90 percent of what the radicals are screaming about would be over. We can't win it by holding back, so I say let's get the hell out. It started all the way back under JFK, God rest his soul. He sent in the advisors. Then under Johnson they asked for more and you had Tonkin Gulf. Mario Savio started screaming, and the black people in the South started pushing for the rights they deserved. Things didn't change fast enough and groups like the Panthers and SDS began feeding on the people's unhappiness, and the cities exploded in riots. So they pushed us in to try and clean up what they had allowed to become rotten ghetto slums. We had to do the dirty work for the Establishment.

"The war kept getting worse, and then when Kennedy and King got killed the young people began listening even more to these radicals. You have to give these animals credit for eating off the suffering, but they're out to destroy us nonetheless. So the young kids start trying to forget everything with drugs. I saw a survey that showed in a forty-block area of Harlem there are eighteen thousand narcotics addicts. Now here's where I worry—that's scary. We've got to do something to rehabilitate these people. But then there's more rioting—not just the blacks, but upper-class white kids—and after they get disillusioned and start throwing bricks, we're moved in to quell the thing. Again we're the scapegoats.

"We've lost touch with the people in a lot of areas. Back in the '50's the policeman was on the beat, but today he's more mechanized. He's left the streets and is part of a mobile force. Squad cars are needed for mobility to fight crime—the beat man just couldn't cover enough ground. But the direct contact with the average people is lost, like "Hi Officer Kelly, hi Officer Smith, oh hi Mrs. Jones." We live in a mechanized society, men on the moon, but you can't take the place of the contact between the beat patrolman and the people. Something's missing today.

"When things went really bad at home we went on welfare. As a child, that branded me. We wore welfare knickers, which were like cheesecloth. They had a flap with a button on them. But if your father worked, you had elastic in your knickers and you wore ankle socks. Uncle Sam branded us, because with our union suits, they knew who we were. I remember going down skinny-dipping and stripping, and the kids would say, 'Look at Terry Galvin and his welfare underwear.' This kind of thing worked on our minds. The social worker who was supposed to help us did more harm than you could imagine. I remember my mother buying a little radio and having to hide it because this obnoxious bitch, who was probably a political appointee, used to come into the house without warning, lifting up everything and snooping around in our private things to see if we had taken too much. There was no such thing as dignity then.

"My mother tried hard to make life normal but we had nothing. I never got a Christmas present in my whole life until I was in my teens. I remember on Easter Sunday how I used to feel. My two friends Billy Keough and Tommy Ryan had new shoes from Flagg Brothers. I had nothing—I had to wear last year's. We used our mother's old stockings as socks to wear with our knickers. In the winter the ice would form inside the windows. I remember my mother heating up bricks for us to keep at the foot of our beds. We would line up and race to see who would get the hottest brick.

"I really wanted to learn as a kid, but the schools were no good. Finally I gave up and they sent me to a discipline school. It wasn't a reform place, it was part of the regular public school system. They shoved you away in another city school if you were screwing up. They still carried you on the rolls and you read funny books until they farmed you out to high school. By the time I hit high school, I was completely unprepared. I mean you can't have a kid drawing cartoons until he's thirteen years old and expect him to be ready for higher learning. So after two years I quit and went to work.

"At sixteen I got a job—illegally, because I was five years underage—as an ambulance orderly at City Hospital. We used to go on the contagious disease runs—smallpox, consumption, things like that. I used to give all of my pay check to my father except for about ten dollars. I stayed there at the hospital for three years. Then I worked as a carpenter's helper. My wife laughs, because to this day we don't own a hammer. Later, when I was about twenty, I worked as a furniture mover and then I worked double shifts at a factory that made floor tiles and linoleum. After the Marine Corps, I signed on as a cop."

On his feet now, Galvin keeps a steady line of cars moving from a ramp off an adjacent expressway. A pedestrian swinging a large transistor radio passes by, and Galvin hears a helicopter report tell commuters, "Traffic is heavy on the main arteries but moving well." Galvin keeps his eyes moving, distracted occasionally by leggy young secretaries who bounce among the crowd of early shoppers and businessmen. "Will you look at *that*," he inhales, pirouetting to ogle a pretty young blonde. He knows he is all talk and no action, a good father who secretly worships his wife. But at nine A.M. every morning this is one way to get the sleep out of his eyes.

By 9:15 the commuting business traffic is exhausted; in less than an hour, downtown will be engulfed by a tidal wave of shoppers. Galvin drives his wagon about six blocks to his regular beat on Washington Street, in the heart of the

Combat Zone, near Hayward and Avery. He stops outside the Avery Hotel in a towaway area. At fifteen dollars a week for a garage spot, there is nowhere else to park.

On Washington Street—in a two-block area just up from the bistros and pulp joints, small drug stores, curiosity shops, movie houses, and banks—the traffic has picked up. Galvin steps off the curb to control it. This is his beat.

"I was assigned to the Traffic Division from the Academy, but I wouldn't put in for a transfer. I'm out in the street, I meet the people. I know everybody in my area. I prefer it to the cruiser. When I'm out there, I'm protecting the walking public, and I have a feeling of accomplishment doing my job. We have a good relationship. A traffic officer anywhere in the country is as much a policeman as someone on a crime patrol. He prevents crime by his very presence, people feel safer when they see him. Some critics say, "He does traffic in front of office buildings. We should put civilian directors out," and that bit. But there's no substitute for the visible policeman, no matter where he might be. How much crime he deters in a given three-block area, no one will ever know."

The traffic moves by steadily with a brief lull at midmorning. There will be another at midafternoon. From somewhere along the brick and asphalt horizon they come; thousands of them, twenty cars a minute, twelve hundred an hour, each hour, every working day. When the movement of vehicles slows to the point where the spacing between cars is three or more car lengths, Galvin lets the lights take over. Two big yellow standing signals on opposite sides of Washington at Hayward and Avery blink continuously, regardless of a policeman's presence. Green for one minute, amber caution for five seconds, caution and stop for ten more, forty-five seconds of red, then green again—an electronic cycle that Galvin has come to rely on for the small measure of security it affords.

The lights, at least, will always be there to back Galvin up if he has to leave. In February, 1958, with the snow piled high in dirty little drifts on the curbs, he happened to glance up at the top of a neighboring office building and saw a young girl on the ledge, her feet dangling over the side. So he rushed up to the rooftop, and ten minutes later coaxed her out of suicide. This brought him the Department Medal of Honor.

"Because of the medal, I get an extra fifty cents a week on my pay check. Until a few months ago I made $159.50 a week, but now, after our raise, Boston police are the sixth best-paid cops in the country. I'm making $10,300. That's $198.60 a week, but that isn't what I bring home. There's something like thirty-four dollars chopped out—eight a week for Blue Cross, eight for the Patrolman's Pension Fund, two dollars for the Patrolman's Association dues, sixteen to the City of Boston Credit Union. Every city employee is in hock. We can take out loans at only a few percent interest and take years to pay them back. I get the loan paid and I take one out again. That's how I started with my house and bought my car. The Credit Union is a good thing.

"About six years ago, we bought this little cracker box down in Marshfield near the water so the kids would have some place to spend the summer. The whole thing cost seven thousand dollars, at five hundred dollars down. It might seem like a luxury but goddamn it, I need the place in the summer when I get off work, to leave the city and have some little place to go to. When you spend all day breathing in the shit air and eating the carbon monoxide, when you're on your feet all day in the heat and the rain with all the noise, you need a place to run to at night. It's costing us extra and we have to give up other luxuries, but I don't know what I'd do if we didn't have the little place.

"With what it costs us, we wouldn't have anything left for other luxuries or emergencies at the end of the week, so I work details. It's just some overtime work that cops do to supplement their income for a few extras we can't afford after we've taken care of the basics. Before the pay hike I worked two details a week just to keep the kids fed. I was away from my home every Friday and Saturday night for four years to make ends meet. When some bar or dance wanted police protection, I worked it at the rate of $4.50 an hour. I used to take the details no one would want because in my division I couldn't get the good ones. I worked lousy hours, from ten at night to two in the morning, in the stinkingest holes in Boston. I never took my wife out once in four years. But that's over now. With the new contract we get $6.75 an hour for details, so I can work just one a week. God help me, I'll never leave my family home again on weekend nights. But if I was ever transferred to a division that's poor on details, we could be in very bad shape."

At 10:15 A.M. Herb Markham arrives. He will work the corner until six P.M.; Galvin, who came on at eight, will leave at four. They will keep these shifts for two weeks, then alternate. Until they got the new contract, they used to work from eight to six on staggered days. Markham has been Galvin's sidekick for almost a decade. He's a heavy-set man with curly gray hair, bumblebee sunglasses, and a belly that hangs out over his belt and holster. Herb is a very shrewd guy. ("Quiet, but shrewd," says Galvin.) In uniform, they are a tight-knit team, periodically relieving each other on the corner as the day moves by.

Two old ladies in silver hair and blue silk dresses approach Galvin as he crosses Avery Street. They are smiling like grammar-school teachers talking to a cute child. ("Officer, where might we find Red Cross Shoes?" "Up Washington, ma'am, corner of Temple Place.") He tips his hat. A pair of anxious businessmen step into the street in front of him. ("Which way to Locke-Ober's?" "Winter Place, three blocks up, left on Winter Street." "Thanks very much, Officer." "Thank you, sir.")

Markham relieves Galvin, who by now wants very much to get some coffee and get off his feet. Galvin goes into Dalton's, a converted chain cafeteria and his street base of operations. Here, under gaudy electric candelabras and oversized-flower wall decorations, it costs $1.15 for "three country-fresh eggs, any style, with bacon or sausage, home fries, and toast—the Farm Special." The Charbroiled Steak Dinner is $1.49. But Dalton's is a Combat Zone eatery that shoppers avoid. Its clientele are the people of the streets: go-go dancers, small store owners, derelicts, peddlers. And policemen.

Sitting over coffee at the rear table at Dalton's, he never takes his eyes off his corner. Traffic has now slowed to a level where the lights can take over. The University of Avery Street, Galvin calls it. When he leaves the trenches of heavy traffic for his outdoor classes in field sociology, Terrance Galvin changes from soldier to full professor.

Back in the street again, a few minutes after taking over for Markham, he catches four young tow-haired boys darting across Washington Street. A loud "Hey!" freezes them in their tracks, and they turn. He holds his hand up and curls his index finger for them to come toward him. He smiles. ("Listen, fellas, if you shoot out into the street like that, one of you will get it.") He puts his arms around the smallest boy. ("See this little midget here? If he gets hit by a truck, he'll be this small for the rest of his life.") Laughter. ("Next time walk between those white lines, okay?") The boys bob their four heads silently, then turn and move on.

As lunch time nears, traffic thickens. A Pontiac GTO convertible stalls at the corner. To Galvin, the shortest measurable time is the millisecond between the time a car stalls and the time the horns behind start honking. He explodes at the cacophony, and yells over the din. ("All right, all right, cool it, turn it off, turn it off!") Water pours from the GTO's overheated radiator, as the driver appeals to the policeman for assistance. ("You stay on the driver's side and I'll help you push it over to the corner near the fruit stand.") Two passing boys help Galvin, pushing from each side of the convertible as he presses from the trunk, and the intersection is cleared. Over at the side of the street the young driver removes his sunglasses and requests dispensation. ("Can I leave it here until I get the radiator filled?" "Listen, Mack, as long as I'm here, you're okay, but I can't promise you that you might not have a ten-spot ticket on the windshield if I'm off for lunch, and one of those meter maids comes by." "Fair enough, Officer. Thanks." "Leave the hood up to show she's broken down, and down here I suggest you lock it." "Right.") The young man walks down Washington Street to a nearby garage.

"The job can be gratifying. The decent, law-abiding person still respects the policeman, he still cares. He loves the police because they are his protection. But the dissident students, the guys who think it's police brutality every other minute, they're the people who don't respect you. What the hell—you represent authority, they hate the law.

Galvin uses the first part of his lunch hour to gather the morning's scuttlebutt at the Association office. He leaves the office after fifteen minutes and stops in at a pizza place at the corner of Washington and Essex, a greasy twenty-four-hour hangout where, after dark, the Combat Zone comes alive in rock music and neon. ("They have the best subs in Boston there, if you can stand the smell of the place.") Even during the day, the stench seems like a commingling of vomit and beer. But Galvin takes his lunch to go, like the scores of interns from nearby New England Medical Center who stop there. Egg salad on rye with a can of Coke. He carries his lunch in a paper bag to the Astor Theater on Tremont Street and climbs to the balcony, where he eats quietly, and alone. As a modern-day policeman, Galvin is allowed free access to the cinemas, and he often takes in a full-length picture in half-hour segments during successive lunch hours. Sometimes it takes a week to see an entire film. Up in the roped-off balcony, he can unloosen the strings on his shoes and relax. The Astor is one of six or seven reputable theaters in the Combat Zone. Galvin steers clear of the sleazier skin-flick emporia on Washington Street. ("I couldn't take the stink inside.") Today he passes up *Land of the 1001 Nudes* and *Dragstrip Girl* in favor of *Getting Straight* with Elliot Gould and Candice Bergen. ("It's about this campus radical who was big during the ban the bomb days, but who's been away for a few years in the Army. He comes back ready to pick up his Master's. He wants to play it straight now, get his degree and teach, but the campus extremists won't leave him alone.") Professor Galvin gets hot when he thinks about extremists. Then he rasps out with a passionate articulateness that belies his lack of book learning.

"Radicals won't destroy this country, but we'll destroy ourselves if the left wing clashes with the right. Both extremes have to be contained. Let the government adhere to the will of the people. If a guy comes along and he has hair down to his knees and looks like Abraham Lincoln's mother, so what? If he's working through the system, more power to him. If our Association sees a law that's going to hurt us, we're going to do our thing about it and petition our Congressmen to get it changed. I hate to use this phrase, because it's a left-wing slogan, but we need "Power to the People." The people by their apathy have let the power slip away. We've got to get that power back. This country is really in bad shape. People don't trust each other, they're living in fear. We've got a fucking war that we shouldn't be fighting, and it's ripping us apart.

"The system needs rejuvenation, a shot in the arm. I mean we can't have the fervor we had in 1776, when we had a revolution that made us the United States of America. We've lost the fervor. You go to a hearing that benefits the public, up at the State House, and you see apathy. You see ten people in the stands where there should be ten thousand up there making themselves heard. Voices are heard when they're in numbers. Let them be heard in the Congress and in the Senate and the legislatures. People want the government to do so much, but for years there's been this apathy. A long time ago in the major Northern cities, the Irish voted for the Irish, the Italians for the Italians. That's gone out the window. You vote for the guy who's going to do the job. What happens is that these liberals who want to achieve change start working through the system—but they get beat down once and they scatter. They don't stick around to try it again. Look at Eugene McCarthy. He did an amazing thing. He came from nothing and went to knock out Johnson and make people think about the war, but because he didn't go all the way and get elected, he's withdrawn now. He's reading poetry instead of staying in and fighting."

The air-conditioning in the Astor is not working well, and the old theater is musty. Galvin finishes his sandwich, waits for the climax of a bedroom scene with Gould and Bergen, then gets up to leave. Back in the street he relieves Markham again, and Markham heads for Dalton's.

Even during daylight, eight hours in the Combat Zone is a true test of equilibrium. For most Bostonians, the Zone is a place to move through quickly. There's no lingering here, except by the city's maimed and outcast, veterans who know the ropes.

The Combat Zone becomes garish after dark as transients come seeking a dose of honky-tonk recreation: students drawn to the perverse, sailors set free from the Charlestown Navy Yard, and suburban White Hunters, cruising through in expensive cars, searching for a black prostitute who will cost them fifteen bucks—if they're lucky. Police have found more than one well-to-do business-man lying in the gutter the morning after he chased some erotic black fancy and ended up beaten and robbed. You can have your fortune told or score on some heroin in the Combat Zone, four blocks along Washington Street, from Stuart to Avery.

But Terrance Galvin sees this every day, and his senses are affected in other ways. After the first half hour at the corner of Federal and High, his ears begin to throb—from the continuous explosions of the pile drivers working the basement of a new office building, from the jackhammers, the automobile horns, and the jets that use the corridor overhead to enter Logan International Airport, from the drone of revving motors and the rumble below from the subway cars, heading out of the MBTA Orange Line through Roxbury.

By early afternoon the smells begin to irritate Galvin's nose and throat, as carbon monoxide fumes cause a steady soreness in his respiratory passages, and bring on shortness of breath. The janitors have opened the barroom doors, letting out the unpleasant odor of stale beer. Pedestrians pause to light up cigarettes. Galvin backs away from the curb, chatting with Sal at the fruit stand, gets a whiff of burning tobacco, and ignites his eleventh Pall Mall of the day. On the side streets, the restaurant air vents tell what's for lunch: tomato paste and pasta at Vince's Spaghetti House, pepper steaks at the Hi-Fi Deli.

By 2:30, it is the walking that begins to bother Galvin most, an aching sensation, tendons strained from continuous hours on his feet. Galvin has been working in this congested atmosphere for years, through every element. He doesn't even hear the noises anymore, and he's learned to breathe the air. More than anything else it's an unconscious inurement. He's not inclined to worry about something he has been putting up with for fifteen years. But there is nothing unconscious about the pain he feels in his ankles during the afternoon, which now shoots up into his calves and thighs. At three o'clock he ambles over to the white police telephone standing on the corner of Washington and Hayward, and leans against the pole.

"By the end of the day, after you've been on the Zone moving traffic eight hours, you're about ready for the straight jacket. It hits your lungs, your head is buzzing, your legs ache. I really get it in the legs. So when my day is over, I run for the car and just about hit the traffic moving south. Every day I get caught in a nice half-hour jam. During the summer, with cars inching along, and the heat from the sun beating down, and the engines roaring around you, it can get brutal. By the time I reach Route Three—fifteen, sixteen miles from Boston, away from the real traffic—I feel like I've just been flushed out of a cesspool. I still love the job, because of the people, but in a crowded city downtown even the friendliest old ladies can get pissy after a couple of hours. Early in the morning it's cool and great, but as the day goes on, you really want to get out and dive into a good breaker or something. So when I get rolling down to Marshfield, I'm in heaven."

Galvin is relieved by Markham for the last time today. It is three minutes to four. He half runs to his car. During the summer months, Galvin spends a half hour each night driving out to Route Three, heading toward his summer cottage in suburban Marshfield. Tonight, after he has escaped the traffic knot, he spots a hitchhiker and pulls over to the side of the road to pick him up. The shaggy youth is startled when he spots Galvin's uniform. ("Don't worry, pal, I'm not gonna bust you.") The boy gets in. ("Where you going?" "Plymouth." "I'll drive you as far as Marshfield, then I get off." "Okay, if you want." "No problem, I have to go that way anyhow. You in school?" "No, I dropped out of Boston State." "The Army on your ass?" "Yeah, I'm trying for a C. O." "Hope you're luckier than I was.")

Galvin slows the car just before the Marshfield cutoff. ("I'm turning here. Listen I mean it, good luck with the C. O. If you can serve in some hospital, it's just as good as getting your head blown off for nothing.") The boy, his dark-blond hair waving in the breeze, says, "Thanks, man," and gets out.

Galvin moves off toward his summer home, foot pressed hard on the accelerator. He is anxious to put the city fast behind. When the oceanside beach becomes visible, he almost utters a sigh as his fingers relax their grip on the steering wheel and he sucks in a healthy gulp of Marshfield's summer air.

"My God, I love this little place. The ocean, the atmosphere. But also 'cause this area's where the little people live, the average guys who busted ass all their lives and finally scraped up just enough for a little cookie box. You won't find any executives and vice presidents down here. Maybe a few with college degrees, but mostly the working stiffs, the blue-collar man. They're good, average people. My kind. The silent majority, maybe.

"But I'm in fear of that majority someday getting very loud, and then we get a major confrontation between left and right. You'll have a battle right in the street. A big move to the right is very possible in this nation, and it has to be stopped. I don't think we should have Kent State, or anybody taking a life, because life is sacred. But at the same time, we can't let these animals tear up cities. Even if the system turned around tomorrow and did everything they wanted, they still would hate it. If the hard core of left-wing radicals were controlled, the right would stay silent.

"We're just playing into the hands of the Phuey Newtons and the Rap Browns and the Jerry Rubins who are preying on the malcontent. Look at the hard-hat construction workers—good Americans, hard-working, they're the lifeblood, putting up buildings, paving roads. It seems that radicalism from the left is pushing people to the right. After years of organizing and struggle, the hard hat is making good money—six, seven bucks an hour—and he earns it. Now when he sees these kids burning, he feels threatened. His six bucks an hour is in danger, his house and family are in jeopardy. He's just had these things a short while, and he thinks someone's going to take them away. The black people—not the crazy Phuey Newtons, but the great majority of the black people—deserve the rights they've been waiting for for centuries. I go along with the Court there. The average guy deserves a better shake, too. His taxes are too high, he gets clipped when he goes to the store, the dollar isn't worth half a buck any more. And look how dirty Boston is. God. I'm directing traffic all day in the guts of the city and taking in poison with every breath. When I go down to this place on the Cape, I can *feel* the difference. All this environmental shit is good. We need changes. Big changes. And the guys that are in power have done a shitty job. The lace-curtain families have spoiled their kids. They get divorced or go on drunks or gambling and their kids grow up and don't know them. Used to be heroin was something the blacks used in the ghetto. Now it's in the suburbs. The well-to-do have fucked up the economy, the government, the countryside, and their own kids.

"But when the mistakes which have been neglected for years boil over into a riot, who do they send in to stop the thing? Who goes in to put on a Band-Aid when the situation calls for major surgery? Who ends up beating heads to quell the disturbance to restore the order? Who in the end has to make the Constitution work? Us, the goddamn policemen. The guy who hasn't got the education because he isn't getting the pay. The guy who has to make split-second decisions that affect human life and take the courts years to decide. The guy who has to deliver a baby one second and stop a riot the next. The guy who can't go home from work at night, because his job stays with him in his mind. The guy who usually hangs around with other cops because other people can't understand the way he thinks. The guy who lives in danger every time he puts on the uniform. The guy who catches hell in the Jewish suburb for not being tougher on guys that hit a store, but who gets his ass burnt by the civil liberties boys if the next day he roughs up some looters in the inner city. The cop.

"But I say there's still a chance to change things within the system by the voting box. I wouldn't change my job if I could. I love it. You rarely hear about cops quitting. If the policemen are starting to look bad to people, they should think for a minute that maybe we just reflect the kind of job we have to do. Maybe we stand for how bad things are in this country, because we see the sickness first, we're on the front lines. We see the crime and delinquency before it gets out to the nice white suburbs."

Galvin parks his station wagon outside the small red three-room frame cottage that he works overtime to maintain. He takes a deep swig of the sea breeze as he walks through the yard, cluttered with beach toys, past the American flag on the pole he set up himself. His wife is at the door. He gives her a quick kiss on the cheek, then goes to the refrigerator and snaps the top on a Budweiser beer.

FURTHER THOUGHTS

1. Does the label *cop* mean to Galvin and Williams what it means to you? What are the differences and similarities?

2. As you think back over Lasson's article, ask yourself what your image of his cop is. How do you picture Galvin? What detail seems most to represent him for you, to serve as a kind of symbol of him? Is the total image the same as the image you had of cops in general before reading the piece? How do you picture the narrator of Williams's poem?

3. There is a lot of labeling in Lasson's article. The reporter does some, Galvin does more. What label would Galvin give you? What labels would you give yourself? What are the expectations set by each of the labels you would give yourself?

THE HUNDRED NAMES
(CHINA, 2300 B.C.)

Anonymous

trans. Henry Hart

> From break of day
> Till sunset glow
> I toil.
> I dig my well,

I plow my field,
And earn my food
And drink.
What care I
Who rules the land
If I
Am left in peace?

It's pretty clear that creativity and love do not come in neatly labeled packages. They are distilled from the stresses and tensions brewed by the given realities of a job. And they appear in many different forms, wearing social masks. As you read the next selection, watch for varied masks of love and creativity.

The quiet burden of leadership is not a popular topic these days. The following selection is part of the autobiography of a man who accepted that burden.

WHAT HAPPENED WHEN I GAVE UP THE GOOD LIFE AND BECAME PRESIDENT

Eberhard Faber

A rather extraordinary thing happened to me this year. Last spring I was without a job—I'd been without one for two years, in fact—and on the whole was enjoying life immensely. In June, however, I had to go back to work. Since working is a common enough experience among adults, and since I'm thirty-five, I don't expect any special sympathy over my reappearance in the U.S. labor force. But the job I got was something special. I became president and chief executive of a $20-million enterprise in deep trouble.

To be more precise about the state of affairs last spring: I was doing a lot of reading, playing a lot of tennis, chess, and poker, chopping wood, and singing and roughhousing with my two sons, who were five and three. I was also trying to write some fiction, but was not, as my wife often pointed out, wearing out the desk. I know that many men feel restless and unfulfilled when they don't have a job to go to, but I don't seem to have that problem—I felt fine. The setting for this idyllic life was a big old farmhouse in Belle Mead, near Princeton, New Jersey.

The company I've now gone to work for is Eberhard Faber Inc., the family business. It was founded by my great-grandfather in 1849, and is one of the oldest, and I think the best, manufacturer of pencils and other stationery supplies in the U.S. Its domestic operations are based in a plant at Mountaintop, outside Wilkes-Barre, Pennsylvania, but it also has subsidiaries in Germany and Canada, partnerships in Venezuela and Colombia, and licensees in Brazil, Argentina, Peru, El Salvador, Turkey, and the Philippines. The company seemed to be thriving when I was growing up, and it occurred to me at a fairly early age that, if I wanted to, I could run it one day.

The View from Greenpoint

Actually, I have been somewhat ambivalent about this prospect over the years. I remember that in the summer of 1953, just before I went off to college at Princeton, I worked as a stock boy in the shipping department. The company was then located in a sprawling thirteen-building complex in the Greenpoint section of Brooklyn. I used to take my lunch up to the roof, sit under the huge letters of the Eberhard Faber sign there, and gaze across the East River at the United Nations Building, trying to decide what to make of my life. At that point I was inclined to be a man of letters. In college I edited the *Daily Princetonian.* Later I won a Fulbright Teaching Fellowship, under which I taught American literature at the University of Caen in Normandy. And later still I spent two years in Paris writing fiction.

However, I also kept my hand in at the company. In 1960-61, I worked as an executive trainee (unpaid) at the new Mountaintop offices. In the spring of 1965, I came back for another, somewhat longer tour of duty: I worked as assistant treasurer, then assistant secretary, and finally secretary of the corporation. I'd been attending board meetings of the company since I was twenty-one, and in 1966, when I was twenty-nine, I became a director.

Then, in 1969, I decided to leave the company. I was bored with my duties, the enterprise seemed to run perfectly well without me, and I wanted to write. Besides, I felt that I wanted to extract more fun out of life than I'd been doing.

I realize that this last declaration is apt to evoke images of a younger generation frittering away the hard-earned resources of its ancestors. In partial self-justification, let me say that the Fabers have always had a tendency toward fun and games and high living. My great-uncle, John Eberhard Faber, is supposed to have named the well-known MONGOL pencil after his favorite soup, Purée Mongole; the story happens to be apocryphal, but it is revealing that the family always liked it. In any case, it is a fact that my great-uncle was a gourmet, and also a fact that he was president of the American Whist League, a fine golfer, and third basemen for the Alpha Baseball Club, which seems to have won some kind of championship in New York in 1875. My grandfather, according to another cherished family tradition, once won an immense sum at roulette in Monte Carlo when he hit on "nineteen" three times in a row. My father and mother once made a killing playing bridge for 25 cents a point, when they thought they were playing for ¼ cent.

Anyway, in March, 1969, I quit the company and took up the good life in Belle Mead. Unfortunately, the company began running into trouble at about the same time. There was, I'm afraid, no connection between my departure and the company's new problems.

Hard Times in the Pencil Game

Some of the problems were built into the industry. The pencil business itself, which represents almost 40 percent of our revenues, had been substantially depressed during much of the postwar period. It is plagued by overcapacity, the result of seventeen companies sharing a market of only about $40 million, and chronically afflicted by ruinous price wars. The ball-point pen and increased computerization of many office operations have held down the market growth that might have been expected with a rising population. Efforts to diversify have not been entirely successful. In addition to pencils, Eberhard Faber Inc. now makes erasers, rubber bands, felt and porous-tipped markers, a "whiteboard" visual-aid panel for schools, several kinds of adhesives, type cleaners, and more; and profit margins on quite a few of the lines are low.

But some of the company's problems in 1969 went beyond those of the industry. Labor relations deteriorated that year and there was an eleven-week strike. When the dust settled, the company had lost a lot of business, some of it permanently. The size of the final settlement further reduced profit margins on the bulk of the product line. Worst of all, there were indications that, even after the settlement, the union's relations with management were hostile and communication was bad. The directors were not surprised when 1969 turned out to be a loss year. They were shaken when the losses continued, and in fact deepened, during 1970.

Later, when it began to look as though 1971 would be even worse, the company called in Goggi & Race, a New York consulting firm, to get an outside appraisal of the problems. Specifically, the firm was asked what Eberhard Faber Inc. should do to straighten out its labor problems. After a long, hard look at the company, Paul Goggi reported to the board that the real problem wasn't labor—it was management. He went on to make some specific suggestions for improving the company's materials management and sales forecasting, reshaping the organizational structure, using our machinery and space more efficiently. Later, when the suggestions were not implemented rapidly enough, Goggi indicated forcibly that the company needed some executive changes.

For almost a century after it was founded, Eberhard Faber Inc. was run by, as well as owned by, members of the family. But a series of tragedies some three decades ago interrupted the family's managerial role. In 1945 my father and one of his brothers were drowned while trying to rescue me in the rough surf off the New Jersey shore; I was eventually rescued by another uncle, my mother's brother Duncan. Not long afterward, my grandfather died. My father had been the company's executive vice president; my grandfather had been president. In an effort to fill this large management vacuum, my great-uncle John took over as president—although he was in his nineties! Not surprisingly, Uncle John never did get a very firm grip on the company, and when he died in 1949 it was pretty much out of control.

Keeping It in the Family

At this point, all logic pointed to selling the company, but my mother insisted that it stay in the family. She continued to insist on family control even after she had received some attractive offers for the company, and she stuck to this position after she was stricken by cancer and had to undergo major surgery. One potential buyer actually got a representative into her room at the hospital, when her condition was still critical, and attempted to do business right there. It is another cherished family tradition that my Uncle Duncan finally got rid of the man by brandishing a revolver at him. Luckily, my mother has the constitution of a Texas steer and the fighting spirit of an Irish terrier. She recovered, held on to the company, and became a vice president (for many years she handled public relations). She did not attempt to run the company, however, and no other Faber was available in the years after Uncle John's death.

I mention all these details because they help to explain why, when Paul Goggi said the company needed new management, I decided to offer my services as president. I had, of course, some large material reasons for being concerned about the company's future. Almost all my family's resources are tied up in the business. If it fails, the family is in trouble. But I wasn't just making an investment decision; a lot of family history and traditions were fed into the decision too. On top of everything else, I felt an obligation to try to do something for the company's employees, hundreds of whom I knew personally. I thought I could actually help the company.

A Beginning in the Cafeteria

The board accepted my offer, and I took over as president on June 8. The first few hours were fairly rugged. I'd been up almost until dawn the night before I showed up at the office, working on a speech I had to deliver to the employees of Eberhard Faber Inc. I knew that the employees would be tense when they assembled for the meeting. They didn't know what they were going to be told, or even by whom. When they saw me appear at the podium of our cafeteria—it's the largest room available at Mountaintop, and it has to be used for meetings—they would realize the occasion was an important one, possibly an announcement that the company would be sold or moved elsewhere. The first thing I had to tell them, therefore, was that I was speaking to them as president of an ongoing enterprise. That would reassure them to some extent; however, there was no getting around the company's massive problems, and so I also had to let them know about the company's deteriorating financial position. Finally, I wanted to inspire them—to give them a feeling that they could turn the company around.

At Eberhard Faber Inc., the factory gets to work at seven, the office at eight. It was seven-thirty on an outrageously beautiful June morning when I pulled into the parking lot. I had an hour before the speech was to be delivered, and I didn't want to be seen, and start all sorts of rumors, during that hour. I scurried quickly up the stairs to the executive offices, feeling somewhat conspiratorial, and spent the ensuing hour with several other executives, trying to smile through the terror. Paul Mailloux, our new executive vice president, kept assuring me that arrangements for the meeting would go smoothly; I noticed, however, that he seemed unable to light his pipe.

Actually, there was a large complication about speaking to all the employees of our company. There were 523 of them at Mountaintop and the production workers were on two different shifts. The cafeteria, furthermore, holds only about seventy-five. In the end, my speech to the employees had to be delivered *eight times.*

I thought that the first session, which was for the management group, went fairly well. I could feel the sweat coursing down my arms and chest as I prepared for the second session, which was for the union committee. But that one seemed to go fairly well too, and when it was over the union president, Paul Butchko, came over and said, "As long as you play fair with us, we'll play fair with you." He had the same husky tone in his voice that I'd heard in mine during parts of the speech, and I suddenly realized that Butchko, who was about my own age, had a lot of new responsibilities to deal with too.

The speeches went on all through the day, which just got hotter every hour. By the time I'd finished Speech No. 8, for the night shift, I was completely exhausted. It was a Wednesday, and I briefly considered dropping by at the Westmoreland Club in downtown Wilkes-Barre to relax in the club's weekly poker game. But the evening papers were carrying our story, and I just didn't feel strong enough to face a crowd of well-wishers and answer questions about my new situation. I went home and slept like a log.

The Westmoreland Club is a rather important institution for businessmen in Wilkes-Barre. One of its attractions is a five-card stud game on Wednesday, and during my earlier stints at the company I'd become one of the regulars. The stakes are interesting, and the other regulars include some of the more interesting men in town: there are two brothers in the lumber business, an architect, a hardware merchant, an executive at the Wilkes-Barre Publishing Co., a retired dentist, the manager of a tractor agency, and a printer; several of the town's bankers also play, but they have never achieved the status of regulars.

When I finally did make it to the club, on my second week in town, they made me feel right at home. At the plant, I was finding that people I'd known since childhood were respectfully calling me Mr. Faber. At the club there was no such problem. I was "Timmy" (an old nickname), and the opening shot, as I walked through the front door, was delivered by Harry Vivian, one of the lumber dealers. "Well, if it isn't Timmy," he greeted me. "Tell us how you got to where you are by hard work and perseverance, Timmy."

Caging the Paper Tiger

Obviously, I had a lot to learn about running the company, but I did have some advantages when I started out. I had, of course, a lot of help from our management team and from Goggi & Race. Because of my previous tours of duty in the company, I knew where the men's room was, so to speak. I was reasonably familiar with the plant operation, the sales distribution patterns, the organizational structure, and the daily routines. And, of course, I knew the people.

The first thing I had to learn about running the company concerned the mounds of paper that were now dumped on my desk—larger mounds than I'd ever seen in my life. Enormous, incomprehensible data-processing runs arrived daily. Tickler files, based on miscellaneous memoranda of past years, appeared promptly every Thursday, often leaving me mystified about whom to tickle, how to tickle them, and whether it really mattered. Job applications and résumés, acquisition and merger inquiries, advertising and sales bulletins, association newsletters, results from our test labs, interoffice memos, travel schedules of other executives, letters of congratulation on my appointment, brochures on the advantages of alternate plant sites, news about our community services, were all in the mound. Also, it seemed as though everyone in the company thought it prudent to send the new president a copy of every letter he wrote, if only as evidence of hard work.

I let this avalanche pour over me for a while; but finally, guided by a powerful instinct for survival, I took a deep breath, prayerfully apologized to the puritan God of Hard Work, and instructed my secretary to hide most of it in the closet. She now screens my mail ruthlessly. Sometimes letters don't get answered for a week, or at all, and sometimes an important document gets buried in the great mound, but I can't really believe it's affecting the bottom line.

The company's major problem at the time I took over was, of course, to stem the accelerating flow of losses and get onto a breakeven basis, at least. This meant, inevitably, that the operating budget had to be trimmed severely. There was also an urgent need to get a grip on our inventories, which were far too large in several product lines. Thus far we've reduced the budget by 18 percent and reduced the total inventory by about 25 percent. The inventory cutback enabled us to pay off our short-term loan and, in general, lower the pressures represented by our friendly bankers.

Selling the Whiteboard

The single most important business decision we faced concerned our "whiteboard" operations in Lansing, Michigan. We had acquired the Lansing operation in 1967, and it was losing money at a frightening rate. The product itself, which we call the Eberhard Faber-Board visual-aid panel, is a white panel that has some substantial advantages over ordinary composition or slate blackboards. It uses water and xylene-based markers as writing instruments, and the writing is a lot easier to read than anything chalked on blackboards; in addition, there's less glare and no smudging when you erase. Finally, the panel can be used as a projection screen.

Unfortunately, we badly misjudged the market for it. We had felt that its principal use would be in schools and colleges, and that it could easily ride on the coattails of our regular line, much of which is sold through school-supply houses and other educational distributors. We failed to see one large difficulty about selling it, however. The panel would be a capital item for the school, which meant that administrators who wanted to buy it would have to go through a quite different and more complicated approval process than they go through when they buy our pencils and erasers. Given the financial crisis that schools generally have been in recently, there just wasn't much heart to take on new lines. A few schools and colleges—one is the Massachusetts Institute of Technology—have been good customers, but in general we haven't had nearly as many educational sales as we'd counted on. The market has thus far turned out to be in industry and among architects. We've sold the board to just about every major corporation in the U.S., and many have been repeat buyers. The whiteboard was even bought by Grumman for use in planning the production and testing of the lunar modules. (Grumman had the panels on tracks, and used groups of them to keep its people informed about the status of the modules as they went through the production process.)

The fact remained, however, that our total sales volume was not high enough to justify the kind of costs we were running up in the Lansing facility. And so I asked our management committee to meet and ponder three alternatives: sell the whiteboard operation to another company; liquidate it; or move it into the Mountaintop plant (which would reduce total corporate overhead charges). I indicated that the one option we did *not* have was doing nothing—that is, leaving the operation as it was.

At the first meeting the management committee was somewhat disposed to move the operation to Mountaintop. For one thing, moving it would be far less costly than liquidating it. For another, we still felt that the product had an exciting sales potential. At this point, however, we found ourselves confronting a question to which we had no answer: what kind of profit margin could we expect on the product if we did move it to Mountaintop? We asked George Flower, our treasurer, for an answer, and I adjourned the meeting.

At a second meeting on the whiteboard, we had Mr. Flower's projections in front of us. They showed a fair enough margin between our production costs and the selling price; the gross margin was close to the necessary minimum for other products at Mountaintop. But it occurred to me to ask about the cost of selling the panels, and Mr. Mailloux's off-the-cuff reply indicated that it was far higher than our average. Suddenly everyone was scribbling numbers on his pad. I have a lot to learn about management, but I know, at least, that you're supposed to do your homework before meetings, not during them. Somewhat exasperated, principally at myself, I adjourned this meeting too and asked George Flower to project his figures all the way to the bottom line. When the new figures came in, they were clearly unsatisfactory.

The reason our selling expenses were so high was that many of our dealers hadn't been willing to devote much time to selling the panel. Therefore we'd had to direct our own sales and promotion effort directly to the ultimate consumer; on many orders we ended up doing all the selling ourselves. That wouldn't have been so bad except that, after we'd done the work, we were letting the dealers write up the orders—and take their standard commissions. With George Flower's new figures in front of him, our sales manager, Walt Krieger, proposed a selling program that was a lot more equitable. The program produced a projected net profit that seemed to make some sense. The decision to move the Lansing operation to Mountaintop was approved.

The moral I drew from this sequence of events was not to worship the false God of Gross Profit Margin. We now base all our product decisions on models that project to the bottom line.

Getting the Lead Out

I guess no businessman's story is complete these days without an account of his problems with consumer advocates. To my considerable astonishment, Eberhard Faber Inc. has had a problem; it began about the time I took over as president, and dealing with it is one of our public-relations chores today.

The issue has been the lead content of the lacquer used to coat pencils. Last spring New York City's Bureau of Lead Poisoning Control performed tests on pencil lacquer, and reported that about a third of the companies whose products were tested had lead contents substantially above the 1 percent level allowed by the American National Standards Institute. In September the attorney general of New York state demanded the voluntary recall of all pencils with excessive lead in their lacquers. He did not indicate what he regarded as excessive. however, or the names of the brand involved. But he issued a press release implying that lead poisoning among pencil chewers was a serious problem.

What I found maddening about this sequence was that Eberhard Faber Inc. had no lead at all in its lacquer (except for the trace quantities found in almost all substances). We took it out ten years ago, when we first became aware that there might be problems about lead; this was before the A.N.S.I. standard even existed. At the time, the company alerted the Pencil Makers Association to the problem, and it's our impression that many of the members proceeded to get all the lead out of their pencils too. But right now the public has no way of knowing which pencils have too much lead and which don't; we're all under the same cloud.

We also had a disturbing problem about our "internal communications," and I'm afraid it arose largely because of my own inexperience. Last September, after I'd been around for three months, I made another series of speeches to our staff. We had just completed a layoff of an extra packaging shift that we put on in the summer; and I was under the impression that no more men had to go. I said in the speech that we contemplated "no further layoffs at this time." I was horrified to learn a few days later that I'd been wrong—we had to furlough a small group of workers on the night shift; and a few weeks after that a larger group had to go too.

When I visited the factory floor a few days after this second layoff, one of the union men suggested pointedly that I'd double-crossed them. We had a meeting with the union committee, and I think I persuaded its members that it had at least been an honest mistake. The moral I've drawn from this mortifying episode is that you just can't make mistakes when people's jobs are involved.

Waiting for a Verdict

One morning a few weeks back, I was driving to my office and thinking about the day's business. Its main feature was a management-committee meeting with a lot of important business on the agenda—one entry was the future of the whiteboard. Brooding about the potential for big trouble in each of the situations, I suddenly felt that it might be a good idea to pull over to the side of the road. I opened the car door and parted with my breakfast. I was weak and found, to my dismay, that I couldn't stop trembling.

At any previous point in my life, I would have felt that the symptoms justified going home and getting into bed. This time, however, it seemed that that management-committee meeting absolutely had to take place, and that I had to be there for it. I drove to the drugstore, bought a bottle of mouthwash, and went to work.

As the story might indicate, I'm still not entirely at ease in my new way of life. Nevertheless, I'm actually having a lot of fun in the job. The prospect of turning our company around, of succeeding at that challenging task, has exhilarated me, just as it has the people working with me. Thus far we have met our short-term objectives; I believe that we'll meet our long-range ones as well, though it certainly will not be easy. I just hope I don't completely lose the ability to loaf.

FURTHER THOUGHTS

1. What love and creativity did you find in Faber's experiences?
2. Why did he throw up before going on to work?
3. Faber started with some clear hopes and fears. What expectations did he have? What feelings did he have about the expectations others had of him?
4. What connections do you see between Faber's story and the conclusion of the ancient Chinese poem "The Hundred Names"?

There is a nearby pizza place with a TV where we go for lunch—always it seems, about the time one of the perennial soap operas is on. Try as we do, we cannot avoid being drawn into them. Perhaps it is because of the moral that is implicit in them—oddly enough, the same moral expressed by the American novelist William Faulkner: the celebration of sheer endurance.

Love is not the theme of the following parable, nor is creativity. But the selection suggests that there may be a primal virtue without which one can be neither lover nor creator.

THE MYTH OF SISYPHUS

Albert Camus

The gods had condemned Sisyphus to ceaselessly rolling a rock to the top of a mountain, whence the stone would fall back of its own weight. They had thought with some reason that there is no more dreadful punishment than futile and hopeless labor.

If one believes Homer, Sisyphus was the wisest and most prudent of mortals. According to another tradition, however, he was disposed to practice the profession of highwayman. I see no contradiction in this. Opinions differ as to the reasons why he became the futile laborer of the underworld. To begin with, he is accused of a certain levity in regard to the gods. He stole their secrets. Aegina, the daughter of Aesopus, was carried off by Jupiter. The father was shocked by that disappearance and complained to Sisyphus. He, who knew of the abduction, offered to tell about it on condition that Aesopus would give water to the citadel of Corinth. To the celestial thunderbolts he preferred the benediction of water. He was punished for this in the underworld. Homer tells us also that Sisyphus had put Death in chains. Pluto could not endure the sight of his deserted, silent empire. He dispatched the god of war, who liberated Death from the hands of her conqueror.

It is said also that Sisyphus, being near to death, rashly wanted to test his wife's love. He ordered her to cast his unburied body into the middle of the public square. Sisyphus woke up in the underworld. And there, annoyed by an obedience so contrary to human love, he obtained from Pluto permission to return to earth in order to chastise his wife. But when he had seen again the face of this world, enjoyed water and sun, warm stones and the sea, he no longer wanted to go back to the infernal darkness. Recalls, signs of anger, warnings were of no avail. Many years more he lived facing the curve of the gulf, the sparkling sea, and the smiles of earth. A decree of the gods was necessary. Mercury came and seized the impudent man by the collar and, snatching him from his joys, led him forcibly back to the underworld, where his rock was ready for him.

You have already grasped that Sisyphus is the absurd hero. He *is,* as much through his passions as through his torture. His scorn of the gods, his hatred of death, and his passion for life won him that unspeakable penalty in which the whole being is exerted toward accomplishing nothing. This is the price that must be paid for the passions of this earth. Nothing is told us about Sisyphus in the underworld. Myths are made for the imagination to breathe life into them. As for this myth, one sees merely the whole effort of a body straining to raise the huge stone, to roll it and push it up a slope a hundred times over; one sees the face screwed up, the cheek tight against the stone, the shoulder bracing the clay-covered mass, the foot wedging it, the fresh start with arms outstretched, the wholly human security of two earth-clotted hands. At the very end of his long effort measured by skyless space and time without depth, the purpose is achieved. Then Sisyphus watches the stone rush down in a few moments toward that lower world whence he will have to push it up again toward the summit. He goes back down to the plain.

It is during that return, that pause, that Sisyphus interests me. A face that toils so close to stones is already stone itself! I see that man going back down with a heavy yet measured step toward the torment of which he will never know the end. That hour like a breathing-space which returns as surely as his suffering, that is the hour of consciousness. At each of those moments when he leaves the heights and gradually sinks toward the lairs of the gods, he is superior to his fate. He is stronger than his rock.

If this myth is tragic, that is because its hero is conscious. Where would his torture be, indeed, if at every step the hope of succeeding upheld him? The workman of today works every day in his life at the same tasks, and this fate is no less absurd. But it is tragic only at the rare moments when it becomes conscious. Sisyphus, proletarian of the gods, powerless and rebellious, knows the whole extent of his wretched condition: it is what he thinks of during his descent. The lucidity that was to constitute his torture at the same time crowns his victory. There is no fate that cannot be surmounted by scorn.

· · · · · · · · · · · ·

If the descent is thus sometimes performed in sorrow, it can also take place in joy. This word is not too much. Again I fancy Sisyphus returning toward his rock, and the sorrow was in the beginning. When the images of earth cling too tightly to memory, when the call of happiness becomes too insistent, it happens that melancholy rises in man's heart: this is the rock's victory, this is the rock itself. The boundless grief is too heavy to bear. These are our nights of Gethsemane. But crushing truths perish from being acknowledged. Thus, Oedipus at the outset obeys fate without knowing it. But from the moment he knows, his tragedy begins. Yet at the same moment, blind and desperate, he realizes that the only bond linking him to the world is the cool hand of a girl. Then a tremendous remark rings out: "Despite so many ordeals, my advanced age and the nobility of my soul make me conclude that all is well." Sophocles' Oedipus, like Dostoevsky's Kirilov, thus gives the recipe for the absurd victory. Ancient wisdom confirms modern heroism.

One does not discover the absurd without being tempted to write a manual of happiness. "What! by such narrow ways—?" There is but one world, however. Happiness and the absurd are two sons of the same earth. They are inseparable. It would be a mistake to say that happiness necessarily springs from the absurd discovery. It happens as well that the feeling of the absurd springs from happiness. "I conclude that all is well," says Oedipus, and that remark is sacred. It echoes in the wild and limited universe of man. It teaches that all is not, has not been, exhausted. It drives out of this world a god who had come into it with dissatisfaction and a preference for futile sufferings. It makes of fate a human matter, which must be settled among men.

All Sisyphus' silent joy is contained therein. His fate belongs to him. His rock is his thing. Likewise, the absurd man, when he contemplates his torment, silences all the idols. In the universe suddenly restored to its silence, the myriad wondering little voices of the earth rise up. Unconscious, secret calls, invitations from all the faces, they are the necessary reverse and price of victory. There is no sun without shadow, and it is essential to know the night. The absurd man says yes and his effort will henceforth be unceasing. If there is a personal fate, there is no higher destiny, or at least there is but one which he concludes is inevitable and despicable. For the rest, he knows himself to be the master of his days. At that subtle moment when man glances backward over his life, Sisyphus returning toward his rock, in that slight pivoting he contemplates that series of unrelated actions which becomes his fate, created by him, combined under his memory's eye and soon sealed by his death. Thus, convinced of the wholly human origin of all that is human, a blind man eager to see who knows that the night has no end, he is still on the go. The rock is still rolling.

I leave Sisyphus at the foot of the mountain! One always finds one's burden again. But Sisyphus teaches the higher fidelity that negates the gods and raises rocks. He too concludes that all is well. This universe henceforth without a master seems to him neither sterile nor futile. Each atom of that stone, each mineral flake of that night-filled mountain, is in itself forms a world. The struggle itself toward the heights is enough to fill a man's heart. One must imagine Sisyphus happy.

FURTHER THOUGHTS

1. Of Sisyphus' fate Camus says, "It is tragic only at the rare moments when it becomes conscious." What does that statement mean? How can you apply it to your own experiences and your attitude toward them?
2. Like Sisyphus and Oedipus, Camus seems to conclude that "all is well." Does that strike you as a bit simple-minded? perhaps a bit blind? Or can you see some sort of wisdom in it?
3. What does Camus mean when he says, "There is no fate that cannot be surmounted by scorn"? Can you think of experiences you yourself or others have had that might support this conclusion?

One of the things most troubling about the fate of Sisyphus is that Sisyphus is so alone. When survival is at stake, working together for mutual support and for a common end makes it possible to endure even the harshness of a prison camp.

THE SIBERIAN CONVICT

Fyodor Dostoyevsky

Hard labor in our fortress was not an occupation, but an obligation. The prisoners accomplished their task, they worked the number of hours fixed by the law, and then returned to the prison. They hated their work outside. If the convict had not some private work of his own, it would have been impossible for him to support his confinement. How could these persons, all strongly constituted, who had been brought together against their will, after society had cast them off—how could they live in a normal and natural manner? Man cannot exist without work, without legal, natural property. Depart from these conditions, and he becomes a wild beast. Accordingly, every convict, through natural requirements and by the instinct of self-preservation, had a trade—an occupation of some kind.

Consequently each barrack, though locked and bolted, assumed the appearance of a large workshop. The work was not, it is true, strictly forbidden, but it was forbidden to have tools, without which work is evidently impossible. But we laboured in secret, and the administration seemed to shut its eyes. Many prisoners arrived without knowing how to make use of their fingers, but they learnt a trade from some of their companions. We had among us cobblers, tailors, masons, locksmiths, and gilders.

I did not understand till long afterwards why the prison labour was really hard and excessive. It was less by reason of its difficulty than because it was forced, imposed, obligatory; done through fear of the stick. The peasant works certainly harder than the convict, for, during the summer, he works night and day. But it is in his own interest. He has a rational aim, so that he suffers less than the convict who performs hard labour from which he derives no profit. It once came into my head that if it were desired to reduce a man to nothing—to punish him atrociously, to crush him in such a manner that the most hardened murderer would tremble before such a punishment—it would be necessary only to give to his work a character of complete uselessness.

Hard labour, as it is now carried on, presents no interest to the convict; but it has its utility. The convict makes bricks, digs the earth, builds; and all his occupations have a meaning and an end. Sometimes, even the prisoner takes an interest in what he is doing. He then wishes to work more skillfully, more advantageously. But let him be constrained to pour water from one vessel into another, or to carry earth from one place to another and back again, then I am persuaded that at the end of a few days the prisoner would strangle himself or commit a thousand crimes, punishable with death, rather than live in such an abject condition and endure such torments.

· · · · · · · · · · · ·

Behind the fortress on the frozen river were two barges belonging to the Government, which were not worth anything, but which had to be taken to pieces in order that the wood might not be lost. The wood was in itself all but valueless. This work was given us to keep us busy. This was understood on both sides.

At last we reached the bank; a little lower down was the old hulk, which we were to break up, stuck fast in the ice. I expected to see everyone go to work at once. Nothing of the kind. Some of the convicts sat down negligently on wooden beams that were lying near the shore, and nearly all took from their pockets pouches containing native tobacco—which was sold in leaf at the market at the rate of three kopecks a pound—and short wooden pipes. They lighted them while the soldiers formed a circle around them, and began to watch us with a tired look.

"Who the devil had the idea of sinking this barge?" asked one of the convicts in a loud voice, without speaking to anyone in particular.

At last the non-commissioned officer appointed to superintend the work came up with a cane in his hand.

"What are you sitting down for? Begin at once."

"Give us our tasks, Ivan Matveitch," said one of the "foremen" among us, as he slowly got up.

"What more do you want? Take the barge to pieces, that is your task."

Ultimately the convicts got up and went to the river, but very slowly. Different "directors" appeared, "directors," at least, in words. The barge was not to be broken up anyhow. The latitudinal beams were to be preserved, and this was not an easy thing to manage.

"Draw this beam out, that is the first thing to do," cried a convict who was neither a director nor a foreman, but a simple workman. This man, very quiet and a little stupid, had not previously spoken. He now bent down, took hold of a heavy beam with both hands, and waited for someone to help him. No one, however, seemed inclined to do so.

"Not you, indeed, you will never manage it; not even your grandfather, the bear, could do it," muttered someone between his teeth.

"Well, my friend, are we to begin? As for me, I can do nothing alone," said the man who had put himself forward, and who now, quitting the beam, stood upright.

"Unless you are going to do all the work by yourself, what are you in such a hurry about?"

"He couldn't feed three hens without making a mistake, and now he puts himself forward!"

"I was only speaking," said the poor fellow, excusing himself for his forwardness.

Finally the prisoners began work, but with no good-will, and very indolently. The irritation of the under-officer at seeing these vigorous men remain so idle was intelligible enough. While the first beam was being removed it suddenly snapped.

"It broke in pieces," said the convict in self-justification. It was impossible then, they suggested, to work in such a manner. What was to be done? A long discussion took place between the prisoners, and little by little they came to insults; nor did this seem likely to be the end of it. The under-officer shouted again and shook his stick, but the second beam snapped like the first.

After an hour the "foreman" arrived. He listened quietly to what the convicts had to say, declared that the task he gave them was to get out four beams unbroken, and to demolish a good part of the barge. As soon as this was done the prisoners could go back to the house. The task was a considerable one,

but good heavens! how the convicts now went to work! Where now was their idleness, their want of skill? The hatchets soon began to dance, and soon the beams were sprung. Those who had no hatchets made use of thick sticks to push beneath the beams, and thus in due time and in skillful fashion they got them out. The convicts seemed suddenly to have become intelligent. No more insults were heard. Every one knew perfectly what to say, to do, to advise. Just half-an-hour before the beating of the drum, the appointed task was executed, and the prisoners returned to the convict prison fatigued, but pleased to have gained half-an-hour from the working time fixed by the regulations.

FURTHER THOUGHTS

1. What caused the shift in the convicts' attitudes and apparent abilities in the final paragraph?
2. How are the convicts like Sisyphus? How are they different?
3. The American poet Edwin Arlington Robinson once said that "The world is not a 'prison-house' but a kind of spiritual kindergarten, where millions of bewildered infants are trying to spell God with the wrong blocks." How does this statement relate to the pieces by Camus and Dostoevsky? What do *you* think of Arlington's point of view?

Sisyphus toiled because the gods ordered him to, the Russian convicts because the guards ordered them to. But, as you read in the introduction to this section, Yves Simon says the worker "must forever deal with the given realities." That *must* and the fact that those realities are *given* means that work always starts with necessity. We work to get the wherewithal to satisfy our needs. We work because we need to. Work and necessity are bound together—as Sigmund Freud, the Austrian psychoanalyst, and Robert Frost, the American poet, point out in the next two selections.

FROM
CIVILIZATION AND ITS DISCONTENTS

Sigmund Freud

After primal man had discovered that it lay in his own hands, literally, to improve his lot on earth by working, it cannot have been a matter of indifference to him whether another man worked with or against him. The other man acquired the value for him of a fellow-worker, with whom it was useful to live together. Even earlier, in his ape-like prehistory, man had adopted the habit of forming families, and the members of his family were probably his first helpers. One may suppose that the founding of families was connected with the fact that a moment came when the need for genital satisfaction no longer made its appearance like a guest who drops in suddenly, and, after his departure, is heard of no more for a long time, but instead took up its quarters as a permanent lodger. When this happened, the male acquired a motive for keeping the female, or, speaking more generally, his sexual objects, near him; while the female, who did not want to be separated from her helpless young, was obliged, in their interests, to remain with the stronger male. In this primitive family one essential feature of civilization is still lacking. The arbitrary will of its head, the father, was unrestricted. In *Totem and Taboo* [1912-13] I have tried to show how the way led from this family to the succeeding stage of communal life in the form of bands of brothers. In overpowering their father, the sons had made the discovery that a combination can be stronger than a single individual. The totemic culture is based on the restrictions which the sons had to impose on one another in order to keep this new state of affairs in being. The taboo-observances were the first 'right' or 'law'. The communal life of human beings had, therefore, a two-fold foundation: the complusion to work, which was created by external necessity, and the power of love, which made the man unwilling to be deprived of his sexual object—the woman—, and made the woman unwilling to be deprived of the part of herself which had been separated off from her—her child. Eros and Ananke [Love and Necessity] have become the parents of human civilization too. The first result of civilization was that even a fairly large number of people were now able to live together in a community.

TWO TRAMPS IN MUD-TIME

Robert Frost

> Out of the mud two strangers came
> And caught me splitting wood in the yard.
> And one of them put me off my aim
> By hailing cheerily "Hit them hard!"
> I knew pretty well why he dropped behind
> And let the other go on a way.
> I knew pretty well what he had in mind:
> He wanted to take my job for pay.

Good blocks of oak it was I split,
As large around as the chopping block;
And every piece I squarely hit
Fell splinterless as a cloven rock.
The blows that a life of self-control
Spares to strike for the common good,
That day, giving a loose to my soul,
I spent on the unimportant wood.

The sun was warm but the wind was chill.
You know how it is with an April day
When the sun is out and the wind is still,
You're one month on in the middle of May.
But if you so much as dare to speak,
A cloud comes over the sunlit arch,
A wind comes off a frozen peak,
And you're two months back in the middle of March.

A bluebird comes tenderly up to alight
And turns to the wind to unruffle a plume,
His song so pitched as not to excite
A single flower as yet to bloom.
It is snowing a flake: and he half knew
Winter was only playing possum.
Except in color he isn't blue,
But he wouldn't advise a thing to blossom.

The water for which we may have to look
In summertime with a witching wand,
In every wheelrut's now a brook,
In every print of a hoof a pond.
Be glad of water, but don't forget
The lurking frost in the earth beneath
That will steal forth after the sun is set
And show on the water its crystal teeth.

The time when most I loved my task
These two must make me love it more
By coming with what they came to ask.
You'd think I never had felt before
The weight of an ax-head poised aloft,
The grip on earth of outspread feet,
The life of muscles rocking soft
And smooth and moist in vernal heat.

Out of the woods two hulking tramps
(From sleeping God knows where last night,
But not long since in the lumber camps).
They thought all chopping was theirs of right.
Men of the woods and lumberjacks,
They judged me by their appropriate tool.
Except as a fellow handled an ax
They had no way of knowing a fool.

Nothing on either side was said.
They knew they had but to stay their stay
And all their logic would fill my head:
As that I had no right to play
With what was another man's work for gain.
My right might be love but theirs was need.
And where the two exist in twain
Theirs was the better right—agreed.

But yield who will to their separation,
My object in living is to unite
My avocation and my vocation
As my two eyes make one in sight.
Only where love and need are one,
And the work is play for mortal stakes,
Is the deed ever really done
For Heaven and the future's sakes.

FURTHER THOUGHTS

1. Freud presents a basis for different kinds of love—including mother-love and romantic love. Does his explanation seem convincing to you? If not, what bothers you about it? You might find it useful to spend a few minutes jotting down examples of all the different ways you can think of that you use the word *love*.
2. What kind of ties does this short passage from Freud have with Diaz's story? with "The Siberian Convict"?
3. What does this sentence mean: "Eros and Ananke [Love and Necessity] have become the parents of human civilization . . ."?
4. What do the final eight lines of Frost's poem say about love, necessity, and work? What links do you see between his poem and the excerpt from Freud?

1st Interlude

The traditional role for the philosopher is to clear up confusions that surround words we use. Sometimes such clarification is most unwelcome—as Socrates learned when he was condemned to death for his troubles. Bertrand Russell spent a good part of this century trying to straighten out other people's thinking. (At one point his attempts landed him in jail.) In the following piece he turns the power of a philosopher's mind to clarifying terms like *work, satisfactions, construction,* and *skill.*

WORK

Bertrand Russell

Whether work should be placed among the causes of happiness or among the causes of unhappiness may perhaps be regarded as a doubtful question. There is certainly much work which is exceedingly irksome, and an excess of work is always very painful. I think, however, that, provided work is not excessive in amount, even the dullest work is to most people less painful than idleness. There are in work all grades, from mere relief of tedium up to the profoundest delights, according to the nature of the work and the abilities of the worker. Most of the work that most people have to do is not in itself interesting, but even such work has certain great advantages. To begin with, it fills a good many hours of the day without the need of deciding what one shall do. Most people when they are left free to fill their own time according to their own choice, are at a loss to think of anything sufficiently pleasant to be worth doing. And whatever they decide on, they are troubled by the feeling that something else would have been pleasanter. To be able to fill leisure intelligently is the last product of civilization, and at present very few people have reached this level. Moreover the exercise of choice is in itself tiresome. Except to people with unusual initiative it is positively agreeable to be told what to do at each hour of the day, provided the orders are not too unpleasant. Most of the idle rich suffer unspeakable boredom as the price of their freedom from drudgery. At times they may find relief by hunting big game in Africa, or by flying round the world, but the number of such sensations is limited, especially after youth is past. Accordingly the more intelligent rich men work nearly as hard as if they were poor, while rich women for the most part keep themselves busy with innumerable trifles of whose earth-shaking importance they are firmly persuaded.

Work therefore is desirable, first and foremost, as a preventive of boredom, for the boredom that a man feels when he is doing necessary though uninteresting work is as nothing in comparison with the boredom that he feels when he has nothing to do with his days. With this advantage of work another is associated, namely that it makes holidays much more delicious when they come. Provided a man does not have to work so hard as to impair his vigor, he is likely to find far more zest in his free time than an idle man could possibly find.

The second advantage of most paid work and of some unpaid work is that it gives chances of success and opportunities for ambition. In most work success is measured by income, and while our capitalistic society continues, this is inevitable. It is only where the best work is concerned that this measure ceases to be the natural one to apply. The desire that men feel to increase their income is quite as much a desire for success as for the extra comforts that a higher income can procure. However dull work may be, it becomes bearable if it is a means of building up a reputation, whether in the world at large or only in one's own circle. Continuity of purpose is one of the most essential ingredients of happiness in the long run, and for most men this comes chiefly through their work. In this respect those women whose lives are occupied with housework are much less fortunate than men, or than women who work outside the home. The domesticated wife does not receive wages, has no means of bettering herself, is taken for granted by her husband (who sees practically nothing of what she does), and is valued by him not for her housework but for quite other qualities. Of course this does not apply to those women who are sufficiently well-to-do to make beautiful houses and beautiful gardens and become the envy of their neighbors; but such women are comparatively few, and for the great majority housework cannot bring as much satisfaction as work of other kinds brings to men and to professional women.

The satisfaction of killing time and of affording some outlet, however modest, for ambition, belongs to most work, and is sufficient to make even a man whose work is dull happier on the average than a man who has no work at all. But when work is interesting, it is capable of giving satisfaction of a far higher order than mere relief from tedium. The kinds of work in which there is some interest may be arranged in a hierarchy. I shall begin with those which are only mildly interesting and end with those that are worthy to absorb the whole energies of a great man.

Two chief elements make work interesting: first, the exercise of skill, and second, construction.

Every man who has acquired some unusual skill enjoys exercising it until it has become a matter of course, or until he can no longer improve himself. This motive to activity begins in early childhood: a boy who can stand on his head becomes reluctant to stand on his feet. A great deal of work gives the same pleasure that is to be derived from games of skill. The work of a lawyer or a politician must contain in a more delectable form a great deal of the same pleasure that is to be derived from playing bridge. Here of course there is not only the exercise of skill but the outwitting of a skilled opponent. Even where this competitive element is absent, however, the performance of difficult feats is agreeable. A man who can do stunts in an aeroplane finds the pleasure so great that for the sake of it he is willing to risk his life. I imagine that an able surgeon, in spite of the painful circumstances in which his work is done, derives satisfaction from the exquisite precision of his operations. The same kind of pleasure, though in a less intense form, is to be derived from a great deal of work of a humbler kind. All skilled work can be pleasurable, provided the skill required is either variable or capable of indefinite improvement. If these conditions are absent, it will cease to be interesting when a man has acquired his maximum skill. A man who runs three-mile races will cease to find pleasure in this occupation when he passes the age at which he can beat his own previous record. Fortunately there is a very considerable amount of work in which new circumstances call for new skill and a man can go on improving, at any rate until he has reached middle age. In some kinds of skilled work, such as politics, for example, it seems that men are at their best between sixty and seventy, the reason being that in such occupations a wide experience of other men is essential. For this reason successful politicians are apt to be happier at the age of seventy than any other men of equal age. Their only competitors in this respect are the men who are the heads of big businesses.

There is, however, another element possessed by the best work, which is even more important as a source of happiness than is the exercise of skill. This is the element of constructiveness. In some work, though by no means in most, something is built up which remains as a monument when the work is completed. We may distinguish construction from destruction by the following criterion. In construction the initial state of affairs is comparatively haphazard, while the final state of affairs embodies a purpose: in destruction the reverse is the case; the initial state of affairs embodies a purpose, while the final state of affairs is haphazard, that is to say, all that is intended by the destroyer is to produce a state of affairs which does not embody a certain purpose. This criterion applies in the most literal and obvious case, namely the construction and destruction of buildings. In constructing a building a previously made plan is carried out, whereas in destroying it no one decides exactly how the materials are to lie when the demolition is complete. Destruction is of course necessary very often as a preliminary to subsequent construction; in that case it is part of a whole which is constructive. But not infrequently a man will engage in activities of which the purpose is destructtive without regard to any construction that may come after. Frequently he will conceal this from himself by the belief that he is only sweeping away in order to build afresh, but it is generally possible to unmask this pretense, when it is a pretense, by asking him what the subsequent construction is to be. On this subject it will be found that he will speak vaguely and without enthusiasm, whereas on the preliminary destruction he has spoken precisely and with zest. This applies to not a few revolutionaries and militarists and other apostles of violence. They are actuated, usually without their own knowledge, by hated: the destruction of what they hate is their real purpose, and they are comparatively indifferent to the question what is to come after it.

Now I cannot deny that in the work of destruction as in the work of construction there may be joy. It is a fiercer joy, perhaps at moments more intense, but it is less profoundly satisfying, since the result is one in which little satisfaction is to be found. You kill your enemy, and when he is dead your occupation is gone, and the satisfaction that you derive from victory quickly fades. The work of construction, on the other hand, when completed is delightful to contemplate, and moreover is never so fully completed that there is nothing further to do about it. The most satisfactory purposes are those that lead on indefinitely from one success to another without ever coming to a dead end; and in this respect it will be found that construction is a greater source of happiness than destruction. Perhaps it would be more correct to say that those who find satisfaction in construction find in it greater satisfaction than the lovers of destruction can find in destruction, for if once you have become filled with hate you will not easily derive from construction the pleasure which another man would derive from it.

At the same time few things are so likely to cure the habit of hatred as the opportunity to do constructive work of an important kind.

The satisfaction to be derived from success in a great constructive enterprise is one of the most massive that life has to offer, although unfortunately in its highest forms it is open only to men of exceptional ability. Nothing can rob a man of the happiness of successful achievement in an important piece of work, unless it be the proof that after all his work was bad. There are many forms of such satisfaction. The man who by a scheme of irrigation has caused the wilderness to blossom like the rose enjoys it in one of its most tangible forms. The creation of an organization may be a work of supreme importance. So is the work of those few statesmen who have devoted their lives to producing order out of chaos, of whom Lenin is the supreme type in our day. The most obvious examples are artists and men of science. Shakespeare says of his verse: "So long as men can breathe, or eyes can see, so long lives this." And it cannot be doubted that the thought consoled him for misfortune. In his sonnets he maintains that the thought of his friend reconciled him to life, but I cannot help suspecting that the sonnets he wrote to his friend were even more effective for this purpose than the friend himself. Great artists and great men of science do work which is in itself delightful; while they are doing it, it secures them the respect of those whose respect is worth having, which gives them the most fundamental kind of power, namely, power over men's thoughts and feelings. They have also the most solid reasons for thinking well of themselves. This combination of fortunate circumstances ought, one would think, to be enough to make any man happy. Nevertheless it is not so. Michael Angelo, for example, was a profoundly unhappy man, and maintained (not, I am sure, with truth) that he would not have troubled to produce works of art if he had not had to pay the debts of his impecunious relations. The power to produce great art is very often, though by no means always, associated with a temperamental unhappiness, so great that but for the joy which the artist derives from his work, he would be driven to suicide. We cannot, therefore, maintain that even the greatest work must make a man happy; we can only maintain that it must make him less unhappy. Men of science, however, are far less often temperamentally unhappy than artists are, and in the main the men who do great work in science are happy men, whose happiness is derived primarily from their work.

One of the causes of unhappiness among intellectuals in the present day is that so many of them, especially those whose skill is literary, find no opportunity for the independent exercise of their talents, but have to hire themselves out to rich corporations directed by Philistines, who insist upon their producing what they themselves regard as pernicious nonsense. If you were to inquire among journalists in either England or America whether they believed in the policy of the newspaper for which they worked, you would find, I believe, that only a small minority do so; the rest, for the sake of a livelihood, prostitute their skill to purposes which they believe to be harmful. Such work cannot bring any real satisfaction, and in the course of reconciling himself to the doing of it, a man has to make himself so cynical that he can no longer derive whole-hearted satisfaction from anything whatever. I cannot condemn men who undertake work of this sort, since starvation is too serious an alternative, but I think that where it is possible to do work that is satisfactory to a man's constructive impulses without entirely starving, he will be well advised from the point of view of his own happiness if he chooses it in preference to work much more highly paid but not seeming to him worth doing on its own account. Without self-respect genuine happiness is scarcely possible. And the man who is ashamed of his work can hardly achieve self-respect.

The satisfaction of constructive work, though it may, as things are, be the privilege of a minority, can nevertheless be the privilege of a quite large minority. Any man who is his own master in his work can feel it; so can any man whose work appears to him useful and requires considerable skill. The production of satisfactory children is a difficult constructive work capable of affording profound satisfaction. Any woman who has achieved this can feel that as a result of her labor the world contains something of value which it would not otherwise contain.

Human beings differ profoundly in regard to the tendency to regard their lives as a whole. To some men it is natural to do so, and essential to happiness to be able to do so with some satisfaction. To others life is a series of detached incidents without directed movement and without unity. I think the former sort are more likely to achieve happiness than the latter, since they will gradually build up those circumstances from which they can derive contentment and self-respect, whereas the others will be blown about by the winds of circumstance now this way, now that, without ever arriving at any haven. The habit of viewing life as a whole is an essential part both of wisdom and of true morality, and is one of the things which ought to be encouraged in education. Consistent purpose is not enough to make life happy, but it is an almost indispensable condition of a happy life. And consistent purpose embodies itself mainly in work.

FURTHER THOUGHTS

1. In his essay Russell sorts out some ideas in a balanced way. He starts with the general topic "Satisfactions of work" and divides it into two subcategories, "Satisfactions of even dull work" and "Satisfactions of interesting work." Then he gives two examples for each of the two subcategories. A diagram of his hierarchy is shown on page 66.

   Russell uses summary sentences to state and restate the main themes in his argument. Try to find a sentence or two that summarize what he says about topics 1 through 7. Points 8 and 9 represent transitions from one topic to the next. Read the essay carefully to find the sentence or two that provide the link or transition at each of these points.

2. The diagram on page 66 is only partial. Try fitting in some of the other important ideas in the essay. For instance, how would you tie in the discussion of holidays early in the essay? or the later discussion of destruction?

3. What do you think of Russell's analysis of the housewife's situation?

4. What do you think the following two statements—or maxims—mean? "Continuity of purpose is one of the most essential ingredients of happiness in the long run." "The habit of viewing life as a whole is an essential part both of wisdom and of true morality."

5. The following are rank-order questions based on those described by Sidney B. Simon, Leland W. Howe, and Howard Kirschenbaum in their book *Values Clarification* (New York: Hart, 1972), pp. 58-93. Each question asks you to decide among three competing values and to list them in your order of preference—1st, 2nd, 3rd. Be ready to discuss the reasons for your choices. Here is an example of such a question:

   What do you think is most important in a job?
   _____2_____ amount of pay
   _____3_____ the kind of people you work with
   _____1_____ how valuable the worker thinks the work itself is

   The numbers indicate that the answerer thought that the most important thing about a job was how valuable the worker thought the work was, that the second most important thing was the amount of pay, and that the third most important thing was the kind of people you work with.

   Notice that as you focus down on the three given alternatives, you make a number of value judgments and weigh a number of different variables at once. Notice, too, that you tend to think of other alternatives that may seem even more valid than any of the three alternatives offered. As you think about these questions, jot down some of the other alternatives that come to your mind, as notes for discussion.

   a. What kind of work would you find most satisfying?
   _____ putting out burning oil wells for $50,000 a year

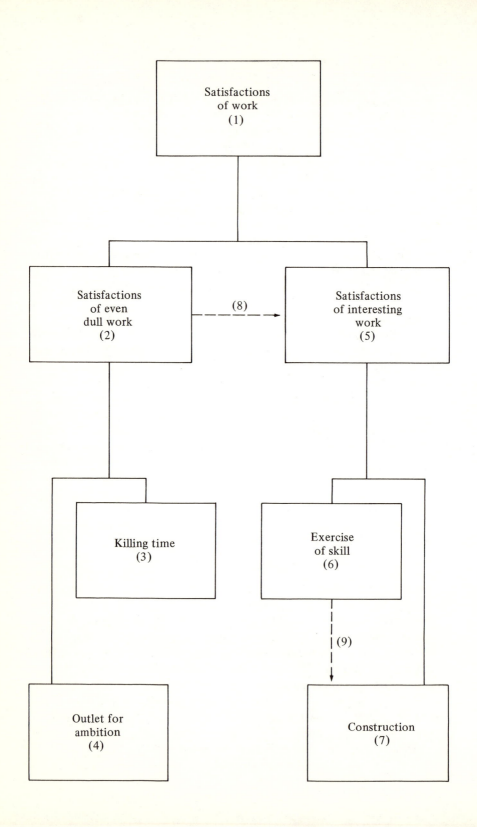

_____ running a movie projector for $10,000 a year

_____ cleaning furnaces and septic tanks for $20,000 a year

b. If you were fired from a good job for reasons not entirely clear to you, what would bother you most?

_____ that you had perhaps failed at the work itself

_____ what your friends or family might think and say

_____ that you had perhaps been treated unfairly by the person who fired you

c. Which would you most like to be?

_____ owner of a successful small delicatessen

_____ a junior executive at General Motors

_____ a highly paid salesman in a small, exclusive jewelry store

d. Make up two questions like those above, dealing with work and its satisfactions.

The Trouble
With Work
And The Need
For Change

There are troubled workers in all jobs—whether in the factory or on the farm, in the office or at home. All of the troubled workers presented in the following pages have one thing in common: Something important is being denied them. What is being denied and the reasons for the denial vary. Sometimes it is forced upon the worker, but often he is denying himself. It can be a denial of creativity, of worth or responsibility, of sociality, of caring and love. Whatever the denial and whatever its source, it creates trouble for the worker—and pressure for change.

Yves Simon reminds us that one of the basic satisfactions of a job is the sense of striving with others against brute necessity: "What the worker is up against are always factual necessities, which he may or may not be able to overcome, and this is where we run again into the problem of pain, difficulty, and irksomeness of work." But what if the factual necessities are jobs that deny man's sociality and make it impossible to feel any sense of striving with others?

After traveling from planet to planet, meeting a conceited man, a king, a businessman, and a tippler, Saint-Exupéry's Little Prince arrives at a tiny planet where a lonely lamplighter lights his lamp for no one, apparently, and to no purpose. To make matters worse, the planet is now turning so fast that sunrise is immediately followed by sunset, and sunset by sunrise, so that the lamplighter is caught in a frantic scramble of lighting and then extinguishing the light. The Little Prince at first concludes that the lamplighter's job is meaningful and even beautiful. But the hapless lamplighter, caught up as he is in its rush and repetition, says, "I follow a terrible profession."

The lamplighter, all alone, caught up in a "terrible profession," can serve as a good symbol of the alienated worker. He is alone, without community, without an opportunity for real human love. The lamp he lights was intended to serve him, but he now must serve it.

FROM
THE LITTLE PRINCE

Antoine de Saint-Exupéry

trans. Katherine Woods

The fifth planet was very strange. It was the smallest of all. There was just enough room on it for a street lamp and a lamplighter. The little prince was not able to reach any explanation of the use of a street lamp and a lamplighter, somewhere in the heavens, on a planet which had no people, and not one house. But he said to himself, nevertheless:

"It may well be that this man is absurd. But he is not so absurd as the king, the conceited man, the businessman, and the tippler. For at least his work has some meaning. When he lights his street lamp, it is as if he brought one more star to life, or one flower. When he puts out his lamp, he sends the flower, or the star, to sleep. That is a beautiful occupation. And since it is beautiful, it is truly useful."

When he arrived on the planet he respectfully saluted the lamplighter.

"Good morning. Why have you just put out your lamp?"

"Those are the orders," replied the lamplighter. "Good morning."

"What are the orders?"

"The orders are that I put out my lamp. Good evening."

And he lighted his lamp again.

"But why have you just lighted it again?"

"Those are the orders," replied the lamplighter.

"I do not understand," said the prince.

"There is nothing to understand," said the lamplighter. "Orders are orders. Good morning."

And he put out his lamp.

Then he mopped his forehead with a handkerchief decorated with red squares.

"I follow a terrible profession. In the old days it was reasonable. I put the lamp out in the morning, and in the evening I lighted it again. I had the rest of the day for relaxation and the rest of the night for sleep."

"And the orders have been changed since that time?"

"The orders have not been changed," said the lamplighter. "That is the tragedy! From year to year the planet has turned more rapidly and the orders have not been changed!"

"Then what?" asked the little prince.

"Then—the planet now makes a complete turn every minute, and I no longer have a single second for repose. Once every minute I have to light my lamp and put it out!"

"That is very funny! A day lasts only one minute, here where you live!"

"It is not funny at all!" said the lamplighter. "While we have been talking together a month has gone by."

"A month?"

"Yes, a month. Thirty minutes. Thirty days. Good evening."

And he lighted his lamp again.

As the little prince watched him, he felt that he loved this lamplighter who was so faithful to his orders. He remembered the sunsets which he himself had gone to seek, in other days, merely by pulling up his chair; and he wanted to help his friend.

"You know," he said, "I can tell you a way you can rest whenever you want to ..."

"I always want to rest," said the lamplighter.

For it is possible for a man to be faithful and lazy at the same time.

The little prince went on with his explanation:

"Your planet is so small that three strides will take you all the way around it. To be always in the sunshine, you need only walk along rather slowly. When you want to rest, you will walk—and the day will last as long as you like."

"That doesn't do me much good," said the lamplighter. "The one thing I love in life is to sleep."

"Then you're unlucky," said the little prince.

"I am unlucky," said the lamplighter. "Good morning."

And he put out his lamp.

"That man," said the little prince to himself, as he continued farther on his journey, "that man would be scorned by all the others: by the king, by the conceited man, by the tippler, by the businessman. Nevertheless he is the only one of them all who does not seem to me ridiculous. Perhaps that is because he is thinking of something else besides himself."

He breathed a sigh of regret, and said to himself, again:

"That man is the only one of them all whom I could have made my friend. But his planet is indeed too small. There is no room on it for two people ..."

What the little prince did not dare confess was that he was sorry most of all to leave this planet, because it was blest every day with 1440 sunsets!

FURTHER THOUGHTS

1. The Little Prince says that the lamplighter is not so absurd as other people he has met, because his work has meaning. But he goes on to say that because the lamplighter's occupation is beautiful, it is useful. Thus he ties together utility, beauty, and meaning. To see how these three things fit together in *your* mind, we suggest that you focus your thinking by trying the following: Draw a circle and imagine that it contains all of the things in the world that you would say have utility—that is, are truly useful to people. Like this:

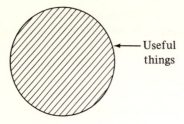

Now draw another circle that contains all of the things in the world that you feel are truly beautiful:

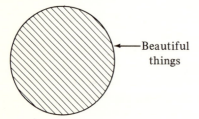

Now the problem is to decide how those two circles relate to one another. Choice A shows one possible relationship between the two:

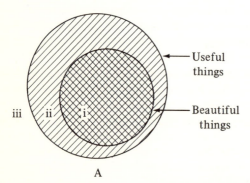

Notice that since A puts the "beautiful" group entirely inside the "useful" group, it says that all beautiful things are useful and that some, but not *all*, useful things are beautiful. Choice A defines three groups of things: (i) things that are both beautiful and useful, (ii) things that are useful but not beautiful, and (iii) things that are neither beautiful nor useful.

When you are dealing with ideas that are as abstract as this, it is always helpful to try to think up some concrete examples. So try to think of examples of things that you think fit into each of the three groups defined by Choice A. Try to get three or four examples in each of the three groups.

Now, notice that Choice A also says, in effect, that there is nothing that is beautiful without being useful. (Check the diagram to make sure that you understand how this point shows up in it.) See if you can think of things that seem to you to be beautiful but of no use at all. (Notice that if you can think of just one such example, then you disagree with Choice A.)

Notice how as you go through this process you tend to keep defining more carefully what you mean by those three original terms.

Now, interpret choices B and C, as you did Choice A.

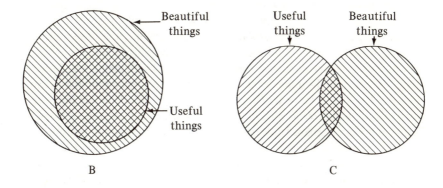

Which choice, if any, seems to you to reflect best the way things are? Can you think of any other choices—that is, any other ways the two circles can be related to one another?

Once you have come up with a relationship between the "useful" group and the "beautiful" group that seems satisfactory to you, put in a third circle representing the "meaningful" group. Notice that now although things get a little more complicated because you are dealing with more groups, the basic strategy remains the same. If you work carefully and methodically through the possibilities—trying always to check your interpretations by thinking of concrete examples—you will in time come up with what amounts to a picture of how you think beauty, utility, and meaning relate to one another. The picture will contain, in compressed form, a lot of your ideas, and you could write out an interpretation of it simply by describing the various groups formed as the circles overlap and by offering good examples for each such group.

2. The lamplighter tells the Little Prince that a month had elapsed during their brief conversation. On the other hand, the poet Theodore Roethke concludes

his poem "I Knew a Woman" with the line "I measure time by how a body sways." What's the essential difference between these two attitudes? How do *you* measure time? What has the passage of time to do with the question of satisfaction?

Every now and then in one of our classes we launch into a favorite historical "explanation" of a particular situation. And every now and then a student objects, "What good is all that history?" And we ask back, "Did you think that mailboxes in the United States of America were always painted red, white, and blue?"

"What has that got to do with anything?"

Well, there was a time after World War II when all mailboxes and mail trucks were painted the color of war—olive drab. And because olive drab is meant to camouflage and distort perspective, funny things would happen. There were an extraordinary number of back-end collisions with mail trucks; other drivers simply misjudged the distance between themselves and the trucks. Some cities painted their litter containers a dark green, and people would put letters in with the litter and litter in with the letters. So, when an Operations Research Team from John Hopkins University was making its recommendations for improving mail service (which was a problem even then), it advised that the mailboxes and the mail trucks be painted red, white and blue.

But the researchers were told that one *couldn't* do that—it was "against the law or something."

At this point they turned to a historian. His assignment: Find out why the government officials think it can't be done. How and when did their resistance to change arise?

The historian dug into the past and discovered that during World War I one of the ways the government geared up for war was by ordering huge quantities of olive drab paint. It ordered so much that when the war ended, they found warehouses full of the paint. An order went out: Paint all the mailboxes and all the mail trucks olive drab. Use up that paint. And so it happened.

But there were only so many boxes and trucks. Years passed before all of the paint was used up. So much time passed that people forgot why that color was being used. They assumed it must be "the law or something." And when the last warehouse of olive drab paint was nearly empty, the government officials reordered, lest they run out.

As soon as the historian presented the story of the olive drab paint (complete with documentation), the bureaucratic inhibition disappeared. And the story ends happily with trucks and boxes painted red, white, and blue. Back-end collisions were dramatically reduced. And letters were no longer deposited in litter.

Many Americans share the late Henry Ford's attitude that "history is bunk." It is bunk if you pretend that you can recapture an event that happened years ago; it is not bunk if you use it to try to make sense of the present. Good history simply extends the range of the here and now. Its practical value is therapeutic—it can relieve an ongoing social system of outmoded restrictions.

There is a tendency to confuse history with tradition. But time itself is amoral and as it goes along, tradition picks up both the stupid and the brilliant. The virtue of the art called history is that it discriminates between the two.

In spite of popular history's obsession with wars and political succession, it may be that the history of work, of crafts and farming, of work and workers, can better help us understand which parts of our tradition are stupid and should be discarded, and which are brilliant and should be cherished.

Consider, for instance, the history of the black worker in America. In the July 1972 issue of *Ebony* Lerone Bennett, Jr. wrote:

> To understand Black is to understand work—and the denial of work. It was work or, to be more precise, it was the white demand for cheap and exploitable labor that brought black people to these shores. And it was in and through the work relationship that the fundamental structures of the black community were formed. . . . It was the unpaid and underpaid work of black men, women and children which changed the flora and fauna of large sections of the New World and created that initial pool of capital which made possible the economic growth from which they were excluded by fraud and violence.
>
> To understand the black experience is to understand that point.

And in their book *Black Rage* psychiatrists William Grier and Price Cobbs document again and again the cost in personal anguish of the black experience of work in white America. In the following selection from their book they bring to public awareness the historical source for the most destructive and damaging set of inhibitions ever laid on a people.

THE SHADOW OF THE PAST

William H. Grier and Price M. Cobbs

Americans characteristically are unwilling to think about the past. We are a future-oriented nation, and facing backward is an impediment to progress. Although these attitudes may propel us to the moon, they are deficient when human conflict needs resolution. They bring white Americans to an impasse when they claim to "understand" black people. After all, the thoughts begin, the Negro is also an American and if he is different it is only a matter of degree. Clichés are brought forth and there is a lengthy recitation of the names of famous Negroes. Long association has bred feelings of familiarity which masquerade as knowledge. But there remains puzzles about black people; all is not understood, something is missing.

For if the black American is to be truly understood, his history must be made intelligible. It is a history that is interwoven with that of this country, although it is rarely reported with candor. In recent years superficial studies of Negroes have been made. For those few who truly search, the past of the black man is seen reflected in his daily life.

It is evident in character structure and child-rearing. It can be heard on a Sunday morning in a Baptist church. It reveals itself in the temper of the ghetto and in the emerging rage now threatening to shatter this nation, a nation the black man helped to build. A few black people may hide their scars, but most harbor the wounds of yesterday.

The black man of today is at one end of a psychological continuum which reaches back in time to his enslaved ancestors. Observe closely a man on a Harlem street corner and it can be seen how little his life experience differs from that of his forebears. However much the externals differ, their inner life is remarkably the same.

On a cold morning one of the authors sat watching a group of black men. They were standing outside an office for casual laborers in clusters of four or five. Some were talking and gesturing, but from a distance one could detect apathy in most.

These were the "hard-core" unemployed. Their difficulties could be blamed on lack of education, personal maladjustments, or just plain laziness and such a judgment would be partially correct. The greater truth was that they were black. Because of this fact, they had little chance of obtaining favorable or permanent work. They were doomed to spend endless gray mornings hoping to secure a day's work.

A truck drove up and they stiffened. There was a ripple of excitement as a white man leaned out of the cab and squinted. As he ran his eyes past the different men, one could almost hear his thoughts.

This one is too thin . . . that dark one looks smartalecky and is probably slow . . . the boy way in the back there might do.

No imagination is required to see this scene as a direct remnant of slavery. Move back in time and this could be an auction block. The manual labor is the same and so is the ritual of selection. The white man involved in the selection feels he is only securing a crew. But, then, so did his forefathers. In addition, the psychic structure of the black men being selected has altered little since slavery. To know this is deeply troubling—and frightening.

A city erupts in fury. Its residents are appalled and outraged. Biracial committees are appointed and scapegoats appear from everywhere. Instead of wretched housing and stifling unemployment, outside agitators and wily Communists are said to be the most important causes. Always the basic reasons are at best minimized and at worst denied. After three centuries of oppression the black man is still thought to need a provocateur to inflame him!

History is forgotten. There is little record of the first Africans brought to this country. They were stripped of everything. A calculated cruelty was begun, designed to crush their spirit. After they were settled in the white man's land, the malice continued. When slavery ended and large-scale physical abuse was discontinued, it was supplanted by different but equally damaging abuse. The cruelty continued unabated in thoughts, feelings, intimidation and occasional lynching. Black people were consigned to a place outside the human family and the whip of the plantation was replaced by the boundaries of the ghetto.

The culture of slavery was never undone for either master or slave. The civilization that tolerated slavery dropped its slaveholding cloak but the inner feelings remained. The "peculiar institution" continues to exert its evil influence over the nation. The practice of slavery stopped over a hundred years ago, but the minds of our citizens have never been freed.

To be a bondsman was to experience a psychological development very different from the master's. Slavery required the creation of a particular kind of person, one *compatible* with a life of involuntary servitude. The ideal slave had to be absolutely dependent and have a deep consciousness of personal inferiority. His color was made the badge of that degradation. And as a final precaution, he was instilled with a sense of the unlimited power of his master. Teachings so painstakingly applied do not disappear easily.

FURTHER THOUGHTS

1. If you accept Grier and Cobbs' historical analysis, who or what is the "villain" in the history of the black worker in America? who or what the "hero"?

2. Slavery is a special kind of relationship between two kinds of people, one called "master," the other called "slave." Think carefully about how the relationship between master and slave is like and different from the following relationships: teacher and student, parent and child, employer and employee, government and citizen. What would you have to do to each of these relationships in order to change it into that between master and slave?

3. What do you think the following sentence means: "The practice of slavery stopped over a hundred years ago, but the minds of our citizens have never been freed"? Does the word *citizens* in the sentence mean black citizens only? Do you agree with this sentence?

Both black and white Americans need to learn the lessons of black history, but the whites have more to learn. As Dan Lacy explains in the preface to *The White Use of Blacks in America*:

> Though the dynamics of that history arise primarily within the black community, which will increasingly shape its own future, most problems that blacks have confronted have been created by whites. Most studies of white actions and attitudes toward blacks in America have treated them as the product of irrational racist emotion and as problems in social psychopathology. Though there has been a marked paranoid component in white racial attitudes, white actions with regard to blacks have not in fact been an aggregation of irrationalities. In their totality they have constituted a deliberate and carefully interlinked set of policies intended to assure the presence and the exploitability of a large semiskilled labor force, primarily in agriculture, whose labor could be commanded at subsistence rates. Changes in the economy that increased or diminished the need for such a labor force have been the principal determinants of racial policy. Indeed, the paranoid elements in American, and especially in Southern, racial attitudes have been in no small part deliberately cultivated as a means of sustaining racial policies having primarily economic objectives.

The selection that follows is from Lacy's book. As its title implies, "It is not, except incidentally, about black history; it is about these questions of white policy. I am myself a white man, a Southerner, and what I have been trying to understand and to recount here are the economic, political, social, and personal policies of my fellow whites and the causes and consequences of our actions."

FROM
THE WHITE USE OF BLACKS IN AMERICA

Dan Lacy

No white man is happy with the situation of blacks in America. There are some who believe that the relative poverty, ignorance, and spiritual exile in which far too many blacks live is a national disgrace and an indictment of American society. But the unhappiness of most is more ambivalent. They denounce blacks as lazy and lacking in ambition while they resent black competition for jobs. They are angered by taxation for relief payments to unemployed Negroes and equally angered by the admission of Negroes to employment formerly reserved for whites. They are disgusted by evidences of black ignorance and resentful of black demands for improved and integrated schools. They are contemptuous of the filth of ghetto slums and fearful of black intrusion into white suburbs. They ridicule black irresponsibility and fear black assertions of responsibility. They resent the burden on white earnings and the threats to white equanimity imposed by the isolation and poverty of blacks, and even more they resent efforts to achieve the integration and the effective black participation in society that would end those burdens and threats.

And yet whites must face the fact that the situation of blacks in America is no accident. The presence here of more than twenty million Negroes, their social, economic, and educational state, indeed the whole condition of their lives, have been in large part determined by deliberate white policy. For more than three centuries it suited the ends of white America to have at its command a large semiskilled labor force, compelled to work for a bare subsistence. For the feudal landlords and the early industrialists of Europe economic necessity provided such a labor force. Landless peasants worked to the landlords' terms or came starving to the city to accept any employment the factory owner offered. But to assemble and hold such a body of laborers in a continent where the open land offered itself to every taker and where every tradition spoke of the freedom and equality of all men required extraordinary measures.

To meet what the dominant whites thought were their needs, they had to create a labor force that was not free to share in the abundance of land or compete for the skilled jobs opening in industry, that did not share in the Declaration's equality of all men or participate in the Address's government by the people, that was denied that determination of one's own destiny that America meant to its other children. To achieve this goal required a vigorous and coherent public policy made up of laws, of folkways, of dilgently implanted attitudes. It required the participation of the state, the churches, the schools, the press, and society generally. Yet for all its complexity and difficulty, such a policy was executed with remarkable effectiveness and with all but complete success. The smooth collaboration of governmental, institutional, and private action is without parallel in our history. We assembled and maintained that labor force—large, productive, and consuming only at the margins of subsistence—through all the kaleidoscopic changes of our history: through the colonial period, through revolution and independence, through the tidal sweep to the Pacific, through the Civil War and Reconstruction, through the creation of the vast cities and overwhelming industries of modern America.

In the last generation our goals have changed. The mindless machine can do the work of the unskilled, and the landowners once desperately dependent on black labor now turn from it in indifference. The unskilled or semiskilled labor force that was once a necessity is now an embarrassment, unusable in our economy. The lack of training for more skilled or professional occupations, once deliberately designed to hold blacks in low-paid jobs by barring them from competitive attractions, is now exceedingly costly. The white community is faced with providing a minimal support for the unusable portion of the black community and with the fears and uncomfortable embarrassment arising from the poverty and disorder in the urban slums in which the workers displaced from agriculture have been segregated.

It suits us, therefore, now to reverse our policies and quickly to transform the black labor force into a skilled one, capable of self-supporting integration into our modern technological economy. The new policy is, however, a halting one and inconsistently pursued. Though it has the impassioned support of those relatively small groups in the white community who had denounced our earlier policies as unjust, it still meets with sullen opposition from those determined to avoid the competition of skilled black labor and from those moved by irrational waves of racial fear and hatred. For it was a cunning and necessary part of the general white strategy of exploiting blacks to create among whites a profound revulsion against blacks as such. In no other way could general white support or at least acquiescence have been won for policies and programs that often damaged the interests of poor whites as well as blacks and that offended every American precept of equality and liberty. The disfranchisement of blacks, their exclusion from equal educational and occupational opportunity, their residential and social segregation, the violence perpetrated on them by the forces of law and lawlessness alike—not to mention slavery itself—could never have been enforced without implanting deeply in the subrational emotions of whites the conviction that blacks were a different and inferior group of beings, to be rejected and feared as well as used by the white community.

We live now with this inheritance of fear and aversion, which stands ominously in the way of all the measures required to reintegrate the black labor force into the economy at a new and productive level and to eliminate the other problems and embarrassments presented to the white community by the alienation and poverty of so large a part of the black.

The policy we now seek to follow is represented by such measures as the Job Corps, the Community Action Programs of the Office of Economic Opportunity, the funding of special education programs in areas of poverty, efforts at educational integration, and the special recruiting and training programs of corporations. But, hampered by ambivalence and halfheartedly pursued, this policy has faltered from the beginning. Discouraged that this weak program has not in a few years undone the results of three centuries of a vigorously pursued opposing policy, we are tempted to abandon even our small efforts and to resign ourselves to drift.

But this will not work either. The continued presence in the society of an alienated community of millions not equipped to participate effectively in the economy will present intolerable problems. If we can no longer use in our economy a distinct caste of serfs, we have no choice but to pursue a policy of full economic integration of the black community, with all its implications of political and educational integration as well.

And since, if we are to avoid chaos, our new policies must achieve their results in a fraction of the time we devoted to those policies whose results we must now efface, they must be pursued with at least as total and comprehensive a devotion. To make blacks equal contributors to the economy, equal sharers of its benefits, and equal participants in the government of the people by the people will require as thorough and dedicated a union of public and private efforts as we formerly devoted to excluding blacks from those aspects of equality.

But another dimension has been added to the problem. Hitherto the destiny of blacks in America has been determined largely by the policies of whites. Blacks were brought to America because whites needed them to work the tobacco and rice and indigo and later the cotton fields. They were enslaved by whites because their masters found them easier to control and more profitable as slaves than as indentured servants. They were kept illiterate by white design, subdued by white violence, apprehended in their escapes by white law. They were partly emancipated in 1865 by uneasy white consciences but kept in a state of semiservitude by a new set of white devices. White decisions determined thereafter how much and what kind of education there would be for blacks. White-made laws enforced segregation in public accommodations; white real-estate policy determined where blacks could live; decisions by white employers and white labor unions determined what jobs they could hold. Whites determined whether and where blacks could vote.

But that is changing. By slow determination and sacrifice and by using white consciences, the black community has accumulated substantial economic and educational resources. It has come to share in some, if as yet small, degree in political power. It has been able to recall the Constitution to life to protect its rights. In a country in which nine-tenths of the people are white and more than nineteen-twentieths of the economic resources are white-owned, black policy must always find its way through white realities. But black power to help determine the future of the black community may achieve what the newer and divided white policies could not achieve alone. If so, black power will have been the means of saving our national community as the fit residence of the society we have dreamed of and of restoring to us our role as a nation conceived in liberty and dedicated to the proposition that all men are created equal.

FURTHER THOUGHTS

1. What was there in Lacy's article that surprised you most? What was there in it that didn't surprise you, even though you didn't know it before? Why weren't you surprised?
2. Lacy mentions some of the effects produced by competition for jobs between blacks and whites. What happens when you speculate upon the effects of this

competition between other groups? men vs. women, for instance? or young people vs. old? Would it make sense to argue that compulsory schooling represents, among other things, an attempt on the part of older people to protect their jobs from younger workers?

3. This article suggests some of the hard economic basis for the prejudices of someone like Archie Bunker. The ironies and hurts of the worker in America that "All in the Family" airs with laughter have their source in the competition between the black man in America and the newly immigrated white man from Europe. Or do you agree? What do you think are the effects of this public airing of prejudice?

In *Black Rage* Doctors Grier and Cobbs invite the reader to "observe closely a man on a Harlem street corner." In 1962 and 1963 a young white anthropologist working on his doctoral dissertation did just that. Only it wasn't Harlem. Elliot Liebow stationed himself at the "New Deal Carry-out Shop" on what he calls "Tally's Corner," in downtown Washington, D.C., his hometown. He had grown up there, going to white schools but living in a predominantly black neighborhood, where his father ran a grocery store.

As Liebow points out, "Washington, D.C. has long been one of the principal stopping-off places for Negroes moving up the Eastern seaboard out of Alabama, Georgia, the Carolinas, and Virginia. In 1963 it was the only major city in the country with more Negroes than whites living in it." But he also points out that the official figures ignore the diurnal rhythm of suburban whites coming into offices in the morning and city blacks going out as household help. It is, however, the black women who take part in that daily movement. The black men remain. And so, Tally's corner was a good vantage point for studying men of the street, even for a white anthropologist. Liebow is much too city-wise not to realize the difference his color made in his reporting:

> My field notes contain a record of what I saw when I looked at Tally, Richard, Sea Cat, and the others. I have only a small notion—and one that I myself consider suspect—of what they saw when they looked at me.
>
> Some things, however, are very clear. They saw, first of all, a white man. In my opinion, this brute fact of color, as they understood it in mine, irrevocably and absolutely relegated me to the status of outsider. I am not certain, but I have a hunch that they were more continuously aware of the color difference than I was. When four of us sat around a kitchen table, for example, I saw three Negroes; each of them saw two Negroes and a white man.
>
> Sometimes, when the word "nigger" was being used easily and conversationally or when, standing on the corner with several men, one

would have a few words with a white passerby and call him a "white motherfucker," I used to play with the idea that maybe I wasn't as much of an outsider as I thought. Other events, and later readings of the field materials, have disabused me of this particular touch of vanity.

. . . .

Whether or not there is more to these citations than "Some of my best friends are . . ." or "Yes, but you're different," the wall between us remained, or better, the chain link fence, since despite the barriers we were able to look at each other, walk alongside each other, talk and occasionally touch fingers. When two people stand up close to the fence on either side, without touching it, they can look through the interstices and forget that they are looking through a fence.

Despite the fence, and sometimes perhaps because of it, Liebow helps tell the story of the streets and the workers trapped there.

MEN AND JOBS

Elliot Liebow

The men do not ordinarily talk about their jobs or ask one another about them.[1] Although most of the men know who is or is not working at any given time, they may or may not know what particular job an individual man has. There is no overt interest in job specifics as they relate to this or that person, in large part perhaps because the specifics are not especially relevant. To know that a man is working is to know approximately how much he makes and to know as much as one needs or wants to know about how he makes it. After all, how much difference does it make to know whether a man is pushing a mop and pulling trash in an apartment house, a restaurant, or an office building, or delivering groceries, drugs, or liquor, or, if he's a laborer, whether he's pushing a wheelbarrow, mixing mortar, or digging a hole. So much does one job look like every other that there is little to choose between them. In large part, the job market consists of a narrow range of nondescript chores calling for nondistinctive, undifferentiated, unskilled labor. "A job is a job."

A crucial factor in the street corner man's lack of job commitment is the overall value he places on the job. *For his part, the streetcorner man puts no*

---

[1] This stands in dramatic contrast to the leisure-time conversation of stable, working-class men. For the coal miners (of Ashton, England), for example, "the topic [of conversation] which surpasses all others in frequency is work—the difficulties which have been encountered in the day's shift, the way in which a particular task was accomplished, and so on." Josephine Klein, *Samples from English Cultures,* Vol. I, p.88.

lower value on the job than does the larger society around him. He knows the social value of the job by the amount of money the employer is willing to pay him for doing it. In a real sense, every pay day, he counts in dollars and cents the value placed on the job by society at large. He is no more (and frequently less) ready to quit and look for another job than his employer is ready to fire him and look for another man. Neither the streetcorner man who performs these jobs nor the society which requires him to perform them assesses the job as one "worth doing and worth doing well." Both employee and employer are contemptuous of the job. The employee shows his contempt by his reluctance to accept it or keep it, the employer by paying less than is required to support a family.[2] Nor does the low-wage job offer prestige, respect, interesting work, opportunity for learning or advancement, or any other compensation. With few exceptions, jobs filled by the streetcorner men are at the bottom of the employment ladder in every respect, from wage level to prestige. Typically, they are hard, dirty, uninteresting and underpaid. The rest of society (whatever its ideal values regarding the dignity of labor) holds the job of the dishwasher or janitor or unskilled laborer in low esteem if not outright contempt.[3] So does the streetcorner man. He cannot do otherwise. He cannot draw from a job those social values which other people do not put into it.[4]

Only occasionally does spontaneous conversation touch on these matters directly. Talk about jobs is usually limited to isolated statements of intention, such as "I think I'll get me another gig [job]," "I'm going to look for a construction job when the weather breaks," or "I'm going to quit. I can't take no more of his shit." Job assessments typically consist of nothing more than a noncommittal shrug and "It's O.K." or "It's a job."

One reason for the relative absence of talk about one's job is, as suggested earlier, that the sameness of job experiences does not bear reiteration. Another and more important reason is the emptiness of the job experience itself. The man sees middle-class occupations as a primary source of prestige, pride and

[2] It is important to remember that the employer is not entirely a free agent. Subject to the constraints of the larger society, he acts for the larger society as well as for himself. Child labor laws, safety and sanitation regulations, minimum wage scales in some employment areas, and other constraints, are already on the books; other control mechanisms, such as a guaranteed annual wage, are to be had for the voting.

[3] See, for example, the U.S. Bureau of the Census, *Methodology and Scores of Socioeconomic Status.* The assignment of the lowest SES ratings to men who hold such jobs is not peculiar to our own society. A low SES rating for "the shoeshine boy or garbage man . . . seems to be true for all [industrial] countries." Alex Inkeles, "Industrial Man," p. 8.

[4] That the streetcorner man downgrades manual labor should occasion no surprise. Merton points out that "the American stigmatization of manual labor . . . *has been found to hold rather uniformly in all social classes*" (emphasis in original; *Social Theory and Social Structure,* p.145). That he finds no satisfaction in such work should also occasion no surprise: "[There is] a clear positive correlation between the over-all status of occupations and the experience of satisfaction in them." Inkeles, "Industrial Man," p. 12.

self-respect; his own job affords him none of these. To think about his job is to see himself as others see him, to remind him of just where he stands in this society.[5] And because society's criteria for placement are generally the same as his own, to talk about his job can trigger a flush of shame and a deep, almost physical ache to change places with someone, almost anyone else.[6] The desire to be a person in his own right, to be noticed by the world he lives in, is shared by each of the men on the streetcorner. Whether they articulate this desire (as Tally does below) or not, one can see them position themselves to catch the attention of their fellows in much the same way as plants bend or stretch to catch the sunlight.[7]

Tally and I were in the Carry-out. It was summer, Tally's peak earning season as a cement finisher, a semiskilled job a cut or so above that of the unskilled laborer. His take-home pay during these weeks was well over a hundred dollars—"a lot of bread." But for Tally, who no longer had a family to support, bread was not enough.

"You know that boy came in last night? That Black Moozlem? That's what I ought to be doing. I ought to be in his place."

"What do you mean?"

"Dressed nice, going to [night] school, got a good job."

"He's no better off than you, Tally. You make more than he does."

"It's not the money. [Pause] It's position, I guess. He's got position. When he finish school he gonna be a supervisor. People respect him. . . . Thinking about people with position and education gives me a feeling right here [pressing his fingers into the pit of his stomach]."

"You're educated, too. You have a skill, a trade. You're a cement finisher. You can make a building, pour a sidewalk."

"That's different. Look, can anybody do what you're doing? Can anybody just come up and do your job? Well, in one week I can teach you cement finishing. You won't be as good as me 'cause you won't have the experience but you'll be a cement finisher. That's what I mean. Anybody can do what I'm doing

[5] "[In our society] a man's work is one of the things by which he is judged, and certainly one of the more significant things by which he judges himself. . . . A man's work is one of the more important parts of his social identity, of his self; indeed, of his fate in the one life he has to live." Everett C. Hughes, *Men and Their Work*, pp. 42-43.

[6] Noting that lower-class persons "are constantly exposed to evidence of their own irrelevance," Lee Rainwater spells out still another way in which the poor are poor: "The identity problems of lower class persons make the soul-searching of middle class adolescents and adults seem rather like a kind of conspicuous consumption of psychic riches" ("Work and Identity in the Lower Class," p. 3).

[7] Sea Cat cuts his pants legs off at the calf and puts a fringe on the raggedy edges. Tonk breaks his "shades" and continues to wear the horn-rimmed frames minus the lenses. Richard cultivates a distinctive manner of speech. Lonny gives himself a birthday party. And so on.

and that's what gives me this feeling. [Long pause] Suppose I like this girl. I go over to her house and I meet her father. He starts talking about what he done today. He talks about operating on somebody and sewing them up and about surgery. I know he's a doctor 'cause of the way he talks. Then she starts talking about what she did. Maybe she's a boss or a supervisor. Maybe she's a lawyer and her father says to me, 'And what do you do, Mr. Jackson?' [Pause] You remember at the courthouse, Lonny's trial? You and the lawyer was talking in the hall? You remember? I just stood there listening. I didn't say a word. You know why? 'Cause I didn't even know what you was talking about. That's happened to me a lot."

"Hell, you're nothing special. That happens to everybody. Nobody knows everything. One man is a doctor, so he talks about surgery. Another man is a teacher, so he talks about books. But doctors and teachers don't know anything about concrete. You're a cement finisher and that's your specialty."

"Maybe so, but when was the last time you saw anybody standing around talking about concrete?"

The streetcorner man wants to be a person in his own right, to be noticed, to be taken account of, but in this respect, as well as in meeting his money needs, his job fails him. The job and the man are even. The job fails the man and the man fails the job.

FURTHER THOUGHTS

1. In the statement "A job is a job," does the second *job* mean something different from the first one?
2. Tally suggests that the worth of a job can be measured by how long it can be meaningfully talked about. Does that criterion make any sense to you? What other criteria seem useful here?

   Compare what is said in the footnote on page 83 about "the leisure-time conversation of stable, working-class men" with the following from Barbara Garson's interviews of automobile assembly-line workers in "Luddites in Lordstown" (*Harper's,* June, 1972):

   > "My father worked in auto for thirty-five years," said a clean-cut lad, "and he never talked about the job. What's there to say? A car comes, I weld it. A car comes, I weld it. One hundred and one times an hour."
   >
   > I asked a young wife, "What does your husband tell you about his work [on the automobile assembly-line]?"
   >
   > "He doesn't say what he does. Only if something happened like, 'My hair caught on fire,' or, 'Something fell in my face.' "

How do you account for the apparent differences in the degree to which English coal miners and American assembly-line workers talk about their jobs?

3. Liebow says of the street-corner man that "He cannot draw from a job those social values which other people do not put into it." To begin to explore this question of social values, try this: List five jobs that you personally feel have the greatest value and *should* bring the greatest social prestige to their workers. Now list the five that you feel actually *do* bring the greatest prestige to their workers. Are there any differences between the two lists? What do you think are the reasons for the differences? Are there any of these jobs you would not want to have? Why?

4. List five jobs that you personally feel have the *least* value and should bring the least social prestige. What seem to be crucial differences to you between "top" jobs and "bottom" ones? Is it how much they pay? What training they require? What product or service they provide?

5. Are there any jobs that would not have been on your personal lists of the top and bottom jobs three years ago? Why the change? Are there any jobs that *would* have been on your list three years ago but are not now? Why the change? At the age of eight what would you have listed as "top" and "bottom" jobs?

The shadow of the slave auction does not stop at the street corner. In the following selection Clark Squire tells how the attitudes of the auction block can operate in the white-collar world of the professions.

FROM
LOOK FOR ME IN THE WHIRLWIND: THE COLLECTIVE AUTOBIOGRAPHY OF THE NEW YORK 21

Clark Squire

After college I forced myself to look for a job. One thing I was absolutely sure of—I was not going to be a schoolteacher. I had already decided I would rather pull cotton than submit to the domination, dehumanization, and emasculation that a black Texas schoolteacher had to face. Needless to say this attitude enraged my Moms, especially since there were almost no other jobs for blacks with degrees in Texas.

As the summer wore on, I rejected one teaching job after another.

A few weeks before leaving school, I had filled out a general job-application form in a college scientific publication. These applications were reproduced and circulated nationwide to major companies for a fee of $5. I had also filed applications for every federal job requiring a math background that appeared in the periodic post office listings. The result was that I received offers of employment as a sheet-metal molding instructor, aircraft mechanic, arc welder—and other peculiar jobs at various air bases, weather bureaus, and government installations around Texas. I received offers for almost every kind of job not relating to mathematics. I accepted all the jobs anyway, but I never heard from any of the places again. About this time my sister married her college boyfriend and left for Ohio. I was now the only one left at home, and Mom's disposition grew harsher accordingly.

Then out of the blue came a call from New York. Western Electric Corporation was asking me to come up for an expense-paid interview. After four and a half days—on the back of the bus through Arkansas, Louisiana, Alabama, and Mississippi—eating bread, bologna and candy bars, and studying differential equations all the way, I arrived in New York. At the Port Authority I asked a red cap where I could find a "colored" hotel. He told me to take the A train uptown two stops, exit, and walk two blocks east. I followed directions, came up at 125th Street and dragged my suitcase up to the Theresa Hotel in the heart of Harlem. The hotel clerk told me he had only one suite left, for $25. I asked him if it was for a week, and he indignantly said, no, for a day! I had a total of $16 in my pockets and so I moved on. I found a room in the St. Marie a few blocks down on Seventh Avenue, for $4.20. I called up and made an appointment for my interview the next day, had my blue serge suit pressed, and went out to look over the town.

I arrived the next morning at the stroke of nine, introduced myself, and waited in a booth while someone went to search for my interviewer. His first question was "What is a superhetrodyne receiver?" My mind spun like slick tires on an ice bed, but I couldn't grab onto anything. I thought, "Hell, that's an electronics question!" Finally, I said, "I don't know." He then fired question after question dealing with problems of decreasing difficulty in electronics. To each question I answered, "I don't know." After about fifteen successive don't know's he worked himself down to Ohm's law, which I was familiar with from my first-year physics course. I answered that one and he immediately switched to math and asked the equation of a circle. I also got that one and figured finally we were getting someplace, but he suddenly ended the interview saying I was very good in math but weak in electronics. I stuttered, stammered, and tried to explain that the job concerned computer programming and anyway he had a copy of my transcript and knew in advance I was a math major and had only an elementary basic course in physics—but he just kept on going, instructing me to take a couple more electronic courses and come back in about six months. He pointed to the cashier, who he said would reimburse me for my ticket and hotel.

I stammered a few more words but by now, my voice seemed very heavy and crude compared to the slick, suave roll of this New Yorker. I turned and went to the cashier's office. I figured my total expenses up from Texas had been about $45, and doubling that for expenses back I expected to receive about $90. But the cashier must have taken one look at me and known I was a hick, because he began dictating my expenses. He told me I was flying back, for $150; hotel, $20 a day; meals, $10 a day; etc., etc., and totaled up a bill of $276.00. I thanked him and left. I had known beforehand that win, lose, or draw, I was not going back to Texas, and now I had enough to maneuver on, yet I couldn't get the taste out of my mouth that I had been tricked.

I found a permanent room on Lenox Avenue and 123rd Street, five-by-eight for $7 a week, and began looking around for a job requiring a math background. It didn't take long to find there was no such job in New York for a nineteen-year-old black, no experience, draft-classification 1A, with a heavy Texas accent. So I worked at this factory and that one. Most of the jobs I bought from cheap employment agencies around Chambers Street. You have to pay the agency a $10 minimum down for a job, and then work a few weeks, paying on the balance as slow as possible, because often after paying off the agency you were laid off. Or, after working a few weeks, the union would demand you join, at an astronomical initial fee, and I would have to quit and repeat the process. In between factory jobs I canvassed various city firms for a job in my field, and filed application after application for various federal jobs listed across the country.

After about six months I got a job with NASA in California. I said goodbye to all my friends and took the bus trip West.

FURTHER THOUGHTS

1. How many different "attitudes of the auction block" can you find mentioned in Clarke Squire's story?
2. What parallels can you find between Clarke Squire's story and the selections by Grier and Cobbs, Lacy, and Liebow?

You may think that the plantation culture of the South died with the Civil War and that it is all "gone with the wind." Maybe. But America's large consumer market and large tracts of tillable soil lend themselves to large-scale farming operations. Here is the story of a modern plantation worker, hired by people who can no longer legally own slaves and therefore seem to think they are absolved from any moral obligation to care about those who work for them.

FROM
FAT CITY

Leonard Gardner

Hundreds of men were on the lamplit street, lined for blocks with labor buses, when Billy Tully arrived, still drunk. He had been up most of the night, as he had nearly every other night since the loss of his cook's job; and he had been fired because of absences following nights out drinking. It had been agony getting up after three hours' sleep. After the night clerk's pounding, Tully had remained motionless, shaken, hearing the knocking at other doors, the same hoarse embittered summons down the hall. It had been so demoralizing that he had taken his bottle out with him under the morning stars. In the other pocket of his gray zipper jacket were two sandwiches in butcher paper. He had eaten no breakfast.

The wine calmed his shivering as he passed the dilapidated buses, the hats and sombreros and caps of the men inside silhouetted in the windows. The drivers stood by the doors addressing the crowds.

"Lettuce thinners! Two more men and we're leaving."

"Onion toppers, over here, let's go."

"Cherries! First Picking."

"They ripe?"

"Sure they're ripe."

"How much you paying?"

"A man can make fifteen, twenty dollars a day if he wants to work."

"Shit, who you kidding?"

"Pea Pickers!"

The sky was still black. Only a few lights were on in the windows of the hotels, dim bulbs illuminating tattered shades and curtains, red fire-escape globes. Under the streetlights the figures in ragged overalls, army fatigues, khakis and suit coats all had a somber uniformity. They pushed to board certain buses that quickly filled and rolled away, grinding and backfiring, and in these crowds Billy Tully jostled and elbowed, asking where the buses were going and sometimes getting no answer. He crossed the street, which was crossed continuously by the men and the few women and by trotting preoccupied dogs, and stopped at a half-filled sky-blue bus with dented fenders and a fat young man in jeans at the door.

"Onions. Ever topped before?"

"Sure."

"When was that?"

"Last year."

"Get on."

Tully climbed into the dark shell, his shoes contacting bottles and papers, and waited amid the slumped forms while the driver recruited outside. "If these onions were any good," Tully said, "looks like he could get him a busload."

"They better than that damn short-handle hoe."

"Maybe I ought to go pick cherries."

"You make more topping onions, if we can get this man moving."

The stars paled, the sky turned a deep clear blue. Trucks and buses lurched away. The crowd outside thinned and separated into groups.

"Let's get going, fat boy," Tully yelled.

"Driver, come *on*. I got in this bus to top onions and I want to top onions. I'm an onion-topping fool."

The bus rattled past dark houses, gas stations, neon-lit motels, and the high vague smokestack of the American Can Company, past the drive-in movie, its great screen white and iridescent in the approaching dawn, across an unseen creek beneath ponderous oaks, past the cars and trailers and pickup-truck caravans of the gypsy camp on its bank and out between the wide fields. Near a red-and-white checkered *Purina Chows* billboard, it turned off the highway. Down a dirt road it bumped to a barn, and the crew had left the bus and taken bottomless buckets from a pickup truck when the grower appeared and told them they were in the wrong man's onion field. The buckets clattered back into the truckbed, the crew returned to the bus, and the driver, one sideburn hacked unevenly and a bloodstained scrap of toilet paper pasted to his cheek, drove back to the highway swearing defensively while the crew cursed him among themselves. The sky bleached to an almost colorless lavender, except for an orange glow above the distant mountains. As the blazing curve of the sun appeared, lighting the faces of the men jolting in the bus—Negro paired with Negro, white with white, Mexican with Mexican and Filipino beside Filipino—Billy Tully took the last sweet swallow of Thunderbird, and his bottle in its slim bag rolled banging under the seats.

They arrived at a field where the day's harvesting had already begun, and embracing an armload of sacks, Tully ran with the others for the nearest rows, stumbling over the plowed ground, knocking his bucket with a knee in the bright onion-scented morning. At the row next to the one he claimed knelt a tall Negro, his face covered with thin scars, his knife flashing among the profusion of plowed-up onions. With fierce gasps, Tully removed his jacket and jerked a sack around his bottomless bucket. He squatted, picked up an onion, severed the top and tossed the onion as he was picking up another. When the bucket was full he lifted it, the onions rolling through into the sack, leaving the bucket once again empty.

In the distance stood the driver, hands inside the mammoth waist of his jeans, yelling: "Trim those bottoms!"

There was a continuous thumping in the buckets. The stooped forms inched in an uneven line, like a wave, across the field, their progress measured by the squat, upright sacks they left behind. In the air was a faint drone of tractors, hardly audible above the hum that had been in Tully's ears since his first army bouts a decade past.

He scrabbled on under the arc of the sun, cutting and tossing, onion tops flying, the knife fastened to his hand by draining blisters. Knees sore, he

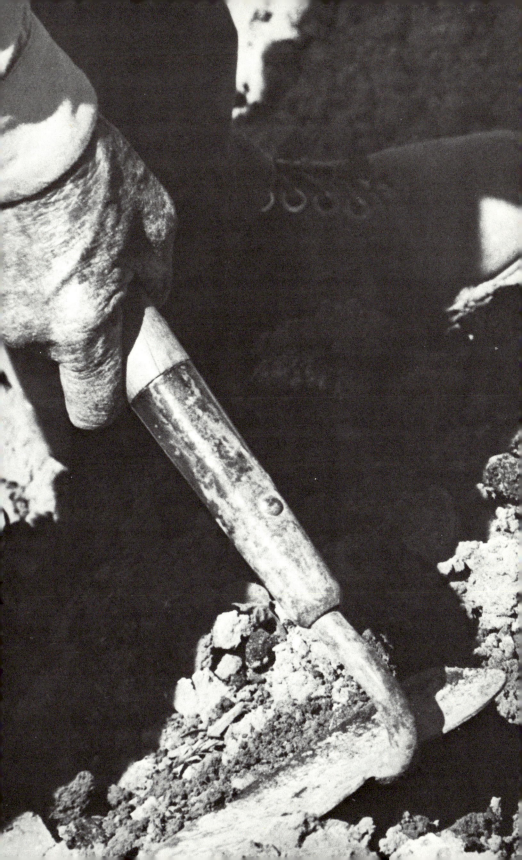

squatted, stood, crouched, sat, and knelt again and, belching a stinging taste of bile, dragged himself through the morning. By noon he had sweated himself sober. Covered with grime, he waddled into the bus with his sandwiches and an onion.

"You got you a nice onion for lunch," a Negro woman remarked through a mouthful of bread, and roused to competition, an old grizzled, white man, with the red inner lining exposed on his sagging lower lids, brought from under his jacket on the seat his own large onion.

"Ain't that a beauty?" All the masticating faces were included in his stained and rotting smile. "Know what I'm going to do with it? I'm going to take that baby home and put it in vinegar." He covered it again with his jacket.

Out in the sun the scarred Negro at the row beside Tully's worked on in a field now almost entirely deserted.

Through the afternoon heat the toppers crawled on, the rows of filled sacks extending farther and farther behind. The old grizzled man, half lying near Tully, his face an incredible red, was still filling buckets though he appeared near death. But Tully was standing. Revived by his lunch and several cupfuls of warm water from the milk can, he was scooping up onions from the straddled row, wrenching off tops, ignoring the bottom fibrils where sometimes clods hung as big as the onions themselves, until a sack was full. Then he thoroughly trimmed several onions and placed them on top. Occasionally there was a gust of wind and he was engulfed by sudden rustlings and flickering shadows as a high spiral of onion skins fluttered about him like a swarm of butterflies. Skins left behind among the discarded tops swirled up with delicate clatters and the high, wheeling column moved away across the field, eventually slowing, widening, dissipating, the skins hovering weightlessly before settling back to the plowed earth. Overhead great flocks of rising and falling blackbirds streamed past in a melodious din.

In the middle of the afternoon the checkers shouted that the day's work was over.

Back in the bus, glib and animated among the workers he had surpassed, the Negro who had topped next to Tully shouted: "It easy to get sixty sacks."

"So's going to heaven."

"If they onions out there I get me my sixty sacks. I'm an onion-topping fool. Now I mean onions. I don't mean none of them little pea-dingers. Driver, let's go get paid. I don't want to look at, hear about, or smell no more onions till tomorrow morning, and if I ain't there then hold the bus because I'm a sixty-sack man and I just won't quit."

"Wherever you go there's always a nigger hollering his head off," muttered the old man beside Tully.

"Just give me a row of good-size onions and call me happy."

"You can have them," said Tully.

"You want to know how to get you sixty sacks?"

"How's that?"

"Don't fool around."

"You telling me I wasn't working as hard as any man in that field?"

"I don't know what you was doing out there, but them onions wasn't putting up no fight against me. Driver, what you waiting on? I didn't come out here to look at no scenery."

They were driven to a labor camp enclosed by a high Cyclone fence topped with barbed wire, and as the crew rose to join the pay line outside, the driver blocked the way. "Now I want each and every one of those onion knives. I want you to file out one by one and I want every one of those knives."

"You going look like a pincushion," said the sixty-sack Negro.

The crew handed over the short, wooden-handled knives, and the driver frowned under the exertions of authority. "One by one, one by one," he repeated, though the aisle was too narrow for departing otherwise.

Tully stepped down into the dust and felt the sun again on his burned neck. Standing in the pay line behind the old man, he looked down the rows of white-washed barracks. A pair of stooped men in loose trousers, and shirts darkened down the backs with sweat, passed between buildings. In the brief swing of a screen door Tully saw rows of iron bunks. A Mexican with both eyes blackened crossed the yard carrying a towel. Tully moved ahead in the line. The paid were leaving the window of the shack and returning to the bus, some lining up again at a water faucet.

"Is that all you picked?" the paymaster demanded of the old man. "What's the matter with you, Pop? If you can't do better than that tomorrow I'm going to climb all over you."

"Well, it takes a while to get the hang of it," came the grieving reply.

Two dimes were laid on the counter under the open window. "Here's your money."

The old man waited. "Huh?"

"That's it."

The creased neck sagged further forward. Slowly the blackened fingers, the crustaceous nails, picked up the dimes. The slack body showed just the slightest inclination toward departing, though the split shoes, the sockless feet, did not move, and at that barely discernible impulse toward surrender, three one-dollar bills were dealt out. With a look of baffled resignation the man slouched away, giving place to Billy Tully, who stepped up to the grinning paymaster with his tally card.

As the bus passed out through the gate, Tully saw, nailed on a whitewashed wall, a yellow poster.

BOXING

ESCOBAR

VASQUEZ

The posters were up along Center Street when the bus unloaded in Stockton. There was one in the window of La Milpa, where Tully laid his five-dollar bill on the bar and drank two beers, eyeing the corpulent waitress under the turning fans, before taking the long walk to the lavatory. He washed his face, blew his dirt-filled nose in a paper towel, and combed his wet hair.

On El Dorado Street the posters were in the windows of bars and barber shops and lobbies full of open-mouth dozers. Tully went to his room in the Roosevelt Hotel. Tired and stiff but clean after a bath in a tub of cool gray water, he returned to the street dressed in a red sport shirt and vivid blue slacks the color of burning gas. Against the shaded wall of Square Deal Liquors, he joined a rank of leaners drinking from cans and pint bottles discreetly covered by paper bags. Across the street in Washington Square rested scores of men, prone, supine, sitting, some wearing coats in the June heat, their wasted bodies motionless on the grass. The sun slanted lower and lower through the trees, illuminating a pair of inert legs, a scabbed face, an outflung arm, while the shade of evening moved behind it, reclaiming the bodies until the farthest side of the park had fallen into shadow. Billy Tully crossed the sidewalk to the wire trash bin full of empty containers and dropped in his bottle. Over the town a dark haze of peat dust was blowing from the delta fields.

He ate fried hot dogs with rice in the Golden Gate Cafe, his shoes buried in discarded paper napkins, each stool down the long counter occupied, dishes clattering, waitresses shouting, the cadaverous Chinese cook, in hanging shirt and spotted khaki pants piled over unlaced tennis shoes, slicing pork knuckles, fat pork roast and tongue, making change with a greasy hand to the slap slap of the other cook's flyswatter.

Belching under the streetlights in the cooling air, Tully lingered with the crowds leaning against cars and parking meters before he went on to the Harbor Inn. Behind the bar, propped among the mirrored faces in that endless twilight was another poster. If Escobar can still do it so can I Tully thought, but he felt he could not even get to the gym without his wife. He felt the same yearning resentment as in his last months with her, the same mystified conviction of neglect.

At midnight he negotiated the stairs to his room, its walls covered with floral paper faded to the hues of old wedding bouquets. Undressing under the dim bulb, he stared at the four complimentary publications on the dresser: *An Hour With Your Bible. El Centinela y Heraldo de la Salud. Signs of the Times—The World's Prophetic Monthly. Smoke Signals—A Renowned Anthropologist Marshals the Facts on What Smoking Does to Life Before Birth.* He wondered if anyone ever read them. Maybe old men did, and wetbacks staying in off the streets at night. And was this where he was going to grow old? Would it all end in a room like this? He sat down on the bed and before him on the wall was the picture of the wolf standing with vaporized breath on a snow-covered hill above a lighted farm. Then the abeyant melancholy of the evening came over him. He sat with his shoulders slumped under the oppression of the room, under the impasse that was himself, the utter, hopeless thwarting that was his blood and bones and flesh. Afraid of a crisis beyond his capacity, he held himself in, his body absolutely still in the passing and fading whine and rumble of a truck. The blue and gold frame, the long cord hanging from the molding, the discolored gold tassel at its apex, all added to the feeling that he had seen the picture in some room in childhood. Though it filled him with despondency he did not think of taking it down, or of throwing out the magazines and pamphlets and removing from the door the sign

IF YOU SMOKE IN BED
PLEASE LET US KNOW
WHERE TO SEND YOUR ASHES.

It did not occur to him that he could, because he did not even feel he lived here.

In the dark he arranged himself with tactical facility in the lumpy terrain of the mattress. When the pounding came again on the door, he lunged up in the blackness crying: "Help!"

Out in the hall the hoarse voice warned: "Four o'clock."

. . . .

Wearing a new straw hat, Billy Tully crawled for seven days in the onion fields, then he was back on the dark morning street among crowds of men left behind by the buses, acridly awake with nothing to do at the impossible hour of 5 a.m. The men grumbled about workers from Mexico, talked of the canneries hiring, passed bottles, knelt in doorways for furtive games of crap, and in the blue light of dawn dwindled away, up Main and Market, along Center and El Dorado, back to the hotels, the lawn and shade of Washington Square, to Chinese and Mexican cafes and to the bars whose doors again were opening.

After reading the paper over coffee and eggs, Tully went back to his room, slept awhile on top of the covers, then took a bus across town. In a crowd of several hundred he stood in the sweet-sour stench of stewing peaches outside a cannery. Trucks passed laden with peach lugs and can-filled cartons. On a vast paved area behind a Cyclone fence, yellow forklifts were stacking lugs into piles the size of barns. Amid the hum of machinery, gleaming empty cans clattered constantly down a conveyor from a boxcar where a man was unstacking and feeding them to the belt with a wooden pitchfork. Blocking the steps to the office, an aged watchman armed with a billy club and a large revolver, his pants hiked above his belly and dewlaps quivering over his buttoned and tieless collar, warned the crowd to keep back from the building.

"Are you hiring or not?" Tully demanded, sweating and irritable now that the sun had cleared the roof.

"You'll just have to wait and hear from them inside."

"It don't do them no good us standing here. Why can't they come out and say if they don't want us?"

"I wouldn't know nothing about that."

"Then let me go in and ask somebody."

"Keep back. No one's going in that office."

"Why not? Who the hell you think you're talking to?"

"I'm just doing what they told me. They told me don't let nobody in the office and nobody's going through that door as long as I'm here. It's none of my doing."

"They're hiring all right," said a man at Tully's side. "I was out here yesterday and they said come back today."

Tully pushed to the front of the crowd and stood with his hands on his hips to prevent anyone from pushing around him. One of the big corrugated steel doors was open; visible in the gloom of the cannery were lines of aproned women. Inside the doorway a forklift had set down a pallet stacked with full lugs, and now a man left the crowd, stepped into the doorway and came back with two peaches. Several men and women followed, returning with handfuls of fruit before the watchman arrived and took the peaches from one final, grinning, capitulating pilferer. At that moment two Negro women sat down on the office steps. The guard ran belligerently back, neck and pelvis forward, squared chin bony from the downward abandonment by its flesh. Arguing, the women rose, and his head turned from them to the open door, from which one more man slipped back to the crowd with a handful of peaches.

"Well, you old fart, are they hiring or not?" shouted Tully.

"Not your kind. You can go home right now."

A whistle blew, the cans stopped rolling from the boxcar, the women inside the building left the line, and the office door was opened by a youthful, sober-faced man in a white short-sleeve shirt with a striped tie.

"The cannery won't be hiring any more personnel at the present time," he announced from the porch. "We've got our full crews for peaches. Come back when the tomatoes are ripe."

A peach banged against the corrugated metal wall several yards to his side—a loud juiceless thump.

"Who did that?" shouted the watchman. He was answered with snickers. The man on the porch stated that throwing peaches would not get anybody a job, and he went back into the office. The crowd fragmented, people walking off down the sides of the street, some running to parked cars, some remaining in the yard as if not believing the announcement. Tully went over to the open cannery door.

"Not hiring!" yelled the watchman.

Nearby in the immense dim room, a girl in jeans and workshirt was seated on a pallet eating a sandwich, her neck round and sloping, with short black curls at the nape.

The watchman arrived wheezing. "Not hiring. Come back when the tomatoes are ripe. Don't take any of that fruit."

Tully took a peach and walked past him into the sunlight. The small chunk he managed to bite away he spit out. When he threw the peach against the front door of a house, it struck with the hardness of stone. Along the sides of the street green peaches lay in the weeds.

The next morning he went out with a busload of tomato thinners. It was a day haul he had many times been warned against, but it paid ninety cents an hour. There was no talk on the ride out of town. The men slept; those with seats to themselves lay down on them. By sunrise they were in the delta.

Preceded by another, the bus jolted down a dirt road to a field bordered by irrigation ditches. With a few groans but mostly in silence, the men climbed out into the sparkling air and selected short-handled hoes from the bed of a pickup truck. Then they jumped a ditch, a foreman already yelling on the other side, and they ranged over the field to continue the previous day's weeding. Bent double, chopping with hoes half a yard long, crossing and uncrossing their legs, they stepped sideways along the rows.

Tully glanced around, saw what was being done, and began chopping, trying to leave an isolated tomato plant every width of a hoe blade. Engulfed by new weeds, grass and dandelion, they were seedlings growing in a double line down each row.

"What the hell kind of weeding you call that?"

Tully turned to a pair of legs in clean khaki. Straightening, he confronted a black mustache on a face he assumed, from its displeasure, was a foreman's. Then he turned to the ground he had cleared: long, leafless gaps, interrupted by infrequent plants, several of which appeared now not to be tomatoes.

"Shape up and get your ass in gear or you can spend the day in the bus."

"Tough shit. A lot I care. Big deal," Tully whispered at the departing back, wanting to hurl his hoe at it. He stooped lower, gripped the handle closer to the blade and hacked on. Instead of spaced plants, for a yard of mounting anxiety he left nothing at all. Sliding his hand all the way down to the blade, he meticulously scraped around the next plant, cutting down grass and weeds in a closer and closer square, plucking with his free hand until the tomato with its two jagged leaves and an adjacent red-rooted weed stood alone; and then in one final minuscule nick both were down. Guiltily, he peered around before propping the tomato plant upright between two clods. Already his back was hurting. The pain began at his waist, spread down the backs of his thighs to the tendons behind the knee joints and up the spine to the shoulders and the back of the neck. A tractor came up his row pulling a disk harrow, and when Tully straightened and moved aside for it to roar past, plowing under the chopped weeds, tiny transparent specks quivered before his eyes. He was falling behind. Soon he was the last stooped man moving across the field, and the foreman, stepping in long strides over the rows, again came threatening dismissal. Tully chopped on with desperate imprecision, dismayed by the lowness of the sun, which seemed to hang stationary. He doubted his back could last, and it was not the loss of the money, a day-long wait or the hitchhiking back he feared. It was the disgrace, for all around him were oaths, moans, bellowed complaints, the brief tableaux of upright wincing men, hoes dangling, their hands on the small of their backs, who were going on under the same torment—some of them winos, donut and coffee men, chain smokers, white-bread eaters, maybe none ever athletes yet all moving steadily on while he fell farther and farther behind, hacking in panic over the desertion of his will. He could not resign himself to the inexorable day; he would have to quit and the others, he felt, were fools in their enduring. Including himself, only three men out of two busloads were white.

He could resolve no more than to clear the next six inches before throwing down his hoe. He straightened up with difficulty and stared hazily at the blue sky that was scrawled with the familiar floating patterns etched for so long now on his eyes. He breathed deeply, stretched, bent back over the row, crouched, knelt, crawled, scrambled up, and all the while the ache in his back continued. He lasted until noon, until the unbelievable half hour of relief. Ten minutes of it he spent waiting in line at a pickup truck to buy bean and potato filled tortillas and a Pepsi-Cola.

"Jesus Christ, you don't care where you eat, do you?" asked one of the two white men passing him where he lay under a pepper tree among a humming profusion of green-glinting flies whose source of delight, he noticed now, lay directly beside him. He had thought the odor was coming from his lunch. With a twinge of embarrassment he rose and entered a bus—sweltering and full of Negroes—and sat next to a man reeking of Sloan's liniment.

Tully was falling asleep while he finished eating, but already the men were hobbling out of the bus and taking up their hoes. Following, he found himself off with the Negroes at one end of the field. Bloated, aching, he again bent over a row. Shuffling sideways, his legs crossing and uncrossing, the short hoe rising and falling, he labored on in the despondency of one condemned, the instrument of his torture held in his own hand. Of all the hated work he had ever done, this was a torment beyond any, almost beyond belief, and so it began to seem this was his future, that this was Work, which he had always tried to evade and would never escape now that his wife was gone and his career was over. And it was as if it were just, as if he deserved no better for the mess he had made of his life. Yet he also felt he could not go on even another hour. He felt his existence had come to a final halt, with no way open to him anywhere. Hand on his back, straightening, he gazed with bleary eyes at all the stooped men inching down the rows, and he felt being white no longer made any difference. His life was being swept in among those countless lives lost hour by captive hour scratching at the miserable earth.

"You call this a living?"

"Uh hum," responded the man he had lunched beside, who, though young, appeared to have lost all his teeth and whose scent of liniment was periodically wafted to Tully's nose.

"How long's it take to get use to this shit anyway?" Tully asked, and was nettled by gleeful forlorn laughter from the chopping and shuffling men.

"What a man want, what a man *need*, is a woman with a good job."

"I had that," Tully said. "But she left."

Again there was that irritating laughter. Tully hoed on in silence, listening to a bantering discussion of divorce, which everyone around him seemed to have undergone.

The wind came up; some of the men across the field masked themselves with bandannas, like bandits, and those who had come with goggles around the crowns of their straw hats drew them over their eyes. The peat dust blew in trails across the field and the blue of the sky was obscured by a gray haze through which the sun shone dully like the lid of a can. Tully forced himself on and the others drew steadily away. Dizzy, the tendons at the back of his knee joints swollen and stiff, he stood upright, watching the foreman. He stumbled across the clods to the water can on the back of a jeep that moved slowly up the rows and idled among the men, and he drank a long time from the sticky tin cup. Rebuked for lingering, he limped back cursing. Even his eyes ached in the downward strain of stooping. He trailed farther and farther behind, the Negroes' voices growing faint, blown by the wind.

The sun sloped down the sky, the bent men moved on across the black earth. Tully was hardly thinking now, his mind fixed on pain and chopping and a vision of quitting time. Seeing a man go to the edge of the field, he rose and went to the foreman, who was suspicious but gave his permission. In the tall grass beside an irrigation ditch, Tully squatted a peaceful moment.

When a white sedan arrived, raising a long trail of dust, Tully was lying in the dirt, propped on one arm, doggedly chopping. He did not understand that its appearance signified the end of the day until some of the crew began leaping over the rows and incredibly racing to the car, where a man now stood at the fender with a small green strongbox.

"Who wants to make a store stop?" the driver asked on the road back to Stockton. So empty cans and bottles clanked along the floor when the bus arrived with its silent motionless passengers in the sunlit town.

"You'll never see me again," declared Tully, and he swayed, leaning oddly backwards, up the street to his hotel, straw cowboy hat cocked forward, his fingers discovering new mounds of muscle in the small of his agonized back.

But the pay was ninety cents a hour, and two days later he was again gripping a short-handled hoe.

FURTHER THOUGHTS

1. Some of the most powerful effects in Gardner's *Fat City* are his concrete descriptions of backbreaking labor. Look at Gardner's descriptions for guidance, then think back to the hardest physical work you've ever done. Now write out a description of it, trying to recapture the smells, the tastes, the sounds, the sights, the feelings on your skin and in your muscles and your bones. Write down all the details you can, not worrying too much about organization and correctness. Just try to get those details.

2. In the introduction to this book we say that there are still jobs that do not satisfy and cannot be made to satisfy, and that, for one reason or another, must be done. Is the work that Gardner describes necessarily an ugly job? What other examples of ugly yet necessary jobs can you think of?

3. Assuming that there are jobs that cannot be satisfying and yet must be done, how do you decide who does them? Many cultures have used slaves for such jobs. What do we use? What could we use? What should we use?

"I am not, of course, Adam Smith," announced the author in his book *The Money Game.* "Mr. Smith lies in a churchyard in Canongate, his tombstone, written by himself, identifying him as the author of *The Wealth of Nations*, and he has been there since he died in 1790, rich in respect and honors, having made himself immortal as the first great free-market economist in all the texts of economic history. Mr. Smith did not think of himself as an economist, but as a moral philosopher." In one short passage the author warns you about himself and about economists.

"Adam Smith" writes for those interested in how money is made by "playing the market." All of the little, individual games played by individual investors and the big investing games played by insurance companies and universities add up to a big game—Smith's Money Game. The game is international and touches nearly everyone, with stakes sometimes so high they are frightening. For if the game gets too wild, individual and institutional disaster threatens. If the stakes get too high, depression looms. And when depression looms large and threatens to be crippling, something even worse can happen—dictators are raised, communes formed, and *somebody stops the game.*

The game is based upon assumptions about workers and buyers, assumptions regularly reaffirmed by dignified men in high offices using imposing charts and earnest tones. But what if either they don't know or they are covering up something that, if known, can endanger the entire money game? In the following selection, from *Supermoney*, "Adam Smith" and a friend called Bill set out to see what is happening back behind the game, back on the assembly line.

PRINCE VALIANT AND THE PROTESTANT ETHIC

Adam Smith

I think it was about five o'clock in the afternoon and the snow was getting worse and I began to ask myself what I was doing in the Pink Elephant Bar in Lordstown, Ohio. The Pink Elephant is on the highway, Route 45, and so is the Seven Mile Inn, and Rod's Tavern is just off the highway, and the highway is the one that goes by the new $250 million General Motors plant that makes Vegas on the world's most automated assembly line. My friend Bill and I go up, cold, to these various characters, some of them indeed with mustaches and long hair and sideburns, and there we are: boy social scientists, amateur pollsters. Can we talk to you? Can we buy you a beer? Rolling Rock or Genesee? Do you work in the Vega plant? Is that a good place to work? I mean, would you tell your brother or your son to get a job there? What do you do there? Does your wife work? Do you want another beer? When you get your paycheck, what do you spend it on? Do you spend it in stores, for things, or do you pay it to people—doctors, barbers, plumbers? What do you think of the kids in the plant? The old guys? The blacks? The foremen? The management? Do you want another beer? What do you want to do with your life?

. . . .

"The revolution of the twentieth century will take place in the United States," writes a French critic, Jean-Francois Revel, "and it has already begun." "There is a revolution coming," writes Charles Reich. "It will not be like revolutions of the past. It will originate with the individual and with culture, and it will change the political structure only as its final act . . . this is the revolution of the new generation."

If *any* of this is true, we cannot simply go back to where we were. Radical change is very hard for most people to contemplate, and money managers are no different. Their attitude is: Sure, changes, we sell something and we buy something else to fit the changes. You say work is going out of style? We'll buy play. Here are my six Leisure Time stocks, and let me tell you how long I've owned Disney. Money managers operate on the theory of displacement: the framework will be the same, but inside you move things around. My favorite is a gentleman I ran into after I got back from the Vega plant. I told him that one problem among others in certain localities was dope addiction, and at one plant—though the number sounded very high to me—the rate was reported to be 14 percent.

"Well," he said, "I haven't owned an auto stock for years. But fourteen percent! Geez, *who makes the needles*?"

The Chairman was pleased to report sharply higher profits for the year, due to increased sales of the entire line of hospital supply equipment. The reasons for the record profitability, said the Chairman, were Medicare, Medicaid, and the sharply increased use of the company's new handy throw-away needle by the burgeoning heroin addiction market.

Now it may be that displacement is all we have to consider. Ah, *things* are out, quality of life is in, back to the countryside; there is a waiting list for ten-speed bicycles, who makes the ten-speed bicycles? Ah, the ecologists are gaining strength, where is our list of water-pollution companies?

That is probably good thinking on the tactical level, but there is also a strategic level, and the strategic level has to consider what the more profound changes are, and in fact it ought to even without the rather parochial justification of buying and selling.

. . . .

In the automobile industry, to consider the parochial side for a moment, rewards and punishments are very tangible, and since the automobile industry is such a fantastic part of America, that would affect us all. General Motors—my God, nobody can comprehend the *size* of General Motors; it makes one out of every seven manufacturing dollars in the country; its sales are bigger than the budget of any of the fifty states, and of any *country* in the world except the United States and the Soviet Union. But even General Motors has problems. As Henry Ford II said, *the Japanese are waiting in the wings.* Someday, he said, they might build all the cars in America. The problem, or one of them, is that imports keep rising, in spite of the theology of Detroit, which always maintained: little cars, fah! Americans won't buy them; Americans want power, a sex symbol, racing stripes, air scoops for nonexistent air, portholes for nonexistent water; they want to leave two big black tire marks going away from the stoplight, rubber on the road. And the names went with the technology: Firebirds and Thunderbirds, Cougars and Barracudas and Impalas, *growrrrr*, nothing about driving a handy little car there—so the handy little cars sold were foreign.

Eventually enough handy little cars were sold that the balance of payments continued in its sickening ways and even Washington began to lean on Detroit, and Detroit figured Okay, we'll build a handy little car. General Motors was not about to have any more of the problems of urban Detroit; it put its $250 million Vega plant in the middle of an Ohio cornfield. And then this work force showed up, the youngest work force around, and *look* at them—hair down to the shoulder blades, mustaches, bellbottoms, the whole bit; it looks like Berkeley or Harvard Square.

It was a Ford official who wrote the following paragraph, but the same thing applies not only everywhere in the automobile industry but probably in much of factory work. The memo is from an industrial relations man to his superiors, and he is talking about the present and the future. This gentleman is nobody's fool, and his memo should be in the sociology texts, not in the filing cabinets. (The memo was xeroxed, and a friend of mine got a xerox and xeroxed it again, so I have one, and I guess the UAW has one, because its vice-president Ken Bannon used some of the same phrases word for word in an interview. Communication by *samizdat*: think what Xerox will do in Russia when it gets going.) The rate of disciplinary cases was going up; turnover was up two and a half times; absenteeism was alarming on Mondays and Fridays. (Hence the useless advice never to buy a car built on a Monday or a Friday. But your dealer will tell you *his* cars are built only on Tuesdays and Thursdays.) Furthermore, the workers weren't listening to the foremen and the supervisors. And why?

For many, the traditional motivations of job security, money rewards, and opportunity for personal advancement are proving insufficient. Large numbers of those we hire find factory life so distasteful they quit after only brief exposure to it. The general increase in real wage levels in our economy has afforded more alternatives for satisfying economic needs. Because they are unfamiliar with the harsh economic facts of earlier years, [new workers] have little regard for the consequences if they take a day or two off ... the traditional work ethic—the concept that hard work is a virtue and a duty—will undergo additional erosion.

General Motors was going to outflank that stuff with the newest, most automated plant; machines would take over a lot of the repetitive jobs; the plant would be in that cornfield in Ohio, near Youngstown, away from all those problems of the, uh, you know, core city. Everything at Lordstown would be made in America, no imported parts, the apogee of American industrialism. The head of Chevrolet buzzed in for a Knute Rockne pep talk. *America* was going to make the small car, by golly, and that was the end of the elves in the Black Forest and the industrious Yellow Peril in Toyota City, who thought they had been in the small-car business. Planeloads of newsmen were flown in. The line is going to do a hundred cars an hour, lots of it without any people; *kachunk* goes the machine that pops the wheel rim into the tire, *pffft* goes the machine that blows up the tire.

So what is all this about trouble in Lordstown? The line is not going at a hundred cars an hour—at least not much of the time—and there are all these characters, all good UAW Local 1112, average age twenty-five, the youngest work force practically anywhere, peace medals, bellbottoms, and hair like Prince Valiant, and the union president is twenty-nine and has a Fu Manchu mustache like the one Joe Namath shaved off, and GM is going up the wall. Where is the *productivity*? Curtis Cox, the supervisor of standards and methods, is getting apoplectic. "I see *foreign cars* in the parking lot," he says. "The owners say they are cheaper. How is this country going to compete?" The GM people practically weep when they think about Japan: all those nice, industrious workers, *singing* the alma mater in the morning ("Hail to Thee, O Mitsubishi"); whistling on their way to work like the Seven Dwarfs, for God's sake—never a strike, never a cross word; playing on the company teams; asking the foreman if it is okay to get engaged to this very nice girl as soon as the foreman meets her.

So I ask General Motors quite routinely if I can go see this apogee of American industrialism, say, Tuesday, and General Motors says *no*, never.

I admit to being a bit stunned. Do they not fly planeloads of people there all the time? Did they not fly alleged same planeloads at the end of the GM strike, together with appropriate refreshment, to watch the first Vega come off the line, with a handout about the Vega was going to Mrs. Sadie Applepie, library assistant of Huckleberry Finn, Illinois, with a quote all ready from Mrs. Applepie: "Oh, I have been waiting so long for my Vega, I can't believe it's finally here, I'm so excited," did they not? What do they mean, No, not that guy? Who the hell do they think I am, Ralph Nader? I begin thumbing my other notebook that has the number of the pay phone in the hallway of Nader's boarding house, and it's off to Lordstown. Because even with plant guards, General Motors is not Russia, and anybody who has graduated from the good ol' U.S. Army knows how to deal with the lower levels of great bureaucracies. (Where you going with that rake? What rake, sir? *That* rake. Oh, *this* rake, the captain, sir, he said take it over there. *What* captain? The other captain. What other captain? Beats me, lieutenant, they just told me take the rake.)

So we are walking around the plant at Lordstown, all $250 million of it very visible, like an iron-and-steel tropical rain forest with the electric drills screaming like parakeets and the Unimate robot welders bending over the Vegas like big mother birds and the Prince Valiants of Local 1112 zanking away with their new expensive electrical equipment. Vegas grow before your eyes. Beautiful. I recommend it, next time you are taking the Howard Johnson tour across the land of the free.

But what are these cars waiting for repair, marked *no high beam signal, dome lite inoperative, no brakes* . . . no brakes? *no brakes.* But what is this on the bulletin board?

> Management has experienced serious losses of production due to poor quality workmanship, deliberate restriction of output, failure or refusal to perform job assignments and sabotage.
>
> Efforts to discourage such actions through the normal application of corrective discipline have not been successful. Accordingly, any further misconduct of this type will be considered cause for severe disciplinary measures, including dismissal.

"Corrective discipline"? My God, you can get *courtmartialed* in this place. They should have an industrial psychologist read the language on the bulletin board. I can hear the Glee Club louder, "Hail to Thee, O Fair Toyota."

Hi there.

Hi.

What is that?

That's the window trim.

Is this a good place to work?

Well, it will be, as soon as we get it shaped up.

Would you buy one of these cars?

Sure, if it wasn't so expensive; it's a well-engineered little car.

Wouldn't you rather be out on your own, say, a garage?

Naw, a garage don't have no benefits.

Say, I don't want to bother you, two of these Vegas just went by without window trim.

Well, they all go by without somethin', this line is moving too fast.

That's productivity, man.

Oh, is that what they call it?

I can give you a few notes of our brilliantly unscientific survey of Lordstown, but they are just that. Our people would rather have had the time off than the overtime. But their wives worked because they needed the extra income. They would tell their brothers to get a job there, and in fact some of them did. Supervisors bugged everybody. Sabotage? Beer cans welded to the inside of a fender? Well, there might be a few hotheads, but that's silly, man, the Vega is our bread and butter—the more Vegas they sell, the better for us. If the foremen bugged our people too much, they would get another job somewhere else; they took for granted there would be such a job.

We asked the older types if the young bucks were any different. They said, "Yes. They're smarter. They don't put up with what we did."

Our favorite Prince Valiant haircut said: "I am not going to bust my ass for anybody. I don't even bust my ass for myself, you know, working around the house."

· · · · · · · · · · · ·

Let us see what we can do with the Protestant Ethic. That phrase describes a devotion to thrift and industry, postponed pleasure and hard work, the hustle as approved by the Lord. It accompanied the Puritan temper, a rather forbidding and pleasure-shy view of life, and is aptly described in the confidential Ford memo together with the complaint that it is disappearing: "the traditional work ethic— the concept that hard work is a virtue and a duty—will undergo additional erosion." (You have already seen the seeds of conflict, because if Prince Valiant at the Pink Elephant says, "I am not going to bust my ass for anybody, I don't even bust my ass for myself," it is safe to say he does not believe that "hard work is a virtue and a duty.")

· · · · · · · · · · · ·

While the literature of the Protestant Ethic has been exhorting everybody for three hundred years in this country to be industrious and thrifty, sober and wise—to "postpone gratification," in the words of the scholars—another literature has sprung up. It is literature really only in the McLuhanesque sense, but it is with us every day, and that is advertising. The purpose of the advertising is not to get you to produce and save but to spend, to buy the goods, and this has been the case since at least fifty years ago, when mass marketing and mass advertising really got going. Now we have commercials in living color, and the populace spends far more time with them than the old populace did with Cotton Mather. What do we see? First of all, we never see anybody *working* except when they are candidates for medication: aspirin, pain relievers, tranquilizers, cold remedies. At least not office or factory work; the White Tornado and the Man From Glad will come and help with the housework. The rest of the time, people are at play: is it possible to sell soft drinks without running into the surf? You only go around once in life, says the beer commercial, so you have to grab everything you can; that character is hanging precariously onto the rigging of his boat because one hand is clutching a beer can. And the airlines—well, there is the bell tolling the end of the Protestant Ethic: Fly now, pay later, Pan Am will take you to an island in the sun where you can be a beachcomber (not a Calling approved by Cotton Mather) and Eastern wants to fly you and Bob and Carol and Ted and Alice *all* to your own little love-nest in Jamaica.

The message of capitalism has been schizophrenic: at work, be hard-nosed, industrious, single-minded, frugal and thrifty, and once you leave work, *whoopee,* have you seen Carol *and* Alice in their bikinis? It may be that some doers can step into a telephone booth and emerge as Clark Kent, but I doubt if it works for a whole society.

The second literature of exhortation, advertising, sometimes recognizes this, and tries to say that the deferred gratification of the Protestant Ethic is a matter of hours, not lifetimes and generations. "You've worked hard, you deserve this," says the clever ad, whether it is a beer, the reward for a day, or a vacation, the reward for a season, or whatever: buy, try, fly.

The less intensive attitude toward work also applies to play. In the winter of 1972 Columbia barely managed to field a basketball team for its Ivy League opener; it could send only six men to Providence to play Brown. "Four members," *The New York Times* reported (January 6) "had resigned, making it a particularly dramatic example of student unhappiness with organized extracurricular pursuits ... Several other college teams have suffered similar player shortages in the last month." Said the team's second-highest scorer as he departed: "My father thinks I'm just a degenerate hippie now, because when I left high school I had all these fantastic ambitions for wealth and fame—and I wanted to be the greatest lawyer in North Carolina. Now I just don't have that."

Oppose this to that paragon of the extreme ethic, Vince Lombardi. You could say, of course, that this is not quite fair: soldiers and professional football players are supposed to win. But the example is not frivolous. When Lombardi died, his death was a major front-page story in all—including the most serious—of newspapers, and personally grieved the President of the United States. Lombardi's hold on the country and the President was that for ten years the teams he had coached had either won championships or come in second. The ethic according to Lombardi, all from *Lombardi* and *Run to Daylight* :

Winning is not everything. It is the only thing.

The will to excell and the will to win, they endure. They are more important than any event that occasions them.

To play this game, you must have that fire in you, and there is nothing that stokes fire like hate.

And from Lombardi's players:

He had us all feeling that we weren't going to win for the Green Bay Packers, but to preserve our manhood ... and we went out and whipped them good and preserved our manhood.

Vinny believes in the Spartan life, the total self-sacrifice, and to succeed and reach the pinnacle he has, you've got to be that way. The hours you put in on a job can't even be considered.

. . . .

If you were told to beat your head against the wall, you did it ... I think we're entering a different period now. I think we now have to give youngsters a good reason to get them to beat their heads against a wall.

Kids today don't fight like we did. They can play football and basketball like hell, but they're very gentle, very kind. They're out playing for fun, and it's not going to interfere with their demonstration for the week or with the things they consider impotrant . . . Those kids don't look at it like the whole world is going to fall apart if you don't bear the Bears.

The examples are so eloquent they need no comment.

Someday we may have such technology and science-and-compound-interest that whether people work hard or not would be marginal, but meanwhile there has been a lot of talk about alienation and unhappiness and The Blue-Collar Blues and, for that matter, The White-Collar Blues. Industry notices this because of absenteeism, turnover and the lack of candidates for foreman, but at bottom nobody really *knows*.

> Five years ago [from 1970] the National Commission on Technology, Automation, and Economic Progress tried to survey existing knowledge on job satisfaction and dissatisfaction under modern industrial conditions. There was pitifully little. With all the talk about alienation, dehumaniza-tion, and the loss of satisfaction from work, you would think that many researchers would be trying to find out the facts, by asking questions and by devising more direct measurements, by trying to figure out what aspects of particular routines are most destructive of satisfaction, and what loss of production would result from changing the routines. But apparently not so. (Robert Solo in *Capitalism Today*)

I suspect, pending the reconvening of the National Commission to fill in the gaps, that two things are true in this country. One is that there are certainly a lot of jobs in this country that are boring, not built to the human spirit or the human body, or not fulfilling in some other way, and that most of American industry is only beginning to pay attention to this. The second is that people like to work, as opposed to not working or hanging around the house. They like to work, or at least they like to go to the place where work is, because they see their friends, they have a beer afterward or a coffee break during, and it gets them into motion, and anyway we have not developed the tradition of playing the lute and counting that as a good afternoon. Given any degree of pleasantness, encouragement and satisfaction, they would go to work even without the exhortations of the Ethic and the prospect of the Shoar of Eternal Blessedness.

It is almost axiomatic in the literature of work that part of the problem comes of bending the men to the machines. But computers are machines too; the pay may be less than that around nonelectronic machinery; yet the blues are not so much heard from this sector, and among the differences may be style, atmosphere and air conditioning.

How hard, or with what care, people work is something else. William H. Whyte, Jr., and the other observers of the fifties told us of the crossover: the executives were working the seventy-hour week and taking work home while the blue-collar hours were going down.

The difference is that both the executive and the blue-collar worker are now conscious of *options* that heretofore they did not think they had. Conscious only, for relatively few have acted on the alternative; behavior and attitude do not necessarily go immediately together. Most of the attention has been paid to the younger generation; at least the future executives were thinking about a balanced life, and the corporations were getting a bit shyer about telling them how demanding corporate life was going to be. Whatever the terrors that haunted the Man in the Gray Flannel Suit—not Making It, not having the House in the Suburb—the terrors do not have quite the same intensity that they used to. The terrors are also less for the industrial workers. For one thing, if you have a house and a car, another house and another car become much less urgent, however pleasant or convenient. (There is a lake within cruising range of the Vega plant in industrial Ohio which is, to put it baldly, a blue-collar lake, which is to say most of the boats belong to union workers from the plants. If they put five more boats on that lake you will not be able to see the water for the boats; thus if you are an industrial worker and don't have a boat to take the kids in, the chances are you have a friend who does, or maybe your old man will lend you his.)

A lack of *things*, unless those things are food, clothing and shelter, does not provide terror except for a Man in a Gray Flannel Suit who has bought a distortion of the old ethic, its tangible evidences without its spirituality. Back to the Ford memo:

> Because they are unfamiliar with the harsh economic facts of earlier years, [new workers] have little regard for the consequences if they take a day or two off.

That's about as succinct as one can be. The harsh economic facts of earlier years were an unpleasant but effective motivator. You do not even have to have gone through a Great Depression yourself, if you heard enough talk about it while you were growing up. Now it has been more than thirty years since the end of the Great Depression, and not only do the Prince Valiants in the plant not know about it, they have not even heard that much about it because granddad does not live with them. I had a series of chats with Daniel Yankelovich, social scientist and the head of the leading marketing research and social science research firm that bears his name, a firm that polls continuously in this area for corporate clients. Only in the last five years has this change in attitude taken place so strikingly. The changing of work goals from salary to interpersonal relationships to content of work has also been documented by Professor Ray Katzell, chairman of the Psychology Department of New York University, and others. It took that long—almost two generations—for the motivation by economic fear to fade.

Granted, all the moonlighting to make ends meet at the current levels; granted, all the places and pockets that have been missed, and some of the unemployment which persists. Mass employment is not a political possibility—almost everyone would agree to that—and the economic whiff of grapeshot (what this country needs to shape up these deadheads is a good depression) has gone out of the lexicon of bargaining. What Yankelovich calls the "sacrifice consensus" is breaking down. The sacrifice part of that phrase means that deferrals for something else are not as popular or necessary: I am doing this for my family, I am working so that my son has a better life than I do. And the consensus, obviously, is that there was agreement that this was a right and proper way of life. The breakdown of this sacrifice consensus does not mean that it is replaced right away with something else, only that now there are many elements present—some sacrificers, some not, but no agreed-upon consensus.

("If women's lib breaks the equation between masculinity and being a good provider, what does that do to motivation? And, say, to insurance?" Yankelovich asked at one point, which started something that made us both late for dinner.)

So: our productivity curve begins to flatten not only because we are becoming a service economy, but because some of the motivations—the spirit and the fear—have gone out of the producers. And maybe our inflation is persistent. If you want the dank side of the extrapolation, some of the workers retire right there on the job and wait for their pension, some take Fridays off. The servicing of all our *things* (and indeed even the services themselves) become so erratic and sloppy that the manufacturers have to work to make them service-free, no checkup for ten thousand miles, and the consumers get so irritated they transfer that irritation into political channels and gladly accept more government regulation of business.

So: it is affluence itself that has taken the edge off our edge. But the President need not exhort us to get out and return to the honesty of a day's work for a day's pay, which he has done on several occasions. Nation Number One will not be unique, because these elements don't stop at the water's edge; at different times, but for the same reasons, they will take place in all the Western industrial countries. The exhortations of Chairman Mao may be to a different end than the Shoar of Blessedness, but the tone is the same. In the capitalist industrial countries, it is the first generation off the farm that provides the longest hours and the most uncomplaining workers. Somebody who has spent sixteen hours a day looking at the wrong end of an ox for sub-subsistence on a patch in Poland may not complain at all when he emigrates with a paper suitcase to a steel mill on the south side of Chicago, but his grandson may not think it is that good a deal. We are the furthest off the farm. Japan had a generation that made its industrial reputation; those glee-club singers in the Matsushita plant think Matsushita is about the most dazzling thing that ever happened, but meanwhile the Germans are using Turks and Spaniards—again, fresher from the farm—to fill out the ranks in the Volkswagen plants. All of which does not solve our problem, but gives us company.

Perhaps that just gives us a challenge. Adolph Berle, among his other activities, was coauthor with Gardiner Means of the granddaddy classic in all this line of thinking, *The Modern Corporation and Private Property.* In one of his later books, *The American Economic Republic,* Berle suggested that we had a flexibility of response which he called the Transcendental Margin, those qualities that accounted for the prosperity of Israel but not Iraq, of the Netherlands but not Bulgaria—a certain creative energy. It propelled our system not towards profits but toward—are you ready?—beauty and truth. In a younger and more optimistic America that did not seem so strange. If we still have it, or something like it, it should be possible to make of work something fulfilling that does not need either the spiritual exhortation or economic fear to motivate it. That is a tall order and a big challenge, but the luckier of our citizens who have experienced something like it know that under those propitious circumstances it can be fun to bust your ass.

We ignore revolutions at our peril. Current evidences may or may not lead to profound changes, but we know that even when changes seem to happen quickly the ideas behind them have been hanging in the air for a long time.

FURTHER THOUGHTS

1. The Cotton Mather "Smith" mentions on page 107 was an American Puritan clergyman (1663-1728) who wrote over 450 works—including histories, biographies, essays, sermons, fables, verses, and treatises on theology, philosophy, science, medicine and "practical piety." In his works on practical piety, he argues fervently that a dedication to hard work is a necessary part of religious faith. In *Supermoney* "Adam Smith" used the following quote as a good example of Mather's feelings on the matter:

   Every Christian hath a GENERAL CALLING which is to Serve the Lord Jesus Christ and Save his own Soul ... and every Christian hath also a PERSONAL CALLING or a certain Particular Employment by which his Usefulness in his Neighborhood is Distinguished ... a Christian at his Two Callings is a man in a Boat, Rowing for Heaven; if he mind but one of his Callings, be it which it will, he pulls the Oar but on one side of the Boat, and will make but a poor dispatch to the Shoar of External Blessedness.

   Interpret this quotation carefully. How adequate is the rowboat image? Is a one-oared rower really in such a dire straits? Aren't there some alternatives even better than two oars? Do you accept Mather's basic distinction between a general and a personal calling? How would you describe these callings—or whatever you see operating in their place? Write out your own image, one that conveys, in more contemporary terms, what you think the case to be concerning a person's callings.

2. "Smith's" selection is organized much like a movie montage that tells a number of stories at once by weaving together scenes from each in a series of

quick cutbacks and sudden juxtapositions. Try to identify the different "stories" he has woven together and write a single sentence for each one, summarizing its main point. A list of these summary sentences would give you a list of the main themes in his argument.

3. Some people work by playing the money game. Is the money game really a game? Poker is a game; but how about playing the market? What—if anything—*is* the difference between gambling and investing? Does it seem fair and right to you that so much should hinge upon what seems to be so much like a mere game? (Why, for that matter, do we tend to speak of *mere* games as opposed to *real* jobs?)

Some people are convinced that it is impossible to make any useful social change. Many of these people are poor whites and blacks who believe themselves powerless. We believe that a person with help can change a system for the better. We remember, for instance, this story of a friend:

"When I was in high school, in social studies class, they taught me that we the people elect representatives to legislatures. These representatives make laws for us so that life can be lived with decency and order. They taught me that the courts of the land uphold those laws, backed by the force of police. (That force was not really stressed, for in the little towns where I grew up, the old Western term "peace officer" was still heard, and keeping the peace was part of the problem.)

"Well, when my father died, I found out a state law had been passed that prevented my mother from getting the retirement money he had earned with twenty-five years of teaching. Angered, I went to the state education association for support to change that unjust law. I was rebuffed. More angered, I scouted the state for cases of inequities under that law, and found them, and also found a young lawyer whose mother had suffered from that same law. The lawyer ran for the legislature. He won. The cases of injustice were presented, the need for change argued. And a new, better law was passed.

"I realize now how in trying to change that law I had made a great act of faith in my high school lessons. I firmly knew, with the faith of the young, that I would change that law. And I believed that changing it would make a difference. I still believe it, though now it is often as much an act of hope as an act of faith. And the anger I felt then comes again whenever an elected or appointed official shames the faith that makes his job possible."

Good lawyers like Ann Fagan Ginger and John George, are making an act of faith—or hope, or both—in the possibilities of change through law and the possibilities of satisfaction in the work of being a lawyer.

PREFACE TO *THE RELEVANT LAWYERS*

Ann Fagan Ginger

Practicing lawyers do not write books about the law. Occasionally one writes a sort of autobiography that tells part of the truth about the cases he won, and perhaps a little about the cases he lost, but very little about the law itself, or about his life as a whole. Reporters who write best sellers about spectacular trials and charismatic lawyers can provide even less of the total picture of the law and the lawyers. Instead, most books about the law are written by scholars and judges who write "hornbooks" and "restatements" laying out what the law is and should be from their vantage points as salaried employees of educational corporations and government, with some leisure and detachment to ponder the fundamental concepts of our legal system. But they leave out the lawyers, and also the clients.

Political scientists and law professors tend to compile casebooks containing excerpts from United States Supreme Court opinions, stressing the legal principles that allegedly are the sole basis for decision and form a logically consistent system. These books are used to train the next generation of law professors and clerks in what to do if they become Supreme Court justices. They don't tell a lawyer who has just passed the bar examination what to advise his first client to do in municipal court.

. . . .

I started the [Tom Paine Summer Law] school to help students answer the practical questions I faced on admission to the bar. I decided to become a lawyer without knowing any lawyers or having any conception of how a lawyer spends his time or pays his bills. I had read books about Clarence Darrow and his client Eugene V. Debs, and had heard my parents discuss grand juries, frame-ups, and injunctions against strikers. I had picked up their historical perspective, their rejection of property ownership as the measure of a person's worth, their disapproval of people seeking to control their relatives through provisions in wills, their belief in buying and selling ideas as well as land and goods.

With this cultural heritage, I entered the pre-law program of the University of Michigan with the idea of learning how to represent unions and the movement for social change. To support myself, I got a part-time job in a typical small-town commercial law firm. As I typed wills and contracts, I quickly concluded that the law as practiced is a dirty business, without the clear-cut victories and villains I had dreamed of.

During this period I read about a famous immigration lawyer, Carol King of New York, and I wrote to her concerning my prospects for becoming a principled woman lawyer. She replied:

> It is hard for anyone to make a living at the law—and even more difficult
> for a woman. I had an easy time making out because I had enough money

to carry me over, so I could do pretty much what I pleased, but if you are going to make a living practicing law, it is going to be dirty, and you can make up your mind to it. I can't quite figure out why that is so dreadful as you seem to think it is. When a picket knocks out a scab on the picket line, it isn't so pretty either; sometimes it is effective, sometimes it isn't.

She added, "If you want to practice law, go ahead and practice law, but if you are going to be fastidious, you had better get a job teaching economics in some workers' school and starve to death." She sent her best wishes along with this advice.

Law school proved to be an unexpected and traumatic experience. It was my first encounter with professors and students who openly accepted and acted on the theory that women are inferior to men.

But more than that, it was my first real encounter with the principles of feudalism and capitalism used as rules of law and public policy to decide disputes between human beings. The few students like myself who wanted to become people's lawyers were put off by the basic courses in Property and Contracts that set forth the law as it slowly evolved from feudalism to laissez-faire capitalism in England and early America through the rule against perpetuities and later the ingenious midwifery that brought forth corporations as citizens having rights under the Constitution. The books and the professors provided no real perspective on the short court opinions; they gave too little historical, economic, and social setting for the continual sale and devise of Blackacre, no explanation of its relevance to the tumultuous strike at Ford Motor Company a few miles away.

We couldn't sign up for a course on Employment Law, although the meaningful property rights and investments of the clients we wanted to serve were all related to their jobs. The complex legal problems of the person who would work for wages all his life (except when unemployed, ill, or retired) were not considered worthy of the minute analysis devoted to the control, sale, and exchange of land and goods covered in Real Property, Corporations, Wills and Trusts, Future Interests, Taxation, and Sales.

Years later, in the 1970s, when conflicts over the methods of law practice sharpened, I remembered Carol King's advice, as well as her remarkable warmth and personal concern for movement lawyers, combined with hard-hitting effectiveness against her opponent in court. The Tom Paine School was my contribution to the debate about law practice. The students were mostly law students, but some were undergraduates and others worked in law offices or in the community.

I asked the lawyers who spoke to emphasize the duality in practicing law: to discuss objective legal questions on which they are experts, and subjective questions on how they run their offices, and how their families fit in with their law practice. Sometimes we didn't get around to the subjective questions at all, and we never did justice to the family. We had some sharp exchanges on income and life style, wondering whether a four-day week is possible for movement lawyers and how they can spend some prime time with their families. We tangled on racism in unions and what is impossible when practicing law from the black perspective. We asked each other: What is a movement lawyer? What is he really after? Fame? Fortune? To make the society work a little better for his clients? Or to change the system in a fundamental sense?

FROM:
ANN FAGAN GINGER'S
THE RELEVANT LAWYERS

SOLO IN SOUL COUNTRY

John George

AFG:　John George is in private practice in Oakland's black community, where he handles both civil and criminal cases—a general practice. I met him years ago when he was working on school integration in Oakland through the NAACP. Then he ran for Congress in 1968 in the Democratic primary. John is known for his subtle sense of humor; his friends listen for it, but acquaintances often miss it under the weight of his rhetoric!

　　After that introduction, John, tell us how you happened to go to law school.

GEORGE:　I drifted through college in the Quiet Fifties, not knowing what I wanted to do. I was taking political science and economics, to learn what makes this country tick, why we are where we are. That was the eternal question being asked even during those Eisenhower years. But we didn't do anything about it. We would just sit around the coffee shops and talk.

　　Somebody came to me after 1954 and said, "The future of the black man is going to be decided in the courts of this country." That was because of the Supreme Court's opinion in *Brown v. Board of Education,* desegregating the schools and saying that separate is inherently unequal. That decision foreshadowed a generation of litigation. So I said, "Well, I guess I'll go to law school." Like if they had said the future of the black man was going to be decided in the schools of architecture, I would have gone to architecture school.

　　Legal education, even when I was coming through, answered all the questions that nobody was asking.

STUDENT:　That's a good line.

GEORGE:　I came out of law school, and my first two years I worked for a lawyer who was also an inheritance-tax appraiser. But my motivation was to do something in civil rights, so I gravitated toward those kinds of cases, which in the West were demonstrations—like the Sheraton-Palace sit-ins.

What I want to tell you about those cases is not my experience in conducting the trials, but what those cases do to the legal system and how the court personnel react when you get involved in them.

You are walking around as a lawyer and you've had the routine case—that is, four counts of murder, two counts of robbery. The DA is your colleague and friend. You go down and discuss equitable disposition, maybe negotiate a plea.

The judge says, "Come on back in chambers," and "Well, what have we got here?"

"Well, Judge, my man has got this going for him," and you name some factors about his life, "and here's what we're trying to accomplish . . ." The judge is your colleague and friend in a certain sense, too.

Then the sit-in cases hit San Francisco. These were political cases. Well, the judges, the DAs, the court personnel just changed almost overnight in dealing with the lawyers on those cases. They treated those sit-ins as if they were hitting at the whole system and they were going to use everything they had to protect it.

Maybe they were perceptive.

See, a guy who goes and murders somebody or robs a store is not threatening the system as a whole; he's just a criminal to be given a jail sentence or probation. But those guys demonstrating were hitting at the very foundations. So all our dealings with the judges became different. And in the sentencing there was almost no talk about straight probation. Those guys were made to serve some time in jail.

I went from those cases to some in Oakland for a guy named Mark Comfort, who was a revolutionary in the early sixties, which was still a quiet time. I couldn't put on an elaborate political defense, because these were just misdemeanors, and we lost them.

STUDENT: What kinds of charges were they?

GEORGE: One was a charge of tending to contribute to the delinquency of a minor. Mark was in a group of speakers that asked high school students to come down to a park to protest police brutality. Now, if a student is absent from school three times without excuse, he becomes a delinquent. So Mark was charged with tending toward contributing to delinquency, because the students were out of school that day without permission. He was found guilty.

Going by the rules, he would have been found guilty no matter what the skill of the lawyer had been. Remember, there is a tendency for radicals to say, "You cannot get justice out of the courts." Yet they want to go to court all the time as a method of focusing attention on the struggle. Then, as the trial comes on, I detect a lingering hope in them that they *are* going to receive justice—that they can beat the rap. They forget that the premise on which the arrest was made indicated that they would never win the case.

I also met Huey Newton at that time. He was going to college then, and we had a few misdemeanor cases. I think we won one and lost two or three. Then they formed the Panthers, and in May 1967 they went to Sacramento to demonstrate. They got arrested for carrying guns, and there was a hard struggle to raise bail money.

There was some talk about why they didn't choose a black lawyer to handle Newton's murder case. My view is that if there had been a skillful black lawyer around who could have handled a case of that magnitude, he would have been chosen. But no black lawyer had ever put himself out for Newton before that, and now that his life was at stake, this was no time for pussyfooting around.

STUDENT: Does a lawyer have to be in a big firm to take a case like that?

GEORGE: Well, a top-notch criminal lawyer, even if he practices alone, would have access to investigators and other lawyers, to do research and legwork for him in a big political case. But the average lawyer would need a pool of resources to handle those cases or he would be wiped out economically.

There's another thing to consider, too. When you get known for doing public-service work, many, many cases come unto you. These clients don't think about your office expenses and bills; they think you are a great public servant, a lawyer, and you can afford it. Other lawyers can establish the image of saying, "You don't have money for me? I'm not going to give you a thing." But he who puts himself out as trying to do something for the community—much is expected of him, and he will receive the rap from people if he doesn't perform. He is like the auspicious intermeddler they tell about in law school: you are under no duty to save a person from drowning, but if you do go out to save him don't do it negligently or you will be sued, and it is no defense to say, "My intentions were good. I tried to do my best."

STUDENT: How many black lawyers are there practicing in the black community here?

GEORGE: In the Bay Area there are about fifty-five admitted to practice.

AFG: Are all of them practicing?

GEORGE: Those are lawyers and judges practicing in government or whatever, but not those doing just real estate or some other business. In private practice there are about thirty or thirty-five. Then there are some with the public defender's office and with Neighborhood Legal Services.

The tragic thing is that there are only about two Mexican-American lawyers in Alameda County.

AFG: Do you know any black women lawyers? What problems of practice do they face?

GEORGE: There are a few in private practice in the Bay Area. One does mostly domestic relations and personal injury, not much criminal law. Another practices in the public defender's office, and one is with Legal Aid in San

Francisco. Then there is Cherie Gaines, a brilliant lady lawyer who is now teaching law.

Not being a woman, I don't know the difficulties of women lawyers. I just think a woman lawyer may be handicapped in criminal law. You have to go into some nitty-gritty places. Even a middle-class man has problems walking into the criminal world. That's why not many middle-class lawyers, black or white, engage in criminal law—you're dealing in many instances with a bad element.

STUDENT: Are white firms opening up to black lawyers today? Are there good opportunities here?

GEORGE: In my opinion, it's not prevalent. And it really depends on what the black lawyer wants to get out of a firm. If he goes into a firm that represents insurance companies, that's the experience he'll get, and if that kind of firm selects him it would probably be because his background indicates that he would fit in with that situation.

Jim Herndon is a black lawyer in a white firm, but it's a firm with "a social conscience," which means he can develop and pursue civil-liberties and other controversial cases. Now, if you go down to one of those big establishment firms in downtown San Francisco . . .

STUDENT: One of the black activists at Boalt Law School took a job with a firm like that. That's why I asked.

GEORGE: I think he probably would have to either sell out or leave that kind of firm.

In the future, I think there is going to be more of a movement of black lawyers creating black firms. Of course, if your practice is based almost exclusively on the black community, that dictates how much you can do. It limits the financial resources you have for handling suits against insurance companies or the district attorney's office. Your clients cannot pay for "fringe benefits" like discovery and investigation costs. That's why these public defenders and Legal Aid offices are popping up, trying to fill the gap.

Money buys a lot of things in this country; housing, education, medicine, law. If you don't have enough money, you may not send for a witness down in Los Angeles; you might not even put an investigator on the case to look for a witness here. If the lawyer is not paid enough, he will not be as diligent in looking for the things that can help his client, even within the present court system. So, the times we could get better treatment within the present system, we miss out for lack of money.

When you are practicing law from a black perspective, you've got to know the community you come from. Otherwise you won't know what rules to apply in that community or how to conduct yourself. Black people are engaged in economic crimes, mostly: burglary, robbery, these type things. That's because the system has created a situation where they have to engage in that sort of conduct. I don't mean to say, "Just excuse that type conduct"; I'm not excusing it, I'm explaining it. The poor are not the cause of poverty;

the system is the cause of poverty, and poverty is the cause of these crimes. Then when poor people are thrown in jail, they aren't fined and given probation the way other people would be, and a lot of talent is wasted. I see guys in county jail who might be some of the best material we have—just wasted.

One of the things we are up against is this: people create institutions and devices to make things more livable and convenient. The creation of these legal systems is a public political act. But the laws are drawn up in many instances to exclude, not to include.

It has been said that politics is the art of making some things impossible for outsiders. They make it impossible for you by putting you on the outside, and then they make rules against outsiders. They dare the outsider to break the rules, and when, on occasion, you break a rule for your survival, the people who judge you—the jury, the prosecutor, the judges—are more in tune with the people who made the rules to exclude you in the first place. You are judged by the rulemakers and you had no say in drawing up those rules. That's what makes it doubly difficult for black people. And if you're poor this falls on you, too.

AFG: For example?

GEORGE: You know how judges are appointed—they are lawyers who worked in a political party. In some instances they may pick a legal scholar, but usually the day before he was appointed the judge was a highly partisan political figure—a county chairman or an assemblyman, maybe. The next day he's the judge, and the lawyer who comes before him is looking for the even hand of justice.

There's also the social atmosphere that judges and lawyers engage in. When you pick up the phone and say to opposing counsel, "Hey, Jim, can we work this out?" and you've just seen him at a luncheon or some other social affair, it helps in your negotiations.

The organization that draws up the rules for the legal profession is the bar association. Now, the people who can be active in the association and can go to the bar conventions are usually the lawyers who are well off, who can take off a few weeks. So somehow it happens that they draw up the minimum-fee schedules based on the practice of most white lawyers. They say the minimum fee for a divorce is $300. Then black lawyers have to take that fee to the black community and try to make it work. Many black people can't afford $300.

Or take another example: a mother doesn't know her son is going to get arrested. She didn't schedule this in her budget. Suddenly one night she has to come up with $150, $200, or her son won't have legal representation. How can she find that money right like that? This is what gets me out there sometimes. Most lawyers won't take the case on credit, because once you become the attorney of record the court is looking to you to carry through on the case.

There is also what I call selective enforcement of the law. The district attorney has great power to select whom to prosecute. For example, in Oakland they've got a statute prohibiting gambling. It's all right to play cards, but not for money. Now, I've never seen any white gamblers being prosecuted. See, if you've got a private club where you go and gamble, then the police don't reach you. But they prosecute black gamblers. They've got experts in the language of gambling, and if you're down in someone's house they've got some informer there playing, too, or listening at the door, and later he comes in and testifies, "Yes, they were talking about money."

I've never seen white prostitutes being prosecuted in Oakland. The rare one who is may be working in black neighborhoods.

STUDENT: Black people get discrimination instead of justice.

GEORGE: But remember: in the practice of criminal law, people are looking for you to get them off, not for justice. If the first words you say to a client are "I can save you from jail, man," then you can be as impatient and insensitive as you want. You can demand the attention and respect of your client. You have what they call great client control.

So, when you practice criminal law in a traditional manner, you strike up a relationship with the district attorney—you discuss matters with him. On a class basis, the black lawyer may be able to communicate better with the DA than he can with his own client who is from a different class. A lawyer has to be very skillful in human psychology to know how to communicate and be understood by his clients. You have to explain difficult things in simple terms. The client is usually in trouble, facing jail, and he does not want to engage in intellectual dialogue or abstract discussion. Even when you try to give him a hypothetical example to show how his case stacks up against others, he'll often say, "But that's not my case. Let's get back to what I did."

You've got 500 cases in your head. His case is the only case in the world to him.

AFG: Do you encourage your client to participate in making decisions about his case?

GEORGE: At a time like this, the routine client is not looking for participatory democracy.

You say to him, "What are we going to do with this case?"

He says, "Well, I came to *you* for that."

He wants you to make an arbitrary decision that you can save him, not to explore the doubts of his case.

He says, "I know I got a weak case; that's why I came to you."

STUDENT: It sounds like you don't have many illusions about your clients.

GEORGE: Many of these guys are hustlers. Some of them are even hustling the lawyer. I had a guy come in, and I asked, "What have they got you charged with?"

"Burglary and receiving stolen property," he says. Then he sits down and says, "That's a nice dictating machine you got there. I like your typewriter." And I start getting leery of my own client.

"Do you know you are only *presumed* to be innocent, and presumptions are easily overcome?"

He says, "What's the retainer fee?"

"It's $200."

"I thought you were one of the brothers who was trying to help out," he says.

Then I look up and say, "You're guilty. The presumption is over."

. . . .

AFG: Are you in practice by yourself now?

GEORGE: Yes, but I share an office with two other lawyers, so we talk things over and we split the office expenses.

AFG: Would you like to have a bigger firm or a more specialized practice?

GEORGE: Yes, both. It's hard keeping up with just search-and-seizure law, much less all the rest of criminal law, domestic relations, patent law, corporations. Most black lawyers are general practitioners. We are corner grocery stores in the supermarket age.

I live from month to month. I don't know where the beans are going to come from in August or the rest of July. I'm hoping it will be like last July or last month, but right now I do not have the money to pay my bills, unless it comes in this week or next. And the office expenses have to be paid almost before the home expenses, because if you don't take care of the office, you may not have your home.

I've been practicing about five years now, and I can make it with a lot of scuffling and volume. But when the clientele you're practicing among is predominantly poor, to make $30,000 gross you've got to handle 500 cases. Compared to the guy who makes $30,000 handling 10 or 100 cases, the service you are giving is another question.

AFG: One of the students was asking how a lawyer can be a decent human being if he has to spend so much of his time working at his profession. Can you ever get away from it, John? Can you relax with your family? Does your wife work? How do you manage?

GEORGE: My wife is a former science teacher. She doesn't work outside the home now. My three children are nine and seven years old and eighteen months.

I'm involved in some political things that do keep me away from home sometimes. I think it's the quality of your relationship with your family that counts, not the quantity. That's my rationalization. I think your children have to be brought up so that they don't constantly have to have their parent around.

You can't schedule robberies. A guy doesn't come to you and say, "I'm going to commit this crime on July eighth. Would you get ready?" You get phone calls at night, on weekends, and you have to go down to the jail. There's no point getting morally outraged when the guy calls you. It would be like a doctor getting mad at a patient for getting sick.

Anyway, by the time your kids get to be fifteen or twenty years old they'll be gone.

AFG: But wait five years, until your nine-year-old is fourteen.

GEORGE: What happens then?

AFG: I found that a parent of teenagers in this time and place has to be in touch with his kid every day. I'm for self-reliance, and my kids do a lot of things on their own; but at a certain age, if you don't give them a chance to talk to you every day, they can get into the damnedest things you would ever dream of. And if a week goes by before you hear about it, it may be more serious by then.

GEORGE: Well, that's a problem, because a lawyer listens to troubles all day and is supposed to deal with them and resolve them as calmly as possible. So then he goes home and he has to listen to more troubles? Home is the place to relax and lounge.

You don't have to smile anymore. Your wife is the only person in the world of whom you can say, "She understands. We know each other's feelings and ways so well that I don't have to explain everything." I can come home and sit down and smoke and kind of shut out. That's true for everybody—teacher, lawyer, physician, bail bondsman, real-estate broker, operating engineer. Home has got to be that sanctuary.

FURTHER THOUGHTS

1. Both John George and Ann Fagan Ginger went into law in part out of their desire to change the system somehow. George mentions the different attitudes prosecutors and judges seem to have towards simple criminals who are not actually trying to change the system, but simply cheat within it and certain activists who are not cheating so much as they are playing the role of spoil sport, calling the entire system into question and trying to get things changed. (Johan Huizinga mentions this same distinction between cheats and spoil sports in the selection from his *Homo Ludens* on page 246.) Jot down the names of some specific criminals you know of. Do the same with some activists. What do you think the "cheats" would think about the "spoil sports," and vice versa? Do *you* feel differently about one or the other? How do you think the distinction between cheats and spoil sports applies to schoolwork? How could it apply to other kinds of work and jobs?

2. In view of what you learn about Ann Fagan Ginger in her selection and what you learn about John George in his, why do you think she asked him that question on page 122 about the lawyer's problems in trying to be a decent human being and a hard-working professional?

3. What things do Ginger and George have to say about people's expectations of roles—especially concerning women, blacks, and political activists? Were you surprised or perhaps angered by any of the expectations that they seemed themselves to have?

Kenneth Lasson's article "The Cop" in Part 1 was taken from his book, *The Workers,* prepared for Ralph Nader's Center for Study of Responsive Law. The book presents portraits of eight other blue-collar workers also—a garbage man, a maid, a baker, a coal miner, a cab driver, a bricklayer, a waitress, and a telephone operator. The following is Ralph Nader's conclusion to the book.

AFTERWORD TO *THE WORKERS*

Ralph Nader

The quest for meaning in work—as distinguished from the quest *for* work—is one of history's least charted courses. Man's struggle to make a living has always overshadowed the interaction of humans with their work and what it does or means for them.

In all societies, different social status has always been attached to different kinds of work. In our country, the principal division has been between blue-collar and white-collar work, with the latter gaining ascendancy earlier in the century when the trend to a service economy became clear. The parallel denigration of blue-collar, manual labor has taken numerous forms which combine to produce a mixture of resignation, boredom, irritation, desperation, and a sense of depreciated self-worth on the part of many manual workers.

It is dismaying how the major institutions which have an impact on blue-collar labor persist in ignoring so many of the issues relating to the worth of the job beyond wages and fringe benefits. Government concerns itself with unemployment rates and aggregate wage rates and labor-management strife. Corporations stress productivity increases and favor highly centralized union bureaucracies. Union leaders emphasize bread and butter gains at the bargaining table. Who concentrates on the relation of the worker to the job and how outside influences—such as inflation, taxes, traffic congestion, the breakdown of community organization, and local citizen expression—affect attitudes and efficiencies on the job? Or how the job affects what workers can do about these and other matters off the job?

Even though there are as yet no enduring answers, these questions have at least been asked with increasing insistency during the past two years. The answers are more likely to be forthcoming when the important issues are identified and made concrete with the facts and feelings of workers as major touchstones. Several of these issues will illustrate the need for a new evaluation of the meaning of work as a human experience rather than a clocked means to simply earn the dollars for afterwork ends.

1. The sense of worth perceived by most blue-collar workers on the job is minimal. Historians explain this as principally a reflection of the shift from craft to assembly line. The laborer often works on but a fraction of the product over

and over again with a mind-numbing drudgery. Pride in workmanship disappears. Moreover, blue-collar work is considered "dirty work" compared to office work. Such is the popular attitude.

How estranged this view is from the relative values of blue-collar work to society! Economists have long shown that production work is a condition precedent to most service work. In recent years the country has had to learn the importance of blue-collar work the hard way, when strikes virtually paralyzed normal living or threatened to do so if the stoppage were allowed to continue very long. It is ironic that workers were reported to have gained a sense of pride when they saw the effect their absence had on a society that deprecatingly had taken them for granted.

Even creativity outside the line of duty receives little recognition. Corporate employers rarely publicize beyond their plant's confines the significant productivity and efficiency gains which frequently result from employee suggestions. Yet these same companies urge and pay for such suggestions.

There are many other signs of a society going out of its way to ignore the blue-collar laborer. The motion picture and television industries operate as if the manual worker didn't exist except as a prop for advertisements or for the well-to-do, or as an intruder on the public scene when he strikes. Although as early post-World War II European films taught Hollywood and its extravaganzas that the lives of ordinary people make subjects of great dramatic interest, blue-collar workers are rarely treated in modern fiction. This is no mere neglect of an indulgence in the activities of over thirty million workers. It is an absence of communication between them and other citizens about their hopes, agonies, fulfillments, and sense of pride or indifference in doing the job that has to be done. In short, being off-stage deprives a group of recognition, dialogue, and a sense of identity.

Blue-collar work need not be romanticized to free it of any stigma or stereotype. As portions of the portraits in this book indicate, even the most routine jobs involve a wide scale of competence with which they can be accomplished to meet valued human needs. Anyone who questions how important these needs are should consider how important the crisis would be if these needs were not met.

2. There are very few outlets for the development of on-the-job citizenship. Every blue-collar job involves an industry as trade whose impact on the public can be improved. Workers know an enormous amount about abuses which they encounter, endorse, observe, or try to avoid every day. Moreover, they often know about them far earlier than their ultimate disclosure—or emergence as public scandals or disasters.

For example, workers know that there is virtually no difference between different brands of gasolines of the same octane level. They know generally which factories dump what pollutants into waterways and that there is more pollution under cover of darkness. They know how car manufacturers fudge inspection on the line. They know how government inspectors tip off coal mines of their impending arrival or how their coworkers smoke in prohibited areas. They know which meat and poultry inspectors are on the take or which fail to exercise their duties. They know how taxi meters and automobile odometers are rigged by design or manipulated to cheat the rider or driver. They know of violations of work safety laws. Indeed, many of the main consumer and environmental problems are rooted in secrets known to hundreds if not thousands of workers. The value of such information can be seen by occasional acts of courage when an assembly line worker discloses evidence of defectively designed products.

Beginning in 1966 Edward Gregory, a quality control worker in GM's Fisher Body plant in St. Louis, reported to the federal government a welding defect affecting over two million Chevrolets which were subsequently recalled in 1969 after exhaust fume leakage claimed a number of lives. If mechanisms can be developed to convey such information about abuses to people and groups who can do something about them, workers can begin to have an opportunity to exercise broader allegiances to principles of fair play and corporate responsibility. Such mechanisms would permit the humblest worker to relate his sense of values to the deeper significance of what is being produced for thousands or millions of citizens as well as to substitute participation for complicity. Whistle-blowing, or the ethic of employees appealing to higher authorities than a negligent, criminal, or stagnant management permits, would lead to internal organizational reforms that would provide greater participation and respect for employees in their work. It should be clear by now that meaningful work for many laborers includes the right and opportunity to apply their sense of justice to their surroundings and the products or services being produced. The feeling of being an automaton is partly due to being denied a normative role on the job. Other countries have experimented with worker councils with some managerial responsibilities at the plant level, and their experiences deserve study.

3. A great deal of manual or blue-collar labor is fatiguing, grimy, hazardous, and boring. Exposure to unsafe working conditions and toxic gases, chemicals, and dust in mines and factories produces thousands of fatalities and millions of injuries and diseases every year. To its credit, the *Wall St. Journal* devoted two lead articles in July, 1971, to describing selected occupations, such as a foundry worker, that wear the body and dull the mind. Given overtime or moonlighting, or even without those additional laboring hours, a worker comes home too tired to think about ways to make a contribution to society in a nonwork capacity. In a twist of the Marxist dictum, work becomes the opiate of the people, draining them of energy to contemplate their citizenship roles in their hours away from the job. Notice how some of the workers described in this book spend their evenings—in utter exhaustion with eyes heavy-lidded before a TV set. This pointedly suggests the desirability of further concentrating the workweek along the lines of the recently touted four-day forty-hour week.

A new study by two British occupational psychologists reported the case of a military officer who left his career in his forties to become a milkman at much lower earnings. However, his workday ends about 2:00 P.M., which allows him to play golf and engage intensively in village political and administrative activities. New life styles in the after-work hours can be developed through participation in community college activities and other educational opportunities which would increase one's options of employment or chances for promotion. Such personal development would also increase the likelihood of postretirement careers in community and citizenship work which would replace the empty, meaningless existence of so many retired people.

4. Neither unions nor government is paying sufficient attention to erosions of wage and fringe benefit gains by inequitable taxes, business frauds, monopolistic practices, crime, pollution, political corruption, or governmental incompetence. What is obtained through employment is seriously depleted outside of employment by deteriorating conditions which have few institutional watchdogs or safeguards. The compelling challenge is how to focus new remedies on the interrelatedness of blue-collar workers with forces beyond their control and often beyond their awareness—forces that reduce the value of their income, impair their health, and safety, inflict psychic stresses on them and their families, and generally reduce the quality of their lives, even as their pay checks increase.

The emergence of black community organizations in the inner cities reflects the dissolution of minimally responsive government. Similarly, the growth of the white urban ethnic movement with its dualism of defense and reform is symptomatic of the obsolescence of the old organizations in and out of government. Some politicians, sensing the potential of rising popular ferment, begin to develop rhetoric that turns the mass of the people against the downtrodden. Other more cautious politicians then begin to drift toward evasion of the issues for fear of alienating a bewildered mass middle class victimized by many of the same forces which bear down so heavily on blacks, Chicanos, and Indians.

Barbara Mikulski of the Southeast Community Organization in Baltimore described the feelings of the urban ethnic portions of the middle class in this way:

The ethnic American is overtaxed and underserved at every level of government. He does not have fancy lawyers or expensive lobbyists getting him tax breaks on his income. Being a home owner, he shoulders the rising property taxes—the major revenue source for the municipalities in which he lives. Yet he enjoys very little from these unfair and burdensome levies.

Because of restrictive eligibility requirements linked either to income or "target areas," he gets no help from Federal programs. If he wants to buy in "the old neighborhood," he cannot get an F.H.A. loan. One major illness in his family will wipe him out. When he needs a nursing home for an elderly parent, he finds that there are none that he can afford, nor is he eligible for any financial assistance.

His children tend to go to parochial schools which receive little in the way of government aid and for which he carries an extra burden. There is a general decline of community services for his neighborhood, e.g., zoning, libraries, recreation programs, sanitation, etc.

His income of $5,000 to $10,000 per year makes him "nearpoor." He is the victim of both inflation and anti-inflationary measures. He is the guy that is hurt by layoffs and by tight money that chokes him with high interest rates for installment buying and home improvements.

Manufacturers, with their price fixing, shoddy merchandise and exorbitant repair bills, are gouging him to death. When he complains about costs, he is told that it is the "high cost of labor" that is to blame. Yet he knows he is the "labor" and that in terms of real dollars he is going backward.

The ethnic American also feels unappreciated for the contribution he makes to society. He resents the way the working class is looked down upon. In many instances he is treated like the machine he operates or the pencil he pushes. He is tired of being treated like an object of production. The public and private institutions have made him frustrated by their lack of response to his needs. At present he feels powerless in his daily dealings with and efforts to change them.

Unfortunately, because of old prejudices and new fears, anger is generated against other minority groups rather than those who have power. What is needed is an alliance of white and black, white collar, blue collar and no collar based on mutual need, interdependence and respect, an alliance to develop the strategy for a new kind of community organization and political participation.

Perhaps the most remarkable context of these expressed grievances is that during the 'sixties there was a booming overall economy which in 1970 amounted to a trillion dollars of gross national product. The contrast between this massive aggregate economic growth and serious problems of poverty, health, housing, pollution, transportation, urban rot and conflict seems to be endemically ignored. The country needs a new political economy giving quality to growth and redirecting resources toward the various problems. The growth ethic is wearing very thin in light of the realities: an increasingly unequal distribution of wealth, and a tragic mismatching of public and private wealth with needs that are acknowledged daily in our newspaper headlines. According to recent statistics covering the post World War II period, the redistribution of income through taxes and the welfare state has simply not occurred. Yet the advertisements of aggregate growth and unreal wage gains inspire persistent myths that automatic progress has occurred as a result. Even buying into their future incomes through the credit economy is interpreted as present gains for workers.

The portraits in the preceding pages reveal a pathetic display of the treadmill effect. These hard-working people are achieving little beyond providing the basic necessities for their families. To do this, they have forfeited the opportunity to develop and contribute as individuals and citizens. But a modern industrial economy is supposed to give workers a greater chance to accomplish just that. The earthy cynicism which some of these workers reveal toward any change for the better indicates the absence of hopes for any alternatives. No system, no ideology, no utopia lights their sense of optimism. Their plea, such as it is, focuses on simple standards of honesty, neighborliness, and decency—with hardly any specific ideas of their role in helping to apply such principles beyond themselves.

Here is the crux of the working person's problem. Most cannot or do not wish to recognize that their wholesale delegation of citizenship duties to elected and appointed officials is failing them badly. At a time when citizenship must receive a new definition and commitment of time and energy—as an obligation to be discharged continually on and off the job, individually and collectively—there is little thinking about replacing past abdications with new resolves. The role of the victim has too often been to bewail his victimization, to the exclusion of doing something about it. This attitude generates despair, discouragement, and disgust. What is needed is indeed rigorous: a citizenship that engages public problems well beyond sporadic elections and develops into a relevant use of human talents. It must become an important portion of what constitutes the human experience, an obligation rather than a freelance hobby for a few determined mavericks.

In concrete terms, the required dedication means an assertion of citizens over larger social organizations. It means organizing to decide, propose, and guide the near and far institutions—corporations, governments, and unions—by the people they are supposed to serve. This kind of initiatory democracy is not an end to itself, but rather a means of placing just values on factual situations through duly constituted channels of power or authority. It is a way of generating a popular demand for skills, resources, and laws to be responsive to people's needs. It is also a way of encouraging independence of activity with accountability for performance. To view the plight of the blue-collar worker in anything less than this broader environment is to permit frustrated emotion to be exploited by calculating power brokers.

A first step toward putting the "demos" back into democracy is accepting the need for professional full-time citizen advocates to represent the interests of the unrepresented. Such advocates—lawyers, economists, scientists, engineers, physicians, and others of various talents—should work outside institutionalized frameworks and outside bureaucracies, to imprint the interests of the mass of citizens on institutions that are not working. One of the greatest ideas of the latter twentieth century will be the one that can organize the funding of such advocates from small contributions by large numbers of the people especially affected by the conditions to be changed, and make these supporters want to participate and contribute their own involvement. Once such movements get underway the workers would have recovered their nerve. And with the recovery of nerve will come the virtues and actions that can change the world for the better.

FURTHER THOUGHTS

1. What is the status of blue-collar workers among people you know? Ask your parents what it was when they were your age. Ask your grandparents the same question. Have any changes occurred over the years?
2. If your parents are not blue-collar workers, how many generations back do you have to go to find blue-collar workers or manual laborers? If you have an informed and talkative older relative who is also willing, sit down with that relative and try to work out a family job-tree.

3. Nader speaks of on-the-job citizenship and "whistle-blowing." If you had a good job, a growing family, and a big mortgage, and you found out that your company was systematically and deliberately cheating the public, what would you do? What if the cheating created a real danger? Are there any kinds of companies you absolutely wouldn't work for? Why?
4. Does it strike you as odd that the word *company* derives from a Latin word meaning "one who eats bread with another"?

Nader's discussion—indeed, Lasson's entire book—raises many valid and important issues about the troubles besetting the blue-collar worker. But blue-collar work is actually declining in America. Fewer than 2 per cent of American workers work on an assembly line, for instance. And as Irving Kristol points out in *The Wall Street Journal*:

> More and more, as the American economy becomes a "post-industrial," service-oriented economy, fewer and fewer people are engaged in blue-collar factory work, in blue-collar work of any kind, in manufacturing altogether. The factory is following the farm as *yesterday's* typical place of employment. Today, there are more insurance salesmen than blue-collar steelworkers in America, and the insurance "industry" as a whole probably employs more people than does automobile manufacturing. There are more white-collar than blue-collar workers in the American labor force, and by 1980 the ratio will reach an overwhelming 5:3. Moreover, by 1980, some 25% of these white-collar workers will be either in the "professional-technical" category (teachers, engineers, scientists, etc.) or in the "managerial" (public and private) category.

The white-collar worker frequently has his own troubles. Like the blue-collar worker he is troubled by the loss of creativity brought on by an increased division of labor and fragmentation of responsibility. He too is troubled by the thinning out of his job and its satisfactions by Parkinson's Law which states, "Work expands so as to fill the time available for its completion. . . . The thing to be done swells in importance and complexity in a direct ratio with the time to be spent."

Most white-collar jobs are within hierarchies, and thus very often the white-collar worker finds his situation aggravated by an institutionalized failure of imagination brought on by something like the Peter Principle: "In a hierarchy every employee tends to rise to his level of incompetence." This means that from the top down in a hierarchy, "In time, every post tends to be occupied by an employee who is incompetent to carry out its duties" (Peter's Corollary). Thus the white-collar worker all too often finds himself in a situation in which any work that gets done "is accomplished by those employees who have not yet reached their level of incompetence" (Peter again)—a situation sure to produce frustration and cynicism. Theodore Roethke's poem "Dolor" describes the feelings of the troubled white-collar worker. And though we can't be sure of the narrator's occupation in Tran Te Xuong's "Me," he too seems to speak for the worker whose sources of satisfaction have been thinned out of existence.

DOLOR

Theodore Roethke

I have known the inexorable sadness of pencils,
Neat in their boxes, dolor of pad and paper-weight,
All the misery of manilla folders and mucilage,
Desolation in immaculate public places,
Lonely reception room, lavatory, switchboard,
The unalterable pathos of basin and pitcher,
Ritual of multigraph, paper-clip, comma,
Endless duplication of lives and objects.
And I have seen dust from the walls of institutions,
Finer than flour, alive, more dangerous than silica,
Sift, almost invisible, through long afternoons of tedium,
Dropping a fine film on nails and delicate eyebrows,
Glazing the pale hair, the duplicate gray standard faces.

ME

Tran Te Xuong (Vietnam)

trans. Burton Raffel

The world is full of useful tasks,
Teaching, digging ditches, farming.
But this? This nonentity
Goes out with his umbrella, in the morning,
And then at night he brings it back.

FURTHER THOUGHTS

1. Do you see any particular reason for the pencils in "Dolor" being *neat*? How does that word tie in with other words in the poem?

2. Even if you've never worked in an office, you've probably been in the kinds of places and experienced the feelings that Roethke describes—in school buildings, if nowhere else. Try writing a "Dolor" of your own experiences. You might try modeling it after Roethke's structure and rhythm for example:

> I have known the inexorable sadness of Mondays,
> Hard upon weekends, dolor of bell and morning-ache,
> All the misery of attendance-taking and toothpaste taste. . . .

And so on.

3. What do teaching, digging ditches, and farming have in common that might have caused Tran Te Xuong to list them as useful tasks? Clearly the farming in *Fat City* didn't seem to be too satisfying. What happened to make unsatisfying drudgery out of a useful task? What other kinds of work would you call useful tasks? When you combine this list of yours with those of other people, what patterns do you begin to see?

When dolor strikes, it's time for a change, whether one has a blue-collar or a white-collar job. In the following three prose sketches Ann Bayer describes some workers who grew dissatisfied with their jobs and decided to start over. A salesman became a teacher in Alaska, a veterinarian became a worker on a receiving dock, and a policeman became a painter.

BEGINNING AGAIN IN THE MIDDLE

Ann Bayer

For many men the years from 35 to 50 turn into grim routine; they are the years of heightened susceptibility to alcohol, heart attack, worry and divorce. The kind of work one does can aggravate these crises—a profession that was appealing at 20 may have soured to appalling in another 20 years. In the old days there was almost no way for a man to change direction. He had invested too much time and talent getting where he was, and he stood to lose too much if he started at the bottom somewhere else. Today, the switch is easier and there are even some incentives. One is the contagious enthusiasm of the under-25 generation, who have made it fashionable to scorn security. Another is the great national affluence that has made it possible to stop one job long enough to train for another. A third is the lessened stigma of old age: companies are becoming increasingly interested in hiring older, qualified men as consultants.

More and more men are changing jobs today. Columbia University recently completed an experimental program just to help them change. There seem to be no limits to the leap; account executives have quit to become ministers, ministers have become engineers, and engineers have turned to raising chickens.

Jack Fuller, Salesman

Eight years ago Jack Fuller of Akron, Ohio was selling graduation accessories (caps and gowns and fraternity pins). He was spending an average of four nights a week on the road "going like the hammers of hell," had picked up 30 extra pounds of flab and complained of a nervous stomach. He was making more than $30,000 a year.

On their 16th wedding anniversary Fuller and his wife Lee (short for Lenore) opened a bottle of champagne. "All of a sudden," says Fuller, "we realized that we'd been married 16 years and never done any of the things we'd meant to do. I had always wanted to go to Alaska, and Lee wanted just as badly to go to the Virgin Islands. So we said let's do something before it's too late." Years before, Fuller had been a high school football coach, and Lee had a teaching certificate. It occurred to him that he and Lee still had a chance to live out their plans: they could become teachers, first in Alaska for two years, and then in the Virgin Islands.

Before that evening the Fullers had never thought seriously about leaving Akron; afterward they could think of nothing else. Jack wrote to the Bureau of Indian Affairs asking for any position above the Arctic Circle. He enrolled at Akron University for his teaching certificate. Eventually the BIA found them teaching jobs in an Arctic whaling village called Point Hope. And a year and a half after that bottle of champagne, ignoring the cries of their friends ("We have a new tennis club and a new swimming pool, and you're *leaving*?"), the Fullers rented their colonial house, stored their furniture and took off.

Fuller is a gregarious ex-Marine and in Point Hope he quickly acquired the name *Sugunaporuk,* Eskimo for "strong, friendly man." Whenever he felt he needed to be alone, he would simply hitch up his dog team and ride off to the tundra. "I'd always wanted to prove I could survive, that I could meet the elements head-on," says Fuller. "For me, being alone in all that vastness is definitely a profound feeling, like being closer to God."

The Fullers' two young daughters, who soon learned to speak fluent Eskimo, also fared well in the Arctic, but for Lee the adjustment was harder. "If I'd known it was going to be the emotional upheaval it was," she says frankly, "I couldn't have done it." At first the family lived in a federal housing project with no telephone and no plumbing. In the winter they melted ice for water; in summer they hauled it from a well. Actually, this life without TV or restaurants or other such amenities was a hardship they rather enjoyed. "Lee and I have always been pretty self-contained," says Fuller. "We could make our own fun." They stayed in Point Hope two years, then taught for three more in an even more remote village called Gambell on St. Lawrence Island, just 45 miles east of Siberia.

The Fullers now live in Nome (average January temperature: 3.4°) in comparative comfort. Jack, who is 48 no longer teaches school but makes $14,000 as a full-time captain in the National Guard Eskimo Scouts. Lee earns $6,000 working part time for the Selective Service.

Fuller is fond of walrus hunting, and in the summer he and an Eskimo partner run a service that takes trophy hunters into the ice floes of the Bering Sea in search of the big bulls. Lee stays at their camp at Savoonga, another village on St. Lawrence Island, and prepares such specialties as a reindeer stew, seal liver and *muktuk* (raw whale). Fuller says his new life has taught him to slow down. "If something's goofed up, I don't get ready to chew somebody out. Down below I used to be so intent on making a buck, that's all there was time for." And he has almost entirely lost touch with life in the lower 48. What happened to the Virgin Islands? "I bought my wife a sun lamp," says Fuller, "and we forgot about it."

Larry Rogers, Veterinarian

Larry Rogers of Dallas wanted to be a veterinarian from the time when he was 12 and watched his dog treated for distemper. He grew up to become a vet. After he had been one for 22 years, however, he discovered that suddenly he'd had enough of "telephones and people tracking me down and dogs and cats and the complexities and uncertainties of medicine." Rogers was luckier than some men. At 42, he had invested a little in the stock market and had a modest outside income. His wife Joan had a part-time job that she enjoyed. Having no desire to "amass a million dollars," he began to think about what he'd really like to do. He thought of going into some specialized aspect of veterinary medicine. He considered becoming a meat inspector or working for a drug company as a salesman. Somehow, though, none of these ideas appealed to him. All he was after was some "plain old physical work without a lot of responsibility and with no tensions and pressures."

He talked it over with his wife and she said she was for any change that would make him happy. "I knew she was the kind who wasn't a prestige seeker," says Rogers, "or I wouldn't have married her in the first place."

So with Joan's approval, he quit his job on January 1, 1968. For three weeks he hung around the house painting, putting up shelf paper and—he now admits—feeling a little odd about being out of work. Then he read that Titche's, a department store in suburban Northpark shopping center, was getting ready for its semiannual inventory and needed extra help. Thinking he might as well give it a try, he applied and was hired for one week. He found the work agreeable, and when the week was up he went to see the assistant store manager about a permanent job. "I said I didn't want sales, I didn't want a lot of public, I didn't want telephones, I didn't want paper work and I didn't want to be the key man.

The assistant manager scratched his head and said, 'That sort of restricts things, doesn't it?' The only thing he could think of was something down on the receiving dock. He said he didn't want to misrepresent this, it was just plain old physical work. I said, 'Great.'"

Rogers has been there ever since, mostly loading and unloading trucks and lending the saleswomen a hand with the heavier merchandise. The store has offered three times to make him supervisor, but Rogers obstinately refuses to quit his $2.50-an-hour job.

Some of Rogers' friends insist on introducing him to people as a retired veterinarian rather than a man who works on a receiving dock—"as if," says Rogers, "they associate working on a dock with something bad." But most people seem to admire what he's doing and often go out of their way to tell him they're glad he's sticking to his guns.

Rogers thinks many men would never even consider making his kind of career change because, as he puts it, "they love the fast-paced world of tensions and pressures." But he maintains that others secretly long to copy him, and he has a number of theories about why they don't simply go ahead and do it: fear of what other people might think; having too many children to support (the Rogerses have no children); being poor money managers; just never getting around to it; or being discouraged by their wives. "Many women would go all to pieces," says Larry, "so the husband stays on in a job he hates, thinking 'I'll pacify my wife even if I have to die of a bleeding ulcer.' "

All told, the Rogers' income amounts to about $15,000; $5,000 from stocks and $5,000 each from Larry's and Joan's salaries. They find it more than enough to live on, and each month a little goes into a special travel account.

Larry, who is now 44, intends to play the rest of his life "by ear." Whether or not he stays on the receiving dock, he's happy just knowing he can keep clear of the tensions and pressures that bothered him so much in the past. "It's all a matter," he says, "of discovering who you really are and what you can and can't do."

Martin Ahrens, Policeman

When Martin Ahrens, age 36, was in the homicide division of the New Orleans police department, an artist friend told him, "Martin, do you realize that you're getting mean? It's gotten so a person can't even have a cup of coffee with you." The friend suggested that the best way for Ahrens to improve his disposition was to find a hobby. Part of Ahrens' job was to make sketches of the scene of a crime, and since there wasn't much else he could do at two in the morning—the hour he frequently got home—he took up drawing. His friend's criticism of Ahrens' early attempts was not exactly calculated to encourage a budding artist: "Terrible! You're nothing but a stupid cop, but keep working."

Meanwhile, his drawing was doing nothing to help Ahrens' meanness. He was exhausted from overwork. "We have a more than ample number of murders here," says Ahrens, "and a like number that aren't murders only because the victim refused to die." He was earning $7,200 with overtime, he hadn't had a real vacation in years, and he hardly ever got to see his wife Karen and their two children.

Then one night last July "everything became too much" and Ahrens hauled off and slammed his fist into a wall, breaking two fingers and two knuckles. Before Karen could drive him to the hospital, he sat down and tried to draw with his left hand. It didn't occur to him to see if he could pull out his gun with his left hand, just whether or not he could draw.

The following month, Ahrens' long overdue vacation was canceled. By this time his paintings had won a number of prizes and he felt he'd progressed enough to make a living as an artist. He promptly handed in his resignation and brought a carbon copy home to his wife, who said, "How about that! What do you want for supper?"

Ahrens now pays a $5.25 yearly license fee for the right to hang his pictures on two sections of the iron fence surrounding Jackson Square, a kind of open-air art gallery in New Orleans' French Quarter. He paints mostly in a style he calls "well-done realism, a kind of mystic realism, but not so mystic that it's way out" which he hopes will appeal to tourists. So far, it has. His work has been selling so rapidly he expects to make at least $10,000 this year. And in the 10 months since he quit the force, not once has he been accused of being mean.

FURTHER THOUGHTS

1. Do you notice any common elements in the dissatisfactions of Jack Fuller, Larry Rogers, Martin Ahrens, and the narrators of "Dolor" and "Me"?
2. Do you notice any common elements in the satisfactions Fuller, Rogers, and Ahrens found after changing their jobs? How do creativity and love, or sociality, enter in? Do you see signs of upcoming dissatisfactions with their new lives?
3. Imagine that when you reach age fifty, you discover that you have acquired most of the goods you really want and that your children are raised and away from home. You have, in short, a good chance to start over. What new things would you consider doing for a living? Think about the reasons for your choices.
4. The three men in the sketches by Bayer represent three quite different solutions to the kind of question posed in Number 3: the first went to a very different land and took very different work; the second stayed home but turned his back on his training and special skills in order to reduce the social responsibilities and pressures placed on him; the third also stayed home and dramatically changed for his own reasons the nature of his work. Go back and look at the three sketches. Who of the three men seems to you to have made the most satisfactory choice? Who seems to have made the least satisfactory choice? Be ready to discuss and defend—if need be—your rank-ordering. Do you see any other alternatives different from the three described?

VIEW FROM A SUBURBAN WINDOW

Phyllis McGinley

> When I consider how my light is spent,
>   Also my sweetness, ditto all my power,
> Papering shelves or saving for the rent
>   Or prodding grapefruit while the grocers glower,
> Or dulcetly persuading to the dentist
>   The wailing young, or fitting them for shoes,
> Beset by menus and my days apprenticed
>   Forever to a grinning household muse;
>
> And how I might, in some tall town instead,
>   From nine to five be furthering a Career,
>   Dwelling unfettered in my single flat,
> My life my own, likewise my daily bread—
>   When I consider this, it's very clear
>   I might have done much worse. I might, at that.

FURTHER THOUGHTS

1. Why does McGinley capitalize *Career* in her poem?
2. Try to imagine yourself as the husband of the speaker of "View from a Suburban Window." Imagine him at his work—perhaps in an office, surrounded by clattering typewriters and never-ending paperwork. Imagine him staring out of his window into the window of a similar office across the street. Now try composing a poem that expresses how you think he feels. Try to come as close as possible to the shape and form of McGinley's poem. (She, after all, was herself writing a parody of John Milton's sonnet on his blindness.) Don't be afraid to "borrow" anything from her poem that fits yours. For example:

> When I consider how my light is spent
> Also my manhood, ditto all my power,
> Shuffling papers while slaving for the rent
> Or adding totals while the bosses glower,

In her article "Black Liberation and Women's Lib" Linda J. M. La Rue says, "There is always a market for a movement. For Women's Liberation, the market will see to it that, in great quantity and unceasing redundancy, the message of 'liberation' gets pushed in a way that women want to hear it, see it and believe it." Her point is that women use the word *oppression* to make common cause with blacks, claiming that women are also oppressed. " 'Common oppression' is fine for rhetoric," she says, "but it does not reflect the actual distance between the oppression of the black man and woman who are unemployed and the 'oppression' of the American White woman who is 'sick and tired' of *Playboy* fold-outs, of Christian Dior lowering hemlines or adding ruffles or of Miss Clairol telling her that blondes have more fun." However, although the women of America may not be oppressed, they certainly have reason to claim they are repressed—and this very real repression is caused by a denial also. It is a denial of creativity, a denial of worth and responsibility, qualitatively, though not quantitatively, much like the oppression of blacks. It is a denial of sociality, a denial, really, of caring and love.

Myth is a curious word. The way it is used in the next selection suggests that a myth is simply a lie. But if that were all the word meant, then a myth couldn't be as powerful as some in fact are. It may be true that a particular fireman may be less than courageous or a particular cop less than honest; an exception does not alter the power of a myth to shape our expectations about particular roles in life. Thus the myths that are the subject of this selection are not falsehoods but, to quote the author, "assumptions" that have determined the roles women are allowed or not allowed to play, and the selection should be read with that in mind.

MYTHS ABOUT WOMEN AT WORK

Marijean Suelzle

The increase in women's employment is a case of moving in, not up. Top positions for women are too few relative to their increased educational attainments over the past 50 years. There are many reasons for the pay and status differentials, most of them based on hoary stereotypes concerning women's work. But these attitudes and practices are fostered not only by the employer but the woman employee herself. For even though many of these myths have been shattered by serious investigation, there are few truths that make their way easily and quickly into public knowledge to become new myths. Some of the current myths are these:

Myth 1: Women naturally don't want careers, they just want jobs.

As a generalization about women entering or in the job market in 1970, the statement may or may not be accurate. It is a myth because of the "naturally." There is nothing natural about the low aspirations of women, any more than the low aspirations of ethnic minorities in public life. To assume that "ambition" is unfeminine is to admit no individual variability: it depends on the person, not the sex.

In a recent study Matina Horner administered a story completion test to female and male undergraduates. Women were asked to write a story based on the sentence "After first-term finals, Anne finds herself at the top of her medical-school class." (Men were given the same task, but with the word "John" replacing the word "Anne" in the sentence.) Over 65 percent of the girls told stories which reflected strong fears of social rejection, fears about definitions of womanhood or denial of the possibility that any mere woman could be so successful:

> Anne is pretty darn proud of herself, but everyone hates and envies her.

> Anne is pleased. She had worked extraordinarily hard, and her grades showed it. "It is not enough," Anne thinks. "I am not happy." She didn't even want to be a doctor. She is not sure what she wants. Anne says to hell with the whole business and goes into social work—not hardly as glamorous, prestigious or lucrative; but she is happy.

> It was luck that Anne came out on top because she didn't want to go to medical school anyway.

In contrast, less than 10 percent of the boys showed any signs of wanting to avoid success. Rather, they were delighted at John's triumph and predicted a great career for him.

Generalized statements about women's ambivalence, about ambition, based on findings such as the above, become part of a myth system when they are used to make predictions and decisions about individual women. It is always necessary to allow for individual differences no matter how true the generalization. Nearly 10 percent of the boys in Horner's study *did* show a tendency to avoid success. And nearly 35 percent of the girls *did not* as the following story indicates:

> Anne is quite a lady—not only is she tops academically, but she is liked and admired by her fellow students—quite a trick in a man-dominated field. She is brilliant—but she is also a woman. She will continue to be at or near the top. And . . . always a lady.

Especially pernicious is the tendency to take a generalization beyond the level of description to make assumptions that the differences are biologically determined. This amounts to blindness to the statistical probability that most women will work for a large part of their adult lives.

Women's Image

At the present time there is an elaborate educational system designed to teach women to underestimate themselves. Society's expectations enter the teaching process before girls reach school, but once they do, school textbooks continue to keep a ceiling on the aspirations of little girls. A recent study of five social studies textbooks written for grades one to three revealed that men were shown or described in over 100 different jobs and women in less than 30. Almost all the women's jobs are those traditionally associated with women. Women are shown as having so few jobs of interest available to them that they might as well stay home and have children. But even their work at home is downplayed. Women are not shown teaching or disciplining their children, baking complicated dishes or handling money in a knowledgeable way. Because the father is making money and therefore the more important member of the family, a house is where Mr. Brown "and his family live." Even pictures show men or boys seven times as often as women or girls.

Moreover, examination of any toy catalog will show page after page of dolls and household appliances for little girls, but no little girls' outfits for engineer, chemist, lawyer or astronaut. TV commercials (bear in mind the length of time the average American child spends before the TV set) endlessly show women helpless before a pile of soiled laundry until the male voice of authority overrides hers to tell how brand X with its fast-acting enzymes will get her clothes cleaner than clean.

If a woman desires or has to work, and if her early socialization hasn't "taken," then for the mature woman there are such venerable institutions as Dr. Spock to make her feel guilty for doing so, especially if she has children.

"Why can't a woman," asked Dr. Benjamin M. Spock, "be less like a man? . . .

The absurd thing is that men go into pediatrics and obstetrics because they find them interesting and creative, and American women shun childbearing and childrearing because they don't . . . .

Man is the fighter, the builder, the trap-maker, the one who thinks mechanically and abstractly. Woman has stayed realistic, personal, more conservative.

Everybody can disprove me by saying these are culturally determined, but I can disprove them by saying that these are emotionally determined."

This type of rhetoric, reinforcing male vanity, has been used until recently to prevent Third World people from taking themselves seriously in occupational terms also, as the following paraphrase by Karen Oppenheim illustrates:

"Why can't a Negro," asked Dr. Benjamin M. Spock, "be less like a white? . . .

The absurd thing is that whites go into agricultural science and overseeing because they find them interesting and creative, and American Negroes shun cotton picking and plant pruning because they don't. . . .

Whites are the fighters, the builders, the leaders, the ones who think mechanically and abstractly. Negroes have stayed rhythmic, personal, more happy-go-lucky.

Everybody can disprove me by saying these are culturally determined, but I can disprove them by saying that these are emotionally determined."

To the influence of textbooks, the media and books on child care we can add the fact that many young women have never had the experience of dealing with a woman in a responsible position of authority. School guidance counsellors assist in the cooling-out process by discouraging women from entering nontraditional fields of employment.

Myth 2: If women do pursue a career they tend to be more interested in personal development than in a career as a way of life.

Another form of this myth is "She will only get married, have children and drop out of the labor force anyway." Figures from the Women's Bureau show the fallacy in this line of reasoning. *One-tenth* of *all* women remain single, and these women work for most of their lives. In fact, those who enter the labor force by age 20 and remain unmarried will work 45 years on the average—*longer* than the 43-year average for men. In addition, *one-tenth* of all *married* women do not have children. If they enter the labor force by age 20, they will work 35 years on the average, eight years less than men. Although it is difficult to estimate the average time spent in the labor force by women with children (the tendency is to work, drop out when the children are small and then reenter), the average woman today will be in her mid-thirties by the time her youngest child is in school. If she reenters the labor force at age 35 and has no more children, she will average another 24 years of work. Women in the labor force who are widowed, separated or divorced at age 35 will work on the average another 28 years (17 percent of women in the population aged 16 or over were widowed or divorced in 1967; 15 percent of those were in the labor force).

Apart from those women who are single, widowed, divorced, married with no children or married with their youngest child in school, there are women with pre-school age children who are motivated to work either due to financial necessity or to the desire for a continuous career pattern. For all of these women it is not only (or perhaps not even primarily) their lack of motivation that prevents their career advancement so much as it is institutionalized assumptions concerning the normality of marriage, motherhood and the inevitability of withdrawal from the labor force. A striking example of this was reported by journalist Jane Harriman who wrote in a recent *Atlantic* article that she was fired from her job when she asked her boss to give her leave to have a baby. That the baby was to be illegitimate only underscores the assumptions and expectations that people have about motherhood. Why, for that matter, shouldn't there be paternity leaves, or paternity firings?

A related, equally serious, result of assuming women to be a marginal and uncommitted work force is the lack of adequate day care facilities. In 1965 the Census Bureau conducted a national study of women who had worked 27 weeks or more in 1964, either full- or part-time, and who had at least one child under 14 years of age living at home. The 6.1 million mothers surveyed had 12.3 million children under 14 years of age, of whom 3.8 million were under six years. But licensed public and private day care facilities available three years later could provide for only about a half a million of those children!

The California Advisory Commission on the Status of Women, for example, had to report that the actual unmet need for children's center services was an unknown quantity. Most districts reported waiting lists from 50 to 100 percent of their present capacity. A two-year delay after being placed on a waiting list was not unusual. One out of every five poverty level residents not in the labor force, but who wanted a regular job, listed inability to obtain child care as the primary reason for not looking for work. Even the available facilties were found to be inadequate. The problems encountered in existing programs and services included obsolete and unsafe facilities, lack of a state-level child care coordinating council, staff shortages, lack of continuity of funding, segregation of children by economic class, lack of adequate licensing standards, transportation and lack of facilities for children under two, for school-aged children up to the age of 12 years and for sick children.

Myth 3: There will be a higher absenteeism and turnover rate amongst women than amongst men, due to the restrictions imposed by children on working mothers.

The third myth is used to rationalize discriminatory employment practices related to women. However, in a 1969 study the Women's Bureau found labor turnover rates more influenced by the skill level of the job, the age of the worker, the worker's record of job stability and the worker's length of service with the employer than by the sex of the worker. Indeed a study of occupational mobility of individuals 18 years of age and over showed that men changed occupations more frequently than women. Between January 1965 and

January 1966, 10 percent of the men, as against 7 percent of the women, were employed in different occupations. Similiarly, women on the average lose more workdays due to acute conditions than do men, but men lose more workdays due to chronic conditions such as heart trouble, arthritis, rheumatism and orthopedic impairment. Considering both conditions, during a one-year period, *women lost less time* than men because of illness or injury (5.3 days for women versus 5.4 days for men 17 years of age and over).

Myth 4: Women are only working for pin money, for extras.

The fourth myth is used to justify discrimination in employment when a job is given to a less qualified man because "she didn't need the money anyway." The Women's Bureau found 1.5 million female family heads—more than one-tenth of all families were headed by a woman in 1966—were the the sole breadwinners for their families. Moreover, families headed by women were the most economically deprived: in 1967 almost one-third of such families lived in poverty, and they were the most persistently poor. Their median income was only $4,010 rising to $5,614 if the woman head was a year-round full-time worker. The income is substantially lower than the $8,168 median income of male-head families in which the male head worked full-time year-round but the wife was not in the labor force. Even where both husband and wife are working, the woman's income is often not for frivolous luxuries but means the difference between economic survival or not. In March 1967, 43 percent of those wives whose husbands' incomes were between $5,000 and $7,000 were in the labor force; 41 percent where husbands' incomes were between $3,000 and $5,000; 33 percent between $2,000 and $3,000; 27 percent between $1,000 and $2,000; and 37 percent when husbands' incomes were under $1,000.

At the state level, the California Advisory Commission on the Status of Women found nearly one in ten families in California headed by a woman. Similar to the national findings, in California economic need is the most compelling reason to work for the great majority of women with young children. The two factors most responsible for the need are the amount and the regularity of the husband's earnings. Women's earnings are not supplementary but basic to the maintenance of their family. Women comprise 35.7 percent of the California labor force, and the California economy depends significantly on women workers.

Myth 5: Women control most of the power and wealth in American society.

The inference that is supposed to be drawn from this notion is that women are "the power behind the throne," the major controllers of economic wealth even though they do not earn it. A weak form of the argument, for example, is that women are the major American stockholders. The argument is false. The Women's Bureau found 18 percent of the total number of shares of stock reported by public corporations were owned individually by women, 24 percent individually by men. The remaining 58 percent were held or owned by institutions, brokers and dealers. In estimated market value, stock registered in women's names was 18 percent of the total, in men's names 20 percent. A glance at the board of directors of public corporations will reveal an almost totally male membership, casting great doubt on how much social control women have, even over the stock they do own.

Women may spend a major portion of their husbands' earnings, but the expenditures are typically for the smaller consumer items. Major purchases such as those of a house or a car will be decided by the husband or by the husband and wife together, rarely by the wife alone. Most women do not even know the exact amount of their husbands' income, so it is he who has the ultimate power over how much of it she can spend. In any event, the amount of power over expenditure is nonexistent when the most important buying decision to be made is that between brand X and brand Y of detergent. Job discrimination, the inability to realize one's true potential, is a high price to pay for the dubious privilege of deciding what color socks he will wear.

Myth 6: It will be too disruptive to an efficient work orientation if women and men are permitted to mingle on the job

Studies have repeatedly shown that traditional attitudes such as these are illogical, based on bias and prejudice, rather than on fact. With respect to the ego threat implied by a woman co-worker or supervisor, men are likely to report that they would feel their masculinity threatened, if they do not have a working wife or if they have never worked for a female supervisor. If they have had the experience, however, their view changes to the positive. Relevant here is the fact that it is much harder for women to get the title than to get the work. Too often, women end up in clerical dead-end jobs, keep getting assigned more and more authority and responsibility as their experience and competence increase, but with no corresponding title or salary increase. They may run the office, but it will be in the old "helpmate" pattern, in the private sense of adjunct to the boss rather than in the public sense of official recognition (social or economic) from others.

The problem of women entering male fields is similar, especially if the field is one of higher status than women are usually allowed to enter. Women and men work compatibly without disruptive sexual involvement as graduate students, laboratory technicians and bank tellers. The real problem with women entering the male-dominated trades or professions, or with men entering the clerical field, would seem to be the salaries. This would create the problem of women being paid "too much" and men "too little" for what has come to be defined as appropriate for women and men.

In brief, myths concerning sexuality on the job are mostly invoked when there is a danger of a crossing-over of female and male status and pay differentials on the job. Although the principle of "equal pay for equal work" is widely accepted and sometimes even legally enforced, great care is taken to ensure that women and men are not given the same job titles and corresponding opportunities for advancement.

Myth 7: Women are more "human-oriented," less mechanical, and they are better at tedious, boring or repetitive tasks than men are.

The myth embodies the dual notion that women's place is in the (human-oriented) home and that women are innately inferior to men in intellectual capacity. When feminists were demanding the right to an education in the last century, educators such as Dr. Edward H. Clarke in a book entitled *Sex in Education* published in 1873, expressed learned judgments that the demand for equality in education was physically impossible. A boy could study six hours a day, according to Dr. Clarke, but if a girl spent more than four the "brain or special apparatus will suffer . . . leading to those grievous maladies which torture a woman's earthly existence, called leucorrhoea, amenorrhoea, dysmenorrhoea, chronic and acute ovaritis, prolapsus uteri, hysteria, neuralgia, and the like." While this quaint wording makes us smile at the ignorance of an earlier generation, it should be noted that Dr. Clarke was only painfully seeking a rationalization for making the value judgment that "what is" must inevitably, innately, biologically—and therefore logically—"continue to be so." Dr. Clarke was Professor of Materia Medica at Harvard from 1855 to 1872 and for five succeeding years an Overseer. He opposed the suggestion that women be admitted to Harvard College. Women were not educated equally with men; women could not be educated equally with men.

Yet few people today smile at the ignorance of today's generation in denying women equal access to a scientific education. The young woman who wants to be an engineer, astronaut, or scientist will be ridiculed out of her decision by her family, school counselors, textbooks, and teachers, and by her peers. The woman who wants a technical education will find many colleges and trade schools do not accept women in pre-employment apprenticeship courses in fields such as carpentry and electronics. The woman who works in a factory will find herself assigned to the tedious, repetitive, boring jobs, denied on-the-job training, placed on a separate seniority list than men (last hired, last promoted, first fired) and, of course, paid less. Women are not educated equally with men; women cannot be educated equally with men. The scientific and technical arena is the last hold out of Dr. Clarke's earlier philosophy. The woman who is unable to become an engineer or a carpenter and the woman who is assigned to the tedious factory position are both being discriminated against by the same myth.

Employers still advertise separate male and female help wanted columns; unions still advertise for journey-women and journeymen. The journeywoman is given less training, her promotional ladder is shorter or non-existent, and she is paid less. The woman in the factory, i.e., the woman at the lowest level in the hierarchy of this form of discrimination, suffers the greatest economic deprivation. She is the least educated, most unskilled, and often her job is necessary for her sheer physical survival. Union leadership is often absent or unresponsive to her plight. If she has a family to support or is a single head of household, she does not have the time to attend union meetings that a man, because he also has a wife who is his caretaker, does. The lack of opportunity for on-the-job training and her social education to a more passive role than her male counterpart also militate against her organizing in her own self-interest as long as her wages remain at the survival level, i.e., as long as she has something—anything—to lose.

As Marjorie B. Turner points out, we know nothing about the comparative propensity of women and men to join unions on an industry-wide basis. The Women's Bureau reports that 1 out of 7 women in the nation's labor force, but 1 out of 4 men workers, belonged to a union in 1966. Whether this is a reflection of sex labelling in jobs, discrimination, segregated locals, or difficulty or disinterest in organizing women is unknown.

The evidence regarding innate sex differences in mechanical and verbal aptitudes is sufficiently contradictory that no generalizations are warranted. Through the preschool and early school years, girls exceed boys in both verbal performance and ability with numbers. By high school, boys fairly consistently excel at mathematics. In addition, boys more accurately assess their abilities and performance by high school, whereas girls seem to show an earlier decline in tested performance. Such differences could, of course, be genetic. However, it seems equally or more plausible to suggest that they are related to social pressures operating differently on women and men to mold them into the adult roles they are assigned by tradition to play. As children, girls are taught to be passive and submissive, and this is conducive to grade school performance. By high school, boys are taught to prepare for careers, and this is conducive to high school performance. The cultural interpretation is consistent with Matina Horner's findings regarding the stronger motive to avoid success in college women than in college men. Until a culture evolves in which both sexes are treated as *people* with equal opportunities and expectations, the question of genetic differences in intellectual functioning will have to remain moot.

Even granting that sex differences may have a genetic base, the statistical picture that emerges is still one of highly overlapping curves for women and men, rather than separate ones. We would be led to predict perhaps a 60:40 or smaller split in the sexes among certain occupations, but not one that is 100:0. Clearly, whether or not sex differences in mechanical aptitude are genetically determined, the current labor market certainly assumes that they are. But evidence to support the opposite conclusion was provided by the demonstrated competence of women in a wide range of occupations during World Wars I and II. Even today, the Women's Bureau reports that by mid-1968 women were being or had been trained as apprentices in 47 skilled occupations. Many of the apprenticeships, such as that of cosmetologist or dressmaker, reflected traditional roles. But some women were being trained as clock and watch repairman, electronic technician, engraver, optical mechanic, precision lens grinder, machinist, plumber, draftsman, electrical equipment repairer, electronic subassembly repairer and compositor.

Women's entry into traditionally male apprenticeship fields illustrates the fallacy of the myth that women are better than men at tedious, boring or repetitive tasks. It is doubtful whether the boredom, repetitiveness or tediousness differs greatly between a clock and watch repairman (male) and a typist (female) or between a precision lens grinder (male) and a dental technician (female). As Caroline Bird has documented, women's work in one part of the world or at one historical period may be man's work in another part of the world or at another time. What doesn't change is that whatever men do is regarded as more important, and gets more rewards, than what women do. The boundaries are defined by status, not aptitude, for even in traditionally female fields the persons in the highest positions of authority are most likely to be male.

Myth 8: Women need to be "protected" because of their smaller size.

There is no question but that women are physically smaller on the average than are men, but the inferences drawn from, and the restrictions imposed by, the biological fact are socially determined. In other cultures and at other times it has been women who have pulled the plows or carried burdens on their heads because of their presumed superior physical strength. Today it is men who suffer from hernias, back troubles and a shorter life expectancy because of the heavier physical tasks they are expected to assume. The industrial revolution made most, if not all, heavy physical work unnecessary, providing employers are willing to invest in the necessary laborsaving equipment. As long as there is a marginal, exploitable, male labor force (as has been the case with Third World peoples in America), it is often cheaper for the employer to use manual labor than to provide the requisite equipment.

Protective laws with respect to lifting should be extended to cover all *people* not restricted to one sex. Where lifting is required, a person's physical ability to hold the job should be medically, not sexually, determined. There may be some jobs involving lifting which only a few women—or men—would be able to perform. At the present time there seems little inclination for women to enter such fields as professional football. (There is one exception, and she may truly prove the rule: she was squashed by an opposing guard.) There has, however, been much resistance to women jockeys, whose smaller size is a decided asset.

As long as there are protective laws governing women only, and not protective laws for workers in general, such laws can be used to perpetuate discrimination. A job requiring heavy lifting can be placed in the lower rung of a promotional hierarchy, even if experience at the job bears no relation to subsequent positions in the hierarchy. It has the effect of preventing women from entering *any* of the positions in the hierarchy becuase they are not allowed to enter the one with the weight-lifting restriction at the bottom.

With respect to restrictions on night work ostensibly concerning the safety of women going to and from their jobs, the rationalization only seems to occur when the overtime or shift work involved would place her in a higher status occupational category as well. As baby-sitter, as charwoman, as librarian, as telephone operator, as nurse, as keypuncher, the woman working at night is considered perfectly capable of looking after her own safety. It is well worth remembering that men often place women on pedestals only so they do not have to look us in the eye!

Vicious Circle

The myth systems that perpetuate sexual discrimination bring us round full circle. Women are stereotyped as lacking in aggressive and managerial qualities; if they do have the qualities or the opportunity to learn them, laws and customs are invoked to prevent their being used. Women and men are not judged as individuals based on demonstrated competence, but on the basis of sexual stereotypes. Moreover, women's underestimation of their own abilities combines with others' underestimation of their abilities to produce the declining status of women in today's labor force.

As Cynthis Fuchs Epstein points out, success is difficult for women because of the nature of informal channels of support and communication. Breaking a color, ethnic or sex occupational barrier means that the newcomers have not shared the same worlds as their colleagues. Casual chats, informal rituals, jokes, shared experiences—all become strained and serve to keep the newcomer in the psychological position of "the stranger."

It is true that women are becoming more emancipated, but it is an emancipation from the home and not towards higher status in the labor force.
Although the mass media provide great fanfare for women as they become "firsts" in traditionally male fields, the publicity obscures the overall decline in women's status in the labor force. The Horatio Alger myth of American society was always a cruel hoax. Perpetuated with respect to women, it is simply laughable, when the average woman with five years of college can expect to earn the equivalent of a man with a high school education.

FURTHER THOUGHTS

1. Ms. Suelzle lists and tries to refute eight myths that hinder women in the working world. Do you find any of her refutations unconvincing? Would you add any other myths to the ones she deals with?
2. Compile a list of similar myths that have led to stereotyped roles and expectations for other groups of people—students, for instance. How about retired people? American Indians? Mexican-Americans?

2nd Interlude

The alienation of a worker caught in an unsatisfying job is, as Erich Fromm says in the following selection, a kind of idolatry. When man comes to value too highly the produce of his own work, it becomes his idol. And when he worships it, as if it were some golden calf, he becomes enslaved by it. In Fromm's words: "The more man transfers his own powers to the idols, the poorer he himself becomes, and the more dependent on the idols, so that they permit him to redeem a small part of what was originally his. . . . Idolatry is always the worship of something into which man has put his own creative powers, and to which he now submits, instead of experiencing himself in his creative act."

Out of this idolatry, this alienation, comes a breakdown in the community of workers. And there comes, too, an estrangement between the worker and his own creativity. The alienation is complete: The community, the love, is gone, and so is the creativity, the sense of bringing order from chaos. The original control the worker had over his work is reversed. The job dominates him now: He becomes a whimpering subordinate to something that he in fact created.

ALIENATION

Erich Fromm

The concept of the active, productive man who grasps and embraces the objective world with his own powers cannot be fully understood without the concept of the *negation of productivity: alienation*. For Marx the history of mankind is a history of the increasing development of man, and at the same time of increasing alienation. His concept of socialism is the emancipation from alienation, the return of man to himself, his self-realization. Alienation (or "estrangement") means, for Marx, that man does *not* experience himself as the acting agent in his grasp of the world, but that the world (nature, others, and he himself) remain alien to him. They stand above and against him as objects, even though they may be objects of his own creation. Alienation is essentially experiencing the world and oneself passively, receptively, as the subject separated from the object.

The whole concept of alienation found its first expression in Western thought in the Old Testament concept of idolatry.[1] The essence of what the prophets

---

[1] The connection between alienation and idolatry has also been emphasized by Paul Tillich in *Der Mensch im Christentum und im Marxismus,* Dusseldorf, 1953, p. 14. Tillich also points out in another lecture, "Protestantisch Vision," that the concept of alienation in substance is to be found also in Augustine's thinking. Lowith also has pointed out that what Marx fights against are not the gods, but the idols, [K. Lowith, *Von Hegel zu Neitzche* (Stuttgart, 1941), p. 378].

call "idolatry" is not that man worships many gods instead of only one. It is that the idols are the work of man's owns hands—they are things, and man bows down and worships things; worships that which he has created himself. In doing so he transforms himself into a thing. He transfers to the things of his creation the attributes of his own life, and instead of experiencing himself as the creating person, he is in touch with himself only by the worship of the idol. He has become estranged from his own life forces, from the wealth of his own potentialties, and is in touch with himself only in the indirect way of submission to life frozen in the idols.[2]

The deadness and emptiness of the idol is expressed in the Old Testament: "Eyes they have and they do not see, ears they have and they do not hear," etc. The more man transfers his own powers to the idols, the poorer he himself becomes, and the more dependent on the idols, so that they permit him to redeem a small part of what was originally his. The idols can be a godlike figure, the state, the church, a person, possessions. Idolatry changes its objects; it is by no means to be found only in those forms in which the idol has a so-called religious meaning. Idolatry is always the worship of something into which man has put his own creative powers, and to which he now submits, instead of experiencing himself in his creative act. Among the many forms of alienation the most frequent one is alienation in language. If I express a feeling with a word, let us say, if I say "I love you," the word is meant to be an indication of the reality which exists within myself, the power of my loving. The *word* "love" is meant to be a symbol of the *fact* love, but as soon as it is spoken it tends to assume a life of its own, it becomes a reality. I am under the illusion that the saying of the word is the equivalent of the experience, and soon I say the word and feel nothing, except the *thought* of love which the word expresses. The alienation of language shows the whole complexity of alienation. Language is one of the most precious human achievements; to avoid alienation by not speaking would be foolish—yet one must be always aware of the danger of the spoken word, that it threatens to substitute itself for the living experience. The same holds true for all other achievements of man; ideas, art, any kind of man-made objects. They are man's creations; they are valuable aids for life, yet each one of them is also a trap, a temptation to confuse life with things, experience with artifacts, feeling with surrender and submission.

The thinkers of the eighteenth and nineteenth centuries criticized their age for its increasing rigidity, emptiness, and deadness. In Goethe's thinking the very same concept of productivity that is central in Spinoza as well as in Hegel and Marx, was a cornerstone. "The divine," he says, "is effective in that which is alive, but not in that which is dead. It is in the which in becoming and evolving,

---

[2]This is, incidentally, also the psychology of the fanatic. He is empty, dead, depressed, but in order to compensate for the state of depression and inner deadness, he chooses an idol, be it the state, a party, an idea, the church, or God. He makes this idol into the absolute, and submits to it in an absolute way. In doing so his life attains meaning, and he finds excitement in the submission to the chosen idol. His excitement, however, does not stem from joy in productive relatedness; it is intense, yet cold excitement, built upon inner deadness or, if one would want to put it symbolically, it is "burning ice."

but not in that which is completed and rigid. That is why *reason*, in its tendency toward the divine, deals only with that which is becoming, and which is alive, while the *intellect* deals with that which is completed and rigid, in order to use it."[3]

We find similar criticisms in Schiller and Fichte, and then in Hegel and in Marx, who makes a general criticism that in his time "truth is without passion, and passion is without truth."[4]

Essentially the whole existentialist philosophy, from Kierkegaard on, is, as Paul Tillich puts it, "an over one-hundred-years-old movement of rebellion against the dehumanization of man in industrial society." Actually, the concept of alienation is, in nontheistic language, the equivalent of what in theistic language would be called "sin": man's relinquishment of himself, of God within himself.

The thinker who coined the concept of alienation was Hegel. To him the history of man was at the same time the history of man's alienation (Entfremdung). "What the mind really strives for," he wrote in *The Philosophy of History*, "is the realization of its notion; but in doing so it hides that goal from its own vision and is proud and well satisfied in this alienation from its own essence."[5] For Marx, as for Hegel, the concept of alienation is based on the distinction between existence and essence, on the fact that man's existence is alienated from his essence, that in reality he is not what he potentially is, or, to put it differently, that *he is not what he ought to be, and that he ought to be that which he could be.*

For Marx the process of alienation is expressed in work and in the division of labor. Work is for him the active relatedness of man to nature, the creation of a new world, including the creation of man himself. (Intellectual activity is of course, for Marx, always work, like manual or artistic activity.) But as private property and the division of labor develop, labor loses its character of being an expression of man's powers; labor and its products assume an existence separate from man, his will and his planning. "The object produced by labor, its product, now stands opposed to it as an *alien being,* as a *power independent* of the producer. The product of labor is labor which has been embodied in an object and turned into a physical thing; this product is an *objectification of labor.*"[6] Labor is alienated because the work has ceased to be a part of the worker's nature and "consequently, he does not fulfill himself in his work but denies himself, has a feeling of misery rather than well-being, does not develop freely his mental and physical energies but is physically exhausted and mentally debased. The worker therefore feels himself at home only during his leisure time, whereas at work he feels homeless."[7] Thus, in the act of production the

---

[3] Eckermann's conversation with Goethe, February 18, 1829, published in Leipzig, 1894, page 47. [My translation—E.F.]
[4] *18th Brumaire of Louis Bonaparte.*
[5] *The Philosophy of History,* translated by J. Sibree, The Colonial Press, New York 1899.
[6] Karl Marx, *Economic and Philosophical Manuscripts,* trans. T. B. Bottomore, in Erich Fromm, *Marx's Concept of Man* (New York: Ungar, 1966), p. 95.
[7] *E.P. MSS.,* p. 98.

relationship of the worker to his own activity is experienced "as something alien and not belonging to him, activity as suffering (passivity), strength as powerlessness, creation as emasculation."[8] While man thus becomes alienated from himself, the product of labor becomes "an alien object which dominates him. This relationship is at the same time the relationship to the sensuous external world, to natural objects, as an alien and hostile world."[9] Marx stresses two points: (1) in the process of work, and especially of work under the conditions of capitalism, man is estranged from his own creative powers, and (2) the *objects* of his own work become alien beings, and eventually rule over him, become powers independent of the producer. "The laborer exists for the process of production, and not the process of production for the laborer."[10]

A misunderstanding of Marx on this point is widespread, even among socialists. It is believed that Marx spoke primarily of the *economic* exploitation of the worker, and the fact that his share of the product was not as large as it should be, or that the product should belong to him, instead of to the capitalist. But as I have shown before, the state as a capitalist, as in the Soviet Union, would not have been any more welcome to Marx than the private capitalist. He is not concerned primarily with the equalization of income. He is concerned with the liberation of man from a kind of work which destroys his individuality, which transforms him into a thing, and which makes him into the slave of things. Just as Kierkegaard was concerned with the salvation of the individual, so Marx was, and his criticism of capitalist society is directed not at its method of distribution of income, but its mode of production, its destruction of individuality and its enslavement of man, not by the capitalist, but the enslavement of man—worker *and* capitalist—by things and circumstances of their own making.

Marx goes still further. In unalienated work man not only realizes himself as an individual, but also as a species-being. For Marx, as for Hegel and many other thinkers of the enlightenment, each individual represented the species, that is to say, humanity as a whole, the universality of man: the development of man leads to the unfolding of his whole humanity. In the process of work he "no longer reproduces himself merely intellectually, as in consciousness, but actively and in a real sense, and he sees his own reflection in a world which he has constructed. While, therefore, alienated labor takes away the object of production from man, it also takes away his *species life,* his real objectivity as a species-being, and changes his advantage over animals into a disadvantage in so far as his inorganic body, nature, is taken from him. Just as alienated labor transforms free and self-directed activity into a means, so it transforms the species life of man into a means of physical existence. Consciousness, which man has from his species, is transformed through alienation so that species life becomes only a means for him."[11]

---

[8] *E.P. MSS.,* p. 99.
[9] *E.P. MSS.,* p. 99.
[10] Karl Marx, *Capital* I (Chicago: Charles H. Kerr and Company, 1906), p. 536.
[11] *E.P. MSS.,* pp. 102-3.

As I indicated before, Marx assumed that the alienation of work, while existing throughout history, reaches its peak in capitalist society, and that the working class is the most alienated one. This assumption was based on the idea that the worker, having no part in the direction of the work, being "employed" as part of the machines he serves, is transformed into a thing in its dependence on capital. Hence, for Marx, "the emancipation of society from private property, from servitude, takes the political form of the *emancipation of the workers;* not in the sense that only the latter's emancipation is involved, but because this emancipation includes the *emancipation of humanity as a whole.* For all human servitude is involved in the relation of the worker to production, and all types of servitude are only modifications or consequences of this relation."[12]

Again it must be emphasized that Marx's aim is not limited to the emancipation of the working class, but the emancipation of the human being through the restitution of the unalienated and hence free activity of all men, and a society in which man, and not the production of things, is the aim, in which man ceases to be "a crippled monstrosity, and becomes a fully developed human being."[13] Marx's concept of the alienated product of labor is expressed in one of the most fundamental points developed in *Capital,* in what he calls "the fetishism of commodities." Capitalist production transforms the relations of individuals into qualities of things themselves, and this transformation constitutes the nature of the commodity in capitalist production. "It cannot be otherwise in a mode of production in which the laborer exists to satisfy the need of self-expansion of existing values, instead of on the contrary, material wealth existing to satisfy the needs of development on the part of the laborer. As in religion man is governed by the products of his own brain, so in capitalist production he is governed by the products of his own hands."[14] "Machinery is adapted to the weakness of the human being in order to turn the weak human being into a machine."[15]

The alienation of work in man's production is much greater than it was when production was by handicraft and manufacture. "In handicrafts and manufacture, the workman makes use of a tool; in the factory the machine makes use of him. There the movements of the instrument of labor proceed from him; here it is the movement of the machines that he must follow. In manufacture, the workmen are parts of a living mechanism; in the factory we have a lifeless mechanism, independent of the workman, who becomes its mere living appendage."[16] It is of the utmost importance for the understanding of Marx to see how the concept of alienation was and remained the focal point in the thinking of the young Marx who wrote the *Economic and Philosophical Manuscripts,* and of the "old" Marx who wrote *Capital.* Aside from the examples

[12] *E.P. MSS.,* p. 107.
[13] *Capital I,* l.c. p. 396.
[14] *Capital I,* l.c. p. 680-1.
[15] *E.P. MSS.,* p. 143.
[16] *Capital I,* l.c. p. 461-2.

already given, the following passages, one from the *Manuscripts,* the other from *Capital,* ought to make this continuity quite clear:

"This fact simply implies that the object produced by labor, its product, now stands opposed to it as an *alien being,* as a *power independent* of the producer. The product of labor is labor which has been embodied in an object and turned into a physical thing; this product is an *objectification* of labor. The performance of work is at the same time its objectification. The performance of work appears in the sphere of political economy as a *vitiation* of the worker, objectification as a *loss* and as *servitude to the object,* and appropriation as *alienation.*"[17]

This is what Marx wrote in *Capital:* "Within the capitalist system all methods for raising the social productiveness of labor are brought about at the cost of the individual laborer; all means for the development of production transform themselves into means of domination over, and exploitation of, the producers; they mutilate the laborer into a fragment of a man, degrade him to the level of an appendage of a machine, destroy every remnant of charm in his work and turn it into a hated toil; they estrange from him the intellectual potentialities of the labor process in the same proportion as science is incorporated in it as an independent power."[18]

Again the role of private property (of course not as property of objects of use, but as capital which hires labor) was already clearly seen in its alienating functioning by the young Marx: *"Private property,"* he wrote, "is therefore the product, the necessary result, of *alienated labor,* of the external relation of the worker to nature and to himself. *Private property* is thus derived from the analysis of the concept of *alienated labor;* that is, alienated man, alienated labor, alienated life, and estranged man."[19]

It is not only that the world of things becomes the ruler of man, but also that the *social and political circumstances* which he creates become his masters. "This consolidation of what we ourselves produce, which turns into an objective power above us, growing out of our control, thwarting our expectations, bringing to naught our calculations, is one of the chief factors in historical development up to now."[20] The alienated man, who believes that he has become the master of nature, has become the slave of things and of circumstances, the powerless appendage of a world which is at the same time the frozen expression of his own powers.

For Marx, alienation in the process of work, from the product of work and from circumstances, is inseparably connected with alienation from oneself, from one's fellow man and from nature. "A direct consequence of the alienation of man from the product of his labor, from his life activity and from his species life

[17] *E.P. MSS.,* p. 95.
[18] *Capital I,* l.c. p. 708.
[19] *E.P. MSS.,* pp. 105-6.
[20] Karl Marx and F. Engels, *German Ideology,* ed. R. Pascal (London: Lawrence, 1939), p. 23.

is that *man* is *alienated* from other men. When man confronts himself, he also confronts *other* men. What is true of man's relationship to his work, to the product of his work and to himself, is also true of his relationship to other men, to their labor and to the objects of their labor. In general, the statement that man is alienated from his species life means that each man is alienated from others, and that each of the others is likewise alienated from human life."[21] The alienated man is not only alienated from other men; he is alienated from the essence of humanity, from his "species-being," both in his natural and spiritual qualities. This alienation from the human essence leads to an existential egotism described by Marx as man's human essence becoming "a *means* for his *individual existence*. It [alienated labor] alienates from man his own body, external nature, his mental life and his *human* life."[22]

Marx's concept touches here the Kantian principle that man must always be an end in himself, and never a means to an end. But he amplifies this principle by stating that man's human essence must never become a means for individual existence. The contrast between Marx's view and Communist totalitarianism could hardly be expressed more radically; humanity in man, says Marx, must not even become a *means* to his individual existence; how much less could it be considered a means for the state, the class, or the nation.

Alienation leads to the perversion of all values. By making economy and its values—"gain, work, thrift, and sobriety"—the supreme aim of life, man fails to develop the truly moral values, "the riches of a good conscience, of virtue, etc., but how can I be virtuous if I am not alive, and how can I have a good conscience if I am not aware of anything?"[24] In a state of alienation each sphere of life, the economic and the moral, is independent from the other, "each is concentrated on a specific area of alienated activity and is itself alienated from the other."[25]

Marx recognized what becomes of human needs in an alienated world, and he actually foresaw with amazing clarity the completion of this process as it is visible only today. While in a socialist perspective the main importance should be attributed "to the *wealth* of human needs, and consequently also to a *new mode of production* and to a new *object* of production," to "a new manifestation of *human* powers and a new enrichment of the human being,"[26] in the alienated world of capitalism needs are not expressions of man's latent powers, that is, they are not *human* needs; in capitalism "every man speculates upon creating a *new* need in another in order to force him to a new sacrifice, to place him in a new dependence, and to entice him into a new kind of pleasure and thereby into economic ruin. Everyone tries to establish over others an *alien* power in order to find there the satisfaction of his own egoistic need. With the mass of objects,

[21]*E.P. MSS.*, p. 103.
[22]*E.P. MSS.*, p. 103.
[23]*E.P. MSS.*, p. 146.
[24]*E.P. MSS.*, p. 146.
[25]*E.P. MSS.*, p. 146.
[26]*E.P. MSS.*, p. 140.

therefore, there also increases the realm of alien entities to which man is subjected. Every new product is a new *potentiality* of mutual deceit and robbery. Man becomes increasingly poor as a man; he has increasing need of *money* in order to take possession of the hostile being. The power of his *money* diminishes directly with the growth of the quantity of production, i.e., his need increases with the increasing *power* of money. The need for money is therefore the real need created by the modern economy, and the only need which it creates. The *quantity* of money becomes increasingly its only important quality. Just as it reduces every entity to its abstraction, so it reduces itself in its own development to a *quantitative* entity. Excess and immoderation become its true standard. This is shown subjectively, partly in the fact that the expansion of production and of needs becomes an *ingenious* and always *calculating* subservience to inhuman, depraved, unnatural, and *imaginary* appetites. Private property does not know how to change crude need into *human* need; its *idealism* is *fantasy, caprice* and *fancy*. No eunuch flatters his tyrant more shamefully or seeks by more infamous means to stimulate his jaded appetite, in order to gain some favor, than does the eunuch of industry, the entrepreneur, in order to acquire a few silver coins or to charm the gold from the purse of his dearly beloved neighbor. (Every product is a bait by means of which the individual tries to entice the essence of the other person, his money. Every real or potential need is a weakness which will draw the bird into the lime. Universal exploitation of human communal life. As every imperfection of man is a bond with heaven, a point at which his heart is accessible to the priest, so every want is an opportunity for approaching one's neighbor with an air of friendship, and saying, 'Dear friend, I will give you what you need, but you know the *conditio sine qua non.* You know what ink you must use in signing yourself over to me. I shall swindle you while providing your enjoyment.') The entrepreneur accedes to the most depraved fancies of his neighbor, plays the role of pander between him and his needs, awakens unhealthy appetites in him, and watches for every weakness in order, later, to claim the remuneration for this labor of love."[27] The man who has thus become subject to his alienated needs is "a *mentally* and *physically dehumanized* being. . .the *self-conscious* and *self-acting commodity.*"[28] This commodity-man knows only one way of relating himself to the world outside, by having it and by consuming (using) it. The more alienated he is, the more sense of having and using consitutes his relationship to the world. "The less you *are,* the less you express your life, the more you *have,* the greater is your *alienated* life and the greater is the saving of your alienated being."[29]

There is only one correction which history has made in Marx's concept of alienation; Marx believed that the working class was the most alienated class, hence that the emancipation from alienation would necessarily start with the liberation of the working class. Marx did not foresee the extent to which alienation was to become the fate of the vast majority of people, especially of

[27]*E.P. MSS.*, pp. 140-2.
[28]*E.P. MSS.*, p. 111.
[29]*E.P. MSS.*, p. 144.

the ever-increasing segment of the population which manipulate symbols and men, rather than machines. If anything, the clerk, the salesman, the executive, are even more alienated today than the skilled manual worker. The latter's functioning still depends on the expression of certain personal qualities like skill, reliability, etc., and he is not forced to sell his "personality," his smile, his opinions in the bargain; the symbol manipulators are hired not only for their skill, but for all those personality qualities which make them "attractive personality packages," easy to handle and to manipulate. They are the true "organization men"—more so than the skilled laborer—their idol being the corporation. Bur as far as consumption is concerned, there is no difference between manual workers and the members of the bureaucracy. They all crave for things, new things to have and to use. They are the passive recipients, the consumers, chained and weakened by the very things which satisfy their synthetic needs. They are not related to the world productively, grasping it in its full reality and in this process becoming one with it; they worship things, the machines which produce the things—and in this alienated world they feel as strangers and quite alone. In spite of Marx' underestimating the role of the bureaucracy, his general description could nevertheless have been written today: "Production does not simply produce man as a *commodity,* the *commodity-man,* man in the role of *commodity;* it produces him in keeping with this role as a *spiritually* and physically *dehumanized* being— [the] immorality, deformity, and hebetation of the workers and the capitalists. Its product is the *self-conscious* and *self-acting commodity.* . . the human commodity."[30]

To what extent things and circumstances of our own making have become our masters, Marx could hardly have foreseen; yet nothing could prove his prophecy more drastically than the fact that the whole human race is today the prisoner of the nuclear weapons it has created, and of the political institutions which are equally of its own making. A frightened mankind waits anxiously to see whether it will be saved from the power of the things it has created, from the blind action of the bureaucracies it has appointed.

SELF-EMPLOYED

David Ignatow

(For Harvey Shapiro)

> I stand and listen, head bowed,
> to my inner complaint.
> Persons passing by think
> I am searching for a lost coin.

[30]*E.P. MSS.,* p. 111.

You're fired, I yell inside
after an especially bad episode.
I'm letting you go without notice
or terminal pay. You just lost
another chance to make good.
But then I watch myself standing at the exit,
depressed and about to leave,
and wave myself back in wearily,
for who else could I get in my place
to do the job in dark, airless conditions?

FURTHER THOUGHTS

1. In Fromm's essay, the concept of alienation is set in different relationships with other ideas—sometimes as an opposite, sometimes as a cause, sometimes as something else. For instance, in the first paragraph Fromm says that alienation is the negation—that is, in a sense, the opposite—of productivity. Pin down and describe the kind of relationship Fromm posits between alienation and socialism, self-realization, estrangement, idolatry, language, sin, money, human needs, work, values, and creativity.

2. Compare what Fromm says about alienation and work in the paragraph starting with "For Marx" on pp. 152-153 with the one starting with "For Marx" on pp. 155-156.

3. The long paragraph starting with "Marx recognized" on pp. 156-157 deals with the roles of money, human needs, and consumerism in an alienated culture. How accurate do you feel this analysis is?

4. When in your own life have you experienced anything like the feeling that Ignatow describes in his poem. Compare and contrast your experience with the one presented by Ignatow.

5. How is Ignatow's poem related to what Fromm says about alienation?

6. After reading the instructions on page 65, answer the following questions:
   a. Which would you least like to be?
      _____ suffering from a crippling, but not fatal, disease
      _____ living in extreme poverty
      _____ being badly disfigured
   b. Which job would you least like to have?
      _____ putting the chrome trim on the left side of new Vegas
      _____ guarding prisoners in a federal penitentiary
      _____ collecting garbage in a rich suburb

c. Where would you least like to live?

_____ Watts

_____ San Francisco's Chinatown

_____ a small town just outside Birmingham, Alabama

d. Which animal would you least like to be?

_____ snake

_____ ant

_____ donkey

e. Write two questions like those above which deal with work and dissatisfactions.

The Kinds
Of Work

The alienation among workers, and between the individual worker and his creativity, is the grim aspect of work. How do we improve the chances that our
work will lead to love and creativity rather than to alienation and sterility?

A society's social imagination defines the jobs it offers. And these jobs are
the roles it gives its people. "That's the story of my life," says a tired waitress,
picking up a dime tip. As one of our fellow teachers, David Burt, says:

> In the long run, and probably also in the short, jobs, the things that people
> can find to do, that they can do and will do, depend directly upon
> society's imaginations of reality. To limit those imaginations to the
> current marketplace is to deprive people of a sense of work, to deprive
> them of work that is of worth to them or anyone else, and eventually to
> deprive them of any work at all. Cybernation and automation, for
> example, are not the villains. Failure to conceive of new production lines,
> and failure to implement these alternative ideas are the villains. Thus the
> failures are failures of imagination on the part of society, accompanied by
> our failures to imagine the sociality of our work.

The phrase "social imagination" might suggest that society is some single entity with a mind apart from and above yours and mine. This metaphor has its uses
but must not be extended beyond its usefulness. The imagination each of us is
responsible for is his own. And what we imagine is based on what we know.

There is a boy named Christopher in the town of Ellensburg, Washington. The
first book he remembers liking was about road building. His parents remember
how he loved that book when he was two and a half and how he imagined himself building roads. Later he was attracted by the story of Cowboy Small, and
he thought that that might be a nice way to be. When he was five, he discovered money and turned his rock collection into a miniature business enterprise.
When he was six, he heard about Napoleon and speculated about being a military officer. But he wasn't quite sure, because in the stories he heard Napoleon
wasn't always the hero. When Christopher was nine, he discovered snakes and
speculated about becoming a world-renowned expert on snakes.

One hopes that Christopher will continue to find things he can be, even though his schools and his parents and television present a limited number of roles drawn from a culture less fragmented, less interdependent, and less mobile than the one he will work in. It is difficult to advise the young about jobs—in part because few of us are aware of the enormous range and complexity of those currently available jobs. And few can read the future, with its promise of hundreds of different kinds of jobs in the next few years, jobs that have not even been invented yet. The psychologist Abraham Maslow says:

> Part of learning who you are, part of being able to hear your inner voices, is discovering what it is that you want to do with your life. Finding one's identity is almost synonymous with finding one's career, revealing the altar on which one will sacrifice oneself. . . . In our schools, however, many vocational counselors have no sense of the possible goals of human existence, or even of what is necessary for basic happiness. All this type of counselor considers is the need of the society for aeronautical engineers or dentists. No one ever mentions that if you are unhappy with your work, you have lost one of the most important means of self-fulfillment.

And when it comes to "discovering what it is that you want to do with your life," there are, alas, no magic formulas. "There ain't no easy runs," sings Johnny Cash in his ballad about truckers and trucklines.

But there are some questions that can be asked. What am I like? is such a question. And, What do I really need? So too, How will you and I work together best? What are we like, working together? And, What is it like? What is the job itself like? You can look into your needs, expectations, and preferences, and into the demands of the various jobs available to you. As Larry Rogers—veterinarian turned receiving-dock worker—says on page 136: "It's all a matter of discovering who you really are and what you can and can't do."

The results of such attempts to match your preferences and skills with the demands of the jobs you might do are far from foolproof. The most to be hoped for is that your questioning and analysis will encourage you to think more about jobs. One of the most important things to be learned from such a process is just how complex real people and the jobs they really do can be.

SIXTEEN PREFERENCES AND ONE HUNDRED JOBS

Earlier we suggested that though the issue is a baffling one, there are some questions that are basic when speculating on a job for yourself. Two of those questions were What am I like? and How will you and I work together best?

As a step toward answering those two questions, look carefully at the following sixteen. Answer each one either *yes, no,* or *no preference*. The questions are serious enough to warrant your spending a little time thinking about each answer.

The Sixteen Preferences[1]

1. Would you prefer a job that places considerable responsibility on you?

2. Is it important to you to be able to express and make use of your own ideas on the job?

3. Would you be willing to take, perhaps even prefer, a job in which you were closely supervised?

4. Would you prefer to work alone, more or less independently?

5. Would you be willing, and able, to take a job that required considerable physical exertion?

6. Would you prefer to work cooperatively, as a member of a team?

7. Would you be interested in a job in which you had to compete with other people?

8. Would it be important to you to have a job in which you directly helped other people?

9. Would you be willing, and able, to take a job that required you to work closely with and to get along with other people?

10. Would you be interested in, and in your opinion fairly skillful at, a job that required you to motivate other people?

---

[1] These questions and the chart on pages 165-168 are adapted from Donald Dillion's "Toward Matching Personal and Job Characteristics," *Occupational Outlook Quarterly* XV (Winter 1971): 11-21.

11. Would you want a job in which you would be called upon to direct the activities of other people?

12. Would you prefer a job in which you worked with ideas rather than with things?

13. Or would you prefer a job in which you worked with things rather than ideas?

14. Would you prefer a job that would show you a tangible, physical product for your efforts?

15. Would you want, and do you think you would be fairly skillful at, a job that required you to work closely with details?

16. Would you be interested in a job that involved considerable repetition?

One Hundred Jobs

The following chart lists nearly one-hundred jobs, to which the sixteen preferences considered in the questions on the preceding pages may be applied. It also indicates the number of openings estimated for each job for each year up to 1980.[2] One way to use the chart is to answer the sixteen questions and then circle the numbers at the top of the chart corresponding to the numbers of the questions answered *yes*. Then, using a straightedge and a felt-tip highlighter pen, highlight the column for each of the numbers you've circled.

If a plus mark falls within one of your highlighted columns, your preferences coincide with the demands of the job. Any time your *yes's* and the job's plus marks match exactly, your preferences exactly correspond to the demands made by that job.

Some jobs may fulfill all your preferences but make additional demands—that is, there will be plus marks in columns you haven't highlighted. An important question in such cases would seem to be how important those discrepancies are. For instance, did you answer the question at issue with a *no* or a *no preference*?

You might find some jobs that have plus marks only in your highlighted columns but not in all of them. How important are those discrepancies?

---

[2] Estimates of annual openings are taken from Neal Rosenthal, "The Occupational Outlook Handbook in Brief," *Occupational Outlook Quarterly* XVI (Spring 1972): 12-33.

TABLE 1
OCCUPATIONS AND PERSONAL PREFERENCES

Occupation	Preferences																Average Annual Openings to 1980
	1	2	3	4	5	6	7	8	9	10	11	12	13	14	15	16	
Accountants				+								+			+	+	31,200
Air-conditioning, refrigeration, and heating mechanics				+									+	+			7,900
Aircraft mechanics		+			+								+		+		6,000
All-round machinists				+	+								+	+	+	+	16,600
Appliance servicemen				+									+	+			11,000
Assemblers			+		+								+			+	44,000
Automobile body repairmen				+	+								+	+			4,500
Automobile mechanics				+	+								+	+			6,000
Bank clerks			+		+										+	+	29,600
Bank officers	+			+			+	+		+					+		11,000
Barbers						+	+							+		+	7,700
Bartenders				+		+	+										8,700
Bookkeeping workers			+		+										+	+	74,000
Bricklayers					+	+							+	+			8,500
Building custodians				+	+	+							+				70,000
Business machine servicemen				+									+	+			6,000
Carpenters					+	+							+	+			46,000
Cashiers			+	+				+							+	+	64,000
Cement masons					+	+				+			+	+			3,500
Chemists		+		+							+				+		9,400
Civil engineers	+	+			+					+	+		+	+			10,000
College and university teachers			+		+			+	+	+	+	+					10,800
Construction electricians					+	+							+	+			12,000
Construction laborers			+		+	+							+			+	25,500
Construction machinery operators		+			+	+							+	+			15,000

Occupation	1	2	3	4	5	6	7	8	9	10	11	12	13	14	15	16	Average Annual Openings to 1980
Cooks and chefs						+		+			+		+				4,900
Cosmetologists								+	+					+			43,000
Dental assistants			+			+		+	+							+	9,200
Dentists	+	+		+				+	+				+	+			5,400
Draftsmen			+			+						+		+			16,300
Electrical engineers		+				+				+	+		+	+			12,200
Electronic computer operating personnel			+			+							+		+	+	34,200
Elevator constructors				+	+								+	+			6,000
Engineering and science technicians			+			+							+		+		33,000
File clerks			+			+							+		+	+	15,300
Firefighters				+	+		+						+				11,800
Foremen	+		+			+			+		+						56,500
Gasoline service station attendants				+	+			+					+				13,300
Guards and watchmen	+			+	+												15,700
Home economists			+	+				+	+	+	+						6,700
Hospital attendants			+			+		+	+								111,000
Industrial engineers	+	+			+				+	+	+			+			8,000
Industrial machinery repairmen				+	+								+	+			9,000
Insurance agents and brokers				+			+	+	+	+				+			19,000
Insurance claims adjusters				+				+	+					+			4,500
Instrument repairmen				+									+	+			5,900
Kindergarten and elementary school teachers	+	+		+			+	+	+	+	+					+	52,000
Lawyers	+	+		+		+	+		+		+			+			14,000
Librarians				+				+						+			11,500
Library technicians					+			+						+			7,200
Licensed practical nurses			+			+		+	+					+			58,000
Life scientists			+	+							+			+			9,900
Local truckdrivers				+	+							+					35,000
Machine tool operators				+	+								+	+	+	+	9,600

Occupation	Preferences																Average Annual Openings to 1980
	1	2	3	4	5	6	7	8	9	10	11	12	13	14	15	16	
Maintenance electricians				+									+				11,000
Manufacturers' salesmen	+			+		+	+	+							+		25,000
Manufacturing inspectors			+	+	+								+		+	+	29,700
Meat cutters			+	+									+			+	5,000
Mechanical engineers	+			+							+	+		+	+		10,100
Medical laboratory workers	+	+		+									+		+		13,500
Musicians and music teachers		+				+	+	+*				+					11,100
Office machine operators			+		+								+		+	+	20,800
Over-the-road truck drivers				+	+								+				21,000
Painters and paperhangers				+	+								+	+			22,000
Personnel workers	+				+		+	+		+					+		9,100
Pharmacists	+		+				+						+		+		5,100
Physicians	+	+		+			+	+						+	+		22,000
Plumbers and pipefitters				+	+								+	+			20,000
Police officers	+		+	+			+	+							+		17,000
Power truck operators			+		+								+			+	5,100
Private household workers			+	+	+			+					+				16,000
Programers				+							+	+			+		34,700
Protestant clergymen			+				+	+	+	+							9,700
Radiologic technologists	+		+		+	+							+		+		7,700
Real estate salesmen and brokers	+			+		+	+	+							+		14,800
Receptionists				+		+	+										23,500
Registered nurses	+	+		+			+	+			+				+		69,000
Retail trade salesworkers				+		+	+	+	+								131,000
Secondary school teachers	+	+	+			+	+	+	+	+							38,000
Securities salesmen	+			+		+	+	+			+						11,800

*Music teachers only.

Occupation	1	2	3	4	5	6	7	8	9	10	11	12	13	14	15	16	Average Annual Openings to 1980
Shipping and receiving clerks			+		+	+							+		+		12,000
Social workers	+		+			+	+	+	+								18,000
Stationary engineers			+										+		+		4,500
Stenographers and secretaries		+	+										+	+	+	+	247,000
Stock clerks		+		+	+								+				23,000
Telephone operators			+				+						+				28,000
Television and radio service technicians			+				+						+	+	+		4,500
Tellers		+	+				+	+							+		14,700
Truck and bus mechanics				+	+								+				5,200
Typists		+	+										+	+	+	+	61,000
Waiters and waitresses					+	+		+	+								67,000
Welders and oxygen and arc cutters				+	+								+	+			22,000
Wholesale trade salesworkers			+			+	+	+	+						+		27,700

OCCUPATIONAL OUTLOOK HANDBOOK
OCCUPATIONAL OUTLOOK QUARTERLY

If your work with the questions and the chart has suggested some jobs that seem to be promising prospects, you need to get more information on them. Two good sources are the *Occupational Outlook Handbook* and the *Occupational Outlook Quarterly.* Both are official publications of the United States Department of Labor and are available in most libraries and sometimes in counseling offices.

The 1972-73 *Handbook* lists over 800 different occupations and tells something about the nature of the work, the places of employment, the training and qualifications required, the employment outlook, earnings and working conditions, and sources of additional information.

The *Occupational Outlook Quarterly* contains articles not only about the current jobs described in the *Handbook,* but also about jobs which are disappearing, new and emerging jobs, new educational and training opportunities, and other changes that are taking place or can be expected. In addition to providing the latest data on jobs, the *Quarterly* routinely lists and describes recent publications dealing with jobs and vocational choice.

Perhaps the major problem with the Handbook *and* Quarterly *is that they offer so much information, it is hard to know how to begin to put any of it to use. One useful strategy is to start with Neal Rosenthal's article "The Occupational Outlook in Brief" in the Spring 1972 issue of the* Quarterly *(pages 12-33). The following table is an excerpt from the article that includes some of the many jobs listed under Health Service Occupations:*

TABLE 2
HEALTH SERVICE OCCUPATIONS

Occupation	Estimated Employment 1970	Average Annual Openings to 1980	Employment Prospects
Chiropractors	16,000	900	Favorable outlook although only a small growth in demand is expected. Anticipated number of new graduates will be inadequate to fill openings.
Dental assistants	91,000	9,200	Excellent opportunities, especially for graduates of academic programs.
Dental laboratory technicians	33,500	2,900	Very good outlook for well-qualified technicians and trainees. Best opportunities for salaried positions in commercial laboratories and the Federal Government.
Dental hygienists	16,000	3,100	Supply will continue to be inadequate to meet demands of the growing population. Very good opportunities both for full-time and part-time workers.

Occupation	Estimated Employ-ment 1970	Average Annual Openings to 1980	Employment Prospects
Dentists	103,000	5,400	Very good opportunities. Limited capacity of dental schools will restrict supply of new graduates.
Dietitians	30,000	2,300	Very good opportunities for both full-time and part-time workers due to expanding programs in hospital and nursing facilities and in other institutions.
Electrocardio-graphic technicians	9,500	1,600	Excellent opportunities due to increased reliance by physicians upon electrocardiograms in diagnosing heart disease and upon electrocardiographs in monitoring patients under intensive care.
Electroencephalo-graphic technicians	3,000	950	Excellent opportunities as EEG's are used more to diagnose brain disease and to monitor brain activity.
Hospital administrators	17,000	1,000	Very good opportunities for those who have master's degrees in hospital administration. Applicants without graduate training will find it increasingly difficult to enter this field.
Medical assistants	175,000	20,000	Excellent opportunities, especially for graduates of 2-year junior college programs. The shortage of physicians, the increasing complexity of medical practice, and the growing volume of paperwork will add to demand.

From Rosenthal's article you might move to the Handbook *article on medical assistants:*

MEDICAL ASSISTANTS

Nature of the Work Medical assistants help physicians examine and treat patients, as well as keep abreast of the reams of paperwork that flow in the wake of current medical treatment.

Medical assistants carry out routine tasks such as preparing patients for examination, medical treatment, and surgery. They may help examine patients by checking weight, height, temperature, blood pressure, and making simple laboratory tests. Medical assistants help in treatment by instructing patients about medication and self-treatment at home, administering injections, applying surgical dressings, and taking electrocardiograms and X-rays, as well as sterilizing and cleaning instruments and other supplies. Medical assistants also perform a variety of clerical jobs. They keep patients' medical records, fill out medical and insurance forms, handle correspondence, schedule appointments, and act as receptionists. Other office duties include dictation, bookkeeping, billing, and receiving payments on bills. Medical assistants may also arrange instruments and equipment in the examining room, check office and laboratory supplies, and maintain the waiting, consulting and examination rooms in neat and orderly condition.

Places of Employment An estimated 175,000 medical assistants were employed in 1970, almost all of whom were women. The large majority work in the offices of physicians in private practice. The remainder work in hospitals and medical clinics.

Training, Other Qualifications, and Advancement Most medical assistants employed in 1970 qualified for the occupation through training received in physicians' offices. A small number were trained in on-the-job programs sponsored by the Manpower Development and Training Act (MDTA). Further information about MDTA opportunities is available from State Employment Services. Some were trained in vocational programs offered by high schools, or by vocational institutes and junior colleges. Others learned their skills in adult education courses provided by post-secondary schools.

In general, applicants for on-the-job training or for post-secondary school academic training must be high school graduates or have equivalent education. High school courses in mathematics, sciences, and office practices are desirable for students seeking admission to medical assistant programs.

Junior college programs for medical assistants are being established in increasing numbers. Most are 2-year programs, leading to an associate degree; the others are 1-year programs and graduates receive a diploma. The programs require completion of designated academic courses, as well as supervised on-the-job clinical experience. Among courses required are biology, chemistry, anatomy, and physiology; laboratory techniques and use of medical machines; medical assistant administrative and clinical procedures; medical terminology; medical office practices; reception of patients; and typing, shorthand, and accounting.

Students wishing to continue their education and obtain a bachelor's degree must realize that not all 4-year colleges accept the same type and amount of credits from different junior colleges. Therefore, it is important for students to apply for admission to a junior college in which they can complete the kind of courses and number of credits acceptable for transfer to a 4-year college.

Medical assistants who meet the standards of the American Association of Medical Assistants (AAMA) may apply for the title of Certified Medical Assistant. An applicant for certification must pass a written examination and have a high school education. She must also be employed as a medical assistant and have at least 3 years' experience in the field. An applicant who has an associate degree in medical assisting need have only one year of experience. Certification is not a license and is not required for AAMA membership; however, Certified Medical Assistants are usually considered by physicians to be high-calibre workers.

Persons who wish to become medical assistants should be able to get along with people, since they will be required to work closely with a variety of people. They should also be thorough, accurate, dependable, and conscientious.

Employment Outlook   Opportunities for medical assistants are expected to be excellent through the 1970's particularly for graduates of 2-year junior college programs. Rapid growth in the occupation is anticipated during the decade. Many more medical assistants will be needed to help doctors engaged in patient care because of the shortage of physicians in most areas of the country and the increasing complexity of medical practice combined with a growing volume of paper work that must be completed in doctors' offices. Other general factors expected to contribute to an increasing demand for medical assistants include those which underly the overall growth in medical care in the United States such as a rapidly growing population; an increasing number of older persons, the people most in need of medical care; improved standards of living including a growing demand for more and better health care; expanding coverage under prepayment programs which enable persons to pay for hospital and medical care; increasing expenditures by Federal, State, and local governments for health care services; and advances in medical technology which enable physicians to treat and cure more illnesses.

In addition to job openings resulting from growth of the profession, many openings will arise because of the need to replace workers who die, retire, or leave the occupation for other reasons.

Earnings and Working Conditions   In 1970, weekly salaries generally ranged from $90 to $125 for inexperienced medical assistants and from $125 to $160 for experienced assistants, according to limited information available. The salaries of beginners depended on their training and other qualifications. Junior college graduates generally received higher starting salaries than those paid workers without any training.

Medical assistants usually have a 40-hour workweek. Their hours, however, may be irregular. They may work evenings and Saturdays. If so, they receive equivalent time off during weekdays.

Sources of Additional Information   General information on a career as a medical assistant, and on the certification program, may be obtained from:

American Association of Medical Assistants, 200 East Ohio Street, Chicago, Ill. 60611.

Information on training programs for medical assistants may be obtained from:

American Medical Association, Council on Medical Education, 535 North Dearborn Street, Chicago, Ill. 60610.

If after looking at the Handbook *article you found your interest still holding, you could spend a few minutes looking through recent issues of the* Quarterly, *in which case you would run across the following article by Gloria Stevenson, which deals with a new variation on the standard notion of medical assistant.*

PHYSICIAN'S ASSISTANT

Steve Joyner works long and hard at providing medical care for the 3,500 townspeople of Ayden, N.C.

On the average workday, he reports to the local hospital at 8 a.m. to make rounds, examine the patients, take histories on new admissions, prepare discharge summaries, and help perform other medical duties. He's in the office from 10 a.m. to 5 p.m. giving routine physical examinations, treating cuts and burns, performing laboratory tests on blood and other body contents, and applying casts to simple fractures. He returns to the hospital at 7 p.m. and finishes his duties there at about 8:30.

A typical busy day for a small town doctor? Yes, but Mr. Joyner is not a doctor. The name plate on his door shows that he is a physician's assistant, a highly skilled worker who, under the supervision of a licensed physician, performs many of the routine duties usually carried out only by doctors.

Mr. Joyner works with Dr. Elliott Dixon, a general practitioner. When a sick patient comes into the office, Mr. Joyner finds out what his symptoms are, examines him, and gathers pertinent facts about his medical background. Then he presents his findings to Dr. Dixon. The physician reviews the information and may order laboratory tests or other diagnostic procedures, or else may diagnose the illness immediately and prescribe treatment. Mr. Joyner may then help carry out treatment procedures.

At the hospital, Mr. Joyner takes care of much of the paperwork involved in patient care. Following Dr. Dixon's directions, he also gives both scheduled and emergency treatment.

Since his assistant has assumed many of the physician's routine tasks, Dr. Dixon has had time to treat more patients every day and to devote more attention to serious and complicated cases.

Pioneer Field   The job of physician's assistant is new to American medicine. It is so new in fact, that ideas about what physician's assistants do—or should do— are still emerging. In mid-1970, fewer than 100 persons had completed physician's assistant training programs; many of the programs were still in pilot or experimental stages.

Training programs differ considerably, according to the training institution's concept of what a physician's assistant should be. Some programs offer general training that prepares the assistant to perform a wide range of medical procedures. Others, on the contrary, train assistants for special fields, such as child health care, radiology, or emergency room treatment. Training is offered in varied educational settings, medical schools, hospitals, and 2- and 4- year colleges. Some programs are open to high school graduates; others require several years of college or training and/or experience in the medical field. Length of training programs varies from 1 year (for persons with previous medical experience) to 5 years.

In general, however, the purpose of all physician's assistant programs is the same, to increase the doctor's ability to provide patient care by training new workers to assume some of his tasks. Training is less extensive than that given physicians, but more advanced than that of technicians in the medical field.

Precedents   The occupation has precedents in other nations. Perhaps the oldest type of assistant still functioning is the Russian feldsher, a profession that dates back to about 1700. Feldsher training consists of 2½ years of academic and practical medical work for students who have completed secondary school, and 3½ years of training for those who have not. Training is broad and does not limit the feldsher to a specific type of medical work after graduation. In urban areas, the feldsher generally performs technical duties such as laboratory work under the close supervision of a physician. The rural feldsher may work in a feldsher midwife station where he independently performs many of the duties of a family doctor.

In this country, interest in training physician's assistants developed in the early 1960's and is still gathering momentum because of the continuing shortage of physicians.

Current estimates indicate that the Nation needs 50,000 more doctors. The shortage of family doctors—general practitioners, pediatricians, and general internists—is especially acute, particularly in rural and ghetto areas. Moreover, factors such as population growth and wider hospitalization and surgical insurance plan coverage are expected to bring even greater demands for physicians throughout the 1970's. (For a detailed description of the current and projected outlook for medical manpower, see the Winter 1970 issue of the *Occupational Outlook Quarterly*.) The use of physicians' assistants who require fewer years of training than a doctor but who can perform many of his less complicated duties is seen as one way of narrowing the gap between the supply of doctors and the growing demand for their services.

Training Programs Currently, fewer than 2 dozen training programs are in operation. Others are in the planning stages. These exclude programs specifically designed to extend the role of the registered nurse. The following descriptions of a few assistant training programs illustrate the variety of approaches.

The Nation's pioneering physician's assistant training program—the one in which Steve Joyner received his training—began in 1965 at the Duke University Medical Center in Durham, N.C. Students first receive 9 months of classroom training covering all aspects of the basic medical sciences. Subjects studied include anatomy, physiology, pharmacology, chemistry, and clinical medicine.

Students spend the next 15 months in rotating assignments within various departments of the medical school. During this time, they take histories, use medical equipment and instruments, perform diagnostic laboratory procedures, and help treat various ailments. This phase provides both general training and specialty training in fields such as pediatrics, surgery, and radiology. Duke University awards successful program graduates a physician's assistant certificate. Students who enter the program with 2 years or more of college may apply credits earned during training toward a bachelor of health science degree.

Qualifications To enter the program, an applicant needs a high school diploma; previous experience in the health field, including at least 1 year of extensive direct patient contact; and three character evaluations, including one from a doctor for whom he has worked. He must also make suitable scores on the Scholastic Aptitude Test of the College Entrance Examination Board.

So far, 42 persons have completed the Duke program, and another 30 are scheduled to finish in August. Graduates work in private physicians' offices, in clinics, and at Duke Hospital. Significantly, some are now working at other medical schools where programs to train physician's assistants are being established. Starting salaries generally range between $10,000 and $12,000 a year.

A different type of training program is located on the west coast. In Seattle, the University of Washington Medical School is training former military medical corpsmen for civilian medical duty.

The potential of this manpower source is indicated by estimates that 30,000 medically trained personnel are discharged from the armed services each year.

Many of these persons already have received hundreds of hours of medical instruction. Many have had from 3 to 20 years of medical experience. In getting this experience, some have functioned independently on battlefields, aboard ship, and in isolated posts. Until now, however, virtually the only civilian medical job open to these persons has been that of hospital orderly.

At the University of Washington, the program—and its students—are called Medex, a term from the French words meaning "physician extension." Ex-corpsmen enrolled in Medex have been qualified for independent medical duty. In the program, they first brush up on civilian medical procedures in a 3-month classroom course. Each then receives a year of on-the-job training from a private general practitioner who has agreed to hire him after the year's training. Salaries range from $8,000 to $12,000 a year.

While in training, the Medex carries out routine functions such as performing physical examinations, applying and removing casts, and suturing minor cuts under the physician's close supervision.

The Medex program, funded under the demonstration grant from the Department of Health, Education, and Welfare (HEW), pays students up to $500 a month during the 15-month training period. This program, begun in June 1969, has now graduated 14 persons. Another 65 to 75 former medics are scheduled to be trained each year during 1971, 1972, and 1973.

As of the beginning of this year, three other Medex programs—in California, North Dakota, and New Hampshire—also had been funded by HEW.

The contrasting specialized type of physician's assistant program is illustrated by a pilot child health associate program, begun at the University of Colorado School of Medicine, Denver, in July 1969. This program is designed to train persons to care for children suffering from relatively common medical problems. Examples are respiratory ailments, minor injuries, communicable diseases, allergies, and various infections. In addition, these associates are being trained for family counseling, health education, and care of children who are not sick. They will not treat severe or complicated illnesses or problems that may handicap a child or threaten his life.

Candidates for the program must have completed at least 2 years of college that included courses in chemistry, biology, psychology, and English literature. Associate training consists of 2 years of instruction at the University of Colorado Medical Center and a 1-year internship. The first year at the medical center emphasizes courses in the basic sciences, and the second includes clinical experience. The latter takes place in the center's pediatric wards, nurseries, and outpatient department, as well as in various community health facilities. Clinical work includes taking histories, performing examinations, and ordering, conducting, and evaluating laboratory tests.

The year-long internship includes the care of both well and sick children in various hospitals, emergency centers, physicians' offices, and public health facilities.

Degree Awarded   Students who successfully complete the first 2 years of training will receive a bachelor of arts degree from the University of Colorado. To be licensed to work under the supervision of a physician whose practice is largely pediatrics, the child health associate must complete the internship and pass an examination given by the Colorado State Board of Medical Examiners. At the beginning of this year, 23 persons—22 women and one man—were in training.

One physician's assistant program which is training high school graduates—both those with and those without previous medical backgrounds—is the medical services associate program being offered jointly by the Brooklyn-Cumberland (New York) Medical Center and the Brooklyn Campus of Long Island University.

Currently operating as a demonstration project, the program is training 39 persons to assist physicians in general practice. Enrollees have been recruited primarily from Brooklyn's Fort Greene and Bedford-Stuyvesant areas, low-income communities with severe shortages of doctors. It is expected that program graduates will help with the special problem of expanding medical services in these areas and in other ghetto neighborhoods.

Training includes a year of classroom study with courses in human anatomy, physiology, pathology, pharmacology, English, mathematics, sociology, psychology, medical ethics, and medical terminology. Trainees also receive a year of clinical experience at the Brooklyn-Cumberland Medical Center.

After completing the program, the medical services associate will be prepared to take medical histories, conduct routine physical examinations, and perform some laboratory tests while ordering others. He will also be able to take part in daily hospital rounds with the physician, make his own rounds of patients assigned to his care, maintain patients' records, operate major medical equipment like cardiac monitors, and perform such procedures as changing dressings, administering intravenous fluids, and performing spinal taps.

Type A Assistant Criteria for accrediting physician's assistant training programs have not been established yet. Steps are being taken, however, to unify concepts of the position and to formulate training standards.

Last year, in an effort to unify concepts, a panel of the National Academy of Sciences' Board on Medicine described two types of highly skilled assistants and suggested appropriate training. The panel defined the Type A assistant as one with a broad foundation in general medicine who can take a patient's medical history, examine him, and present the findings to the supervising physician. The doctor then can visualize the medical problem and determine appropriate diagnostic steps or treatment. This same assistant can help to carry out the procedures called for by the physician and coordinate the work of technicians. Although he must work under the doctor's general supervision and responsibility, the Type A assistant may perform some duties without immediate supervision. He is "distinguished by his ability to integrate and interpret findings on the basis of general medical knowledge and to exercise a degree of independent judgment."

The panel recommended that the Type A assistant receive the equivalent of 2 years of professional-level training in combined classroom and clinical work. While noting that many Type A assistants are likely to have 2 years of college, the panel emphasized that a college background should not be considered necessary for admission to Type A training programs. Students in this type of program, however, should be able to communicate effectively in both speech and writing and should have an aptitude for scientific work.

To help develop a unified approach to training and certification of qualified Type A assistants, representatives of several medical institutions which offer physician's assistant training last year set up the American Registry of Physician's Associates.

Type B Assistant   As described by the Board of Medicine panel, the Type B assistant is a specialist with exceptional skills in either one clinical specialty, pediatrics, for example, or in certain procedures within a specialty. In fact, he may be more skilled in his area than physicians not engaged in that specialty. Nevertheless, because his skills are relatively narrow, he is less qualified for independent action than the Type A assistant.

The panel recommended that a significant portion of the Type B assistant's training be given by physicians specializing in the assistant's area of concentration. Length of training would vary according to the specialty involved.

Last year, in preparation for development of training criteria, a unit of the American Medical Association (AMA), in cooperation with groups of private physicians in various medical specialties, began to study the responsibilities, limitations, and supervision of the physician's assistant. After an overall concept is developed and approved by AMA units concerned with health manpower, the AMA's Council on Medical Education and appropriate medical specialty groups are expected to establish standards for accrediting programs.

Another event that may help standardize concepts of the physician's assistant's job took place late last year when the position was established in the Federal service. Most positions there will be developed in the Veterans' Administration, but some will exist in the Public Health Service, the District of Columbia Government, and the military services.

Entrance-level positions (GS-7) pay $8,582 a year. The Civil Service Commission announcement of the new position said candidates

> ... typically must have completed a specialized 12-month course of study designed to provide the knowledge and skills required of professional-caliber physician's assistants. In addition, they must have a broad prior background or medical knowledge. This knowledge could be acquired by a bachelor's degree in a health care occupation such as nursing, or by 3 years of responsible experience such as serving as independent-duty medical corpsman in the military service.

Unanswered Questions   Besides the issues of what a physician's assistant is and how he should be trained, other unanswered questions surround the occupation. A major one concerns legal recognition.

State governments have the responsibility for regulating the practice of medicine. However, most have no official guidelines on just how much direct patient care can be given by someone who, though not a licensed physician, is doing much of the doctor's job. Several States are studying this question now, and a few have passed legislation which bring physicians' assistants into the State's legal medical framework. Colorado, for example, already has passed legislation licensing and regulating the practice of child health associates.

Although many persons involved in the training of physicians' assistants feel that clear legal recognition of these new workers is desirable, most caution against legislation that would rigidly define the assistant's duties. The theory is that this kind of regulation could halt innovative approaches to the use of physicians' assistants and thus prevent the most effective use of these workers.

Other questions being asked about the physicians' assistant concept include these:

(1) Will patients feel they are getting second-class care if they are examined by assistants rather than doctors? So far, experience indicates a high degree of public acceptance, although limited studies by Duke University indicate that middle-income patients are more confortable with assistants than are high- or low-income persons.

(2) Will physicians be receptive to the use of assistants? Indications to date are that they will. The idea of developing new categories of health workers to assist the physician has the backing of the AMA and other professional organizations. Last year, AMA President Walter Bornemeier said, "The relatively simple concept of physician's assistants, we of the AMA believe, will go a long way toward answering one of the major problems faced by this country."

In a study of Wisconsin practicing physicians, 42 percent of the respondents said they would use assistants. Furthermore, persons involved in several training programs say job offers for graduates have been plentiful. Duke officials, for example, say there are about six offers for each graduate.

(3) Where will the assistant fit into the nurse-doctor health team? If an assistant has fewer years of training than a nurse, should he be paid less than a nurse?

(4) Exactly how effective can assistants be in improving the scope and amount of health care services? The National Academy of Sciences' Board on Medicine pointed out the need for objective data in this area, including measurements of the assistant's effect on the quality and quantity of health care services delivered in various settings. Some studies have been undertaken by training institutions, and further data will become available as additional assistants are trained and gain experience in work situations.

(5) Will physician's assistants have opportunities for advancement? The Board on Medicine panel recommended that Type A assistants be able to apply their professional training toward a bachelor's degree, and a joint report of the AMA and the National Institutes of Health recommended that eligible assistants with a bachelor's degree be given high priority in admission to medical school.

Despite the number of issues still to be resolved, the concept of the physician's assistant is gaining increased attention and acceptance. In the words of *RN* magazine, assistant training programs are "springing up like mushrooms after a rain." In view of the continuing shortage of physicians, those mushrooms could be important fare in the health manpower diet of the 1970's.

Further information about the concept of the physician's assistant and a list of training programs is available from:

American Medical Association, Department of Health Manpower, 535 North Dearborn Street, Chicago, Ill. 60601

The October 1970 issue of *RN* magazine, which is available in many public libraries, carries a list of training programs for physician's assistants. Programs designed specifically to extend the role of registered nurses are included. Information also is provided on prerequisites, length and cost of training, and certificate or degree awarded.

A compilation of *Selected Training Programs for Physician Support Personnel* is available upon request from:

Division of Physician Manpower, Bureau of Health Professions, Education and Manpower Training, National Institutes of Health, Department of Health, Education, and Welfare, Bethesda, Md. 20014

This publication lists program titles, training institutions, program directors, curriculums, entrance requirements, and degree or certificate awarded.

Former medical corpsmen interested in applying for admission to the Medex program should contact:

Medex Communications Center, Suite 203, 444 Northeast Ravenna Boulevard, Seattle, Wash. 98115

Persons who wish to learn more about opportunities for physician's assistants in the Federal Service should contact:

U.S. Civil Service Commission, 1900 E Street, NW., Washington, D.C. 20415

As we suggested earlier, first read from Rosenthal's article for a quick overview, proceed to the Handbook *for more detail, and then to the* Quarterly *for a look into a closely related field. On pages 182-190 this strategy is applied again.*

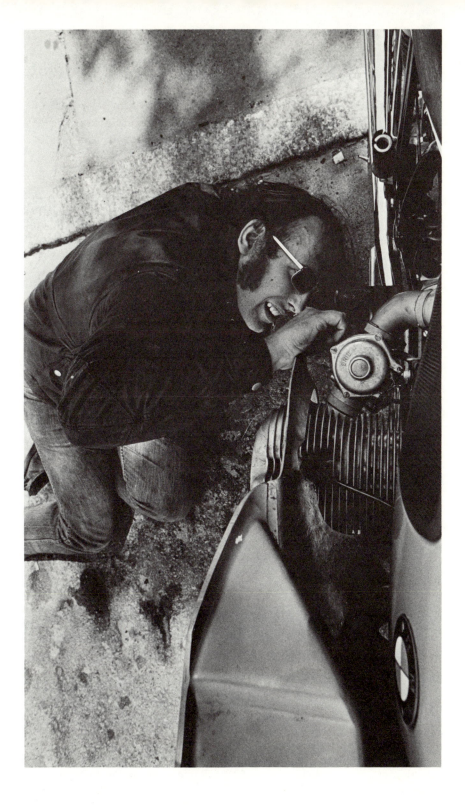

TABLE 3
MECHANICS AND REPAIRMEN

Occupation	Estimated Employment 1970	Average Annual Openings to 1980	Employment Prospects
Air-conditioning, refrigeration, and heating mechanics	115,000	7,900	Very rapid increase in air-conditioning mechanic employment due primarily to continued growth of home air-conditioning. Oil burner mechanics may find openings limited since relatively few new homes have oil heating systems.
Aircraft mechanics	140,000	6,000	Rapid growth because of substantial increase in the number of aircraft in operation. Openings will occur in both firms providing general aviation services and in independent repair shops.
Appliance servicemen	220,000	11,000	Rapid increase as a result of growth in the number and variety of household appliances.
Automobile body repairmen	100,000	4,500	Moderate increase as a result of growing number of traffic accidents.
Automobile mechanics	610,000	23,300	Moderate increase as a result of more automobiles and added features such as air-conditioning and exhaust control devices. Greater shop efficiency will limit growth.
Bowling-pin-machine mechanics	6,000	140	Little or no change in employment due to improved pinsetting machines which require fewer repairs. A small number of openings will occur as a result of retirements or deaths.
Business machine servicemen	80,000	6,000	Very rapid growth. Outlook particularly favorable for those trained to service computers and associated equipment.
Diesel mechanics	85,000	4,100	Rapid increase due to expansion of industries that are major users of diesel engines.
Electric sign servicemen	8,000	450	Rapid increase due to business expansion and increasing use of electric signs.

Occupation	Estimated Employment 1970	Average Annual Openings to 1980	Employment Prospects
Farm equipment mechanics	53,000	1,400	Slow increase due to declining number of farms and increased reliability of farm machinery.
Industrial machinery repairmen	180,000	9,000	Rapid increase due to growing amount of machinery needed to fabricate, process, assemble, and inspect industrial production materials.
Instrument repairmen	95,000	5,900	Very rapid growth due to the increase in use of instruments for scientific, industrial, and technical purposes.
Jewelers and jewelry repairmen	15,000	500	Little or no employment change. Despite growing demand for jewelry, greater efficiency will limit the need for new workers. Turnover will create a small number of openings.
Maintenance electricians	250,000	11,000	Moderate increase mostly from the need to replace workers who retire or die.
Millwrights	80,000	3,100	Moderate increase, related to new plants, additions of new machinery, changes in plant layout, and maintenance of increasing amounts of complex machinery.

This is an article from the Occupational Outlook Handbook.

AUTOMOBILE BODY REPAIRMEN

Nature of the Work Automobile body repairmen are skilled craftsmen who repair damaged motor vehicles by straightening bent frames, removing dents from fenders and body panels, welding torn metal, and replacing badly damaged parts. Body repairmen usually are qualified to repair all types of vehicles, although most work mainly on automobiles and small trucks. Some specialize in repairing large trucks, buses, or truck trailers.

Before making repairs, body repairmen generally receive instructions from their supervisors, who determine which parts are to be restored or replaced, and who estimate the amount of time the repairs should take. When repairing damaged fenders and other body parts, the body repairman may first remove body hardware, window operating equipment, and trim in order to gain access to the damaged area. To reshape the metal, he may push large dents out with a hydraulic jack or hand prying bar, or knock them out with a hand tool or pneumatic hammer. He smoothes remaining small dents and creases by holding a small anvil against one side of the damaged area while hammering the opposite side. Very small pits and dimples are removed from the metal by pick hammers and punches.

The body repairman may remove badly damaged sections of body panels with a pneumatic metalcutting gun or acetylene torch, and weld in new sections. If the damage tears the metal, he welds the torn edges. He shrinks stretched metal by repeatedly heating the area with an acetylene torch and striking it with a hammer to restore the metal's original shape.

The automobile body repairman uses solder or plastic to fill small dents that he cannot work out of the metal. Before applying solder, he cleans and coats it with liquid tin so that the solder will adhere to the surface. He softens the solder with a torch and uses a wooden paddle or other tool to mold it to the desired shape. When the solder has hardened, the body repairman files or grinds it down to the level of the adjacent metal.

After being restored to its original shape, the repaired surface is sanded in preparation for painting. In most shops, automobile painters do the painting. (These workers are discussed elsewhere in the *Handbook*.) Some smaller shops employ workers who are combination body repairmen and painters.

The automobile body repairman uses special machines to align damaged vehicle frames and body sections. He chains or clamps the machine to the damaged metal and applies hydraulic pressure to straighten it. He also may use special devices to align damaged vehicles that have "unit-bodies" instead of frames. In some shops, the straightening of frames and unit-bodies is done by a body repairman who specializes in this type of work.

The body repairman's work is characterized by variety because the repair of each damaged vehicle presents a different problem. Therefore, in addition to having a broad knowledge of automobile construction and repair techniques, he also must develop appropriate methods for each repair job. Most body repairmen find their work challenging and take pride in being able to restore damaged automobiles.

Automobile body repairmen usually work by themselves with only general directions from foremen. In some shops, they may be assisted by helpers.

Places of Employment   More than 100,000 automobile body repairmen were employed in 1970. Most of them worked in shops that specialized in automobile body repairs and painting, and in the service departments of automobile and truck dealers. Other employers included organizations that maintain their own fleets of motor vehicles, such as trucking companies and buslines, and Federal,

State, and local governments. Motor vehicle manufacturers employed a small number of these workers.

Automobile body repairmen can find employment opportunities in every section of the country. About half of them work in the nine States with the largest number of motor vehicles: California, Texas, New York, Ohio, Pennsylvania, Illinois, Michigan, Florida, and New Jersey.

Training, Other Qualifications, and Advancement Most automobile body repairmen learn the trade on-the-job. Young persons usually start as helpers and pick up the skills of the trade from experienced workers. Helpers begin by assisting body repairmen in tasks such as removing damaged parts, installing repaired surfaces in preparation for painting. They gradually learn how to remove small dents and make other minor repairs, and progress to more difficult tasks as they gain experience. Generally, 3 to 4 years of on-the-job training is necessary to become a fully qualified body repairman.

Although most workers who become automobile body repairmen pick up the skills of the trade informally through on-the-job experience, most training authorities recommend the completion of a 3- or 4-year formal apprenticeship program as the best way for young men to learn this trade. These programs include both on-the-job and related classroom instruction.

Training programs for unemployed and underemployed workers for entry automobile body repairmen jobs are in operation in many cities under provisions of the Manpower Development and Training Act. These programs, which last up to a year, stress the fundamentals of automobile body repair. Persons who complete these programs need additional on-the-job or apprenticeship training before they can qualify as skilled body repairmen.

Young persons interested in becoming automobile body repairmen should be in good physical condition and have good eye-hand coordination. Courses in automobile body repair, offered by a relatively small number of high schools, vocational schools, and private trade schools, provide helpful experience, as do courses in automobile mechanics. Although completion of high school is not generally a requirement for an entry job, many employers believe graduation indicates that a young man can "finish a job."

Automobile body repairmen usually are required to own their hand tools, but power tools ordinarily are furnished by the employer. Many of these craftsmen have a few hundred dollars invested in tools, Trainees are expected to accumulate tools as they gain experience.

An experienced automobile body repairman with supervisory ability may advance to shop foreman. Many body repairmen open their own shops.

Employment Outlook Employment of automobile body repairmen is expected to increase moderately through the 1970's. In addition to the job openings resulting from employment growth, more than a thousand openings are expected each year from the need to replace experienced body repairmen who retire or die. Job openings also will occur as some body repairmen transfer to other occupations.

The number of body repairmen is expected to increase primarily as a result of the rising number of motor vehicles damaged in traffic. Accidents are expected to continue to increase as the number of motor vehicles in use grows, even though new and improved highways, driver training courses, added safety features on new vehicles, and stricter law enforcement may slow down the rate of increase.

The favorable employment effect of the rising number of motor vehicle accidents will be offset somewhat by developments that will increase the efficiency of body repairmen. For example, the growing practice of replacing rather than repairing damaged parts, the use of plastics for filling dents, and improved tools will enable these workers to complete jobs in less time.

Earnings and Working Conditions   Body repairmen employed by automobile dealers in 34 cities had average straight-time earnings of $5.51, based on a survey in late 1969. Average hourly earnings of these workers in individual cities ranged from $3.83 in Providence–Pawtucket, R.I., to $7.67 in Detroit, Mich. Skilled body repairmen usually earn between two and three times as much as inexperienced helpers and trainees.

Many experienced body repairmen employed by automobile dealers and independent repair shops are paid a commission, usually about 50 percent of the labor cost charged to the customer. Under this method, a worker's earnings depend mainly on the amount of work he is assigned and how fast he completes it. Employers frequently guarantee their commissioned body repairmen a minimum weekly salary. Helpers and trainees are usually paid an hourly rate until they are sufficiently skilled to work on commission. Body repairmen employed by trucking companies, buslines, and other organizations that maintain their own vehicles usually receive an hourly wage rate. Most body repairmen work 40 to 48 hours a week.

Many employers of body repairmen provide holiday and vacation pay, and additional benefits such as life, health, and accident insurance. Some also contribute to retirement plans. Body repairmen in some shops are furnished with laundered uniforms free of charge.

Automobile body shops are noisy because of the banging of hammers against metal and the whir of power tools. Most shops are well ventilated, but often they are dusty and the odor of paint is noticeable. Body repairmen often work in awkward or cramped positions, and much of their work is strenuous and dirty. Hazards include cuts from sharp metal edges, burns from torches and heated metal, and injuries from power tools.

Many automobile body repairmen are members of unions, including the International Association of Machinists and Aerospace Workers; the International Union, United Automobile, Aerospace and Agricultural Implement Workers of America; the Sheet Metal Workers' International Association; and the International Brotherhood of Teamsters, Chauffeurs, Warehousemen and Helpers of America (Ind.). Most body repairmen who are union members are employed by large automobile dealers and by trucking companies and buslines.

Sources of Additional Information   For further information regarding work opportunities for automobile body repairmen, inquiries should be directed to local employers, such as automobile body repair shops and automobile dealers; locals of the unions previously mentioned; or the local office of the State employment service. The State employment service also may be a source of information about the Manpower Development and Training Act, apprenticeship, and other programs that provide training opportunities.

General information about the work of automobile body repairmen may be obtained from:

Automotive Service Industry Association, 230 North Michigan Ave., Chicago, Ill. 60601

Independent Garage Owners of America, Inc., 624 South Michigan Ave., Chicago, Ill. 60605

Looking through the Occupational Outlook Quarterly *you would find the following article by Hall Dillon.*

Boat-motor Mechanics Keep the Pleasure Fleet Afloat

Boat motors have many things in common with automobile motors, including unannounced breakdowns. A reliable motor is particularly essential in boating. Breakdowns far from shore can leave a boatman stranded for hours—a frustrating and potentially dangerous predicament if the weather turns bad.

To minimize the possibility of breakdowns, motor manufacturers recommend periodic inspections by a qualified mechanic. The mechanic examines the motor and repairs or replaces worn or defective parts. For example, he may replace ignition points, adjust valves, and clean the carburetor. After completing these tasks, the mechanic runs the motor to check for other needed adjustments. These routine maintenance jobs normally make up most of the mechanic's workload.

When breakdowns occur, the mechanic diagnoses the cause and makes the necessary repairs. The ability to make a quick and accurate diagnosis—one of the mechanic's most valuable skills—requires analytical ability as well as a thorough knowledge of the motor's operation. Some jobs require only the replacement of a single item, such as a fuel pump, and may be completed in less than an hour. In contrast, tearing down and reassembling a motor to replace worn valves, bearings, or piston rings may take a day or more.

Mechanics may specialize in either outboard or inboard motors, although many repair both. Portable gasoline-fueled outboard motors are used in most small boats. Inboards, on the other hand, are located inside the boat (much like the engine in a car) and are used primarily in larger craft, such as cabin cruisers and commercial fishing boats. Larger inboard engines and automobile and truck engines are similar in design and operation. A small number of inboards burn diesel fuel rather than gasoline.

In large shops, mechanics usually work only on motors and other running gear. In small shops, however, they may patch and paint hulls, and repair steering mechanisms, lights, and other boat equipment. In addition, they may repair motorcycles, minibikes, snowmobiles, and lawn mower motors and other small gasoline engines.

Mechanics use common handtools such as screwdrivers and wrenches. They also use power and machine tools including drills and grinders. Hoists are used to lift motors and boats. Motor analyzers, compression gages, and other testing devices help mechanics locate faulty parts. Mechanics refer to service manuals for assistance in assembling and repairing motors.

Places of Employment Most of the estimated 10,000 full-time boat-motor mechanics employed in 1971 worked in the shops of boat dealers and marinas. Others worked for motor manufacturers, making final adjustments and repairs at the end of the assembly line. A small number of mechanics were employed by boat rental firms. Marinas operated by Federal, State, and local governments also employed mechanics.

Dealer and marina shops typically employ one to three mechanics; few employ more than 10. Some dealers and marinas that do not do enough business to employ mechanics send repair work to larger shops.

Boat-motor mechanics are employed in every State. Employment is concentrated along coastal areas in New York, California, Texas, Florida, Washington, Massachusetts, and Louisiana, and near the numerous lakes and rivers in Michigan, Illinois, Ohio, Minnesota, Pennsylvania, Missouri, and Indiana. Mechanics who specialize in outboard motors are employed in all areas. Those who specialize in inboard motors are employed mostly near oceans, bays, and large lakes.

Training Boat-motor mechanics learn their skills primarily through on-the-job training. At first, the trainee cleans boats and motors and does other odd jobs. Under the guidance of mechanics, he learns to remove and disassemble motors, replace ignition points and spark plugs, and do other routine tasks. As the trainee gains experience, he progresses to more difficult tasks such as diagnosing the cause of breakdowns and overhauling motors. Generally, an inexperienced beginner needs 2 to 3 years on the job to become skilled in repairing both outboard and inboard gasoline motors. A capable mechanic can learn to repair diesels in an additional year or two.

Employers sometimes send trainees and mechanics to factory-sponsored courses, which usually last 1 to 2 weeks. Trainees learn the fundamentals of motor repair. Mechanics upgrade their skills and learn to repair new models.

When hiring trainees, employers look for young men who have mechanical aptitude, good physical condition, and an interest in boating. High school graduates are preferred, but many employers will hire applicants with less education. High school courses in small engine repair, automobile mechanics, and machine shop are helpful, as are science and mathematics. Before graduating, a young man may be able to get a summer job as a mechanic trainee.

Information about training or work opportunities in this field usually can be obtained from local boat dealers and marinas or local State employment service offices.

In 1971, under provisions of the Manpower Development and Training Act (MDTA), the unemployed and underemployed were trained in a small number of cities for outboard-motor repair and in many cities for small engine and automobile repair which can be applied to boat-motor repair. Information on MDTA programs is available at the local State employment service.

Mechanics usually are required to furnish their own handtools which cost several hundred dollars. Employers provide power tools and test equipment.

Mechanics who have leadership ability can advance to supervisory positions, such as shop foremen or service managers found in larger firms. Mechanics who have the necessary capital may establish their own dealerships or marinas.

Employment Outlook   Several hundred full-time job openings for boat-motor mechanics are expected annually through the 1970's as a result of a moderate increase in employment requirements and the need to replace experienced mechanics who retire, die, or transfer to other occupations.

Increases in population, personal income levels, and leisure time will create a demand for more motor-boats and mechanics. A growing number of new boats will be equipped with automatic tilts, power-trim controls, and other convenience features—all of which increase maintenance requirements. Moreover, growth in the number of mini-bikes and snowmobiles will add to the demand for mechanics. However, expenditures on retail boating will decline as a proportion of expenditures on recreation due to a greater range of recreational choices.

Earnings   Earnings of boat-motor mechanics vary widely and depend on level of skill, geographic location, and employer. Based on information obtained from a limited number of boat dealers and marinas, hourly earnings of experienced mechanics ranged from about $3 to $6 in 1971. Experienced mechanics generally earned two to three times as much as beginning trainees.

Most mechanics are paid an hourly rate or weekly salary. Others are paid a percentage—usually 50 percent of the standardized labor charges that have been established for each job performed. If a mechanic is paid on a percentage basis, his weekly earnings depend on the amount of work he is assigned and how quickly he completes it.

Boating activity increases sharply as the weather grows warmer. Consequently, many mechanics work more than 40 hours a week in spring and summer. During winter, however, they may work less than 40 hours a week; a relatively small number are laid off. In Northern States, some of the winter slack is taken up by repair work on snowmobiles.

Many employers provide holiday and vacation pay and additional benefits such as life, health, and accident insurance. Some also provide paid sick leave, contribute to retirement plans, and furnish laundered uniforms free of charge. A few have profit-sharing programs for their mechanics.

Boat-motor repair work is not hazardous, but mechanics sometime suffer cuts, bruises, and other minor injuries. Shop working conditions vary from clean and spacious to dingy and cramped. All shops are noisy when engines are being tested. Mechanics occasionally must work in awkward positions to adjust or replace parts. For many mechanics, however, these disadvantages are more than compensated for by the variety of work assignments and the satisfaction which comes from solving problems. Moreover, mechanics may enjoy working near water recreation areas.

The *Quarterly* and the *Handbook* can give you some facts about a job, but facts are not enough if you are to choose a job wisely. The late Paul Goodman, poet and critic, reminds us that being "practical" is not necessarily the same as being wise.

VOCATIONAL GUIDANCE

Paul Goodman

In vocational guidance there is a necessary conflict between economists and educators. The economist studies how the economic and technological machine is running and will be running for the next ten years, and he advises how much labor and what kinds of skills will be in demand. He tests for aptitudes to man this machine better. He does not omit the factor of individual satisfaction, since it is evident that workmen are more efficient when the work suits them, just as it is now understood that enterprises are more efficient when working conditions are better, when there are better interpersonal relations and more security. (Relations would be still better if the workmen identified with the enterprise as their "own," but persistent efforts of social engineers to create such a feeling have not been very successful, being too much at variance with the facts of present-day management.) In general, the aim of economists is fairly high use of the productive capital, fairly full employment, and a good rate of expansion.

An educator, on the other hand, attends to the young persons who are to man that machine, and so he has a different aim. He is interested not merely in a boy or girl's finding a job, making a living, and adjusting to society's needs, but also in each individual's actualizing his powers and growing up into a worthwhile person. He deals in longer-range considerations than the economist. He takes into account family and cultural background, and he forecasts the forty or fifty years of working life. He is likely to deal in vague heuristic concepts like "nature" and "alienation from nature," to indicate whether or not a job is a good one for a young person. If there is a good "flowing" relation between a person's nature, background, education, and work, the work will be done with force, grace, intelligence, spontaneity, and inventiveness; it will be a major factor in happiness. But alien work is betrayed by behavior symptomatic of not belonging or pressured conformity, of lack of interest, of merely playing a role or having a job. The ideal is for a youth to find a vocation, a kind of work in the community that is his identity and provides a structure for his life, a use of his powers, a sense of being justified. When the educator tests for skills, therefore, his purpose is to find a job in the economic and technical machine that will be an opportunity for growth. He may urge a youth to try his hand at various likely jobs until he hits on the one that brings out his excellence. And if, as happens, there is no right job in all the *Occupational Handbook*, this is not taken as a failure of the youth, although he is economically a dead loss. The educator—now perhaps called a psychologist—simply redoubles his efforts to bring him out with productive noneconomic activities—now called occupational therapy. In the long run, the aim of the educator is to produce not merely full employment in an expanding economy, but also a productive and inventive society of workers with a noble standard of life.

Such an educator cannot be easily impressed into the service of Society; he must be in conflict. He has a twofold task: to protect the developing human powers that are abused by many of our ways of working, and therefore to try radically to alter much of our economy and society in order to build an educative society. This seems to be very impractical, but is it? Fundamentally, our chief resources are our human resources. If we waste them by having people work at a tiny fraction of their capacities, it is a poor bargain to gain an efficient, even automatic machine—not to mention the morbidly destructive social effects of alienated labor, anomie, delinquency, the sensationally useless American standard of living, and so forth. I do not at all mean that a highly scientific industrial technology is necessarily inhuman and produces anomie; on the contrary, I am persuaded that a scientific, technical way of life can be powerfully cultural and part of a noble humanism. It can be rich with meaning for all its workmen, rather than empty of meaning except for a few top managers, planners, and technicians. This was the ideal of Proudhon, Prince Kropotkin, Karl Marx, Thorstein Veblen, John Dewey. How to implement the ideal in each era of technology must be studied. It is not machines that hurt us but how we use them, our technical and social arrangements, and our low standards for the jobs themselves. By and large, nobody is at fault for our present plight; we have not yet learned how. Modern conditions are too new. But we are at fault if we continue to avoid the problem as a crucial one. Therefore there *ought to be* a conflict between the educators and the engineers, because this will lead to experimentation and finding solutions hitherto unthought of.

Let me mention an example of disagreement within pedagogy itself. Confronted with the emergencies of the Cold War and the need to expand the economy, Dr. James Conant surveyed the junior high schools and the high schools. On the basis of tests and grades, he decided that only 15 per cent of the youth were academically talented enough to study sciences and mathematics. He felt that most should have a realistic vocational training aimed at the actual industries and other jobs in their communities. Characteristically, he was much concerned about centralizing and enlarging the schools in order to have better equipment and more uniform standards. In all of this, Dr. Conant was acting the part of a social engineer.

Remarkably different was the attitude of the conference of distinguished scientists and teachers of science that met at Woods Hole in 1959 to decide on methods and curriculum for teaching science in these same primary and secondary schools. (The conference has been reported in Jerome Bruner's *The Process of Education*.) Since these men were interested in producing scientists and not test passers or technical assistants, they concluded that the methods must be classical progressive-educational methods, unblocking intuition, giving the youth confidence in himself, learning by doing, working with the life interests of each age group. The curriculum, they said, must comprise big structural ideas of the field, not the accumulation of the latest facts and theories. They want to produce men with the habit of science, as Aristotle would have called it, who see the structure *in* their present world, who do not merely know all *about* it. These scientists and educators do not seem to be much concerned about equipment or standard performance—indeed, they encourage guessing—but they insist that the primary textbooks and demonstrations must be prepared by the giants of science, since only such men can convey the simple underlying structures. And with regard to the aptitude of the kids, they insist that almost any child at any age can grasp the most advanced conception. "When I teach well," says one, "I find that seventy-five per cent of the students are above the median!"

Now we cannot call these Woods Hole people "impractical"—they know what they are after, and how hard it is to get. What I would suggest is that, in the broader field of all jobs and vocations, and not merely the scientific, we might well imitate their thinking.

I can propose three or four "impractical" notions that would facilitate the flowing relation of nature, culture, and work so that our machine can be manned by grown-up men and women rather than by cases of arrested development and resignation, or thwarted and resentful potentialities.

One thing that is overlooked by placement engineers is the meaningfulness of the job as such: is it *worth* doing, is the product good for anything? They are so concerned about the economics of the system that they forget that objective utility must be the chief structure and chief motivation for work. When even simple utility is absent, naturally everything degenerates to status seeking and emphasis on methods rather than goals. Young people are quite simple-minded about this. We see that in emergencies, almost everybody comes across with remarkable spirit. But it is impossible to tell oneself, "During the forty years of my working life, I shall spend six to eight hours a day doing what is no good," without profound resignation and alienation. Consider as an ideal case the work camps for youth, whether the Civilian Conservation Corps, or the camps sponsored by Senator Humphrey, or Quaker Youth for Service, or even camps for delinquents: in all these, it is felt that the work must be unmistakably socially useful, whether conservation or urban renewal or painting a poor widow's kitchen. It is only such work that makes a youth feel that he is indispensable and becoming a man. Yet in our present nicely expanding economy, many a job cannot meet this standard.

Another sad fact is that, in many jobs as we do them at present, a person is too small a cog in the machine; he does not know enough what he's doing. Psychologically, for creative experience it is not necessary to know the whole—that might even be a hindrance to growth—but one must know a large mind-sized chunk. Yet our present minute subdivision of labor is not inevitable; indeed, in very many cases it is demonstrably inefficiently centralized, for instance. We must figure out other technical arrangements, more opportunity for the individual to work on, and train for, larger wholes. And he must have more opportunity to criticize and make inventions. Let us keep in mind the wisdom of the Woods Hole scientists, that it is the big structural ideas that are absorbing, motivating, confidence breeding, and stirring to initiative.

This brings me, alas, to an idea that is even more impractical. What is wrong with our society is, in the end, not the kinds of jobs it offers, for nearly all of them are potentially worth while and useful. It is how people work on their jobs. They are not *allowed* to make them useful. It is no secret that initiative is discouraged and common sense often outraged. The use of a man's full energies and capacities is severely frowned on, and plain honesty will sometimes get him fired. Let's face it, the educator who believes in productive life as a great means and goal of human growth will find himself inculcating in the young attitudes of sincerity, understanding, and initiative that will sometimes get them fired. It happens that I am often called to talk to the students of architecture and community planning at various schools. We, and the members of the faculty, agree that it is invaluable training for a young architect to learn to criticize the program for a project rather than merely to carry it out; for the program is often misconceived, based on ignorant assumptions, and it sometimes needlessly prevents a handsome and workable solution. "But what," I ask, "when you are in a big office and the building you have to work on has a bad plan, or the City Planning Commission has hired you for some Urban Renewal that is socially disastrous—ah, then what?" Our present tendency to centralize and department-mentalize is unusual in its effect of excluding, muffling, or baffling original, gifted, and outspoken men.

Finally, I want to make an obvious, but neglected, psychological comment about "getting a job" altogether, especially as it applies to a poor youth in our society. For school drop-outs, unemployment is regarded as predelinquent. The youth who "gets a job," however, is considered to be on the right track and making a normal adjustment. Certainly he is not then a social nuisance, and he does gain some independence from his family. Nevertheless, if the job is not worth while or suited to the young man, and therefore is not educative and does not provide him a new structure of values, "getting a job" tends to be merely a response to the internalized superego demand, "Go out and support yourself," and this is an important factor that keeps him psychologically adolescent. The job may soon rouse a resentment that is often lasting and channeled against later married responsibilities. (I think this situation is often a contributory cause of alchoholism, which spites the demand.) On the job the youth, unprotected even by a union, acts out a relation with the boss that is little different from his childish relation to his father. He is tied to the job, just as he was to his home. Conversely, he rebels against the job out of resentment. Either way, he has no freedom to make rational choices. So the chance of growth through real work and of finding identity in vocation is muddied up by irrelevant emotions, rather than fired by relevant emotions. Nor does it help if the youth enviously sees his more fortunate peers continuing in school and going on to better jobs. Surely we ought to keep all this in mind and manage better.

These are radical ideas. The criterion of socially useful work attacks our profit system. The criterion of a job that exercises capacities and offers a field for real training and subsequent initiative is pretty close to Syndicalism, it threatens management. The need for sincere criticism and energetic performance undermines the conformity of our bureaucratic corporate system and the feather-bedding of labor unions. To support our poor youth requires a better community than we have. Naturally, then, an educator to whom these are basic considerations is in conflict.

It is a troubling situation. For a youth to grow, there must be a fairly stable environment; one cannot change too much too fast. There must be a going concern for him to take his place in. Yet at present that going concern is simply not good enough.

FURTHER THOUGHTS

1. Goodman compares the attitude of what he calls the "economist" with that of the "educator." What are the differences between them? To what extent is a person both an economist and an educator when he thinks about choosing his own work? So what?

2. Goodman offers four "impractical" and "radical" suggestions "that would facilitate the flowing relation of nature, culture, and work." Just how impractical and radical do they seem to you?

3. What suggestions would *you* make for facilitating "the flowing relation of nature, culture, and work" in the 1970s? To answer, think first of what specific problems you are speaking to and second how each suggestion would ease each problem. As you think out these problems and proposed solutions, you might find the following questions useful to focus your mind: Who or

what causes the problem that you are interested in? What exactly is it that this person or thing is doing that creates this problem? Why do they do this thing? What exactly is the link between their action and the problem?

Giving advice these days is a big business. People today seek advice, and whether it is from "Dear Abby" and "The *Playboy* Advisor" or from presidential advisory commissions and industrial consultants, there are plenty of people to give it to them. Among today's big-time advisors is Peter Drucker, a man we find to be most wise, and who seems to have at his command the most pertinent information about jobs today and in the future. In the following selection he warns you that most of today's jobs and most of the jobs of the future involve words and the use of words. He also suggests that you look carefully at a job once you have it to see whether that job matches *your* ambitions.

HOW TO BE AN EMPLOYEE

Peter F. Drucker

Ours has become a society of employees. A hundred years or so ago only one out of every five Americans at work was employed, i.e., worked for somebody else. Today only one out of five is not employed but working for himself. And where fifty years ago "being employed" meant working as a factory laborer or as a farmhand, the employee of today is increasingly a middle-class person with a substantial formal education, holding a professional or management job requiring intellectual and technical skills. Indeed, two things have characterized American society during these last fifty years: the middle and upper classes have become employees; and middle-class and upper-class employees have been the fastest-growing groups in our working population—growing so fast that the industrial worker, that oldest child of the Industrial Revolution, has been losing in numerical importance despite the expansion of industrial production.

This is the one of the most profound social changes any country has ever undergone. It is, however, a perhaps even greater change for the individual young man about to start. Whatever he does, in all likelihood he will do it as an employee; wherever he aims, he will have to try to reach it through being an employee.

Yet you will find little if anything written on what it is to be an employee. You can find a great deal of very dubious advice on how to get a job or how to get a promotion. You can also find a good deal on work in a chosen field, whether it be metallurgy or salesmanship, the machinist's trade or bookkeeping. Every one of these trades requires different skills, sets different standards, and requires a different preparation. Yet they all have employeeship in common. And increasingly, especially in the large business or in government, employeeship is more important to success than the special professional knowledge or skill. Certainly more people fail because they do not know the requirements of being an employee than because they do not adequately possess the skills of their trade; the higher you climb the ladder, the more you get into administrative or executive work, the greater the emphasis on ability to work within the organization rather than on technical competence or professional knowledge.

Being an employee is thus the one common characteristic of most careers today. The special profession or skill is visible and clearly defined; and a well-laid-out sequence of courses, degrees, and jobs leads into it. But being an employee is the foundation. And it is much more difficult to prepare for it. Yet there is no recorded information on the art of being an employee.

The Basic Skill

The first question we might ask is: what can you learn in college that will help you in being an employee? The schools teach a great many things of value to the future accountant, the future doctor, or the future electrician. Do they also teach anything of value to the future employee? The answer is: "Yes—they teach the one thing that it is perhaps most valuable for the future employee to know. But very few students bother to learn it."

This one basic skill is the ability to organize and express ideas in writing and in speaking.

As an employee you work with and through other people. This means that your success as an employee—and I am talking of much more here than getting promoted—will depend on your ability to communicate with people and to present your own thoughts and ideas to them so they will both understand what you are driving at and be persuaded. The letter, the report or memorandum, the ten-minute spoken "presentation" to a committee are basic tools of the employee.

If you work as a soda jerker you will, of course, not need much skill in expressing yourself to be effective. If you work on a machine your ability to express yourself will be of little importance. But as soon as you move one step up from the bottom, your effectiveness depends on your ability to reach others through the spoken or the written word. And the further away your job is from manual work, the larger the organization of which you are an employee, the more important it will be that you know how to convey your thoughts in writing or speaking. In the very large organization, whether it is the government, the large business corporation, or the Army, this ability to express oneself is perhaps the most important of all the skills a man can possess.

Of course, skill in expression is not enough by itself. You must have something to say in the first place. The popular picture of the engineer, for instance, is that of a man who works with a slide rule, T square, and compass. And engineering students reflect this picture in their attitude toward the written word as something quite irrelevant to their jobs. But the effectiveness of the engineer—and with it his usefulness—depends as much on his ability to make other people understand his work as it does on the quality of the work itself.

Expressing one's thoughts is one skill that the school can really teach, especially to people born without natural writing or speaking talent. Many other skills can be learned later—in this country there are literally thousands of places that offer training to adult people at work. But the foundations for skill in expression have to be laid early: an interest in and an ear for language; experience in organizing ideas and data, in brushing aside the irrelevant, in wedding outward form and inner content into one structure; and above all, the habit of verbal expression. If you do not lay these foundations during your school years, you may never have an opportunity again.

If you were to ask me what strictly vocational courses there are in the typical college curriculum, my answer—now that the good old habit of the "theme a day" has virtually disappeared—would be: the writing of poetry and the writing of short stories. Not that I expect many of you to become poets or short-story writers—far from it. But these two courses offer the easiest way to obtain some skill in expression. They force one to be economical with language. They force one to organize thought. They demand of one that he give meaning to every word. They train the ear for language, its meaning, its precision, its overtones—and its pitfalls. Above all they force one to write.

I know very well that the typical employer does not understand this as yet, and that he may look with suspicion on a young college graduate who has majored, let us say, in short-story writing. But the same employer will complain—and with good reason—that the young men whom he hires when they get out of college do not know how to write a simple report, do not know how to tell a simple story, and are in fact virtually illiterate. And he will conclude—rightly—that the young men are not really effective, and certainly not employees who are likely to go very far.

The next question to ask is: what kind of of employee should you be? Pay no attention to what other people tell you. This is one question only you can answer. It involves a choice in four areas—a choice you alone can make, and one you cannot easily duck. But to make the choice you must first have tested yourself in the world of jobs for some time.

Here are the four decisions—first in brief outline, then in more detail:

1) Do you belong in a job calling primarily for faithfulness in the performance of routine work and promising security? Or do you belong in a job that offers a challenge to imagination and ingenuity—with the attendant penalty for failure?

2) Do you belong in a large organization or in a small organization? Do you work better through channels or through direct contacts? Do you enjoy more

being a small cog in a big and powerful machine or a big wheel in a small machine?

3) Should you start at the bottom and try to work your way up, or should you try to start near the top? On the lowest rung of the promotional ladder, with its solid and safe footing but also with a very long climb ahead? Or on the aerial trapeze of "a management trainee," or some other staff position close to management?

4) Finally, are you going to be more effective and happy as a specialist or as a "generalist," that is, in an administrative job?

Let me spell out what each of these four decisions involves:

1: Is "Security" for You?

The decision between secure routine work and insecure work challenging the imagination and ingenuity is the one decision most people find easiest to make. You know very soon what kind of person you are. Do you find real satisfaction in the precision, order, and system of a clearly laid-out job? Do you prefer the security not only of knowing what your work is today and what it is going to be tomorrow, but also security in your job, in your relationship to the people above, below, and next to you, and economic security? Or are you one of those people who tend to grow impatient with anything that looks like a "routine" job? These people are usually able to live in a confused situation in which their relations to the people around them are neither clear nor stable. And they tend to pay less attention to economic security, find it not too upsetting to change jobs, etc.

There is, of course, no such black-and-white distinction between people. The man who can do only painstaking detail work and has no imagination is not much good for anything. Neither is the self-styled "genius" who has nothing but grandiose ideas and no capacity for rigorous application to detail. But in practically everybody I have ever met there is a decided leaning one way of the other.

The difference is one of basic personality. It is not too much affected by a man's experiences; he is likely to be born with the one or the other. The need for economic security is often as not an outgrowth of a need for psychological security rather than a phenomenon of its own. But precisely because the difference is one of basic temperament, the analysis of what kind of temperament you possess is so vital. A man might be happy in work for which he has little *aptitude*; he might be quite successful in it. But he can be neither happy nor successful in a job for which he is *temperamentally* unfitted.

You [used to] hear a great many complaints . . . about the excessive security-consciousness of our young people. My complaint is the opposite: in the large organizations especially there are not enough job opportunities for those young people who need challenge and risk. Jobs in which there is greater emphasis on conscientious performance of well-organized duties rather than on imagination—especially for the beginner—are to be found, for instance, in the inside jobs in banking or insurance, which normally offer great job security but not rapid promotion or large pay. The same is true of most government work, of the railroad industry, particularly in the clerical and engineering branches, and of most public utilities. The bookkeeping and accounting areas, especially in the larger companies, are generally of this type too—though a successful comptroller is an accountant with great management and business imagination.

At the other extreme are such areas as buying, selling, and advertising, in which the emphasis is on adaptability, on imagination, and on a desire to do new and different things. In those areas, by and large, there is little security, either personal or economic. The rewards, however, are high and come more rapidly. Major premium on imagination—though of a different kind and coupled with dogged persistence on details—prevails in most research and engineering work. Jobs in production, as supervisor or executive, also demand much adaptability and imagination.

Contrary to popular belief, very small business requires, above all, close attention to daily routine. Running a neighborhood drugstore or a small grocery, or being a toy jobber, is largely attention to details. But in very small business there is also room for quite a few people of the other personality type—the innovator or imaginer. If successful, a man of this type soon ceases to be in a very small business. For the real innovator there is, still, no more promising opportunity in this country than that of building a large out of a very small business.

2: Big Company or Small?

Almost as important is the decision between working for a large and for a small organization. The difference is perhaps not so great as that between the secure, routine job and the insecure, imaginative job; but the wrong decision can be equally serious.

There are two basic differences between the large and the small enterprise. In the small enterprise you operate primarily through personal contacts. In the large enterprise you have established "policies," "channels" of organization, and fairly rigid procedures. In the small enterprise you have, moreover, immediate effectiveness in a very small area. You can see the effect of your work and of your decisions right away, once you are a little bit above the ground floor. In the large enterprise even the man at the top is only a cog in a big machine. To be sure, his actions affect a much greater area than the actions and decisions of the man in the small organization, but his effectiveness is remote, indirect, and elusive. In a small and even in a middle-sized business you are normally exposed to all kinds of experiences, and expected to do a great many things without too much help or guidance. In the large organization you are normally taught one thing thoroughly. In the small one the danger is of becoming a jack-of-all-trades and master of none. In the large one it is of becoming the man who knows more and more about less and less.

There is one other important thing to consider: do you derive a deep sense of satisfaction from being a member of a well-known organization—General Motors, the Bell Telephone System, the government? Or is it more important to you to be a well-known and important figure within your own small pond? There is a basic difference between the satisfaction that comes from being a member of a family; between impersonal grandeur and personal—often much too personal—intimacy; between life in a small cubicle on the top floor of a skyscraper and life in a crossroads gas station.

3: Start at the Bottom, or . . . ?

You may well think it absurd to say that anyone has a choice between beginning at the bottom and beginning near the top. And indeed I do not mean that you have any choice between beginner's jobs and, let us say, a vice presidency at General Electric. But you do have a choice between a position at the bottom of the hierarchy and a staff position that is outside the hierarchy but in view of the top. It is an important choice.

In every organization, even the smallest, there are positions that, while subordinate, modestly paid, and usually filled with young and beginning employees, nonetheless are not at the bottom. There are positions as assistant to one of the bosses; there are positions as private secretary; there are liaison positions for various departments; and there are positions in staff capacities, in industrial engineering, in cost accounting, in personnel, etc. Every one of these gives a view of the whole rather than of only one small area. Every one of them normally brings the holder into the deliberations and discussions of the people at the top, if only as a silent audience or perhaps only as an errand boy. Every one of these positions is a position "near the top," however humble and badly paid it may be.

On the other hand the great majority of beginner's jobs are at the bottom, where you begin in a department or in a line of work in the lowest-paid and simplest function, and where you are expected to work your way up as you acquire more skill and more judgment.

Different people belong in these two kinds of jobs. In the first place, the job "near the top" is insecure. You are exposed to public view. Your position is ambiguous; by yourself you are a nobody—but you reflect the boss's status; in a relatively short time you may even speak for the boss. You may have real power and influence. In today's business and government organization the hand that writes the memo rules the committee; and the young staff man usually writes the memos, or at least the first draft. But for that very reason everybody is jealous of you. You are a youngster who has been admitted to the company of his betters, and is therefore expected to show unusual ability and above all unusual discretion and judgment. Good performance in such a position is often the key to rapid advancement. But to fall down may mean the end of all hopes of ever getting anywhere within the organization.

At the bottom, on the other hand, there are very few opportunities for making serious mistakes. You are amply protected by the whole apparatus of authority. The job itself is normally simple, requiring little judgment, discretion, or initiative. Even excellent performance in such a job is unlikely to speed promotion. But one also has to fall down in a rather spectacular fashion for it to be noticed by anyone but one's immediate superior.

4: Specialist or "Generalist"?

There are a great many careers in which the increasing emphasis is on specialization. You find these careers in engineering and in accounting, in production, in statistical work, and in teaching. But there is an increasing demand for people who are able to take in a great area at a glance, people who perhaps do not know too much about any one field—though one should always have one area of real competence. There is, in other words, a demand for people who are capable of seeing the forest rather than the trees, of making over-all judgments. And these "generalists" are particularly needed for administrative positions, where it is their job to see that other people do the work, where they have to plan for other people, to organize other people's work, to initiate it and appraise it.

The specialist understands one field; his concern is with technique, tools, media. He is a "trained" man; and his educational background is properly technical or professional. The generalist—and especially the administrator—deals with people; his concern is with leadership, with planning, with direction giving, and with coordination. He is an "educated" man; and the humanities are his strongest foundation. Very rarely is a specialist capable of being an administrator. And very rarely is a good generalist also a good specialist in a particular field. Any organization needs both kinds of people, though different organizations need them in different ratios. It is your job to find out, during your apprenticeship, into which of those two job categories you fit, and to plan your career accordingly.

Your first job may turn out to be the right job for you—but this is pure accident. Certainly you should not change jobs constantly or people will become suspicious—rightly—of your ability to hold any job. At the same time you must not look upon the first job as the final job; it is primarily a training job, an opportunity to analyze yourself and your fitness for being an employee.

The Importance of Being Fired

In fact there is a great deal to be said for being fired from the first job. One reason is that it is rarely an advantage to have started as an office boy in the organization; far too many people will still consider you a "green kid" after you have been there for twenty-five years. But the major reason is that getting fired from the first job is the least painful and the least damaging way to learn how to take a setback. And whom the Lord loveth he teacheth early how to take a setback.

Nobody has ever lived, I daresay, who has not gone through a period when everything seemed to have collapsed and when years of work and life seemed to have gone up in smoke. No one can be spared this experience; but one can be prepared for it. The man who has been through earlier setbacks has learned that the world has not come to an end because he lost his job—not even in a depression. He has learned that he will somehow survive. He has learned, above all, that the way to behave in such a setback is not to collapse himself. But the man who comes up against it for the first time when he is forty-five is quite likely to collapse for good. For the things that people are apt to do when they receive the first nasty blow may destroy a mature man with a family, whereas a youth of twenty-five bounces right back.

Obviously you cannot contrive to get yourself fired. But you can always quit. And it is perhaps even more important to have quit once than to have been fired once. The man who walks out on his own volition acquires an inner independence that he will never quite lose.

When to Quit

To know when to quit is therefore one of the most important things—particularly for the beginner. For on the whole young people have a tendency to hang on to the first job long beyond the time when they should have quit for their own good.

One should quit when self-analysis shows that the job is the wrong job—that, say, it does not give the security and routine one requires, that it is a small-company rather than a big-organization job, that it is at the bottom rather than near the top, a specialist's rather than a generalist's job, etc. One should quit if the job demands behavior one considers morally indefensible, or if the whole atmosphere of the place is morally corrupting—if, for instance, only yes men and flatterers are tolerated.

One should also quit if the job does not offer the training one needs either in a specialty or in administration and the view of the whole. The beginner not only has a right to expect training from his first five or ten years in a job; he has an obligation to get as much training as possible. A job in which young people are not given real training—though, of course, the training need not be a formal "training program"—does not measure up to what they have a right and a duty to expect.

But the most common reason why one should quit is the absence of promotional opportunities in the organization. That is a compelling reason.

I do not believe that chance of promotion is the essence of a job. In fact there is no surer way to kill a job and one's own usefulness in it than to consider it as but one rung in the promotional ladder rather than as a job in itself that deserves serious effort and will return satisfaction, a sense of accomplishment, and pride. And one can be an important and respected member of an organization without ever having received a promotion; there are such people in practically every office. But the organization itself must offer fair promotional opportunities. Otherwise it stagnates, becomes corrupted, and in turn corrupts. The absence of promotional opportunities is demoralizing. And the sooner one gets out of a demoralizing situation, the better. There are three situations to watch out for:

The entire group may be so young that for years there will be no vacancies. That was a fairly common situation in business a few years back, as a result of the depression. Middle and lower management ranks in many companies were solidly filled with men in their forties and early fifties—men who were far too young to be retired but who had grown too old, during the bleak days of the Thirties, to be promotable themselves. As a result the people under them were bottled up; for it is a rare organization that will promote a young man around his older superior. If you find yourself caught in such a situation, get out fast. If you wait it will defeat you.

Another situation without promotional opportunities is one in which the group ahead of you is uniformly old—so old that it will have to be replaced long before you will be considered ready to move up. Stay away from organizations that have a uniform age structure throughout their executive group—old or young. The only organization that offers fair promotional opportunities is one in which there is a balance of ages.

Who Gets Promoted?

And finally there is the situation in which all promotions go to members of a particular group—to which you do not belong. Some chemical companies, for instance, require a master's degree in chemistry for just about any job above sweeper. Some companies promote only engineering graduates, some government agencies only people who majored in economics, some railroads only male stenographers, some British insurance companies only members of the actuaries' association. Or all the good jobs may be reserved for members of the family. There may be adequate promotional opportunities in such an organization—but not for you.

On the whole there are proportionately more opportunities in the big organization than in the small one. But there is very real danger of getting lost in the big organization—whereas you are always visible in the small one. A young man should therefore stay in a large organization only if it has a definite promotional program which ensures that he will be considered and looked at. This may take several forms: it may be a formal appraisal and development program; it may be automatic promotion by seniority as in the prewar Army; it may be an organization structure that actually makes out of the one big enterprise a number of small organizations in which everybody is again clearly visible (the technical term for this is "decentralization").

But techniques do not concern us here. What matters is that there should be both adequate opportunities and fair assurance that you will be eligible and considered for promotion. Let me repeat: to be promoted is not essential, either to happiness or to usefulness. To be considered for promotion is.

Your Life off the Job

I have only one more thing to say: to be an employee it is not enough that the job be right and that you be right for the job. It is also necessary that you have a meaningful life outside the job.

I am talking of having a genuine interest in something in which you, on your own, can be, if not a master, at least an amateur expert. This something may be botany, or the history of your county, or chamber music, cabinetmaking, Christmastree growing, or a thousand other things. But it is important in this "employee society" of ours to have a genuine interest outside of the job and to be serious about it.

I am not, as you might suspect, thinking of something that will keep you alive and interested during your retirement. I am speaking of keeping yourself alive, interested, and happy during your working life, and of a permanent source of self-respect and standing in the community outside and beyond your job. You will need such an interest when you hit the forties, that period in which most of us come to realize that we will never reach the goals we have set ourselves when younger—whether these are goals of achievement or of worldly success. You will need it because you should have one area in which you yourself impose standards of performance on your own work. Finally, you need it because you will find recognition and acceptance by other people working in the field, whether professional or amateur, as individuals rather than as members of an organization and as employees.

This is heretical philosophy these days when so many companies believe that the best employee is the man who lives, drinks, eats, and sleeps job and company. In actual experience those people who have no life outside their jobs are not the really successful people, not even from the viewpoint of the company. I have seen far too many of them shoot up like a rocket, because they had no interests except the job; but they also come down like the rocket's burned-out stick. The man who will make the greatest contribution to his company is the mature person—and you cannot have maturity if you have no life or interest outside the job. Our large companies are beginning to understand this. That so many of them encourage people to have "outside interests" or to develop "hobbies" as a preparation for retirement is the first sign of a change toward a more intelligent attitude. But quite apart from the self-interest of the employer, your own interest as an employee demands that you develop a major outside interest. It will make you happier, it will make you more effective, it will give you resistance against the setbacks and the blows that are the lot of everyone; and it will make you a more effective, a more successful, and a more mature employee.

You have no doubt realized that I have not really talked about how to be an employee. I have talked about what to know before becoming an employee—which is something quite different. Perhaps "how to be an employee" can be learned only by being one. But one thing can be said. Being an employee means working with people; it means living and working in a society. Intelligence, in the last analysis, is therefore not the most important quality. What is decisive is character and integrity. If you work on your own, intelligence and ability may be sufficient. If you work with people you are going to fail unless you also have basic integrity. And integrity—character—is one thing most, if not all, employers consider first.

There are many skills you might learn to be an employee, many abilities that are required. But fundamentally the one quality demanded of you will not be skill, knowledge, or talent, but character.

FURTHER THOUGHTS

1. The bulk of Drucker's article continues, either directly or indirectly, the questioning of your personal preferences begun earlier in this chapter. As you ponder the kinds of questions he raises, do you change any of the attitudes or tentative decisions you arrived at earlier? How significant are the kinds of questions he asks?
2. What do you think of Drucker's notions about getting fired and quitting?
3. Drucker points out that whatever a young person does, "in all likelihood he will do it as an employee." That statement has some sobering implications. First of all, do you agree with it? And if you find it convincing, do you find it at all troubling?

3rd Interlude

Children everywhere thrive on stories. They need them, love them. Stories are, we say, "make-believe"—and indeed they are. Stories are about beliefs. They help children make their beliefs by giving imaginative shape to roles they might play. Children's love and need for stories stem from a natural desire to find a stance toward the world of events.

Behind the love for stories lies the serious question that always needs answering: What does all of that happening out there mean to me? Good stories always pose this tough question and offer tough answers. That is why good stories, no matter how old, are always relevant. And that is why the great themes of marriage, death, survival, crime, guilt, growing up, war, and of virtues in conflict are present even in the most "childish" of good stories. They make the reader ask himself: Is *that* part of what I am? Is *that* what I am to be? Is *that* what it means to me?

In her book *Man's World, Woman's Place,* Elizabeth Janeway describes how we all live by stories and why we need them to help us identify the roles we can assume and the stances we can take toward the world of events. These stories are called myths. But she notes that these stories we tell each other may not match the stories we actually live.

Out of the cast of characters offered by current social myths comes the array of roles available to us. Janeway argues that the myths and roles of today—especially for women but certainly, too, for men and young people—no longer strengthen and liberate but in fact weaken and entrap. She doesn't conclude that myths must be discarded; she feels rather that they must be changed so that they line up more closely with present social reality. The problem is to find myths that provide a sufficiently large, varied, and integrated cast of characters to allow creativity and love to exist in that present reality.

UNDERSTANDING SOCIAL MYTHS (Abridged)

Elizabeth Janeway

> Whenever you begin, you will have to begin again twice over. (Erik Erikson, *Childhood and Society*)

Exploring social mythology is easier said than done. The word *myth* itself, to most people, has come to mean only an archaic story, pretty, false, and totally unrelated to life. It is not, therefore, anything to take seriously. Others use it differently. Agreeing that the mythmaking urge did not die out with the

Greeks or the Norsemen, they see the products of this process as simply false representation of life—the racial myths of Nazi Germany, for instance. The only reason for taking such myths seriously (this view of them supposes) is to disprove them and so put an end to superstitious nonsense.

I shall have to ask my readers to consider mythology and mythmaking from a quite different point of view. They are, in the first place, to be taken very seriously indeed, because they shape the way we look at the world. The urge to make, spread and believe in myths is as powerful today as it ever was. If we are going to understand the society we live in, we shall have to understand the way mythic forces arise, grow and operate. I do not believe we shall ever get rid of them and, in fact, I do not believe that we could get on without them: they are the product of profound emotional drives, drives that are basic to life. Sometimes these drives are able to act directly and effectively on the world of events. Sometimes they succeed in gaining their ends rationally and by logic. But sometimes (and particularly when they are thwarted) they substitute for action a will to believe that what they desire exists—or should exist. That is mythic thinking. It is illogical—or, at least, pre-logical; but from this very fact it gains a certain strength: logic may disprove it, but it will not kill it.

Logic is an incomparable tool, once a problem has been isolated and the data that are relevant determined. But how do we decide the context of a myth? It doesn't come down to facts, as a scientific problem does, where logic helps us to form hypotheses and then test our hypotheses so that we arrive at demonstrable conclusions. Myth incorporates emotions, and against these logic will not automatically prevail. Facts can be disproved, and theories based on them will yield in time to rational arguments and proof that they don't work. But myth has its own, furious, inherent reason-to-be because it is tied to desire. Prove it false a hundred times, and it will still endure because it is true as an expression of feeling.

We must, in short, tackle myth with different techniques and ask it different questions, questions that are anathema to scientific analysis and both useless and misleading for the criticism and evaluation of art, music and literature. Now, a number of people, if they think of myth at all, think of it as being some vague sort of art form. It isn't, and the difference will tell us quite a bit about what myth is. The questions we can ask of myth and shouldn't ask of art have to do with *motivation.*

Motives matter to art and science only as *motors* driving the producer to produce. If we ask about them, we find that we are dealing with the internal and psychological problems quite different from critical valuation. Why for instance, do dedicated, hardworking individuals produce kitsch and nonsense more often than they do art? Why do curious investigators pore over mathematical formulas for years and predict the end of the world last Friday? Sometimes the same brain, operating the same way, turns out both sense and nonsense. During the years when Isaac Newton was working out his greatest discoveries, he was also conducting lengthy experiments in alchemy, seeking the philosopher's stone and the elixir of life with the same painstaking care that he devoted to the laws of motion. His motives were the same, his curiosity as intense, his labors as unremitting; what differed was the product. In the one case he brought forth the theoretical underpinnings of modern science, in the other, magical twaddle.

The point is that he did produce objective results and that these can be judged without regard to the motivation behind them. This gives us a clearer view of myth, in contrast to art and science. Myth does not detach itself from its creator and move into the world of reality on its own. It remains attached to the mythmaker, and when it affects the world of reality, it is because those who believe in it act to make it come true. If, for example, the Nazi myths had been scientifically accurate, the "superior" Aryans would hardly have found it necessary to wipe out the "inferior" Jews.

This brings us another step forward. If it is characteristic of mythic thinking to be wishful, it is characteristic of mythic action to be inappropriate to the end it desires to achieve. Killing the Jews did not produce a sound and buoyant Third Reich, fit to endure a thousand years. Let us assume that science, art and myth all begin with a sincere and dedicated desire to understand and act on the outside world. Scientific experiment is directly pinned down to fact, art completes itself in an emotional resolution which reflects some aspect of reality, but myth can do neither. Based on the same inner tension, its actions do not relieve the tension. The desire remains; the engine drives on, fueled by longing. The logic of the outer world may prove myth wrong, but it cannot reach the engine within and shut it off.

One more point. If we tend to overlook the distinction between art and myth, it is because we usually know the latter by means of the former: mythic themes inspire art, and art owes a great deal to the tension of mythic longing. But in art something happens to transmute the one into the other. *Oedipus Tyrannus* is not a myth, but a conscious finished drama by a great artist. In the process of art a theme, often a mythic theme, is taken out of the dark and placed in a context that jibes with the world as it is seen and understood by both artist and audience. The theme is tested as a scientific hypothesis is tested: by confronting it with reality. Our involvements are worked out in action, they arrive at a climax and are resolved. The tragedy (or the comedy) which the mythic theme suggests becomes a separate entity. But myth *as* myth is unable to arrive at resolution and culmination, just as the formulas of neurosis cannot solve the crisis situation in the personality which has brought them about.

Then is myth just another form of neurosis? This, my last comparison, is the most crucial of all. Are myth and neurosis the same thing, the latter private, the former simply projected on a grander scale? There is much to make us think so, and certainly psychoanalysts have made great used of myth in exploring and explaining mental illness. Freud was the first, but only the first, to discover a correspondence between mythic formulations and the patterns and rhythms of unconscious processes as revealed by dream analysis and pathological behavior.

Both the form and the content of myth have helped to light up the labyrinth of the unconscious mind. The opposite twins, the shape-changer, the cannibal lovers and the dark goddess present themselves as figures in both and represent efforts to deal with overwhelming emotions, efforts to identify them, and thus control them, by symbolization. The figures and symbols of myth have built themselves up over millenniums as human situations have repeated themselves. They are abbreviations of emotional crisis, characters in an elementary calligraphy of feeling. No wonder that therapists find them useful for comprehending and interpreting the symbols which appear in neurotic formations. But can we reverse this process? Does an understanding of neurosis help us to comprehend myth?

Many, many analysts (beginning once more with Freud) have tried to do this, to explore the patterns of feeling that have crystallized into myths by means of the techniques worked out in their practice. If myth and neurosis are aspects of the same thing, one ought to be able to connect them backward and forward. When he named the child's attachment to his mother the Oedipus complex, Freud used myth—successfully—to identify the ground from which neurotic formulation can spring. Then he tried it the other way around, in *Totem and Taboo* (to cite one obvious example), and the result was sadly different and thoroughly unconvincing. What Freud did was to imagine primitive society as being similar to a family in structure, and primitive people as being similar to children. The guilt of rebellious sons who killed their father was then declared to be the reason for the ban against incest which is found in all societies. From its publications in 1913 to today, anthropologists have vociferously disagreed with him.

This is not to say that they are always right and Freud always wrong. But his attempt to explain the myth which forbids incest runs into a problem that tells us a great deal about the difference between the two processes. Neurosis begins as internal and individual and in effect it remains so. If it uses mythic figures to express itself, it's because these exist already. But myths, in essence, are not simply common to a group of people reacting in the same way to the pressures of a given society, they are *public*: that is, they structure themselves for action in the real world instead of being merely defensive. They may start with private feelings, but they address themselves to public situations and they are understood by other members of the society in question. This can only mean that in myth there exists some reflection of, or correspondence with, reality as it affects whole groups of people who respond as a group.

One more point of difference between the proper approach to neurosis and a useful effort to understand myth and the way it works: analysts try to understand neuroses *because they want to heal their patients.* But myth is not an illness, and society is not a patient to be cured in any simple, primary sense. It's terribly easy—and shatteringly wrong—to see myth and neurosis are similar distortions of thought and set out to cure society of its ills by getting rid of this kind of "sickness." But distortions within a society have a basis that is more than psychological. They may be so in part, but they are always bound up with social or economic difficulties. What arrogance to imagine that changing minds will remake the world! What a leap to conclusions! What—in fact—an indulgence in mythic thinking, the sort of thinking that declares, "This is wrong, and I will cure it, because it is all in your mind." Psychologists know better than that, in dealing with sick minds; they understand that the sickness involves a relationship with the outer world and that cure will come only as the relationship is adjusted. Social analysts would do well to realize that they won't even be able to analyze a situation correctly if they begin by prescribing a cure, for their own intentions will distort what they see.

To sum up, the purpose of studying social mythology is not therapy but simply and solely understanding. Any other approach is touched with megalomania. If we begin by aiming at a cure, we are clearly assuming that we know the rights and wrongs of an enormously complex situation, that we know what needs curing, and how to go about it. We don't. And we never shall, unless we are willing to do nothing but listen and learn, to start without preconceptions—including the basic preconception that the thing to do about social problems is to "cure" them, to make them go away and stop bothering us. This is the sort of misconception which declares that revolutionaries are "sick" and (on the part of the revolutionaries) that getting rid of The Establishment will set the world aright. But, to go back for a moment to the Nazi example, what the Germans needed after the First World War was not therapy, but economic opportunity and some change in the social structure which would have made democratic political processes at the local level more effective and more attractive. The Nazi mythology spread through Germany because it appeared to take account of real problems. Its methods were false and its answers disastrous, but it had its roots in actual needs and desires, actual political and economic difficulties.

If this chapter is rich in digressions, it's because I have taken Erik Erikson's advice and started again twice over. Let us see where this has got us. Our aim is to explore the social myths that surround us, shape and explain our world. and influence our behavior. They show up in things we take for granted and the attitudes we assume without bothering to decide why we assume them. We must take the influence of myths seriously, at the same time that we take their content with a grain of salt. We'll get nowhere by simply disproving them in logical fashion, nor can we cure them by psychotherapy. A neurotic individual has only himself to please with his fantasies, but myths are plausible to many. They gain strength from the connection that they supply to their believers, the shared desires, the joint wishful thinking that backs up one person's fantasies with another's, with those of a like-minded group. They endure because they offer hope, because they justify resentments, but perhaps most of all because they provide a bond of common feeling.

UNDERSTANDING SOCIAL ROLES (Abridged)

Elizabeth Janeway

> A social system is a function of the common culture, which not only forms the basis of the intercommunication of its members, but which defines, and so in one sense determines, the relative statuses of its members. . . . In so far as these relative statuses are defined and regulated in terms of a common culture, the following apparently paradoxical statement holds true: what persons *are* can only be understood in terms of a set of beliefs and sentiments which define what they *ought to be*.
> (Talcott Parsons, "The Superego and the Theory of Social Systems")

Our discussion of mythology has shown us that history does not live by facts alone. Another sort of logic is loose in the world, and we shan't understand the way people act unless we allow for the dynamics of greed and desire and the inertia of complacent power. So far, however, we have been talking very generally, and it is time to begin looking at these ideas in the small rather than in the large. One good reason for changing focus is that, when we look at them in large terms, they are very discouraging: if this is the way the world works, what can we ever do about it? Such disillusion and despair have their own effect on the phenomenal world because they tempt us to draw back from action. In addition, loss of interest means loss of the intense attention with which we follow activities in which we can see ourselves intervening. Someone who's playing in a tennis tournament watches the other matches in a very different fashion from the ordinary spectator. If we see ourselves as mere audience to life, we let events slip by and the connection between them remains unseen.

The world looks very different if we feel we can act upon it. And when we consider how emotional tendencies operate *within individuals*, it becomes possible to think that other individuals may have some effect upon them. Then those who hope to change the world will find "the way things work" operating to their advantage, even if the advantage is only knowing where one is. As Lincoln remarked, knowing where we are is what we need in order to move on.

The way myths affect individuals is through holding up roles for them to play. Talcott Parsons, whom I have quoted above, was one of the first sociologists to explore the concept of social roles, with particular attention to family roles. We shall come to his views on the importance of parental roles in child-raising very shortly, but at the moment I want to point out the clear connection with mythic thinking involved in the whole idea of roles: that we understand who people are only in terms of what we think they ought to be. This is basic to the entire experience of a human being in his world. Unless he knows who else is living in that world with him, he is a lost and frightened creature; but he will not know who these strangers around him are unless he has some idea of what they ought to be. He must tie his feelings about them (and so about himself) into his experience of what he sees them doing and hears them saying, how they behave toward him.

Parson's definition of "role" is tied up in a rather daunting knot of sociological prose, but I shall quote it here because it can be untwined to yield a very useful basis of analysis. A role is "the aspect of what the actor does in his relationship with others seen in the context of its functional significance for the social system." There are three factors here. First, playing a role implies a *relationship* with someone else. It is not, that is to say, individual fantasy or mere pretense. The role of "mother" demands the existence of a child to be mothered, or (a little more complicated) someone who is treated *as if* he were a child to be mothered. The role of "doctor" assumes that there are sick people to be treated and, at a secondary level, nurses to be instructed and a hospital staff to carry through the actions which the doctor prescribes for his patients' cure.

Next, a role is built around an *activity*: what the doctor does to and for his patients in his professional capacity. Out of his actions grow familiarity and then expectation. No single act is enough to establish a role. It demands continuity. The continuity of expected actions within a relationship has an effect on the other person involved. *He* begins to act reciprocally, in response to what the role-player is doing. Thus he becomes a bit more than audience, though he remains that too. The sociologists call him a "role-other." So the pattern of role-playing within a relationship works out to action, acceptance and reciprocal action.

If we take one more glance backwards at the world view of early man, we find on the wall of the cave of Les Trois Frères in the Pyrenees a painting of a half-human, half-animal figure, apparently engaged in a stamping dance. He has been named the Sorcerer, and he wears a mask, horns, tail and animal skins.

We, of course, can only guess what his performance was supposed to accomplish, and our ignorance brings us to the third element involved in role-playing: the *social system* within which the activity takes place and the relationship between role-player and role-others exists. This underlies and is part of the "common culture" of shared belief which allows each member of the relationship to understand what is going on between them. Both parties, actor and participating audience, need to share an interpretation of the meaning of the role and the purpose of the activity proper to it. Doctor and patient, for example, agree that the first intends to cure the second, and anything the doctor does is satisfactory to the patient as long as the latter feels that it jibes with this intention.

It is the surround of awareness and agreement which permits the actor to act effectively and the other person in the relationship to go along with the actions of the first. Without this grammar of recognition, the meaning of the role vanishes and the status of the actor changes sharply. So dramatic is a shift like this that drama has treated it often: Oedipus on the road to Colonus has fallen from his high estate to become a blind old man; Lear, after renouncing his kingdom, is a mad old man, raving and nonsensical, his occupation gone. How many such old men has America seen, who left their native lands to find themselves mocked by newer generations! The role of "elder" recognized and respected by sons and daughters, which they had seen their fathers play, had been left behind the old country.

A role, then, is both public and private. It is not just action, but action-plus-expressive gesture, action undertaken in a way that is understandable to others. The weight of such actions can be enormous. In Parsons' view, for instance, children learn about the world and the culture in which they live by growing up in the subsystem of that culture which we call the nuclear family. In this are included the four roles of father, mother, son and daughter or, from the point of view of the child, brother and sister. As he grows, he learns and incorporates within himself a comprehension of his relationship to each other member of the family, and with it an understanding of who and what each other member of the family is.

Later he also learns that the members of his family represent social situations and relationships that are common to the rest of the world he lives in. What his father does is generalized to "what fathers do." Eventually his own behavior as a father will hark back to what he learned as a son. It may echo his own father's actions, or it may go in quite the opposite direction, depending on how the son feels about his upbringing, but either way he has learned what a father *ought to be*, and his judgment on his own father derives from this. He is seeing (in Parsons' words), what his father was in terms of what he ought to have been.

Outside the family the expressive side of the role is even more important than within it, where members are so deeply familiar with each other. Appearance counts most, that is, where people are stangers to each other. Erving Goffman, a sociologist who has done a great deal of work on encounters between individuals and on the way they work together in groups, sums this up clearly: "In performing a role, the individual must see to it that the impressions of him that are conveyed in the situation are compatible with role-appropriate personal qualities effectively imputed to him," that is, with what people expect. "A judge is supposed to be deliberate and sober; a pilot in a cockpit to be cool; a bookkeeper to be accurate and neat in doing his work. These personal qualities . . . combine with a person's title, when there is one, to provide a basis of self-image for the incumbent and . . . for the image that . . . others will have of him."

All this is obvious: we judge people by how they fit into what we expect of them. What is interesting is Goffman's view of the effect of this on the role-player. "A self," he goes on, "virtually awaits the individual entering a position; he need only conform to the pressures on him and he will find a *me* ready-made for him. In the language of Kenneth Burke, doing is being." Now this equation of "role" with "ready-made me" touches a note which is disturbing to the lay reader. It suggests that a role has its own dynamism and that, if we enter upon it, we will be carried along by its demands willy-nilly, caught in the nightmare situation in which the mask takes over the individual face behind it, in which a life becomes only a meaningless series of gestures from which spontaneity and reality are absent.

Is such a fear justified? It is very much what Betty Friedan described, in *The Feminine Mystique*, as being a typical situation for middle-class women who feel themselves cut off from life, though it is certainly not a feeling confined to women alone. In replying, we must, I think, recognize that we are not only pondering the difference between the private and public sides of role-playing, but also whether the two aspects are compatible with each other at all. This is a very large problem indeed. It involves social judgments on a vast scale, and it may well be that any society—particularly the one we know best in this very moment of time—is capable of forcing private, feeling individuals to play public roles that are grindingly unsympathetic, overdemanding and dehumanizing. When this is the case, such a society is conniving at its own breakdown, for the choice of a "ready-made me" that it offers the child who is growing into man or woman is too far away from his own natural self to be endurable.

The resolution of this huge problem is beyond the scope of my inquiry; but it may throw some light on it to consider the advantages which an identifiable role offers when the demands it makes are not too heavy; that is, when role-playing is functioning in a useful and healthy way. If one's public role is satisfying and comfortable to the private self, one profits by the fact that it has been molded by the expectations of others and is clear and satisfying to them. One has a place in the social system and there are prescribed actions which will win approval for the role-player if they are well done. Even more, there are pre-existing standards of judgment by which a verdict of "well-done" can be pronounced on him. He is not only presented with a self, he is given a map of the world and the heavens, and a moral compass to guide himself along its coordinates. One can hesitate to take on a new self, but it is harder to refuse a whole universe where one's activities are accepted as meaningful and valuable, in which it is clear from the start that *this* behavior is appropriate and *that* is out of place. Most of all, it is hard to refuse a set of values that can be trusted to avoid paralyzing moral dilemmas by indicating what is worthy of respect and esteem. In a world where the public and private aspects of roles are not too far apart, a young doctor feels he knows what a good doctor is and does. His ideas may not agree with those of his teachers, but he has a grip on them and they on him. He has his work and his work tells him who he is; knowing this, he knows how to approach his patients. This is the "ready-made me" that has been waiting for him, and though it may give him a mask, it also sets up bulwarks against chaos. For ideally and in its origins, a role is not false, nor does it oppose or misrepresent the activity which it surrounds. Rather, it is a way of communicating to other people the meaning of the activity. It makes actions or situations or attitudes public and communal by tying them into a known and recognizable pattern of events and emotions. Consequently, like all means of communication, it must use terms that are common and recognizable to the public. Of course, therefore, it will never be quite precise, and its margin of imprecision will always be untrue. But this is the case with language itself: as T.S. Eliot's Sweeny said unhappily, "I've gotta use words when I talk to you." Any word, any gesture, any way of behaving can *become* false to a damaging extent if it becomes inappropriate to what is being done in its name, and thus inexpressive of reality.

What should make us wary is the continuation of inappropriate images. If people in power keep making this kind of mistake, if we ourselves, in our daily lives, find that we can't really explain what we're doing or why, and that lying is easier than looking for the heart of a muddled truth, then we have landed ourselves in a situation where reality must certainly be very different from what we think it is. Role-playing loses its usefulness if it communicates nothing but falsehoods. A child who is told only lies will distrust language—which must certainly have happened to many school dropouts. As the black community begins to find an identity for itself, it is willing to use in public the private language it used to save for its own members; and the use of this language is a measure of its distrust and dislike of the white language. Such distrust, however, is not inherent in role-playing, but springs up whenever language, including the language of behavior, begins to seem false.

As long as we need to act within a group, however, we shall have to have some way of showing the others in the group what we are doing. To do that, we must resort to ways of behaving that can be understood because they are familiar: we must play roles. If we don't, our behavior becomes frightening because it is strange. It's apt to be classed as "deviant" or crazy. The rest of the group grow confused and then hostile. Thus, even for those who want to break new ground, playing a role can be very useful indeed. It offers the protection of familiar behavior. Behind this behavior, innovation can take place as long as what is done is not *inappropriate* to what the rest expect. If the role-player is trusted, he can act to meet new situations within an old role and, if he turns out to be right about them, he can even change the role to keep it in tune with reality. A role should not be only a mask. It can be a shield, and an instrument too. Playing a role allows an individual to avoid the hostility that greets strange behavior. Sometimes one plays a role out of fear, but its primary purpose is quite different—to get something done without kicking up a fuss.

Role behavior has another use: it is a device for learning. We have noted Talcott Parsons' theory that the family is a center for teaching children their own social roles and, beyond this, the place of such roles in the structure of society. School and community together continue the process, for a great deal of education is not factual, but emotional and behavioral. "This is what people do, this is the way they feel," the child of a traditional society is taught, "in this situation or that—when grandparents die, when you go to work, when you travel abroad—expect this, don't be surprised at that, respond in this way, go to a priest or a rabbi for help if you are puzzled." So every individual finds the world structured and explained by other people's experience. It has been imagined for him in the shape of his native culture by those who lived before him. He may disagree with these findings, but at least he has a body of knowledge to argue against and a place to begin.

The value of a particular role, in a particular time, is quite a separate thing, then, from the value of role-playing in general. Role-playing is a complex activity necessary to society and useful in many ways to the individual. But the virtue of any special role depends on its closeness to the mental and emotional makeup of the performer and to its appropriateness to his situation. Does the behavior proper to this role fit with the action that needs to be taken in the external world, or does it oppose it? Does it fit the player comfortably and yet loosely enough for him to move about within its protection and adapt his posture to changing circumstances? Does it, on the other hand, clamp him so tightly that it denies him any feeling of choice, or opportunity for imaginative innovation, or pleasure in achievement? Does it belittle his hopes and deny him full human status? If the negative element is too great, the individual who has put on a role will cease to be a performer and become a puppet, moved wholly by the demands of his role and feeling that his fate has gone out of his control. Society can survive that for a while, for the puppet still acts and still expresses the meaning of his actions. But the individual is no longer a person, only a bundle of prescribed gestures with nothing inside to tie them together; and too many of these robots a changing society cannot afford, for they do not adapt to change.

FURTHER THOUGHTS

1. Toward the end of the selection Ms. Janeway discusses the advantages of having public roles to play. What are these advantages? Do you agree with her description here?

2. What roles do you think society provides for you to play? Ms. Janeway says that "the virtue of any special role depends on its closeness to the mental and emotional makeup of the performer and to its appropriateness to his situation." Which of your roles seem to be useful? in what ways? Which seem to be useless, even damaging? Why?

3. Ms. Janeway compares and contrasts myth with some other social phenomena—science, for instance, and art, and neurosis. Take a clean sheet of paper and divide it into three columns, the left-hand one only an inch or so wide. Then divide the sheet into three equal parts horizontally. In the upper left-hand box write "Myth and Science"; in the middle left-hand box write "Myth and Art," and in the lower left-hand box "Myth and Neurosis." Label

the two wide columns "Alike" and "Different." Then go back through the selection looking for specific ways in which myth is either like or different from each of the three—science, art, and neurosis. Jot down your findings in the proper boxes. Add your own ideas, too. Be ready to discuss—or perhaps even to write about—your findings.

4. If this is the first time you've encountered the kinds of questions asked in this exercise, go back to page 65 and read the instructions there.

   a. Which would you most like to be?

   _____ a Black lawyer in California
   _____ a Black lawyer in Nigeria
   _____ a Black lawyer in Sweden

   b. Which would you trust least?

   _____ a politician
   _____ a used-car salesman
   _____ an orthodontist

   c. Which seems to you to be worst?

   _____ someone who murders another person in a fit of passion
   _____ someone who sells drugs to support his own habit
   _____ an ugly and shy man who commits rape

   d. Which would you most want as a neighbor?

   _____ a circus clown
   _____ a famous poet
   _____ a professional football player

   e. Write two questions like those above which deal with social roles and myths.

Work
And Play

This whole business of work can get very serious if you aren't careful. But even on the most solemn of jobs, playfulness will break in. People do things "for the hell of it", they say—a curious phrase, for if ever there were a place where play is outlawed, it must be hell. Play is supposed to be physical and earthy, but it is also touchingly beautiful. Somewhere deep in the playful is the aesthetic.

And somewhere deep in aesthetic experience is the willingness to dare and to laugh. We were on a picnic with our families and had stopped at a playground, a favorite because it featured a high, long, curved and bumpy slide. It was much too high for Meg, the youngest child, but she watched the others, noisy, laughing, giddy, swoosh down. We must have been less than alert, for as happens so often to parents, an abrupt silence warned us that something was wrong. Meg had climbed the high slide and was poised at the top—a small, determined three-year-old on a suddenly dangerous toy. There are no safe playgrounds. A thoroughly safe and sanitized playground ceases to be a place to play. Without the risk of going beyond control, without the risk of being hurt, there is no opportunity for joy. You can learn to gauge the margin of risk and reduce it to some extent, but if you erase the margin completely, you also eliminate the possibilities for joy.

Meg started down the slide, afraid and happy until the last, large bump where she lost control, and was caught by her frightened and chastened father. "I almost made it, Dad." "Yes, you did, but let's not try it again today. Your father isn't up to it." "Next time?" "Maybe, if I am here."

One of the satisfactions of play is also found in craftsmanship—a sense of control, of expanding, joyful control. The satisfactions of play depend on the degree to which the sense of expanding control is part of your working life. What play means to you depends on what your work means to you. The less your work can give you, the more you need the release of play, in which expanding control—or even losing it—is necessary. The catch is that demeaning work can diminish your capacity to imagine what joy and play can be, and your expectations of a full life—in all realms of living.

"Keep your nose to the grindstone," our elders said, "and your shoulder to the wheel." But there are limits to such dedicated contortions. A job, no matter how satisfying, is seldom enough for a full life. Man's needs include the need for play. This idea is made clear in the following fable by E. M. Forster, which gives new meaning to a cliché, the image of work as a race—an image drawn originally from the world of play.

THE OTHER SIDE OF THE HEDGE

E. M. Forster

My pedometer told me that I was twenty-five; and, though it is a shocking thing to stop walking, I was so tired that I sat down on a milestone to rest. People outstripped me, jeering as they did so, but I was too apathetic to feel resentful, and even when Miss Eliza Dimbleby, the great educationist, swept past, exhorting me to perservere, I only smiled and raised my hat.

At first I thought I was going to be like my brother, whom I had had to leave by the roadside a year or two round the corner. He had wasted his breath on singing, and his strength on helping others. But I had travelled more wisely, and now it was only the monotony of the highway that oppressed me—dust under foot and brown crackling hedges on either side, ever since I could remember.

And I had already dropped several things—indeed, the road behind was strewn with the things we all had dropped; and the white dust was settling down on them, so that already they looked no better than stones. My muscles were so weary that I could not even bear the weight of those things I still carried. I slid off the milestone into the road, and lay there prostrate, with my face to the great parched hedge, praying that I might give up.

A little puff of air revived me. It seemed to come from the hedge; and, when I opened my eyes, there was a glint of light through the tangle of boughs and dead leaves. The hedge could not be as thick as usual. In my weak, morbid state, I longed to force my way in, and see what was on the other side. No one was in sight, or I should have not have dared to try. For we of the road do not admit in conversation that there is another side at all.

I yielded to the temptation, saying to myself that I would come back in a minute. The thorns scratched my face, and I had to use my arms as a shield, depending on my feet alone to push me forward. Halfway through I would have gone back, for in the passage all the things I was carrying were scraped off me, and my clothes were torn. But I was so wedged that return was impossible, and I had to wriggle blindly forward, expecting every moment that my strength would fail me, and that I should perish in the undergrowth.

Suddenly cold water closed round my head, and I seemed sinking down for ever. I had fallen out of the hedge into a deep pool. I rose to the surface at last, crying for help, and I heard someone on the opposite bank laugh and say: 'Another!' and then I was twitched out and laid panting on the dry ground.

Even when the water was out of my eyes, I was still dazed, for I had never been in so large a space, nor seen such grass and sunshine. The blue sky was no longer a strip, and beneath it the earth had risen grandly into hills—clean, bare buttresses, with beech trees in their folds, and meadows and clear pools at their feet. But the hills were not high, and there was in the landscape a sense of human occupation—so that one might have called it a park, or garden, if the words did not imply a certain triviality and constraint.

As soon as I got my breath, I turned to my rescuer and said:

'Where does this place lead to?'

'Nowhere, thank the Lord!' said he, and laughed. He was a man of fifty or sixty—just the kind of age we mistrust on the road—but there was no anxiety in his manner, and his voice was that of a boy of eighteen.

'But it must lead somewhere!' I cried, too much surprised at his answer to thank him for saving my life.

'He wants to know where it leads!' he shouted to some men on the hill side, and they laughed back, and waved their caps.

I noticed then that the pool into which I had fallen was really a moat which bent round to the left and to the right, and that the hedge followed it continually. The hedge was green on this side—its roots showed through the clear water, and fish swam about in them—and it was wreathed over with dog-roses and Traveller's Joy. But it was a barrier, and in a moment I lost all pleasure in the grass, the sky, the trees, the happy men and women, and realized that the place was but a prison, for all its beauty and extent.

We moved away from the boundary, and then followed a path almost parallel to it, across the meadows. I found it difficult walking, for I was always trying to out-distance my companion, and there was no advantage in doing this if the place led nowhere. I had never kept step with anyone since I left my brother.

I amused him by stopping suddenly and saying disconsolately, 'This is perfectly terrible. One cannot advance: one cannot progress. Now we of the road ———'

'Yes. I know.'

'I was going to say, we advance continually.'

'I know.'

'We are always learning, expanding, developing. Why, even in my short life I have seen a great deal of advance—Transvaal War, the Fiscal Question, Christian Science, Radium. Here for example—'

I took out my pedometer, but it still marked twenty-five, not a degree more.

'Oh, it's stopped! I meant to show you. It should have registered all the time I was walking with you. But it makes me only twenty-five.'

'Many things don't work in here,' he said. 'One day a man brought in a Lee-Metford, and that wouldn't work.'

'The laws of science are universal in their application. It must be the water in the moat that has injured the machinery. In normal conditions everything works. Science and the spirit of emulation—those are the forces that have made us what we are.'

I had to break off and acknowledge the pleasant greetings of people whom we passed. Some of them were singing, some talking, some engaged in gardening, hay-making, or other rudimentary industries. They all seemed happy; and I might have been happy too, if I could have forgotten that the place led nowhere.

I was startled by a young man who came sprinting across our path, took a little fence in fine style, and went tearing over a ploughed field till he plunged into a lake, across which he began to swim. Here was true energy, and I exclaimed: 'A cross-country race! Where are the others?'

'There are no others,' my companion replied; and, later on, when we passed some long grass from which came the voice of a girl singing exquisitely to herself, he said again: 'There are no others.' I was bewildered at the waste in production, and murmured to myself, 'What does it all mean?"

He said: 'It means nothing but itself'—and he repeated the words slowly, as if I were a child.

'I understand,' I said quietly, 'but I do not agree. Every achievement is worthless unless it is a link in the chain of development. And I must not trespass on your kindness any longer. I must get back somehow to the road, and have my pedometer mended.'

'First, you must see the gates,' he replied, 'for we have gates, though we never use them.'

I yielded politely, and before long we reached the moat again, at a point where it was spanned by a bridge. Over the bridge was a big gate, as white as ivory, which was fitted into a gap in the boundary hedge. The gate opened outwards, and I exclaimed in amazement, for from it ran a road—just such a road as I had left—dusty under foot, with brown crackling hedges on either side as far as the eye could reach.

'That's my road!' I cried.

He shut the gate and said: 'But not your part of the road. It is through this gate that humanity went out countless ages ago, when it was first seized with the desire to walk.'

I denied this, observing that the part of the road I myself had left was not more than two miles off. But with the obstinacy of his years he repeated: 'It is the same road. This is the beginning, and though it seems to run straight away from us, it doubles so often, that it is never far from our boundary and sometimes touches it.' He stooped down by the moat, and traced on its moist margin an absurd figure like a maze. As we walked back through the meadows, I tried to convince him of his mistake.

'The road sometimes doubles, to be sure, but that is part of our discipline. Who can doubt that its general tendency is onward? To what goal we know not—it may be to some mountain where we shall touch the sky, it may be over precipices into the sea. But that it goes forward—who can doubt that? It is the thought of that that makes us strive to excel, each in his own way, and gives us an impetus which is lacking with you. Now that man who passed us—it's true that he ran well, and jumped well, and swam well; but we have men who can run better, and men who can jump better, and who can swim better. Specialization has produced results which would surprise you. Similarly, that girl——'

Here I interrupted myself to exclaim: 'Good gracious me! I could have sworn it was Miss Eliza Dimbleby over there, with her feet in the fountain!'

He believed that it was.

'Impossible! I left her on the road, and she is due to lecture this evening at

Tunbridge Wells, Why, her train leaves Cannon Street in—of course my watch has stopped like everything else. She is the last person to be here.'

'People always are astonished at meeting each other. All kinds come through the hedge, and come at all times—when they are drawing ahead in the race, when they are lagging behind, when they are left for dead. I often stand near the boundary listening to the sounds of the road—you know what they are—and wonder if anyone will turn aside. It is my great happiness to help someone out of the moat, as I helped you. For our country fills up slowly, though it was meant for all mankind.'

'Mankind have other aims,' I said gently, for I thought him well-meaning; 'and I must join them.' I bade him good evening, for the sun was declining, and I wished to be on the road by nightfall. To my alarm, he caught hold of me, crying: 'Your are not to go yet!' I tried to shake him off, for we had no interests in common, and his civility was becoming irksome to me. But for all my struggles the tiresome old man would not let go; and, as wrestling is not my specialty, I was obliged to follow him.

It was true that I could have never found alone the place where I came in, and I hoped that, when I had seen the other sights about which he was worrying, he would take me back to it. But I was determined not to sleep in the country, for I mistrusted it, and the people too, for all their friendliness. Hungry though I was, I would not join them in their evening meals of milk and fruit, and, when they gave me flowers, I flung them away as soon as I could do so unobserved. Already they were lying down for the night like cattle—some out on the bare hillside, others in groups under the beeches. In the light of an orange sunset I hurried on with my unwelcome guide, dead tired, faint for want of food, but murmuring indomitably: 'Give me life, with its struggles and victories, with its failures and hatreds, with its deep moral meaning and its unknown goal!'

At last we came to a place where the encircling moat was spanned by another bridge, and where another gate interrupted the line of the boundary hedge. It was different from the first gate; for it was half transparent like horn, and opened inwards. But through it, in the waning light, I saw again just such a road as I had left—monotonous, dusty, with brown crackling hedges on either side, as far as the eye could reach.

I was strangely disquieted at the sight, which seemed to deprive me of all self-control. A man was passing us, returning for the night to the hills, with a scythe over his shoulder and a can of some liquid in his hand. I forgot the destiny of our race. I forgot the road that lay before my eyes, and I sprang at him, wrenched the can out of his hand, and began to drink.

It was nothing stronger than beer, but in my exhausted state it overcame me in a moment. As in a dream, I saw the old man shut the gate, and heard him say: 'This is where your road ends, and through this gate humanity—all that is left of it—will come in to us.'

Though my senses were sinking into oblivion, they seemed to expand ere they reached it. They perceived the magic song of nightingales, and the odour of invisible hay, and stars piercing the fading sky. The man whose beer I had stolen lowered me down gently to sleep off its effects, and, as he did so, I saw that he was my brother.

FURTHER THOUGHTS

1. What are the major differences between life on the road and life in the country beyond the hedge? Is it simply a case of one being a life of work and the other a life of play?
2. What is the goal for which the racers are striving? How do they know when they've achieved it? Is the only answer to drop out of the race? What's the goal in the country beyond the hedge?
3. Was the life of the racer a playful life? How about the life beyond the hedge?

The myths of the Greeks, of the Romans, of the Middle Ages, even those of the early American West—all describe models of humanity in moments of bravery, strength, intense feeling, truth, beauty.

What are the sources of myths today? Certainly not war—as it was for so many centuries. It seems that Korea and Vietnam have affected our capacity for grounding our myths in war.

So where do the myths of today come from?

One possibility is the world of play. But if play is to begin to assume mythic dimensions, it must provide a fine balance of control and order on the one hand, and freedom and unpredictability on the other. There has to be enough order and convention to make craftsmanship possible and thus to make it possible to experience joy in mastery and control. But there must be enough freedom for excess; there must be room for the individual player to put his own mark on the game, to rise to the level of hero. Out of this balance of freedom and control come both craft and the possibility of heroism. Out of it comes a sense of control over a situation, at times an ecstatic control. And out of this balance comes, too, the possibility of creating myth.

For many fans professional football exemplifies exactly this balance of order and freedom. It has the power of an epic. And it takes place in a setting that lends itself to epic perspectives: crowds of people on hand, millions of devoted followers in the wings; men larger than life, even without the padding; great rewards riding on the outcome.

To someone who isn't a fan it may seem an empty-headed notion, but think about it. Don't mistake what comes out of your tube every Sunday—live and in color, with too much empty commentary and too many silly commercials—for the myth. Myth doesn't emerge from the instant of battle—or play. Myth emerges, like all poetry, in reflection and recollection, out of the forms and images in which we preserve the battle and the play. You can perhaps begin to see this in the many television programs that present edited highlights of important games. There the editing creates striking images and juxtapositions. And the fact that it has all become history distances things enough for reflection. History blends into myth in the editing room. The film editor—working in recollection— scans the action in the manner of the epic poet: getting the spectator into the middle of the action, focusing in on a crucial confrontation, heightening the role of the hero, emphasizing the turning point, stressing the "moral."

In recollection and with reflection events become symbols. Television images become poetic metaphors. The Minnesota Vikings' Joe Kapp sags to the ground late in the game against Kansas City, a battered man, but more than that, a defeated advocate of a new style, the usurper brought down. Joe Namath slips those passes through the Baltimore Colts, and the joker becomes a hero. Bart Starr squeezes through the Dallas Cowboys' line to win the NFL championship in 1967—and "goodness" triumphs. The Packers' Jerry Kramer describes that play: "And I can still feel the pure pleasure of the scoring play, when Ken Bowman and I blocked Jethro Pugh, the ecstasy of seeing Bart Starr squeeze by me into the end zone, the slaps on the back and the yells and the blood pumping so hard right into the locker room. And then that night, I got silly drunk, singing songs with Fuzzy in his restaurant, with the heating system broken and the temperature down to twenty-two below, and all the wives and the dates and the nonplayers shivering, and the rest of us still warmed by the heat of victory" (*Jerry Kramer's Farewell to Football,* ed. Dick Schaap [New York: Bantam Books, 1969], p. 5)

This is the world that beckoned George Plimpton. He decided to see what it would be like for a mere mortal to work out and play with the modern demigods of professional football. *Paper Lion* is the elegant and funny account of his weeks as a pretend rookie with the Detroit Lions. The selection that follows describes the day he left training camp—the league management was getting nervous.

FROM
PAPER LION

George Plimpton

I went back to Cranbrook early. I decided to leave camp the next day. In two weeks the Lions had a big exhibition game with the New York Giants at Cleveland, part of a doubleheader, but the commissioner's edict was sure to continue. I packed that night and made reservations to leave Detroit at noon the next day. I put the football back in the suitcase, and the high-school coaching manuals on basic principles of team play, which I had not opened. There were some sweatshirts with DETROIT LIONS across the front which George Wilson had given me, and I took those, thinking how when I got back to New York the shirts would look out in the winter pickup touch-football games in Central Park.

When I had packed my suitcase, I went down the dormitory corridor to look in on some of the players to say goodbye. It was quiet that night. A few of the players were already asleep. But one or two of the rooms were lively, the players still working off the excitement of the day. I joined them. Hearing that I was leaving the next day, there was some murmuring that I should stay. They knew how much I wanted to get in a league game, and they began plotting how I could be secretly inserted in the Giant game in Cleveland. "We'll just sit on ol' Milt Plum a bit, just *hem* him in on the sidelines," someone said. "And another group doing the same to Earl Morrall, and by the time they're loose, and Wilson's on to it, you can reel off a good quick series."

I knew that if such a thing was done some of them would get into trouble. The temptation was strong, and as we conspired in that small dormitory room the consideration of *writing* about such a subterfuge was almost irresistible. But it would not have set well. I never forgot that in Pontiac, just before the scrimmage was to begin, John Gordy had shouted as the huddle broke, "Let's everyone lie down, and let him go through, let him get his touchdown." I had shouted, "No, it's got to be straight—no fake, *straight.*" Gordy, with the others, not only played it straight, but he shot out of his offensive guard position with such vehemence that he bowled me over. He told me afterward that my being in there at all had upset him. Keyed up as he was by the vigor of his profession, he felt it wasn't *natural* to have an amateur like me involved. That was fooling around. There was no combining the two attitudes—it had to be one or the other.

The talk shifted to the afternoon's game. They began talking about Reeberg's play. "He had a fair afternoon with the guy opposite," someone said. "But anybody good—like Katcavage on the Giants—why the Kat'd rape him."

Just at that moment, quite abruptly, so that a sentence a player was speaking trailed off, the doorway filled, and we looked up and saw the coaches standing there—Wilson in front, Doll on one side, and the Hawk on the other, with a clipboard.

"Bedcheck," said Wilson.

He had the familiar glum look on his dark face that came when he was forced to do something, usually in the name of discipline, which he felt beneath his dignity.

"Anybody missing in here?" asked the Hawk. He looked at his clipboard. "Where's Whitlow? He bunks in here, doesn't he?"

"He's down taking a shower," someone said without much conviction.

The Hawk made some sort of mark on the clipboard. "That shower's pretty full up tonight, from what I've been told. There's maybe ten, twenty men must be down in there according to my records." He looked down at his clipboard. "That had to be a mighty dusty bus ride coming back from Detroit. We're going to be awful low on soap."

Nobody seemed much amused.

"Where's Morrall at?" the Hawk asked. "That him singing down in the shower?" He cocked a hand to his ear derisively. We all stared sullenly at nothing in particular.

"It's long after eleven," Wilson said. "Can't you men stick to the goddamn rules? You think the coaches like to make Holy Rollers out of you? You think it gives us some sort of goddamn pleasure?"

He turned away abruptly. We heard their footsteps go down the hall, and the murmur rise from the next room where they had stopped to check.

After a while, John Gonzaga said: "This is the time when you want to pack and go back to your wife. At least you don't get some guy turning up with a clipboard and peering into your bedroom to see if you're there."

"What are Holy Rollers?" I asked.

"That's what they call the guys doing the grass sprints," someone said. "You hang around long enough tomorrow and you'll see. The sprints are a type of punishment. It's better than a fine. But not much. A guy will miss a bedcheck, maybe three or four guys, like tonight, and the coaches'll put them to it the next day. It doesn't sound hard. You have to sprint for twenty yards, then on hands and knees for ten, then down and roll for ten more, then up again and sprint for twenty—keeping this up in succession down the length of the field and back until maybe you've done two hundred yards. It's sort of funny at the start, everybody leap-frogging and grinning, and the spectators all laughing and pointing. But you have to do the drill at top speed, and the rolling in particular gets you dizzy and sick feeling. There're not many who can do a hundred yards of it without puking. Then it's not so funny any more."

"I can imagine," I said.

Someone said, "George Wilson doesn't call it but once or twice in the training season. But the guy before him, Buddy Parker, he used to have the Holy Rollers performing like it was a weekly benefit. This one time he put the entire squad to it. I've forgotten what for—must have been bad. Bobby Layne was the team leader then, and he was madder than a tick. He had this gut that poked out, a regular pot, which made it tough on him in the rolling—but he was the leader and the toughest, and while he was rolling himself along, and leaping up and down in those sprints, he was shouting and swearing at the others to keep up with him and finish it out or he'd see to it that they never drew another breath. He pulled them all through, just like he did in the games on Sunday. Then what does Layne do but line up the Holy Rollers like a platoon and he's going to march them up towards the gym, singing some damn song, just to show Buddy Parker that he hadn't broken their spirit."

"It's like some sort of bad movie," I interjected.

"Well, Parker was no mild-mannered bozo neither," the veteran went on. "He looked at this singing and marching as indicating some form of disrespect. He blew his whistle and ordered Layne and his guys to do the sprints *again.* There was damn near a mutiny. But they went through it. Layne finished the course; hardly nobody else. He wanted his men to sing and march, but they weren't so sure. And then Layne saw something."

"What was that?"

"Well, he looked over and he saw Parker standing there, calm and collected, wearing a nice shirt, all clean, and a golfing hat, and a whistle on a white cord, and I mean Layne wasn't a complete dummy. I mean it was no contest. All Parker had to do was lift that whistle a couple of inches up to his mouth to blow it, and rolling and sprinting for a hundred yards was no match for *that.* So Bobby Layne lost that one. He just trotted up towards the gym, and the others straggled along behind him."

One of the veterans stirred and recalled that at Chicago when Hunk Anderson, an awesome disciplinarian, was there, recalcitrants used to run what were called "fat-man" races, and Anderson had a little wooden paddle he eased onto the posteriors of linemen going by who he felt needed to be picked up in spirit.

"You see," one of the veterans said to me, "you needn't feel too bad about leaving camp tomorrow."

I came in late to breakfast the next morning. A few players were there, and they said that the word was around that I was leaving. "The report is you're chickening out on the grass sprints," they said.

Wilson came up and said that the team and the coaches had planned a little ceremony in which I was to be presented with a gold football mounted on a wooden pedestal that read THE BEST ROOKIE IN DETROIT LION HISTORY. The trophy was not ready, so they would have to send it through the mail. John Gordy, standing nearby, said that the real reason I was leaving was because I didn't have the nerve to accept such an award for the brand of football I had displayed at Cranbrook. "I haven't got one damn trophy," he said with a big grin, "and you're getting one for the worst football I *ever* seen played."

Wilson said he hoped if I had time that morning I'd come down to the practice. When I had the bags in the car, I started through the school grounds for the practice field. I had a half hour or so. It was hot and quiet, the lawn sprinklers ticking back and forth. I thought about the Holy Rollers. I went down past the tennis courts and the pine grove, walking gingerly to keep my street shoes clear of the hot powder dust.

When I stepped out from the sidelines the players all came and crowded around to say goodbye.

George Wilson said, "You want to try one last play. One more?"

"Sure," I said. "Absolutely."

The defense began shouting happily. Joe Schmidt said, "We get one last shot at him. One last shot. That'll do it. One mighty jumbo, men, that'll do it fine."

Scooter McLean blew his whistle. "O.K.," he shouted. "Let's get settled. Offense huddle up! George, go on in there and call your play."

The teams separated. The helmets were tugged on. I went in among the offensive huddle, feeling slight in my street clothes. "I expect protection," I said, grinning at them. Their helmets were turned toward me, so as always the faces were hooded and expressionless.

"Let's turn them inside out with a pass play," I said. "Green right, three right, ninety-three on *three*!"

I said it distinctly, and with the right rhythm, and they broke sharply with a crack of hands, and moved up to the line. I went up briskly behind Whitlow. I looked out at the defense. I stood in closer to the center. That had been one of my troubles in Pontiac—standing too far back and reaching for the ball. At *three* the ball came back cleanly slapping hard into my palm, and I hurried back, surefooted, seven yards, and turned to look downfield. Just in front I could see the haunches of the blockers around the rim of the protective pocket as they strained forward with their cleats churning up dust, but their bodies bent upright by the shock of the defensive tackles and ends working at them in a flail of arms; beyond them I saw Pietrosante cutting across, downfield about fifteen yards from me; he was looking over. I cut loose the pass, and it hit him just right, so that he could gather the ball in at a height at which the defending linebacker could not reach over to bat it down. With his legs pumping he moved the ball a few more yards downfield before he was brought down.

A great roar went up, not only from the offense, but also from the defensive people. The crowds along the sidelines stirred curiously, craning to see.

I heard the Hawk yelling: "Anything wrong with that? Any complaints about that?"

"Duck soup," I called out. "Damn cinch. Child's play." I snapped my fingers.

"Give him the game ball," said Wilson.

The helmets were off. Everyone was standing around grinning.

"Too bad about this trade with Baltimore—me for John Unitas," I said. "I suppose Bill Ford and Anderson know what they're doing."

I shook hands with some of them. I said what a fine time I had enjoyed there at Cranbrook. Then I left them and walked up through the pine trees, the scent warm and strong in the noonday heat. On the tennis court two girls were playing desultory singles—awkward at it, using their game for gossip; but they were lovely to watch, each in startling white tennis outfits that set off their tanned bodies. I had a few minutes to spare. Their game consisted mostly of double-faults. One of them called to the other: "I tell you Timmy's car seats come *off*—I mean you sit there for a while on that hot leather and it comes off on your legs." She served, a high arched shot like a lob. The other girl set herself, measuring her shot, and when she swung her racquet through she hit the ball with her thumb. The ball glanced off and she dropped the racquet to the court with a clatter. "You absolute fiend!" she said. She inspected her hand. The score went unannounced. One girl served, then the other, in some helter-skelter fashion, whoever held the ball it seemed. "God, at least," said the girl with the bruised thumb, "Timmy plays a banjo. You know what?"

"What?"

"His coat pockets are full of picks—those little fingernail-like things?" She bent and tried to scoop up a tennis ball with her racquet.

"What?" The other girl had her hands on her hips, her head cocked prettily, a bell of hair falling to her shoulder.

"Picks," came the answer. "Those things he *plinks* with. Plink! Plink! Plink!" She began strumming her racquet, her feet shuffling on the court. "He has hundreds."

I stood and watched them. It was quiet in the pine grove. And then an odd sound drifted up from the distant practice field, invisible behind the barriers of trees. I could see in my mind's eye what was going on—the coaches' whistles going, and the players beginning to congregate from the reaches of that enormous field. Then one of them, as he trotted in, offered up a despairing croak, as if he had run too far, or belted the tackling dummies too hard, or his uniform felt soggy and itchy from sweat. With hours more of physical discomfort to come, the anguish erupted from him, and as if empathetic, his yell was caught up by the others and repeated, so that a chorus rose up through the pine grove—a medley of despair, boredom, frustration, exhaustion—a sound I'd never heard before at Cranbrook. They were the same loud grunts of resentment that went up along the line when troops were called up out of the comfortable roadside grass after a break in a long dusty march. The coaches' whistles began shrilling very loudly, as if to drown out the resentment. I wondered what had happened. Perhaps the players knew that the coaches were going to order the grass drills.

I often thought about the sound, wondering about it. It was an inhuman, melancholy noise. Then it died out abruptly. The players had apparently grouped around the coaches. The hum of insects rose up out of the hot pines. One of the girls began bouncing a tennis ball against the court; the sound was pleasant and summery. "Jiminy, d'ja hear *that*?" she called across the net. "That's the craziest . . . "

The other girl was still turned, her head tilted, as if the sound would come again, and she could diagnose it this time—her face puzzled and vacant as she waited, her mouth half open. Then, quite abruptly, she seemed to shake herself, a shiver of movement that tossed the hair at her shoulders, and she turned and called: "Who's serving? Who's serving? I'll serve!"—and dismissing the past in a quick rush of breath, she threw the ball so high in the air that she had to maneuver under it, her racquet poised.

FURTHER THOUGHTS

1. The introduction to Plimpton's selection contains the third more or less distinct use of the word *myth* in this book. Marijean Suelzle used it to mean something like falsehood or misconception. Elizabeth Janeway used it to describe the kind of stories a society tells itself, true or not, that produce the social roles it gives its members to play. Now we are using it to refer to those tales of the Greeks—and the forms and images in a football game. What do all these meanings have in common? How do they differ?
2. How many different kinds of playing—and playing at—are going on in Plimpton's selection?
3. Do professional football players play football?
4. Is professional football yet another male chauvinist social institution? What role do women play in it? What is its counterpart for women?

AT THE BALL GAME

William Carlos Williams

The crowd at the ball game
is moved uniformly

by a spirit of uselessness
which delights them—

all the exciting detail
of the chase

and the escape, the error
the flash of genius—

all to no end save beauty
the eternal—

So in detail they, the crowd,
are beautiful

for this
to be warned against

saluted and defied—
It is alive, venomous

it smiles grimly
its words cut—

The flashy female with her
mother, gets it—

The Jew gets it straight—it
is deadly, terrifying—

It is the Inquisition, the
Revolution

It is beauty itself
that lives

day by day in them
idly—

This is
the power of their faces

It is summer, it is the solstice
the crowd is

cheering, the crowd is laughing
in detail

permanently, seriously
without thought

BILLIARDS

Geo. Dumitrescu

trans. Roy MacGregor-Hastie

Billiards—what a splendid game it is.

I take my head and put it on the green baize.
It is a detachable head. I strike it with the cue,
sending it, slowly at first then faster,
towards the adversary ball
which always has a black spot on it.

The ball rolls, no longer either immobile
or lonely. But it is not enough
to hit the adversary ball
and send it moving about the table;
what matters is to find the red ball,
setting off
a lively movement of all three;
this is the way to make
four points,
the four cardinal points.

Don't strike the ball too hard; the balls
could jump off the table and you would lose time
and a certain number of points.

Let us play billiards, then. After each game
things all around seem to make more sense,
be more coherent, all rolling,
with a free, planetary movement,
looking for the red ball.

Billiards—it is a splendid game.
You can play with words, too,
or even with stars,
with black balls and green balls,
you can even play with thoughts, white or bluish,
but the essential thing is to find the red ball,
that is the heart of the game
in which single movements are joined together,
without which
you cannot make the four points.

Let us play billiards! When things
don't make sense any more, seem incoherent,
I go to play billiards,
better to understand the world.
I take my head and put it on the green baize.
Fortunately it is a detachable head,
because it is the only ball I can play with,
the only ball with which I can find the red ball,
the sun-ball. . . .

The last five words of the title of the next selection pretty well explain what it's about—and why it's in this section. The first word in the title may not be so clear. *Metalogue* is a word coined by Gregory Bateson to refer to "a conversation about some problematic subject. This conversation should be such that not only do the participants discuss the problem but the structure of the conversation as a whole is also relevant to the same subject." This particular metalogue is between Bateson—who has worked in anthropology, biology, cybernetics, and psychiatry—and his nine-year-old daughter, who manages to hold her own—at least. Like the George Plimpton selection, this metalogue notices that *rules* have something to do with fun and games, and they have something to do with play, too. Here the play is with ideas, which can be played with as readily as a tennis ball, but what are the rules for that play? And what are limits of control?

METALOGUE: ABOUT GAMES AND BEING SERIOUS

Gregory Bateson

DAUGHTER: Daddy, are these conversations serious?

FATHER: Certainly they are.

D: They're not a sort of game that you play with me?

F: God forbid . . . but they are a sort of game that we play together.

D: Then they're *not* serious!

. . . .

F: Suppose you tell me what you would understand by the words "serious" and a "game."

D: Well . . . if you're . . . I don't know.

F: If I am what?

D: I mean . . . the conversations are serious for me, but if you are only playing a game . . .

F: Steady now. Let's look at what is good and what is bad about "playing" and "games." First of all, I don't mind—not much—about winning or losing. When your questions put me in a tight spot, sure, I try a little harder to think straight and to say clearly what I mean. But I don't bluff and I don't set traps. There is no temptation to cheat.

D: That's just it. It's not serious to you. It's a game. People who cheat just don't know how to *play*. They treat a game as though it were serious.

F: But it *is* serious.

D: No, it isn't—not for you it isn't.

F: Because I don't even want to cheat?

D: Yes—partly that.

F: But do you want to cheat and bluff all the time?

D: No—of course not.

F: Well then?

D: Oh—Daddy—you'll *never* understand.

F: I guess I never will.

F: Look, I scored a sort of debating point just now by forcing you to admit that you don't want to cheat—and then I tied onto that admission the conclusion that therefore the conversations are not "serious" for you either. Was that a sort of cheating?

D: Yes—sort of.

F: I agree—I think it was. I'm sorry.

D: You see, Daddy—if I cheated or wanted to cheat, that would mean that I was not serious about the things we talk about. It would mean that I was only playing a game with you.

F: Yes, that makes sense.

· · · · · · · · · · · ·

D: But it doesn't make sense, Daddy. It's an awful muddle.

F: Yes—a muddle—but still a sort of sense.

D: How, Daddy?

· · · · · · · · · · · ·

F: Wait a minute. This is difficult to say. First of all—I think that we get somewhere with these conversations. I enjoy them very much and I think you do. But also, apart from that, I think that we get some ideas straight and I think that the muddles help. I mean—that if we both spoke logically all the time, we would never get anywhere. We would only parrot all the old cliches that everybody has repeated for hundreds of years.

D: What is a cliché, Daddy?

F: A cliché? It's a French word, and I think it was originally a printer's word. When they print a sentence they have to take the separate letters and put them one by one into a sort of grooved stick to spell out the sentence. But for words and sentences which people use often, the printer keeps little sticks of letters ready made up. And these ready-made sentences are called clichés.

D: But I've forgotten now what you were saying about clichés, Daddy.

F: Yes—it was about the muddles that we get into in these talks and how getting into muddles makes a sort of sense. If we didn't get into muddles, our talks would be like playing rummy without first shuffling the cards.

D: Yes, Daddy—but what about those things—the ready-made sticks of letters?

F: The clichés? Yes—it's the same thing. We all have lots of ready-made phrases and ideas, and the printer has ready-made sticks of letters, all sorted out into phrases. But if the printer wants to print something new—say, something in a new language, he will have to break up all that old sorting of the letters. In the same way, in order to think new thoughts or to say new things, we have to break up all our ready-made ideas and shuffle the pieces.

D: But, Daddy, the printer would not shuffle all the letters? Would he? He wouldn't shake them all up in a bag. He would put them one by one in their places—all the *a*'s in one box and all the *b*'s in another, and all the commas in another, and so on.

F: Yes—that's right. Otherwise he would go mad trying to find an *a* when he wanted it.

· · · · · · · · · · · ·

F: What are you thinking?

D: No—it's only that there are so many questions.

F: For example?

D: Well, I see what you mean about our getting into muddles. That that makes us say new sorts of things. But I am thinking about the printer. He has to keep all his little letters sorted out even though he breaks up all the ready-made phrases. And I am wondering about our muddles. Do we have to keep the little pieces of our thought in some sort of order—to keep from going mad?

F: I think so—yes—but I don't know *what* sort of order. That would be a terribly hard question to answer. I don't think we could get an answer to that question today.

· · · · · · · · · · · ·

F: You said there were "so many questions." Do you have another?

D: Yes—about games and being serious. That's what we started from, and I don't know how or why that led us to talk about our muddles. The way you confuse everything—it's sort of cheating.

F: No, absolutely not.

· · · · · · · · · · · ·

F: You brought up two questions. And really there are a lot more . . . We started from the question about these conversations—are they serious? Or are they a sort of game? And you felt hurt that I might be playing a game, while you were serious. It looks as though a conversation is a game if a person takes part in it with one set of emotions or ideas—but not a "game" if his ideas or emotions are different.

D: Yes, it's if your ideas about the conversation are different from mine . . .

F: If we *both* had the game idea, it would be all right?

D: Yes—of course.

F: Then it seems to be up to me to make clear what I mean by the game idea. I know that I am serious—whatever that means—about the things that we talk about. We talk about ideas. And I know that I play with the ideas in order to understand them and fit them together. It's "play" in the same sense that a small child "plays" with blocks . . . And a child with building blocks is mostly very serious about his "play."

D: But is it a *game*, Daddy? Do you play *against* me?

F: No. I think of it as you and I playing together against the building blocks—the ideas. Sometimes competing a bit—but competing as to who can get the next idea into place. And sometimes we attack each other's bit of building, or I will try to defend my built-up ideas from your criticism. But always in the end we are working together to build the ideas up so that they will stand.

• • • • • • • • • • • •

D: Daddy, do our talks have *rules*? The difference between a game and just playing is that a game has rules.

F: Yes. Let me think about that. I think we do have a sort of rules . . . and I think a child playing with blocks has rules. The blocks themselves make a sort of rules. They will balance in certain positions and they will not balance in other positions. And it would be a sort of cheating if the child used glue to make the blocks stand up in a position from which they would otherwise fall.

D: But what rules do *we* have?

F: Well, the ideas that we play with bring in a sort of rules. There are rules about how ideas will stand up and support each other. And if they are wrongly put together the whole building falls down.

D: No glue, Daddy?

F: No—no glue. Only logic.

• • • • • • • • • • • •

D: But you said that if we always talked logically and did not get into muddles, we could never say anything new. We could only say ready-made things. What did you call those things?

F: Clichés. Yes. Glue is what clichés are stuck together with.

D: But you said "logic," Daddy.

F: Yes, I know. We're in a muddle again. Only I don't see a way out of this particular muddle.

• • • • • • • • • • • •

D: How did we get into it, Daddy?

F: All right, let's see if we can retrace our steps. We were talking about the "rules" of these conversations. And I said that the ideas that we play with have rules of logic . . .

D: Daddy! Wouldn't it be a good thing if we had a few more rules and obeyed them more carefully? Then we might not get into these dreadful muddles.

F: Yes. But wait. You mean that I get us into these muddles because I cheat against rules which we don't have. Or put it this way. That we might have rules which would stop us from getting into muddles—as long as we obeyed them.

D: Yes, Daddy, that's what the rules of a game are for.

F: Yes, but do you want to turn these conversations into *that* sort of a game? I'd rather play canasta—which is fun too.

D: Yes, that's right. We can play canasta whenever we want to. But at the moment I would rather play this game. Only I don't know what sort of a game this is. Nor what sort of rules it has.

F: And yet we have been playing for some time.

D: Yes. And it's been fun.

F: Yes.

. . . .

F: Let's go back to the question which you asked and which I said was too difficult to answer today. We were talking about the printer breaking up his clichés, and you said that he would still keep some sort of order among his letters—to keep from going mad. And then you asked "What sort of order should we cling to so that when we get into a muddle we do not go mad?" It seems to me that the "rules" of the game is only another name for that sort of order.

D: Yes—and cheating is what gets us into muddles.

F: In a sense, yes. That's right. Except that the whole point of the game is that we do get into muddles, and do come out on the other side, and if there were no muddles our "game" would be like canasta or chess—and that is not how we want it to be.

D: Is it *you* that make the rules, Daddy? Is that fair?

F: That, daughter, is a dirty crack. And probably an unfair one. But let me accept it at face value. Yes, it is I who make the rules—after all, I do not want us to go mad.

D: All right. But, Daddy, do you also change the rules? Sometimes?

F: Hmm, another dirty crack. Yes, daughter, I change them constantly. Not all of them, but some of them.

D: I wish you'd tell me when you're going to change them!

F: Hmm—yes—again. I wish I could. But it isn't like that. If it were like chess or canasta, I could tell you the rules, and we could, if we wanted to, stop playing and discuss the rules. And then we could start a new game with the new rules. But what rules would hold us between the two games? While we were discussing the rules?

D: I don't understand.

F: Yes. The point is that the purpose of these conversations is to discover the "rules." It's like life—a game whose purpose is to discover the rules, which rules are always changing and always undiscoverable.

D: But I don't call that a *game* Daddy.

F: Perhaps not. I would call it a game, or at any rate "play." But it certainly is not like chess or canasta. It's more like what kittens and puppies do. Perhaps. I don't know.

. . . .

D: Daddy, why do kittens and puppies play?

F: I don't know—I don't know.

FURTHER THOUGHTS

1. Someone once observed that true art goes beyond the rules—maybe that applies to the art of thinking, too. One of the "muddles" the father and

daughter discover is the one that confuses "logic" with "thought." Here is one paraphrase of the muddle: "Logic is a useful game because it lets you see where your thinking has been. But it is back-looking; it must start and end with the ideas being examined. Bringing in new ideas is cheating. And so, useful as it is, logic is not thought, but a way of seeing what patterns thought has achieved. What, then, is thought?" Try your own paraphrase, or try one of the other muddles.

2. How successfully does this metalogue realize Bateson's notion that its structure should be relevant to its topic?

3. In the metalogue Bateson describes life as "a game whose purpose is to discover the rules, which rules are always changing and always undiscoverable." Do you agree with this description? Why? Whether you agree with it or not, can you recall in your own life certain experiences that might lead to such a conclusion?

4. One cluster of important words in this metalogue is *playing, games,* and *serious.* Another is *muddles, clichés,* and *logic.* What is the connection between these two clusters of ideas? How do the notions about rules and cheating enter in?

As you would expect in a conversation between thinking people, Gregory Bateson and his daughter keep getting into muddles. In a similar situation in the first section we introduced the philosopher Bertrand Russell, whose job it was to help sort out muddles. In this situation we will turn to the scholar Johan Huizinga.

In his book *Homo Ludens* Huizinga offers a scholarly discussion of the role of play in human culture. In the selection included here he outlines some of the formal characteristics of play, making it clear that play differs sharply from labor. But play does not contrast so clearly with work. Work, to the degree that it allows the playful, is to that degree not labor. Play, like work, can make it possible for us to find a sense of community and creativity. Indeed, creativity, we are reminded again and again, depends for its very life on playfulness. Carl Jung said, "The dynamic principle of fantasy is play, which belongs also to the child, and as such it appears to be inconsistent with the principle of serious work. But without this playing with fantasy no creative work has ever yet come to birth. The debt we owe to the play of imagination is incalcuable."

FROM
HOMO LUDENS
Johan Huizinga

First and foremost, then, all play is a voluntary activity. Play to order is no longer play: it could at best be but a forcible imitation of it. By this quality of freedom alone, play marks itself off from the course of the natural process. It is something added thereto and spread out over it like a flowering, an ornament, a garment. Obviously, freedom must be understood here in the wider sense that leaves untouched the philosophical problem of determinism. It may be objected that this freedom does not exist for the animal and the child; they *must* play because their instinct drives them to it and because it serves to develop their bodily faculties and their powers of selection. The term "instinct", however, introduces an unknown quantity, and to presuppose the utility of play from the start is to be guilty of a *petitio principii*. Child and animal play because they enjoy playing, and therein precisely lies their freedom.

Be that as it may, for the adult and responsible human being play is a function which he could equally well leave alone. Play is superfluous. The need for it is only urgent to the extent that the enjoyment of it makes it a need. Play can be deferred or suspended at any time. It is never imposed by physical necessity or moral duty. It is never a task. It is done at leisure, during "free time". Only when play is a recognized cultural function—a rite, a ceremony— is it bound up with notions of obligation and duty.

Here, then, we have the first main characteristic of play: that it is free, is in fact freedom. A second characteristic is closely connected with this, namely, that play is not "ordinary" or "real" life. It is rather a stepping out of "real" life into a temporary sphere of activity with a disposition all of its own. Every child knows perfectly well that he is "only pretending," or that it was "only for fun." How deep-seated this awareness is in the child's soul is strikingly illustrated by the following story, told to me by the father of the boy in question. He found his four-year-old son sitting at the front of a row of chairs, playing "trains." As he hugged him the boy said: "Don't kiss the engine, Daddy, or the carriages won't think it's real." This "only pretending" quality of play betrays a consciousness of the inferiority of play compared with "seriousness", a feeling that seems to be something as primary as play itself. Nevertheless, as we have already pointed out, the consciousness of play being "only a pretend" does not by any means prevent it from proceeding with the utmost seriousness, with an absorption, a devotion that passes into rapture and, temporarily at least, completely abolishes that troublesome "only" feeling. Any game can at any time wholly run away with the players. The contrast between play and seriousness is always fluid. The inferiority of play is continually being offset by the corresponding superiority of its seriousness. Play turns to seriousness and seriousness to play. Play may rise to heights of beauty and sublimity that leave seriousness far beneath. Tricky questions such as these will come up for discussion when we start examining the relationship between play and ritual.

As regards its formal characteristics, all students lay stress on the *disinterestedness* of play. Not being "ordinary" life it stands outside the immediate satisfaction of wants and appetites, indeed it interrupts the appetitive process. It interpolates itself as a temporary activity satisfying in itself and ending there. Such at least is the way in which play presents itself to us in the first instance: as an intermezzo, an *interlude* in our daily lives. As a regularly recurring relaxation, however, it becomes the accompaniment, the complement, in fact an integral part of life in general. It adorns life, amplifies it and is to that extent a necessity both for the individual—as a life function—and for society by reason of the meaning it contains, its significance, its expressive value, its spiritual and social associations, in short, as a culture function. The expression of it satisfies all kinds of communal ideals. It thus has its place in a sphere superior to the strictly biological processes of nutrition, reproduction and self-preservation. This assertion is apparently contradicted by the fact that play, or rather sexual display, is predominant in animal life precisely at the mating-season. But would it be too absurd to assign a place *outside* the purely physiological, to the singing, cooing and strutting of birds just as we do to human play? In all its higher forms the latter at any rate always belongs to the sphere of festival and ritual—the sacred sphere.

Now, does the fact that play is a necessity, that it subserves culture, or indeed that it actually becomes culture, detract from its disinterested character? No, for the purposes it serves are external to immediate material interests or the individual satisfaction of biological needs. As a sacred activity play naturally contributes to the well-being of the group, but in quite another way and by other means than the acquisition of the necessities of life.

Play is distinct from "ordinary" life both as to locality and duration. This is the third main characteristic of play: its secludedness, its limitedness. It is "played out" within certain limits of time and place. It contains its own course and meaning.

Play begins, and then at a certain moment it is "over." It plays itself to an end. While it is in progress all is movement, change, alternation, succession, association, separation. But immediately connected with its limitation as to time there is a further curious feature of play: it at once assumes fixed form as a cultural phenomenon. Once played, it endures as a new-found creation of the mind, a treasure to be retained by the memory. It is transmitted, it becomes tradition. It can be repeated at any time, whether it be "child's play" or a game of chess, or at fixed intervals like a mystery. In this faculty of repetition lies one of the most essential qualities of play. It holds good not only of play as a whole but also of its inner structure. In nearly all the higher forms of play the elements of repetition and alternation (as in the *refrain*), are like the warp and woof of a fabric.

More striking even than the limitation as to time is the limitation as to space. All play moves and has its being with a play-ground marked off beforehand either materially or ideally, deliberately or as a matter of course. Just as there is no formal difference between play and ritual, so the "consecrated spot" cannot be formally distinguished from the play-ground. The arena, the card-table, the magic circle, the temple, the stage, the screen, the tennis court, the court of justice, etc., are all in form and function play-grounds, i.e. forbidden spots, isolated, hedged round, hallowed, within which special rules obtain. All are temporary worlds within the ordinary world, dedicated to the performance of an act apart.

Inside the play-ground an absolute and peculiar order reigns. Here we come across another, very positive feature of play: it creates order, *is* order. Into an imperfect world and into the confusion of life it brings a temporary, a limited perfection. Play demands order absolute and supreme. The least deviation from it "spoils the game," robs it of its character and makes it worthless. The profound affinity between play and order is perhaps the reason why play, as we noted in passing, seems to lie to such a large extent in the field of aesthetics. Play has a tendency to be beautiful. It may be that this aesthetic factor is identical with the impulse to create orderly form, which animates play in all its aspects. The words we use to denote the elements of play belong for the most part to aesthetics, terms with which we try to describe the effects of beauty: tension, poise, balance, contrast, variation, solution, resolution, etc. Play casts a spell over us; it is "enchanting", "captivating". It is invested with the noblest qualities we are capable of perceiving in things: rhythm and harmony.

The element of tension in play to which we have just referred plays a particularly important part. Tension means uncertainty, chanciness; a striving to decide the issue and so end it. The player wants something to "go," to "come off"; he wants to "succeed" by his own exertions. Baby reaching for a toy, pussy patting a bobbin, a little girl playing ball—all want to achieve something difficult, to succeed, to end a tension. Play is "tense", as we say. It is this element of tension and solution that governs all solitary games of skill and application such as puzzles, jig-saws, mosaic-making, patience, target-shooting, and the more play bears the character of competition the more fervent it will be. In gambling and athletics it is at its height. Though play as such is outside the range of good and bad, the element of tension imparts to it a certain ethical value in so far as it means a testing of the player's prowess: his courage, tenacity, resources and, last but not least, his spiritual powers—his "fairness"; because, despite his ardent desire to win, he must still stick to the rules of the game.

These rules in their turn are a very important factor in the play-concept. All play has its rules. They determine what "holds" in the temporary world circumscribed by play. The rules of a game are absolutely binding and allow no doubt. Paul Valéry once in passing gave expression to a very cogent thought when he said: "No scepticism is possible where the rules of a game are concerned, for the principle underlying them is an unshakable truth. . . ." Indeed, as soon as the rules are transgressed the whole play-world collapses. The game is over. The umpire's whistle breaks the spell and sets "real" life going again.

The player who trespasses against the rules or ignores them is a "spoil-sport." The spoil-sport is not the same as the false player, the cheat; for the latter pretends to be playing the game and, on the face of it, still acknowledges the magic circle. It is curious to note how much more lenient society is to the cheat than to the spoil-sport. This is because the spoil-sport shatters the play-world itself. By withdrawing from the game he reveals the relativity and fragility of the play-world in which he had temporarily shut himself with others. He robs play of its *illusion*—a pregnant word which means literally "in-play" (from *inlusio*, *illudere* or *inludere*). Therefore he must be cast out, for he threatens the existence of the play-community. The figure of the spoil-sport is most apparent in boys' games. The little community does not enquire whether the spoil-sport is guilty of defection because he dares not enter into the game or because he is not allowed to. Rather, it does not recognize "not being allowed" and calls it "not daring." For it, the problem of obedience and conscience is no more than fear of punishment. The spoil-sport breaks the magic world, therefore he is a coward and must be ejected. In the world of high seriousness, too, the cheat and the hypocrite have always had an easier time of it than the spoil-sports, here called apostates, heretics, innovators, prophets, conscientious objectors, etc. It sometimes happens, however, that the spoil-sports in their turn make a new community with rules of its own. The outlaw, the revolutionary, the cabbalist or member of a secret society, indeed heretics of all kinds are of a highly associative if not sociable disposition, and a certain element of play is prominent in all their doings.

A play-community generally tends to become permanent even after the game is over. Of course, not every game of marbles or every bridge-party leads to the founding of a club. But the feeling of being "apart together" in an exceptional situation, of sharing something important, of mutually withdrawing from the rest of the world and rejecting the usual norms, retains its magic beyond the duration of the individual game. The club pertains to play as the hat to the head. It would be rash to explain all the associations which the anthropologist calls "phratria"—e.g. clans, brotherhoods, etc.—simply as play-communities; nevertheless it has been shown again and again how difficult it is to draw the line between, on the one hand, permanent social groupings—particularly in archaic cultures with their extremely important, solemn, indeed sacred customs—and the sphere of play on the other.

The exceptional and special position of play is most tellingly illustrated by the fact that it loves to surround itself with an air of secrecy. Even in early childhood the charm of play is enhanced by making a "secret" out of it. This is for *us*, not for the "others." What the "others" do "outside" is no concern of ours at the moment. Inside the circle of the game the laws and customs of ordinary life no longer count. We are different and do things differently. This temporary abolition of the ordinary world is fully acknowledged in child-life, but it is no less evident in the great ceremonial games of savage societies. During the great feast of initiation when the youths are accepted into the male community, it is not the neophytes only that are exempt from the ordinary laws and regulations: there is a truce to all feuds in the tribe. All retaliatory acts and vendettas are suspended. This temporary suspension of normal social life on account of the sacred play-season has numerous traces in the more advanced civilizations as well. Everything that pertains to saturnalia and carnival customs belongs to it. Even with us a bygone age of robuster private habits than ours, more marked class-privileges and a more complaisant police recognized the orgies of young men of rank under the name of a "rag." The saturnalian licence of young men still survives, in fact, in the ragging at English universities, which the *Oxford English Dictionary* defines as "an extensive display of noisy and disorderly conduct carried out in defiance of authority and discipline."

The "differentness" and secrecy of play are most vividly expressed in "dressing up." Here the "extra-ordinary" nature of play reaches perfection. The disguised or masked individual "plays" another part, another being. He *is* another being. The terrors of childhood, open-hearted gaiety, mystic fantasy and sacred awe are all inextricably entangled in this strange business of masks and disguises.

Summing up the formal characteristics of pay we might call it a free activity standing quite consciously outside "ordinary" life as being "not serious", but at the same time absorbing the player intensely and utterly. It is an activity connected with no material interest, and no profit can be gained by it. It proceeds within its own proper boundaries of time and space according to fixed rules and in an orderly manner. It promotes the formation of social groupings which tend to surround themselves with secrecy and to stress their difference from the common world by disguise or other means.

FURTHER THOUGHTS

1. This selection from Huizinga's *Homo Ludens* is basically a list of play's characteristics. Notice that he starts out by numbering the characteristics. The items on the list are linked to one another in different ways. The diagram on page 249 suggests one way of indicating some of these relationships. Try to fill in the blank boxes and to find other links like the three in the diagram that you can identify and label. You should find the summary in the final paragraph of the selection very useful here.
2. The paragraph beginning "The player" on page 246 contains an important discussion of the differences between a spoil-sport and a cheat. Where would you place this discussion on the diagram above? How would you relate it to and link it with the rest of the diagram?
3. The word *ludens* in the title is a form of a Latin word meaning game or play. It shows up in several other modern English words, such as *ludicrous, interlude, delude,* and *illusion.* How are the meanings of these words related?

Play is:

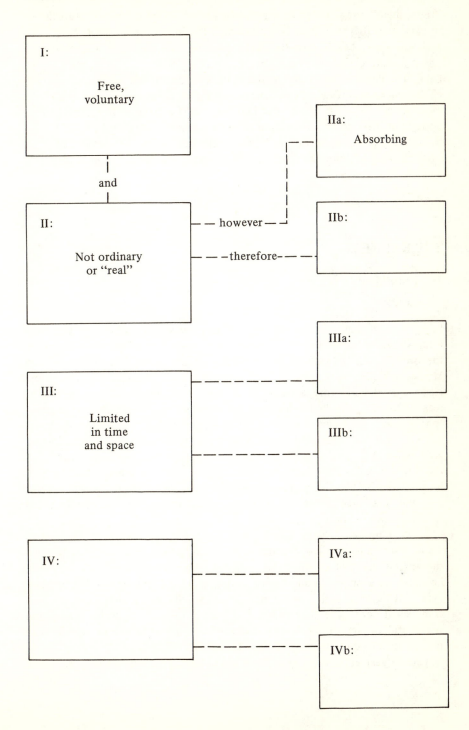

"Here, then," wrote Johan Huizinga, "we have our first main characteristic of play: that it is free, is in fact freedom." The images of freedom change with the times. At one time the image of cast-off chains served. Currently, on movie and television screens, images of play are once again the symbol of being free. People, usually young, run in the surf, or through a meadow, exuberant, joyous—free. Yet perhaps one of the shoddiest tricks we play on ourselves is believing in instant freedom. We say, "I want to be free, free right now!" Free from what? "Free from all those confining roles, all those things other people expect of me." But expectations are hard to get free of. The following selection is a story about a liberated man who needed to play— a lonely liberated man.

THE HARNESS

John Steinbeck

Peter Randall was one of the most highly respected farmers of Monterey County. Once, before he was to make a little speech at a Masonic convention, the brother who introduced him referred to him as an example for young Masons of California to emulate. He was nearing fifty; his manner was grave and restrained, and he wore a carefully tended beard. From every gathering he reaped the authority that belongs to the bearded man. Peter's eyes were grave, too; blue and grave almost to the point of sorrowfulness. People knew there was force to him, but force held caged. Sometimes, for no apparent reason, his eyes grew sullen and mean, like the eyes of a bad dog; but that look soon passed, and the restraint and probity came back into his face. He was tall and broad. He held his shoulders back as though they were braced, and he sucked in his stomach like a soldier. Inasmuch as farmers are usually slouchy men, Peter gained an added respect because of his posture.

Concerning Peter's wife, Emma, people generally agreed that it was hard to see how such a little skin-and-bones woman could go on living, particularly when she was sick most of the time. She weighed eighty-seven pounds. At forty-five, her face was as wrinkled and brown as that of an old, old woman, but her dark eyes were feverish with a determination to live. She was a proud woman, who complained very little. Her father had been a thirty-third degree Mason and Worshipful Master of the Grand Lodge of California. Before he died he had taken a great deal of interest in Peter's Masonic career.

Once a year Peter went away for a week, leaving his wife alone on the farm.

To neighbors who called to keep her company she invariably explained, "He's away on a business trip."

Each time Peter returned from a business trip, Emma was ailing for a month or two, and this was hard on Peter, for Emma did her own work and refused to hire a girl. When she was ill, Peter had to do the housework.

The Randall ranch lay across the Salinas River, next to the foothills. It was an ideal balance of bottom and upland. Forty-five acres of rich level soil brought from the cream of the county by the river in old times and spread out as flat as a board; and eighty acres of gentle upland for hay and orchard. The white farmhouse was as neat and restrained as its owners. The immediate yard was fenced, and in the garden, under Emma's direction, Peter raised button dahlias and immortelles, carnations and pinks.

From the front porch one could look down over the flat to the river with its sheath of willows and cottonwoods, and across the river to the beet fields, and past the fields to the bulbous dome of the Salinas courthouse. Often in the afternoon Emma sat in a rocking-chair on the front porch, until the breeze drove her in. She knitted constantly, looking up now and then to watch Peter working on the flat or in the orchard, or on the slope below the house.

The Randall ranch was no more encumbered with mortgage than any of the others in the valley. The crops, judiciously chosen and carefully tended, paid the interest, made a reasonable living and left a few hundred dollars every year toward paying off the principal. It was no wonder that Peter Randall was respected by his neighbors, and that his seldom spoken words were given attention even when they were about the weather or the way things were going. Let Peter say, "I'm going to kill a pig Saturday," and nearly every one of his hearers went home and killed a pig on Saturday. They didn't know why, but if Peter Randall was going to kill a pig, it seemed like a good, safe, conservative thing to do.

Peter and Emma were married for twenty-one years. They collected a houseful of good furniture, a number of framed pictures, vases of all shapes, and books of a sturdy type. Emma had no children. The house was unscarred, uncarved, unchalked. On the front and back porches footscrapers and thick cocoa-fiber mats kept dirt out of the house.

In the intervals between her illnesses, Emma saw to it that the house was kept up. The hinges of doors and cupboards were oiled, and no screws were gone from the catches. The furniture and woodwork were freshly varnished once a year. Repairs were usually made after Peter came home from his yearly business trips.

Whenever the word went around among the farms that Emma was sick again, the neighbors waylaid the doctor as he drove by on the river road.

"Oh, I guess she'll be all right," he answered their questions. "She'll have to stay in bed for a couple of weeks."

The good neighbors took cakes to the Randall farm, and they tiptoed into the sickroom, where the little skinny bird of a woman lay in a tremendous walnut bed. She looked at them with her bright little dark eyes.

"Wouldn't you like the curtains up a little, dear?" they asked.

"No, thank you. The light worries my eyes."

"Is there anything we can do for you?"

"No, thank you. Peter does for me very well."

"Just remember, if there's anything you think of——"

Emma was such a tight woman. There was nothing you could do for her when she was ill, except to take pies and cakes to Peter. Peter would be in the kitchen, wearing a neat, clean apron. He would be filling a hot water bottle or making junket.

And so, one fall, when the news traveled that Emma was down, the farm-wives baked for Peter and prepared to make their usual visits.

Mrs. Chappell, the next farm neighbor, stood on the river road when the doctor drove by. "How's Emma Randall, doctor?"

"I don't think she's so very well, Mrs. Chappell. I think she's a pretty sick woman."

Because to Dr. Marn anyone who wasn't actually a corpse was well on the road to recovery, the word went about among the farms that Emma Randall was going to die.

It was a long, terrible illness. Peter himself gave enemas and carried bedpans. The doctor's suggestion that a nurse be employed met only beady, fierce refusal in the eyes of the patient; and, ill as she was, her demands were respected. Peter fed her and bathed her, and made up the great walnut bed. The bedroom curtains remained drawn.

It was two months before the dark, sharp bird eyes veiled, and the sharp mind retired into unconsciousness. And only then did a nurse come to the house. Peter was lean and sick himself, not far from collapse. The neighbors brought him cakes and pies, and found them uneaten in the kitchen when they called again.

Mrs. Chappell was in the house with Peter the afternoon Emma died. Peter became hysterical immediately. Mrs. Chappell telephoned the doctor, and then she called her husband to come and help her, for Peter was wailing like a crazy man, and beating his bearded cheeks with his fists. Ed Chappell was ashamed when he saw him.

Peter's beard was wet with his tears. His loud sobbing could be heard throughout the house. Sometimes he sat by the bed and covered his head with a pillow, and sometimes he paced the floor of the bedroom bellowing like a calf. When Ed Chappell self-consciously put a hand on his shoulder and said, "Come on, Peter, come on, now," in a helpless voice, Peter shook his hand off. The doctor drove out and signed the certificate.

When the undertaker came, they had a devil of a time with Peter. He was half mad. He fought them when they tried to take the body away. It was only after Ed Chappell and the undertaker held him down while the doctor stuck him with a hypodermic, that they were able to remove Emma.

The morphine didn't put Peter to sleep. He sat hunched in the corner, breathing heavily and staring at the floor.

"Who's going to stay with him?" the doctor asked. "Miss Jack?" to the nurse.

"I couldn't handle him, doctor, not alone."

"Will you stay, Chappell?"

"Sure, I'll stay."

"Well, look. Here are some triple bromides. If he gets going again, give him one of these. And if they don't work, here's some sodium amytal. One of these capsules will calm him down."

Before they went away, they helped the stupefied Peter into the sitting-room and laid him gently down on the sofa. Ed Chappell sat in an easy-chair and and watched him. The bromides and a glass of water were on the table beside him.

The little sitting-room was clean and dusted. Only that morning Peter had swept the floor with pieces of damp newspaper. Ed built a little fire in the grate, and put on a couple of pieces of oak when the flames were well started. The dark had come early. A light rain spattered against the windows when the wind drove it. Ed trimmed the kerosene lamps and turned the flames low. In the grate the blaze snapped and crackled and the flames curled like hair over the oak. For a long time Ed sat in his easy-chair watching Peter where he lay drugged on the couch. At last Ed dozed off to sleep.

It was about ten o'clock when he awakened. He started up and looked toward the sofa. Peter was sitting up, looking at him. Ed's hand went out toward the bromide bottle, but Peter shook his head.

"No need to give me anything, Ed. I guess the doctor slugged me pretty hard, didn't he? I feel all right now, only a little dopey."

"If you'll just take one of these, you'll get some sleep."

"I don't want sleep." He fingered his draggled beard and then stood up. "I'll go out and wash my face, then I'll feel better."

Ed heard him running water in the kitchen. In a moment he came back into the living-room, still drying his face on a towel. Peter was smiling curiously. It was an expression Ed had never seen on him before, a quizzical, wondering smile. "I guess I kind of broke loose when she died, didn't I?" Peter said.

"Well—yes, you carried on some."

"It seemed like something snapped inside of me," Peter explained. "Something like a suspender strap. It made me all come apart. I'm all right, now, though."

Ed looked down at the floor and saw a little brown spider crawling, and stretched out his foot and stomped it.

Peter asked suddenly, "Do you believe in an afterlife?"

Ed Chappell squirmed. He didn't like to talk about such things, for to talk about them was to bring them up in his mind and think about them. "Well, yes. I suppose if you come right down to it, I do."

"Do you believe that somebody that's—passed on—can look down and see what we're doing?"

"Oh, I don't know as I'd go that far—I don't know."

Peter went on as though he were talking to himself. "Even if she could see me, and I didn't do what she wanted, she ought to feel good because I did it when she was here. It ought to please her that she made a good man of me. If I wasn't a good man when she wasn't here, that'd prove she did it all, wouldn't it? I was a good man, wasn't I, Ed?"

"What do you mean, 'was'?"

"Well, except for one week a year I was good. I don't know what I'll do now. . . . " His face grew angry. "Except one thing." He stood up and stripped off his coat and his shirt. Over his underwear there was a web harness that pulled his shoulders back. He unhooked the harness and threw it off. Then he dropped his trousers, disclosing a wide elastic belt. He shucked this off over his feet, and then he scratched his stomach luxuriously before he put on his clothes again. He smiled at Ed, the strange, wondering smile, again. "I don't know how she got me to do things, but she did. She didn't seem to boss me, but she always made me do things. You know, I don't think I believe in an after-life. When she was alive, even when she was sick, I had to do things she wanted but just the minute she died, it was—why like that harness coming off! I couldn't stand it. It was all over. I'm going to have to get used to going without that harness." He shook his finger in Ed's direction. "My stomach's going to stick out," he said positively. "I'm going to let it stick out. Why, I'm fifty years old."

Ed didn't like that. He wanted to get away. This sort of thing wasn't very decent. "If you'll just take one of these, you'll get some sleep," he said weakly.

Peter had not put his coat on. He was sitting on the sofa in an open shirt. "I don't want to sleep. I want to talk, I guess I'll have to put that belt and harness on for the funeral, but after that I'm going to burn them. Listen, I've got a bottle of whiskey in the barn. I'll go get it."

"Oh no," Ed protested quickly. "I couldn't drink now, not at a time like this."

Peter stood up. "Well, I could. You can sit and watch me if you want. I tell you, it's all over." He went out the door, leaving Ed Chappell unhappy and scandalized. It was only a moment before he was back. He started talking as he came through the doorway with the whiskey. "I only got one thing in my life, those trips. Emma was a pretty bright woman. She knew I'd've gone crazy if I didn't get away once a year. God, how she worked on my conscience when I came back!" His voice lowered confidentially. "You know what I did on those trips?"

Ed's eyes were wide open now. Here was a man he didn't know, and he was becoming fascinated. He took the glass of whiskey when it was handed to him. "No, what did you do?"

Peter gulped his drink and coughed, and wiped his mouth with his hand. "I got drunk," he said. "I went to fancy houses in San Francisco. I was drunk for a week, and I went to a fancy house every night." He poured his glass full again. "I guess Emma knew, but she never said anything. I'd've *busted* if I hadn't got away."

Ed Chappell sipped his whiskey gingerly. "She always said you went on business."

Peter looked at his glass and drank it, and poured it full again. His eyes had begun to shine. "Drink your drink, Ed. I know you think it isn't right—so soon, but no one'll know but you and me. Kick up the fire. I'm not sad."

Chappell went to the grate and stirred the glowing wood until lots of sparks flew up the chimney like little shining birds. Peter filled the glasses and retired to the sofa again. When Ed went back to the chair he sipped from his glass and pretended he didn't know it was filled up. His cheeks were flushing. It didn't seem so terrible, now, to be drinking. The afternoon and the death had receded into an indefinite past.

"Want some cake?" Peter asked. "There's half a dozen cakes in the pantry."

"No, I don't think I will thank you for some."

"You know," Peter confessed, "I don't think I'll eat cake again. For ten years, every time Emma was sick, people sent cakes. It was nice of 'em, of course, only now cake means sickness to me. Drink your drink."

Something happened in the room. Both men looked up, trying to discover what it was. The room was somehow different that it had been a moment before. Then Peter smiled sheepishly. "It was that mantel clock stopped. I don't think I'll start it any more. I'll get a little quick alarm clock that ticks fast. That clack-clack-clack is too mournful." He swallowed his whiskey. "I guess you'll be telling around that I'm crazy, won't you?"

Ed looked up from his glass, and smiled and nodded.

"No, I will not. I can see pretty much how you feel about things. I didn't know you wore that harness and belt."

"A man ought to stand up straight," Peter said. "I'm a natural sloucher." Then he exploded: "I'm a natural fool! For twenty years I've been pretending I was a wise, good man—except for that one week a year." He said loudly, "Things have been dribbled to me. My life's been dribbled out to me. Here, let me fill your glass. I've got another bottle out in the barn, way down under a pile of sacks."

Ed held out his glass to be filled. Peter went on, "I thought how it would be nice to have my whole river flat in sweet peas. Think how it'd be to sit on the front porch and see all those acres of blue and pink, just solid. And when the wind came up over them, think of the big smell. A big smell that would almost knock you over."

"A lot of men have gone broke on sweet peas. 'Course you get a big price for the seed, but too many things can happen to your crop."

"I don't give a damn," Peter shouted. "I want a lot of everything. I want forty acres of color and smell. I want fat women, with breasts as big as pillows. I'm hungry, I tell you, I'm hungry for everything, for a lot of everything."

Ed's face became grave under the shouting. "If you'd just take one of these, you'd get some sleep."

Peter look ashamed. "I'm all right. I didn't mean to yell like that. I'm not just thinking these things for the first time. I been thinking about them for years, the way a kid thinks of vacation. I was always afraid I'd be too old. Or that I'd go first and miss everything. But I'm only fifty, I've got plenty of vinegar left. I told Emma about the sweet peas, but she wouldn't let me. I don't know how she made me do things," he said wonderingly. "I can't remember. She had a way of doing it. But she's gone. I'm going to slouch, Ed—slouch all over the place. I'm going to track dirt into the house. I'm going to get a big fat housekeeper—a big fat one from San Francisco. I'm going to have a bottle of brandy on the shelf all the time."

Ed Chappell stood up and stretched his arms over his head. "I guess I'll go home now, if you feel all right. I got to get some sleep. You better wind that clock, Peter. It don't do a clock any good to stand not running."

The day after the funeral Peter Randall went to work on his farm. The Chappells, who lived on the next place, saw the lamp in his kitchen long before daylight, and they saw his lantern cross the yard to the barn half an hour before they even got up.

Peter pruned his orchard in three days. He worked from first light until he couldn't see the twigs against the sky any more. Then he started to shape the big piece of river flat. He plowed and rolled and harrowed. Two strange men dressed in boots and riding breeches came out and looked at his land. They felt the dirt with their fingers and ran a post-hole digger deep down under the surface, and when they went away they took little paper bags of dirt with them.

Ordinarily, before planting time, the farmers did a good deal of visiting back and forth. They sat on their haunches, picking up handsful of dirt and breaking little clods between their fingers. They discussed markets and crops, recalled other years when beans had done well in a good market, and other years when field peas didn't bring enough to pay for the seed hardly. After a great number of these discussions it usually happened that all the farmers planted the same things. There were certain men whose ideas carried weight. If Peter Randall or Clark DeWitt thought they would put in pink beans and barley, most of the crops would turn out to be pink beans and barley that year; for, since such men were respected and fairly successful, it was conceded that their plans must be based on something besides chance choice. It was generally believed but never stated that Peter Randall and Clark DeWitt had extra reasoning powers and special prophetic knowledge.

When the usual visits started, it was seen that a change had taken place in Peter Randall. He sat on his plow and talked pleasantly enough. He said he hadn't decided yet what to plant, but he said it in such a guilty way that it was plain he didn't intend to tell. When he had rebuffed a few inquiries, the visits to his place stopped and the farmers went over in a body to Clark DeWitt. Clark was putting in Chevalier barley. His decision dictated the major part of the planting in the vicinity.

But because the questions stopped, the interest did not. Men driving by the forty-five acre flat of the Randall place studied the field to try to figure out from the type of work what the crop was going to be. When Peter drove the seeder back and forth across the land no one came in, for Peter had made it plain that his crop was a secret.

Ed Chappell didn't tell on him, either. Ed was a little ashamed when he thought of that night; ashamed of Peter for breaking down, and ashamed of himself for having sat there and listened. He watched Peter narrowly to see whether his vicious intentions were really there or whether the whole conversation had been the result of loss and hysteria. He did notice that Peter's shoulders weren't back and that his stomach stuck out a little. He went to Peter's house and was relieved when he saw no dirt on the floor and when he heard the mantel clock ticking away.

Mrs. Chappell spoke often of the afternoon. "You'd've thought he lost his mind the way he carried on. He just howled. Ed stayed with him part of the night, until he quieted down. Ed had to give him some whiskey to get him to sleep. But," she said brightly, "hard work is the thing to kill sorrow. Peter Randall is getting up at three o'clock every morning. I can see the light in his kitchen window from my bedroom."

The pussywillows burst out in silver drops, and the little weeds sprouted up along the roadside. The Salinas River ran dark water, flowed for a month, and then subsided into green pools again. Peter Randall had shaped his land beautifully. It was smooth and black; no clod was larger than a small marble, and under the rains it looked purple with richness.

And then the little weak lines of green stretched out across the black field. In the dusk a neighbor crawled under the fence and pulled one of the tiny plants. "Some kind of legume," he told his friends. "Field peas, I guess. What did he want to be so quiet about it for? I asked him right out what he was planting, and he wouldn't tell me."

The word ran through the farms, "It's sweet peas. The whole God-damn' forty-five acres is in sweet peas!" Men called on Clark DeWitt then, to get his opinion.

His opinion was this: "People think because you can get twenty to sixty cents a pound for sweet peas you can get rich on them. But it's the most ticklish crop in the world. If the bugs don't get it, it might do good. And then come a hot day and bust the pods and lose your crop on the ground. Or it might come up a little rain and spoil the whole kaboodle. It's all right to put in a few acres and take a chance, but not the whole place. Peter's touched in the head since Emma died."

This opinion was widely distributed. Every man used it as his own. Two neighbors often said it to each other, each one repeating half of it. When too many people said it to Peter Randall he became angry. One day he cried, "Say, whose land is this? If I want to go broke, I've got a damn good right to, haven't I?" And that changed the whole feeling. Men remembered that Peter was a good farmer. Perhaps he had special knowledge. Why, that's who those two men in boots were—soil chemists! A good many of the farmers wished they'd put in a few acres of sweet peas.

They wished it particularly when the vines spread out, when they met each other across the rows and hid the dark earth from sight, when the buds began to form and it was seen the crop was rich. And then the blooms came; forty-five acres of color, forty-five acres of perfume. It was said that you could smell them in Salinas, four miles away. Busses brought the school children out to look at them. A group of men from the seed company spent all day looking at the vines and feeling the earth.

Peter Randall sat on his porch in a rocking-chair every afternoon. He looked down on the great squares of pink and blue, and on the mad square of mixed colors. When the afternoon breeze came up, he inhaled deeply. His blue shirt was open at the throat, as though he wanted to ge the perfume down next his skin.

Men called on Clark DeWitt to get his opinion now. He said, "There's about ten things that can happen to spoil that crop. He's welcome to his sweet peas." But the men knew from Clark's irritation that he was a little jealous. They looked up over the fields of color to where Peter sat on his porch, and they felt a new admiration and respect for him.

Ed Chappell walked up the steps to him one afternoon. "You got a crop there, mister."

"Looks that way," said Peter.

"I took a look. Pods are setting fine."

Peter sighed. "Blooming's nearly over," he said. "I'll hate to see the petals drop off."

"Well, I'd be glad to see 'em drop. You'll make a lot of money, if nothing happens."

Peter took out a bandana handkerchief and wiped his nose, and jiggled it sideways to stop an itch. "I'll be sorry when the smell stops," he said.

Then Ed made his reference to the night of the death. One of his eyes drooped secretly. "Found somebody to keep house for you?"

"I haven't looked," said Peter. "I haven't had time." There were lines of worry about his eyes. But who wouldn't worry, Ed thought, when a single shower could ruin his whole year's crop.

If the year and the weather had been manufactured for sweet peas, they couldn't have been better. The fog lay close to the ground in the mornings when the vines were pulled. When the great piles of vines lay safely on spread canvasses, the hot sun shone down and crisped the pods for the threshers. The neighbors watched the long cotton sacks filling with round black seeds, and they went home and tried to figure out how much money Peter would make on his tremendous crop. Clark DeWitt lost a good part of his following. The men decided to find out what Peter was going to plant next year if they had to follow him around. How did he know, for instance, that this year'd be good for sweet peas? He *must* have some kind of special knowledge.

When a man from the upper Salinas Valley goes to San Francisco on business or for a vacation, he takes a room in the Ramona Hotel. This is a nice arrangement, for in the lobby he can usually find someone from home. They can sit in the soft chairs of the lobby and talk about the Salinas Valley.

Ed Chappell went to San Francisco to meet his wife's cousin who was coming out from Ohio for a trip. The train was not due until the next morning. In the lobby of the Ramona, Ed looked for someone from the Salinas Valley, but he could see only strangers sitting in the soft chairs. He went out to a moving picture show. When he returned, he looked again for someone from home, and still there were only strangers. For a moment he considered glancing over the register, but it was quite late. He sat down to finish his cigar before he went to bed.

There was a commotion at the door. Ed saw the clerk motion with his hand. A bellhop ran out. Ed squirmed around in his chair to look. Outside a man was being helped out of a taxicab. The bellhop took him from the driver and guided him in the door. It was Peter Randall. His eyes were glassy, and his mouth open and wet. He had no hat on his mussed hair. Ed jumped up and strode over to him.

"Peter!"

Peter was batting helplessly at the bellhop. "Let me alone," he explained. "I'm all right. You let me alone, and I'll give you two bits."

Ed called again, "Peter!"

The glassy eyes turned slowly to him, and then Peter fell into his arms. "My old friend," he cried. "Ed Chappell, my old, good friend. What you doing here? Come up to my room and have a drink."

Ed set him back on his feet. "Sure I will," he said. "I'd like a little night-cap."

"Night-cap, hell. We'll go out and see a show, or something."

Ed helped him into the elevator and got him to his room. Peter dropped heavily to the bed and struggled up to a sitting position. "There's a bottle of whiskey in the bathroom. Bring me a drink, too."

Ed brought out the bottle and the glasses. "What you doing, Peter, celebrating the crop? You must've made a pile of money."

Peter put out his palm and tapped it impressively with a forefinger. "Sure I made money—but it wasn't a bit better than gambling. It was just like straight gambling."

"But you got the money."

Peter scowled thoughtfully. "I might've lost my pants," he said. "The whole time, all the year, I been worrying. It was just like gambling."

"Well, you got it, anyway."

Peter changed the subject, then. "I been sick," he said. "I been sick right in the taxicab. I just came from a fancy house on Van Ness Avenue," he explained apologetically, "I just had to come up to the city. I'd'a busted if I hadn't come up and got some of the vinegar out of my system."

Ed looked at him curiously. Peter's head was hanging loosely between his shoulders. His beard was draggled and rough. "Peter—" Ed began, "the night Emma—passed on, you said you was going to—change things."

Peter's swaying head rose up slowly. He stared owlishly at Ed Chappell. "She didn't die dead," he said thickly. "She won't let me do things. She's worried me all year about those peas." His eyes were wondering. "I don't know how she does it." Then he frowned. His palm came out, and he tapped it again. "But you mark, Ed Chappell, I won't wear that harness, and I damn well won't ever wear it. You remember that." His head dropped forward again. But in a moment he looked up. "I been drunk," he said seriously. "I been to fancy houses." He edged out confidentially toward Ed. His voice dropped to a heavy whisper. "But it's all right, I'll fix it. When I get back, you know what I'm going to do? I'm going to put in electric lights. Emma always wanted electric lights." He sagged sideways on the bed.

Ed Chappell stretched Peter out and undressed him before he went to his own room.

FURTHER THOUGHTS

1. Notice the kind of words used early in the story to describe Peter Randall: *respected, example, grave, restrained, safe, conservative.* Consider them in the light of what you know about him by the end of the story. And notice, by way of contrast, the words used to describe Emma.
2. What else in Peter's life was like that harness he took off? What are your harnesses? What does the story suggest to you about the need for play?
3. Why, do you think, did Peter plant forty-five acres of sweet peas?
4. Suppose that tomorrow you were freed from the burden of expectations others have of you. What would you do?
5. Are there certain expectations that come only from yourself, expectations that no one else taught you? Check your dreams carefully. Are there other people in them? What do you expect of them?

"To grow," says Erik Erikson in the following selection, "means to be divided into different parts which move at different rates"—an idea that Forster's racers would probably find puzzling. Furthermore, says Erikson, play is very important to this complicated process of growing—a statement that might be even more puzzling to the racers. Play is more than simply diversion from labor. Erikson provides a psychologist's definition, concluding that through play we can turn the normal limitations of our daily reality into toys—things like gravity, fate, time, or our own bodily drives.

TOYS AND REASONS

Erik Erikson

Let us take as our text for the beginning of this more reassuring chapter a play episode described by a rather well-known psychologist. The occasion, while not pathological, is nevertheless a tragic one: a boy named Tom Sawyer, by verdict of his aunt, must whitewash a fence on an otherwise faultless spring morning. His predicament is intensified by the appearance of an age mate named Ben Rogers, who indulges in a game. It is Ben, the man of leisure, whom we want to observe with the eyes of Tom, the working man.

> He took up his brush and went tranquilly to work. Ben Rogers hove in
> sight presently—the very boy, of all boys, whose ridicule he had been

dreading. Ben's gait was the hop-skip-and-jump—proof enough that his heart was light and his anticipations high. He was eating an apple, and giving a long, melodious whoop, at intervals, followed by a deep-toned ding-dong-dong, ding-dong-dong, for he was personating a steamboat. As he drew near, he slackened speed, took the middle of the street, leaned far over to starboard and rounded to ponderously and with laborious pomp and circumstance—for he was personating the *Big Missouri*, and considered himself to be drawing nine feet of water. He was boat and captain and engine-bells combined, so he had to imagine himself standing on his own hurricane-deck giving the orders and executing them:

. . . "Stop the stabboard! Ting-a-ling-ling! Stop the labboard! Come ahead on the stabboard! Stop her! Let your outside turn over slow! Ting-a-ling-ling! Chow-ow-ow! Get out that head-line! *Lively* now! Come—out with your spring-line—what're you about there! Take a turn round that stump with the bight of it! Stand by that stage, now—let her go! Done with the engines, sir! Ting-a-ling-ling! *Sh't! sh't! sh't!*" (trying the gauge-cocks).

Tom went on whitewashing—paid no attention to the steamboat. Ben stared a moment, and then said:

"Hi-*yi! You're* up a stump, ain't you! . . . You got to work, hey?"

My clinical impression of Ben Rogers is a most favorable one, and this on all three counts: organism, ego, and society. For he takes care of the body by munching an apple; he simultaneously enjoys imaginary control over a number of highly conflicting items (being a steamboat and parts thereof, as well as being the captain of said steamboat, and the crew obeying said captain); while he loses not a moment in sizing up social reality when, on navigating a corner, he sees Tom at work. By no means reacting as a steamboat would, he knows immediately how to pretend sympathy though he undoubtedly finds his own freedom enhanced by Tom's predicament.

Flexible lad, we would say. However, Tom proves to be the better psychologist: he is going to put Ben to work. Which shows that psychology is at least the second-best thing to, and under some adverse circumstances may even prove superior to ordinary adjustment.

In view of Ben's final fate it seems almost rude to add interpretation to defeat, and to ask what Ben's play may mean. I presented this question to a class of psychiatric social-work students. Most of the answers were, of course, of the traumatic variety, for in what other way could Ben become accessible to "case work"? Ben must have been a frustrated boy, the majority agreed, to take the trouble to play so strenuously. The possible frustrations ranged from oppression by a tyrannical father from whom he escapes in fantasy by becoming a bossy captain, to a bedwetting or toilet trauma of some kind which now made him want to be a boat drawing nine feet of water. Some answers concerned the more obvious circumstance that he wanted to be big, and this in the form of a captain, the idol of his day.

My contribution to the discussion consisted of the consideration that Ben is a growing boy. To grow means to be divided into different parts which move at different rates. A growing boy has trouble in mastering his gangling body as well as his divided mind. He wants to be good, if only out of expediency, and always finds he has been bad. He wants to rebel, and finds that almost against his will he has given in. As his time perspective permits a glimpse of approaching adulthood he finds himself acting like a child. One "meaning" of Ben's play could be that it affords his ego a temporary victory over his gangling body and self by making a well-functioning whole out of brain (captain), the nerves and muscles of will (signal system and engine), and the whole bulk of the body (boat). It permits him to be an entity within which he is his own boss, because he obeys himself. At the same time, he chooses his metaphors from the tool world of the young machine age, and anticipates the identity of the machine god of his day: the captain of the *Big Missouri*.

Play, then, is a function of the ego, an attempt to synchronize the bodily and the social processes with the self. Ben's fantasy could well contain a phallic and locomotor element, a powerful boat in a mighty stream makes a good symbol. A captain certainly is a fitting father image, and beyond that, an image of well-delineated patriarchal power. Yet the emphasis, I think, should be on the ego's need to master the various areas of life, and especially those in which the individual finds his self, his body, and his social role wanting and trailing. To hallucinate ego mastery and yet also to practice it in an intermediate reality between phantasy and actuality is the purpose of play—but play, as we shall see presently, is the undisputed master of only a slim margin of existence. What is play—and what is it not? Let us consult language, and then return to children.

The sunlight playing on the waves qualifies for the attribute "playful" because it faithfully remains within the rules of the game. It does not really interfere with the chemical world of the waves. It insists only on an intermingling of appearances. These patterns change with effortless rapidity and with a repetitiveness which promises pleasing phenomena within a predictable range without ever creating the same configuration twice.

When man plays he must intermingle with things and people in a similarly uninvolved and light fashion. He must do something which he has chosen to do without being compelled by urgent interests or impelled by strong passion; he must feel entertained and free of any fear or hope of serious consequences. He is on vacation from social and economic reality—or, as is most commonly emphasized: he *does not work*. It is this opposition to work which gives play a number of connotations. One of these is "mere fun"—whether it is hard to do or not. As Mark Twain commented, "constructing artificial flowers . . . is work, while climbing the Mont Blanc is only amusement." In Puritan times and places, however, mere fun always connoted sin; the Quakers warned that you must "gather the flowers of pleasure in the fields of duty." Men of equally Puritan mind could permit play only because they believed that to find "relief from moral activity is in itself a moral necessity." Poets, however, place the emphasis elsewhere: "Man is perfectly human only when he plays," said Schiller. Thus play is a borderline phenomenon to a number of human activities and, in its own playful way, it tries to elude definition.

It is true that even the most strenuous and dangerous play is by definition not work; it does not produce commodities. Where it does, it "goes professional." But this fact, from the start, makes the comparison of adult and child's play somewhat senseless; for the adult is a commodity-producing and commodity-exchanging being, whereas the child is only preparing to become one. To the working adult, play is re-creation. It permits a periodical stepping out from those forms of defined limitation which are his social reality.

Take *gravity*: to juggle, to jump, or to climb adds unused dimensions to the awareness of our body. Play here gives a sense of divine leeway, of excess space.

Take *time*: in trifling, in dallying, we lazily thumb our noses at this, our slave-driver. Where every minute counts, playfullness vanishes. This puts competitive sports on the borderline of play: they seem to make concessions to the pressure of space and time, only to defeat this very pressure by a fraction of a yard or of a second.

Take *fate* and *causality* which have determined who and what we are, and where. In games of chance we re-establish equality before fate, and secure a virgin chance to every player willing to observe a few rules which, if compared with the rules of reality, seem arbitrary and senseless. Yet they are magically convincing, like the reality of a dream, and they demand absolute compliance. Let a player forget that such play must remain his free choice, let him become possessed by the demon of gambling, and playfulness vanishes again. He is a gambler, not a player.

Take *social reality*, and our defined cubicles in it. In play-acting we can be what in life we could not or would not be. But as the play-actor begins to believe in his impersonation he comes closer to a state of hysteria, if not worse; while if he tries, for purposes of gain, to make others believe in his "role" he becomes an impostor.

Take our *bodily drives*. The bulk of the nation's advertising effort exploits our wish to play with necessity, to make us believe, for example, that to inhale and to eat are not pleasurable necessities, but a fanciful game with ever new and sensuous nuances. Where the need for these nuances becomes compulsive, it creates a general state of mild addiction and gluttony, which ceases to transmit a sense of abundance and, in fact, produces an undercurrent of discontent.

Last but not least, in *love life* we describe as sex play the random activities preceding the final act, which permit the partners to choose body part, intensity, and tempo ("what, and with which, and to whom," as the limerick has it). Sex play ends when the final act begins, narrowing choice, dictating tempo, and giving rein to "nature." Where one of the preparatory random acts becomes compelling enough to completely replace the final act, playfulness vanishes and perversion begins.

This list of playful situations in a variety of human endeavors indicates the narrow area with which our ego can feel superior to the confinement of space and time and to the definitiveness of social reality—free from the compulsions of conscience and from impulsions of irrationality. Only with these limitations, then, can man feel at one with his ego; no wonder he feels "only human when he plays." But this presupposes one more most decisive condition: he must play rarely and work most of the time. He must have a defined role in society. Playboys and gamblers are both envied and resented by the working man. We like to see them exposed or ridiculed, or we put them to worse than work by forcing them to live in luxurious cages.

FURTHER THOUGHTS

1. At the end of the selection Erikson says that we "must play rarely and work most of the time." What do you think of this final emphasis? Is it puritanism? realism? or what?
2. How does Erikson's definition of *play* compare with your own? Can you think of activities you would call play that aren't covered by Erikson's definition? Can you think of activities that are covered by his definition but which you would not call play?
4. When we play, says Erikson, we turn some of our normal limitations into toys. He then gives six examples. Can you think of others?

We have checked around a bit and found out that many parents have had the same experience. Their youngster is gulled by the world's greatest pusher, the television advertiser, into wanting a gaudy, overpriced, electromechanical push-button toy. The parent yields, knowing damn well that the toy will disappoint. Maybe that's the lesson—an expensive one—that makes the experience worth something. Even if the toy doesn't break too quickly, it is still discarded shortly after it is unwrapped. Sometimes the box it came in gets played with more than the toy itself. The box gives the imagination some room to work in, something the push-button gadget can never do.

In "Toys and Reason" Erik Erikson says that play allows us to turn the limitations of everyday reality into toys. And that may be the problem. Ready-made, preassembled toys mimic the limitations of everyday reality too closely. The French critic Roland Barthes argues in the following short selection that the quality of the toys to a great extent determines more than the quality of the play: It can determine, too, the quality of the child, and in time the quality of the adult that child grows into.

TOYS

Roland Barthes

French toys: one could not find a better illustration of the fact that the adult Frenchman sees the child as another self. All the toys one commonly sees are essentially a microcosm of the adult world; they are all reduced copies of human objects, as if in the eyes of the public the child was, all told, nothing but a smaller man, a homunculus to whom must be supplied objects of his own size.

Invented forms are very rare: a few sets of blocks, which appeal to the spirit of do-it-yourself, are the only ones which offer dynamic forms. As for the others, French toys *always mean something*, and this something is always entirely socialized, constituted by the myths or the techniques of modern adult life: the Army, Broadcasting, the Post Office, Medicine (miniature instrument-cases, operating theatres for dolls), School, Hair-Styling (dryers for permanent-waving), the Air Force (Parachutists), Transport (trains, Citroens, Vedettes, Vespas, petrol-stations), Science (Martian toys).

The fact that French toys *literally* prefigure the world of adult functions obviously cannot but prepare the child to accept them all, by constituting for him, even before he can think about it, the alibi of a Nature which has at all times created soldiers, postmen and Vespas. Toys here reveal the list of all the things the adult does not find unusual: war, bureaucracy, ugliness, Martians, etc. It is not so much, in fact, the imitation which is the sign of an abdication, as its literalness: French toys are like a Jivaro head, in which one recognizes, shrunken to the size of an apple, the wrinkles and hair of an adult. There exist, for instance, dolls which urinate; they have an oesophagus, one gives them a bottle, they wet their nappies; soon, no doubt, milk will turn to water in their stomachs. This is meant to prepare the little girl for the causality of house-keeping, to 'condition' her to her future role as mother. However, faced with this world of faithful and complicated objects, the child can only identify himself as owner, as user, never as creator; he does not invent the world, he uses it; there are, prepared for him, actions without adventure, without wonder, without joy. He is turned into a little stay-at-home householder who does not even have to invent the mainsprings of adult causality; they are supplied to him ready-made: he has only to help himself, he is never allowed to discover anything from start to finish. The merest set of blocks, provided it is not too refined, implies a very different learning of the world: then, the child does not in any way create meaningful objects, it matters little to him whether they have an adult name; the actions he performs are not those of a user but those of a demiurge. He creates forms which walk, which roll, he creates life, not property: objects now act by themselves, they are no longer an inert and complicated material in the palm of his hand. But such toys are rather rare: French toys are usually based on imitation, they are meant to produce children who are users, not creators.

The bourgeois status of toys can be recognized not only in their forms, which are all functional, but also in their substances. Current toys are made of a graceless material, the product of chemistry, not of nature. Many are now moulded from complicated mixtures; the plastic material of which they are made has an appearance at once gross and hygienic, it destroys all the pleasure, the sweetness, the humanity of touch. A sign which fills one with consternation is the gradual disappearance of wood, in spite of its being an ideal material because of its firmness and its softness, and the natural warmth of its touch. Wood removes, from all the forms which it supports, the wounding quality of angles which are too sharp, the chemical coldness of metal. When the child handles it and knocks it, it neither vibrates nor grates, it has a sound at once muffled and sharp. It is a familiar and poetic substance, which does not sever the child from close contact with the tree, the table, the floor. Wood does not wound or break down; it does not shatter, it wears out, it can last a long time, live with the child, alter little by little the relations between the object and the hand. If it dies, it is in dwindling, not in swelling out like those mechanical toys which disappear behind the hernia of a broken spring. Wood makes essential objects, objects for all time. Yet there hardly remain any of these wooden toys from the Vosges, these fretwork farms with their animals, which were only possible, it is true, in the days of the craftsman. Henceforth, toys are chemical in substance and colour; their very material introduces one to a coenaesthesis of use, not pleasure. These toys die in fact very quickly, and once dead, they have no posthumous life for the child.

FURTHER THOUGHTS

1. Barthes is speaking of French toys. To what extent is what he says applicable to American toys?
2. Barthes says that toys teach the child to accept "all the things the adult does not find unusual." Take a trip through a toy store and see what you can find out about the nature of the adult world.
3. Make a list of the most popular "adult toys" today. What do they teach you about the adult world?
4. Think for a bit about the most popular toys among children today. How do the elements of control and ecstasy enter into the play allowed by such toys?
5. What, precisely, does Barthes mean by his distinction between being a creator and being an owner?

It is just possible that the toys we play with form a large part of what we can be, because they form our expectations of what is to be. If that is so, then what about all those manufactured things that surround us as adults? If our toys are not playful, what does that say about the adult-sized products around us? We close this section with a short passage from Remy Kwant.

FROM
THE PHENOMENOLOGY OF EXPRESSION

Remy Kwant

In present-day society there is a shortage of playfulness. The rigid organization of the world of work left little room for playfulness in the recent past, and the situation existing in the world of work influenced education. The average worker was viewed as someone unable to take an initiative and therefore the labor order left no room for initiative on his part. This view continues to exercise influence even today.

The lack of playfulness in our expression manifests itself also very strongly in many newly built residential sections of cities. Monotony and lack of creative imagination are the predominant feature. Although the situation is improving somewhat, it is still far from satisfactory. Utilitarian provisions are much better, of course, than they used to be, but very little seems to be done about providing for man's fundamental need for playfulness. This condition may be connected with the modern divorce between work and art. In former eras work and art were integrated, at least far more than today, now they are separated. Thus work developed as an artless pursuit, and art became something "eccentric." The building of houses must again become a real art if the residential areas are to leave room for playfulness. The builders must keep in mind that it is very difficult to live playfully in an environment that is not built in a playful way.

FURTHER THOUGHTS

1. Is the building you are in playful in any way? Does laughter seem strange where you are?
2. If you were to design a playful bank, one that laughed at the absurdities of money, yet at the same time acknowledged its seriousness, how would you do it? Is the idea of a playful bank so strange? They make them for youngsters. How about a playful church? (People used to dance in cathedrals; pews are rather late intruders onto the dance floor.) How about a playful hospital? funeral home? How about a playful wedding ceremony?
3. Why are pick-up trucks more playful than sports cars?

4th Interlude

The glory of the ancient Greeks seems to have been based on learning how to loot methodically their part of the Mediterranean Sea. With the leisure they bought that way the citizens of Athens had time to talk, and they began to take their talk very seriously. Some of them tried to decide what it was they now had. Aristotle, the great Greek philosopher and scientist who lived over 2,000 years ago, thought carefully about the meanings of work, play, and leisure.

His thoughts are discussed in the following selection. Aristotle says, briefly, that we play in order to refresh ourselves that we might work, and we work in order to earn for ourselves the fruits of leisure. Leisure becomes the goal. But leisure is, to him, the time when one's energies are devoted to thought, especially to speculative thought. It is the time in which a person tries to understand the nature of the world in which he is working, and the nature of the self that demands play and esteem.

WORK AND LEISURE

from The Great Ideas Today, 1965

Work and leisure are always thought of as opposed to each other. If one is at work, he is by that very fact not at leisure. A leisure class is a class that does not work, and does not have to work. As an extension of this same way of thinking, work becomes identified with activity as such, and leisure then comes to mean free time, that is, a period of time in which one does not have to do anything. Hence also, by a still further extension, leisure gets to mean idleness. Work is then equated with being occupied or employed, and leisure with being unoccupied or unemployed. We thus face the paradoxical conclusion that as society provides more leisure for more people, it also produces more unemployed.

Such a conclusion is as uncomfortable as it is paradoxical. A society in which the great majority of the people had literally nothing to do would be a bored society. Hence, it is not without significance that many people are now calling for a reexamination of the meaning and nature of work and leisure. Toward such a reexamination, the *Great Books*, especially those written by the ancients who were privileged to belong to a leisure class, can make a distinct contribution. In particular, they enable us to make and develop a threefold distinction between: (1) leisure and free time; (2) leisure and subsistence-work; and (3) leisure and play.

Leisure and Free Time

The first distinction is illuminated by the following passage from Aristotle's *Politics*, where he is discussing the best society:

> The whole of life is further divided into two parts, business and leisure, war and peace, and of actions some aim at what is necessary and useful, and some at what is honourable. And the preference given to one or the other class of actions must necessarily be like the preference given to one or other part of the soul and its actions over the other; there must be war for the sake of peace, business for the sake of leisure, things useful and necessary for the sake of things honourable. . . . For men must be able to engage in business and go to war, but leisure and peace are better; they must do what is necessary and indeed what is useful, but what is honourable is better (*Politics* VII, *Great Books of the Western World,* Vol. 9, p. 538a–b).

Leisure, in this passage, is grouped with peace and with actions that aim at the honorable; it is identified as that for the sake of which business and compulsory or useful actions are done. Happiness itself, for Aristotle, consists in activity. The same is true of leisure. In fact, leisure is one of the main constituents of a happy life. The active character of leisure, in Aristotle's view, is more prominent in the original Greek than in the English translation. To contrast leisure with "business" connotes too readily that leisure is merely not being busy—"business" being the positive notion of which leisure is merely the negation. But in Aristotle's Greek, it is the other way round. "Leisure" is the positive term (*scholé*), and its opposite is "nonleisure" (*ascholé*), which is here translated as "business."

Aristotle's view would stand out more clearly if "leisure" in English were a verb as well as a noun, as it is in Greek. Thus it is perfectly natural for Aristotle to talk about the "activity of leisuring" and to claim that "to leisure is better and more perfect than to nonleisure." He may sometimes use "leisure" (*scholé*) as a noun to mean time free from work. But there is no implication that leisure is a mere privation, mere lack of occupation, or idleness. In fact, the sense is all the other way. Leisure is highly active. As we shall see, he wants man "to leisure well" (*scholazein kalos*). For him, there would be nothing paradoxical, as there is for us, in speaking of "leisuring long and hard" and being "tired and worn out from leisuring."

Leisure, for Aristotle, is honorable or noble, whereas work, he says, is "useful and necessary." Yet he also maintains, as we shall see, that leisure, too, is a necessary activity. Obviously, work and leisure must be necessary in two different ways. In fact, we can distinguish three different ways in which an activity may be necessary for us. Some activities are absolutely necessary and cannot be omitted or eliminated, given the kind of creature man is; such are the biological activities of eating, sleeping, and the like. Other activities are necessary but can be eliminated, provided other ways are available for achieving the same result; such is the work of producing food, shelter, and all the economic goods that we need for life. This is work that can be escaped if we possess sufficient wealth or productive property to obtain the necessary goods without working. Finally, some activities are necessary not for life, but for the good life; these might be said to be morally necessary, whereas the previous activities are biologically or economically necessary.

Aristotle, in the passage quoted above, is evidently distinguishing leisure from those activities that are economically necessary—the activities we must engage in just to remain alive. We are not free to do them or leave them undone. Time spent on such compulsory activities is not free time.

Leisure, in contrast, occupies our free time. We pursue it in the time that remains free after we have met the necessary demands of living. This fact helps to explain why leisure is sometimes confused with free time itself. Free time is a condition for leisure. If we had no free time, if all our time were consumed in satisfying merely the biological and economic needs of the body, we would not be able to engage in leisure activities.

The fact that leisure is dependent upon free time is no reason, however, for identifying the two. Thoreau went to Walden Pond to reduce his work to a minimum and found that working six weeks a year was sufficient to provide him with food and shelter. But he did not so drastically reduce his work merely in order to do nothing. He reduced his work load because he had more important things *to do*. Being at leisure was for him anything but being inactive, as his account of life at Walden eloquently testifies.

Leisure and Subsistence-work

Leisure is not opposed to work as inactivity to activity. What, then, is the basis of the opposition between them? To answer this question, it is helpful to consider the simplest form of work. Perhaps the simplest (if not, in fact, also the original) form of work is that of a man working with his hands to provide for his daily sustenance. According to Aquinas, manual labor can be understood as standing for "all human occupations by which man lawfully gains a livelihood." This labor may have subsidiary aims, such as supplying a remedy for idleness, a curb of concupiscence, or a surplus for almsgiving, but its main purpose, according to Aquinas is to provide food to sustain life (GBWW, Vol. 20, p. 667a,c). We might well name this form of work after its primary end and call it subsistence-work.

In the past, subsistence-work has always been associated with toil and drudgery. The *Georgics* of Virgil, for example, are devoted to celebrating the life

of the farmer. That life, as Virgil pictures it, has its delights. But work is not one of them. Although not without its satisfactions and compensations, work is usually described as hard and painful, a laborious drudgery. "Work has conquered all," he declares, but it is only as "remorseless and under the spur of harsh necessity" (GBWW, Vol. 13. p. 41a, lines 145-146). Virgil's adjective here is the Latin word *improbus*, and this means not only remorseless and persistent, but also insatiable, bad, and disliked. Labor is usually associated with what is hard and painful, and with what one would gladly avoid if one could, along with disease, and sad old age, and death (*ibid* p. 69a, lines 67-68). Labor appears with the same associates in the *Aeneid*, where it is shown on the outskirts of the "ghostly realms of Dis," accompanied also by grief and care, fear, and famine, and loathly want (*ibid*. p. 218b, lines 274-276).

Virgil's description of subsistence-work offers further means of distinguishing it from leisure activity. The drudgery lies not only in its being hard and strenuous, but even more in its being recurrent and repetitive; it has to be done over and over again. For this reason its compensation lies not within the activity itself, but in its extrinsic product or result. All these characteristics are caught and summed up in the famous lines in *Georgic* I in which Virgil declares that except for "patient toil," all things, "by fate impelled, speed on to the worse, and, backward borne, glide from us, just as an oarsman rowing his boat against the current, need but relax his arms a moment and with headlong force the current sweeps him down the hurrying tide" (*ibid*. p. 42b, lines 200-203).

Work in the sense of subsistence-work is obviously an evil, and it is not difficult to understand why men should see in its necessity a sign of punishment for some ancient wrong or sin. As Aristotle notes: "That in a well-ordered state the citizens should have leisure and not have to provide for their daily wants is generally acknowledged, but there is a difficulty in seeing how this leisure is to be attained" (*Politics* II, GBWW, Vol. 9, p. 465c). For him, as for the ancient writers in general, such work should be left to slaves, so that the citizens might be free to devote themselves to leisure activities.

In one place in his *Politics* Aristotle declares, with prophetic insight, that slaves would no longer be necessary if men possessed automatic machinery: "If every instrument could accomplish its own work, obeying or anticipating the will of others, like the statues of Daedalus, or the tripods of Hephaestus, . . . if, in like manner, the shuttle would weave and the plectrum touch the lyre without a hand to guide them, chief workmen would not want servants, nor masters slaves" (*ibid.,* p. 447b-c).

We now do possess automated slaves, and nowhere have the results been so dramatic as in agriculture, the basic work of subsistence. We have learned how to produce increasing quantities of food with ever decreasing numbers of men, who thus have been released for other pursuits, and even those still engaged in the production of food have little of the pain and drudgery that once characterized the work of the farmer.

Leisure and Play

Leisure, as we have seen, is not to be confused with free time. It is an activity or use of free time. In this it differs from subsistence-work. Leisure is like such work in being a serious activity. To further characterize it, we need to see how it differs from other free activities, that is, from other uses of our free time. Here again Aristotle merits consideration. As already noted, he regards work, or "business," as a means, serving leisure as an end. Hence, for a full understanding of leisure, we need to consider activities that are pursued as ends, *i.e.*, intrinsically worth doing for their own sake. He provides an analysis of such activities in the following passage from the *Ethics* :

> Those activities are desirable in themselves from which nothing is sought beyond the activity. And of this nature virtuous actions are thought to be; for to do noble and good deeds is a thing desirable for its own sake. Pleasant amusements also are thought to be of this nature; we choose them not for the sake of other things; for we are injured rather than benefited by them, since we are led to neglect our bodies and our property. . . .
> Happiness . . . does not lie in amusement; it would, indeed, be strange if the end were amusement, and one were to take trouble and suffer hardship all one's life in order to amuse oneself. For, in a word, everything that we choose we choose for the sake of something else—except happiness, which is an end. Now to exert oneself and work for the sake of amusement seems silly and utterly childish. But to amuse oneself in order that one may exert oneself, as Anacharsis puts it, seems right; for amusement is a sort of relaxation, and we need relaxation because we cannot work continuously. Relaxation, then, is not an end; for it is taken for the sake of activity (*Ethics* X GBWW, Vol. 9, p. 43 1a-c).

Aristotle is not denying here that a person may subjectively and in his own mind pursue amusement or play for its own sake, without thinking of any further purpose. Men play golf and cards and go to the movies without needing any further justification than the activities themselves. They do so for the pleasure they obtain from them, and pleasure is itself an end of action needing no further justification.

Play, however, is not only and wholly an end. It also serves as a means; in fact, we need it as a means because of the weakness of the flesh. Aristotle is pointing this out when he notes that play and amusement perform a therapeutic function. We are incapable of working or "leisuring" continuously and must turn aside, from time to time, for relaxation, recuperation, recreation. Play for such purposes is therapeutic and a means to other activities.

Yet Aristotle's main reason for not identifying leisure with play lies elsewhere; the point is not that play is a means as well as an end, whereas leisure is wholly an end. Play is not serious enough, Aristotle claims, to count as the end of life. He expands upon this point in another text in which he also further develops the meaning of leisure:

> Nature herself, as has been often said, requires that we should be able, not only to work well, but to use leisure well; for, as I must repeat once again, the first principle of all action is leisure. Both are required, but leisure is better than occupation and is its end; and therefore the question must be asked, what ought we to do when at leisure? Clearly we ought not to be amusing ourselves, for then amusement would be the end of life. But if this is inconceivable, and amusement is needed more amid serious occupations than at other times (for he who is hard at work has need of relaxation, and amusement gives relaxation, whereas occupation is always accompanied with exertion and effort), we should introduce amusements only at suitable times, and they should be our medicines, for the emotion which they create in the soul is a relaxation, and from the pleasure we obtain rest. But leisure of itself gives pleasure and happiness and enjoyment of life, which are experienced, not by the busy man, but by those who have leisure. For he who is occupied has in view some end which he has not attained; but happiness is an end, since all men deem it to be accompanied with pleasure and not with pain (*Politics* VIII, GBWW, Vol. 9, p. 543a–b).

Thus, according to Aristotle, it is by "leisuring well" that we enjoy happiness. In fact, leisure, for him, *is* happiness. Happiness is a serious activity and, hence, not to be equated with a play or amusement. Not the playboy, but the virtuous man is the happy man. For Aristotle the virtues include both the moral and intellectual excellences that develop and perfect both the individual and society, including the activities of love and friendship. They might be called simply the goods of the spirit and of civilization.

To identify leisure with virtuous activity, in Aristotle's sense, implies that it is obligatory, but obligatory morally, and not physically, as subsistence-work is. Play or amusement is not obligatory or necessary in a moral sense, although it may be necessary physically, in that we are so constructed as to be incapable of continuous serious activity. It is simply desirable.

The meaning of leisure is thus clarified by comparing and contrasting it with work and play. Leisure is like both work and play in being an activity, a use of time, and not just the absence of doing anything. It is like work, and unlike play, in being both serious and necessary. But it is not necessary in the same way that work is. Work, understood as that which is needed for our subsistence, is physically necessary, necessary to support life; leisure activity is morally necessary, indispensable for the good life.

In fact, work, as distinguished from play, can be considered as having two forms: subsistence-work and leisure-work. The first of these has its compensations outside of itself, in its product or reward; it is also a compulsory or unfree work which, because of its drudgery, should be lessened as much as possible; and, in fact, is being eliminated through the use of machinery. The second (that is, leisure-work) is intrinsically rewarding and would be pursued even without extrinsic compensation; it is an activity of our free time. In these two respects, leisure is similar to play and opposed to subsistence-work.

The way our life is organized today makes it extremely difficult to find activities that exemplify one and only one of these three kinds of activity. Most work for most people is a combination of subsistence-work and leisure-work—in some respects intrinsically satisfying and yet something for which we also receive an extrinsic compensation. So, too, our play and amusement is often mixed with leisure activity, since it involves both love and friendship. Yet the mere fact that our experience compounds work, play, and leisure is no justification for confusing these important parts of life as though they were not profoundly different from one another.

Once we have succeeded in clarifying and distinguishing them, we can see the relation of work and leisure, on the one hand, to wealth and happiness, on the other. Subsistence-work is pursued for the sake of the economic goods that it obtains. But wealth consists in economic goods, understood broadly as covering whatever is needed to maintain life. Both work and wealth are sought as means to an end beyond themselves. That end, in the most general and also the most ultimate sense, is happiness, and happiness is achieved in and through leisure activity.

FURTHER THOUGHTS

1. Sort out some of your own activities into work, play and leisure. Are there any you can't classify? What seems to be the trouble? Do you seem to need some additional categories? Do you find any activities that seem to want to fit into more than one category? If so, how can you qualify them to specify when they belong in one category and when in another?
2. If you work with tools and play with toys, what do you leisure with?
3. In his essay "Work" Bertrand Russell says, "To be able to fill leisure intelligently is the last product of civilization, and at present very few people have reached this level." In the light of the discussion in "Work and Leisure," how do you respond to Russell's conclusion?
4. Our notion of subsistence depends upon our expectations. The more we expect, or demand, the more we need. One way to get the free time necessary to leisure would be to reduce our expectations, thus reducing our needs, thus reducing the amount of subsistence-work we had to do. Why don't more people do that—rather than constantly increasing their subsistence levels?
5. If this is the first time you've encountered the kinds of questions asked in this exercise, go back to page 65 and read the instructions there.

a. Which would you least like to do?

_____ listen to a live performance of Beethoven's 9th Symphony

_____ watch William Buckley and John Galbraith debate

_____ politics on television

_____ attend a top Broadway play

b. Which would you most like to learn?

_____ how to make your own fabrics or pottery

_____ how to play the electric organ

_____ how to fix household appliances

_____ karate

c. Which would you find it easiest to do?

_____ serve as a volunteer on a Crisis line

_____ raise money for a political campaign

_____ work with retarded adults

d. Which about yourself would you most like to improve?

_____ your on-the-job (or at-school) skills

_____ your off-the-job skills that still involve work (gardening, for instance)

_____ certain play skills (water skiing or poker playing, for instance)

e. Write two questions like those above which deal with jobs and leisure, work and play.

Leisure
And
Time Off

"Work and play! work and play! The order of the universe"—so sang a poet named John Davidson. But there is more to it than work and play. Some of man's greatest achievements come not out of work, not out of play, but out of something best called "leisure."

Leisure is not merely time free from work. Much free time is given over to play, much to necessary rest and idleness. Leisure is free time used for something other than play or idleness. It is a time to try to understand one's self and one's world better. Leisure, according to philosophers like Josef Pieper, is the basis of human culture—of art and science, of philosophy and religion, of all those human creations that require the serious efforts of people freed of the need to labor simply to survive.

According to the Book of Genesis, this labor began in the Garden of Eden.

THE STORY OF EDEN

Genesis 2:4–3:19

At the time when God Yahweh made earth and heaven—no shrub of the field being yet in the earth and no grains of the field having sprouted, for God Yahweh had not sent rain upon the earth and no man was there to till the soil; instead, a flow would well up from the ground and water the whole surface of the soil—God Yahweh formed man from clods in the soil and blew into his nostrils the breath of life. Thus man became a living being.

God Yahweh planted a garden in Eden, in the east, and placed there the man whom he had formed. And out of the ground God Yahweh caused to grow various trees that were a delight to the eye and good for eating, with the tree of life in the middle of the garden and the tree of knowledge of good and bad.

A river rises in Eden to water the garden; outside, it forms four separate branch streams. The name of the first is Pishon; it is the one that winds through the whole land of Havilah, where there is gold. The gold of that land is choice; there is bdellium there, and lapis lazuli. The name of the second river is Gihon; it is the one that winds through all of the land of Cush. The name of the third river is Tigris; it is the one that flows east of Asshur. The fourth river is the Euphrates.

God Yahweh took the man and settled him in the garden of Eden, to till and tend it. And God Yahweh commanded the man, saying, "You are free to eat of any tree of the garden, except only the tree of knowledge of good and bad, of which you are not to eat. For the moment you eat of it, you shall be doomed to death."

God Yahweh said, "It is not right that man should be alone. I will make him an aid fit for him." So God Yahweh formed out of the soil various wild beasts and birds of the sky and brought them to the man to see what he called them; whatever the man would call a living creature, that was to be its name. The man gave names to all cattle, all birds of the sky, and all wild beasts, yet none proved to be the aid that would be fit for man.

Then God Yahweh cast a deep sleep upon the man and, when he was asleep, he took one of his ribs and closed up the flesh at that spot. And God Yahweh fashioned into a woman the rib that he had removed from the man, and he brought her to the man. Said the man,

This one at last is bone of my bones and flesh of my flesh.

She shall be called Woman, for she was taken from Man.

Thus it is that man leaves his father and mother and clings to his wife, and they become one flesh.

The two of them were naked, the man and his wife, yet they felt no shame.

Now the serpent was the sliest of all the wild creatures that God Yahweh had made. Said he to the woman, "Even though God told you not to eat of any tree in the garden . . . " The woman interrupted the serpent, "But we may eat of the trees in the garden! It is only about the fruit of the tree in the middle of the garden that God did say, 'Do not eat of it or so much as touch it, lest you die!'" But the serpent said to the woman, "You are not going to die. No, God well knows that the moment you eat of it your eyes will be opened and you will be the same as God in telling good from bad."

When the woman saw that the tree was good for eating and a delight to the eye, and that the tree was attractive as a means to wisdom, she took of its fruit and ate; and she gave some to her husband and he ate. Then the eyes of both were opened and they discovered that they were naked; so they sewed fig leaves together and made themselves loincloths.

They heard the sound of God Yahweh as he was walking in the garden at the breezy time of day; and the man and his wife hid from God Yahweh among the trees of the garden.

God Yahweh called to the man and said to him, "Where are you?" He answered, "I heard the sound of you in the garden; but I was afraid because I was naked, so I hid." He asked, "Who told you that you were naked? Did you, then, taste of the tree from which I had forbidden you to eat?" The man replied, "The woman whom you put by my side—it was she who gave me of that tree, and I ate." God Yahweh said to the woman, "How could you do such a thing?" The woman replied, "The serpent tricked me, so I ate."

God Yahweh said to the serpent:

> "Because you did this,
> Banned shall you be from all cattle
> And all wild creatures!
> On your belly shall you crawl
> And on dirt shall you feed
> All the days of your life.
>
> I will plant enmity between you and the woman,
> And between your offspring and hers;
> They shall strike at your head,
> And you shall strike at their heel."

To the woman he said:

> "I will make intense
> Your pangs in childbearing.
> In pain shall you bear children;
> Yet your urge shall be for your husband,
> And he shall be your master."

To the man he said: "Because you listened to your wife and ate of the tree from which I had forbidden you to eat,

> Condemned be the soil on your account!
> In anguish shall you eat of it
> All the days of your life.
> Thorns and thistles
> Shall it bring forth for you,
> As you feed on the grasses of the field.
> By the sweat of your face
> Shall you earn your bread,
> Until you return to the ground,
> For from it you were taken:
> For dust you are
> And to dust you shall return!"

TO EVERYTHING THERE IS A SEASON

Ecclesiastes 3:1-11

> To everything there is a season,
> And a time to every purpose under the heaven:
> A time to be born, and a time to die;
> A time to plant, and a time to pluck up that which is planted;
> A time to kill, and a time to heal;
> A time to break down, and a time to build up;
> A time to weep, and a time to laugh;
> A time to mourn, and a time to dance;
> A time to cast away stones, and a time to gather stones together;
> A time to embrace, and a time to refrain from embracing;
> A time to seek, and a time to lose;
> A time to keep, and a time to cast away;
> A time to rend, and a time to sew;
> A time to keep silence, and a time to speak;
> A time to love, and a time to hate;
> A time for war, and a time for peace.

What profit hath he that worketh in that wherein he laboureth? I have seen the travail which God hath given to the sons of men to be exercised therewith. He hath made every thing beautiful in its time: also he hath set the world in their heart, yet so that man cannot find out the work that God hath done from the beginning even to the end.

FURTHER THOUGHTS

1. Did Adam and Eve work in Eden before the Fall? Is this story a myth?
2. What is the point of the verse portion of *Ecclesiastes*? What is the point of the very last sentence?
3. What do these two selections have to do with the topics of work and leisure?
4. "The Story of Eden" tells of mankind's loss of innocence, in which the naive child became the knowing adult. This is a process that every individual goes through, too. Everyone learns that he can't be yesterday's child—perhaps because of the death of someone close, perhaps because of the discovery that someone or something is not so pure after all, perhaps because of new responsibilities, of being left on one's own. Write a description of your loss of innocence, trying to describe what things were like before and then after it occurred. Concentrate on precisely what it was that caused your "fall."

Philosophers like Aristotle tell us that leisure is more than simply time away from work, more than simple idleness. But the following selection, from Melville's novel *Moby Dick*, suggests that there is something to be said even for simple idleness.

FROM
MOBY DICK

Herman Melville

THE DART

According to the invariable usage of the fishery, the whale-boat pushes off from the ship, with the headsman or whale-killer as temporary steersman, and the harpooner or whale-fastener pulling the foremost oar, the one known as the harpooneer-oar. Now it needs a strong, nervous arm to strike the first iron into the fish; for often, in what is called a long dart, the heavy implement has to be flung to the distance of twenty or thirty feet. But however prolonged and exhausted the chase, the harpooneer is expected to pull his oar meanwhile to the uttermost; indeed, he is expected to set an example of superhuman activity to the rest, not only by incredible rowing, but by repeated loud and intrepid exclamations; and what it is to keep shouting at the top of one's compass, while all the other muscles are strained and half-started—what that is none know but those who have tried it. For one, I cannot bawl very heartily and work very recklessly at one and the same time. In this straining, bawling state, then, with his back to the fish, all at once the exhausted harpooneer hears the exciting cry—"Stand up, and give it to him!" He now has to drop and secure his oar, turn round on his centre half-way, seize his harpoon from the crotch, and with what little strength may remain, he essays to pitch it somehow into the whale. No wonder, taking the whole fleet of whalemen in a body, that out of fifty fair chances for a dart, not five are successful; no wonder that so many hapless harpooneers are madly cursed and disrated; no wonder that some of them actually burst their blood-vessels in the boat; no wonder that some Sperm whalemen are absent four years with four barrels; no wonder that to many ship owners, whaling is but a losing concern; for it is the harpooneer that makes the voyage, and if you take the breath out of his body how can you expect to find it there when most wanted!

Again, if the dart be successful, then at the second critical instant, that is, when the whale starts to run, the boatheader and harpooneer likewise start to running fore and aft to the imminent jeopardy of themselves and every one else. It is then they change places; and the headsman, the chief officer of the little craft, takes his proper station in the bows of the boat.

Now, I care not who maintains the contrary, but all this is both foolish and unnecessary. The headsman should stay in the bows from first to last; he should both dart the harpoon and the lance, and no rowing whatever should be expected of him except under circumstances obvious to any fisherman. I know that this would sometimes involve a slight loss of speed in the chase; but long experience in various whalemen of more than one nation has convinced me that in the vast majority of failures in the fishery, it has not by any means been so much the speed of the whale as the before described exhaustion of the harpooneer that has caused them.

To ensure the greatest efficiency in the dart, the harpooneers of this world must start to their feet from out of idleness, and not from out of toil.

FURTHER THOUGHTS

1. "The Dart" is really a fable, rather like those of Aesop—and like those of Aesop this fable is meant to illustrate the maxim stated in the final sentence. If you applied that maxim to people in general, what would it mean. What if you applied it to the performance of a student in school?
2. Try to recall an experience you or someone you know has had in which, so to speak, the whale was lost due to the simple exhaustion of the harpooneer.

LYING IN A HAMMOCK AT WILLIAM DUFFY'S FARM IN PINE ISLAND, MINNESOTA

James Wright

Over my head, I see the bronze butterfly,
Asleep on the black trunk,
Blowing like a leaf in green shadow.
Down the ravine behind the empty house,
The cowbells follow one another
Into the distances of the afternoon.
To my right,
In a field of sunlight between two pines,
The droppings of last year's horses
Blaze into golden stones.
I lean back, as the evening darkens and comes on.
A chicken-hawk floats over, looking for home.
I have wasted my life.

DEPRESSED BY A BOOK OF BAD POETRY, I WALK TOWARD AN UNUSED PASTURE AND INVITE THE INSECTS TO JOIN ME

James Wright

Relieved, I let the book fall behind a stone.
I climb a slight rise of grass.
I do not want to disturb the ants
Who are walking single file up the fence post,
Carrying small white petals,
Casting shadows so frail that I can see through them.
I close my eyes for a moment, and listen.
The old grasshoppers
Are tired, they leap heavily now,
Their thighs are burdened.
I want to hear them, they have clear sounds to make.
They have gone to sleep.
Then lovely, far off, a dark cricket begins
In the castles of maple.

FURTHER THOUGHTS

1. The speaker in Wright's "Lying in a Hammock" concludes that he has wasted his life. What do you think he means by that?
2. How do you go about wasting a life, anyhow? What's the difference between wasting a life and spending one?
3. Are these poems dealing with leisure or with idleness?

In the article "Work and Leisure" it was pointed out that Henry Thoreau went to Walden Pond and reduced his work load "because he had more important things *to do*. Being at leisure was for him anything but being inactive . . . ." The following short selection from *Walden* tells you about the more important things that Thoreau had to do with his time.

FROM
WALDEN

Henry David Thoreau

The mass of men lead lives of quiet desperation. What is called resignation is confirmed desperation. From the desperate city you go into the desperate country, and have to console yourself with the bravery of minks and muskrats. A stereotyped but unconscious despair is concealed even under what are called the games and amusements of mankind. There is no play in them, for this comes after work. But it is a characteristic of wisdom not to do desperate things.

When we consider what, to use the words of the catechism, is the chief end of man, and what are the true necessaries and means of life, it appears as if men had deliberately chosen the common mode of living because they preferred it to any other. Yet they honestly think there is no choice left. But alert and healthy natures remember that the sun rose clear. It is never too late to give up our prejudices.

. . . .

Most of the luxuries, and many of the so-called comforts of life, are not only dispensable, but positive hindrances to the elevation of mankind. With respect to luxuries and comforts, the wisest have ever lived a more simple and meagre life than the poor. The ancient philosophers, Chinese, Hindoo, Persian, and Greek, were a class than which none has been poorer in outward riches, none so rich in inward. . . . Our inventions are wont to be pretty toys, which distract our attention from serious things. They are but improved means to an unimproved end, an end which it was already but too easy to arrive at; as railroads lead to Boston or New York. We are in great haste to construct a magnetic telegraph from Maine to Texas; but Maine and Texas, it may be, have nothing important to communicate. Either is in such a predicament as the man who was earnest to be introduced to a distinguished deaf woman, but when he was presented, and one end of her ear trumpet was put into his hand, had nothing to say. As if the main object were to talk fast and not talk sensibly. We are eager to tunnel under the Atlantic and bring the Old World some weeks nearer to the New; but perchance the first news that will leak through into the broad, flapping American ear will be that the Princess Adelaide has the whooping cough. After all, the man whose horse trots a mile in a minute does not carry the most important messages; he is not an evangelist, nor does he come round eating locusts and wild honey. I doubt if Flying Childers ever carried a peck of corn to mill.

One says to me, "I wonder that you do not lay up money; you love to travel; you might take the cars and go to Fitchburg to-day and see the country." But I am wiser than that. I have learned that the swiftest traveller is he that goes afoot. I say to my friend, Suppose we try who will get there first. The distance is thirty miles; the fare ninety cents. That is almost a day's wages. I remember when wages were sixty cents a day for laborers on this very road. Well, I start now on foot, and get there before night; I have travelled at that rate by the week together. You will in the meanwhile have earned your fare, and arrive there some time to-morrow, or possibly this evening, if you are lucky enough to get a job in season. Instead of going to Fitchburg, you will be working here the greater part of the day. And so, if the railroad reached round the world, I think that I should keep ahead of you; and as for seeing the country and getting experience of that kind, I should have to cut your acquaintance altogether.

Such is the universal law, which no man can ever outwit, and with regard to the railroad even we may say it is as broad as it is long. To make a railroad round the world available to all mankind is equivalent to grading the whole surface of the planet. Men have an indistinct notion that if they keep up this activity of joint stocks and spades long enough all will at length ride somewhere, in next to no time, and for nothing; but though a crowd rushes to the depot, and the conductor shouts "All aboard!" when the smoke is blown away and the vapor condensed, it will be perceived that a few are riding, but the rest are run over,—and it will be called, and will be, "A melancholy accident." No doubt they can ride at last who shall have earned their fare, that is, if they survive so long, but they will probably have lost their elasticity and desire to travel by that time. This spending of the best part of one's life earning money in order to enjoy a questionable liberty during the least valuable part of it reminds me of the Englishman who went to India to make a fortune first, in order that he might return to England and live the life of a poet. He should have gone up garret at once.

. . . .

For more than five years I maintained myself thus solely by the labor of my

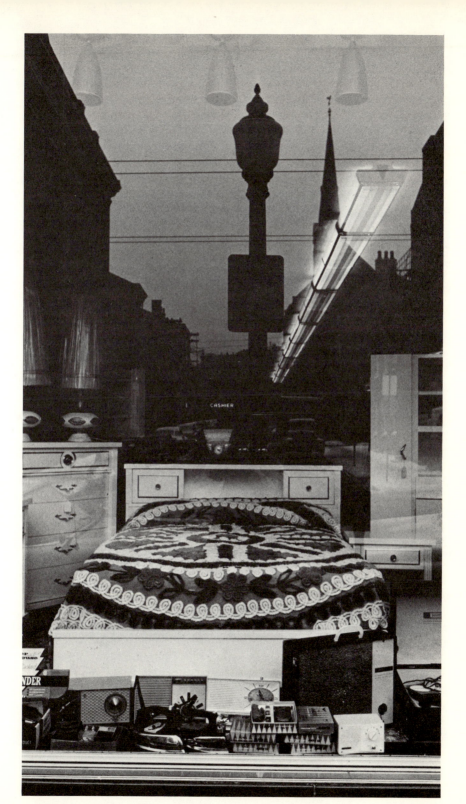

hands, and I found that, by working about six weeks in a year, I could meet all the expenses of living. The whole of my winters, as well as most of my summers, I had free and clear for study. I have thoroughly tried schoolkeeping, and found that my expenses were in proportion, or rather out of proportion, to my income, for I was obliged to dress and train, not to say think and believe, accordingly, and I lost my time into the bargain. As I did not teach for the good of my fellow-men, but simply for a livelihood, this was a failure. I have tried trade; but I found that it would take ten years to get under way in that, and that then I should probably be on my way to the devil. I was actually afraid that I might by that time be doing what is called a good business. When formerly I was looking about to see what I could do for a living, some sad experience in conforming to the wishes of friends being fresh in my mind to tax my ingenuity, I thought often and seriously of picking huckleberries; that surely I could do, and its small profits might suffice,—for my greatest skill has been to want but little,—so little capital it required, so little distraction from my wonted moods, I foolishly thought. While my acquaintances went unhesitatingly into trade or the professions, I contemplated this occupation as most like theirs; ranging the hills all summer to pick the berries which came in my way, and thereafter carelessly dispose of them; so, to keep the flocks of Admetus. I also dreamed that I might gather the wild herbs, or carry evergreens to such villagers as loved to be reminded of the woods, ever to the city, by hay-cart loads. But I have since learned that trade curses everything it handles; and though you trade in messages from heaven, the whole curse of trade attaches to the business.

As I preferred some things to others, and especially valued my freedom, as I could fare hard and yet succeed well, I did not wish to spend my time in earning rich carpets or other fine furniture, or delicate cookery, or a house in the Grecian or the Gothic style just yet. If there are any to whom it is no interruption to acquire these things, and who know how to use them when acquired, I relinquish to them the pursuit. Some are "industrious," and appear to love labor for its own sake, or perhaps because it keeps them out of worse mischief; to such I have at present nothing to say. Those who would not know what to do with more leisure than they now enjoy, I might advise to work twice as hard as they do,—work till they pay for themselves, and get their free papers. For myself I found that the occupation of a day-laborer was the most independent of any, especially as it required only thirty or forty days in a year to support one. The laborer's day ends with the going down of the sun, and he is then free to devote himself to his chosen pursuit, independent of his labor; but his employer, who speculates from month to month, has no respite from one end of the year to the other.

In short, I am convinced, both by faith and experience, that to maintain one's self on this earth is not a hardship but a pastime, if we will live simply and wisely; as the pursuits of the simpler nations are still the sports of the more artificial. It is not necessary that a man should earn his living by the sweat of his brow, unless he sweats easier than I do.

. . . .

Our life is frittered away by detail. An honest man has hardly need to count more than his ten fingers, or in extreme cases he may add his ten toes, and lump the rest. Simplicity, simplicity, simplicity! I say, let your affairs be as two or three, and not a hundred or a thousand; instead of a million count half a dozen, and keep your accounts on your thumbnail. In the midst of this chopping sea of civilized life, such are the clouds and storms and quicksands and thousand-and-one items to be allowed for, that a man has to live, if he would not founder and go to the bottom and not make his port at all, by dead reckoning, and he must be a great calculator indeed who succeeds. Simplify, simplify.

. . . .

I went to the woods because I wished to live deliberately, to front only the essential facts of life, and see if I could not learn what it had to teach, and not, when I came to die, discover that I had not lived. I did not wish to live what was not life, living is so dear; nor did I wish to practise resignation, unless it was quite necessary. I wanted to live deep and suck out all the marrow of life, to live so sturdily and Spartanlike as to put to rout all that was not life, to cut a broad swath and shave close, to drive life into a corner, and reduce it to its lowest terms, and, if it proved to be mean, why then to get the whole and genuine meanness of it, and publish its meanness to the world; or if it were sublime, to know it by experience, and be able to give a true account of it in my next excursion.

FURTHER THOUGHTS

1. Thoreau says that most men "lead lives of quiet desperation." Look up *desperate* and *desperation* in the dictionary; check the meanings, etymology, and any synonymy studies you can find. What kinds of things do you see in our lives that you think would be good examples of "quiet desperation"? What do you think Thoreau means when he says that "it is a characteristic of wisdom not to do desperate things"? How does one *avoid* "quiet desperation"? What hint does Thoreau provide? What other things do you feel would help?
2. Thoreau says that he wanted to live his life "deliberately." Treat this statement the way you treated the quotation in the first question.
3. Thoreau is noted for his full and polished sentences. Copy down six or seven sentences from the selection from *Walden* that speak most strongly to you. What kinds of ideas do you see running through those sentences, either on the surface or hidden underneath as assumptions and implications?

Leisure, as we have said, is a time for speculating on the nature of things. One has little time to think great thoughts when grubbing for food or building shelter for himself and those close to him. One has time and energy for truth-seeking only after a brotherhood or sisterhood is affirmed and is no longer an issue. Without time for leisure the ultimate goals of truth, beauty, and goodness are only fleetingly glimpsed. But some people do manage, as Thoreau puts it, to live deliberately. For some people like Eric Hoffer, leisure is a time for thought and study, a time for truth. For some people like Louis Simpson, it is a time for artistic creation, a time for beauty. For some people like Carolyn See's veterinarian leisure is a time for doing good works.

A VETERINARIAN

Carolyn See

Tom Mehlhoff knew that he did a lot of things for reasons which were obscure even to himself. He feared that he did things for style; the "in thing to do" was the way his mind phrased it, in some leftover cliché which underlined all the things he was trying to avoid.

He'd had a beard as soon as he could grow one; but when it became the style to be hirsute, he'd cut his beard and hair—mercilessly—so that now in the morning as he shaved or tended one or another of the cuts and scratches which were the stock in trade of his profession, he saw entirely too much to suit himself. His face came from a long line of Andy Hardys and Van Johnsons, and made no room anywhere for passion or spite or sorrow or fear.

He was too young to be grown-up, and he leaned away from everything his parents believed, but too old too for the street people; he missed them not by years (twenty-eight is not old) but by that mindless ease, that slack relaxing into sloughs of nonaccomplishment and dumbness. To demonstrate, say, to walk, jostling and hugging, indiscriminate, and wave a sign imprinted with yet another easy cliché, and chant words which had been done, and done, and done . . .

Like many people who consider themselves between generations, he divided himself between two jobs. He was a veterinarian, which he vaguely considered to be his justification to all things living: the stamp (if anybody should ask) of a good man. He was also from time to time a clinical pathologist, a specialist in exfoliative cytology, in what he liked to call a human hospital: the long, thin prongs are pushed deep into some poor dog or cat—or human—and removed, bearing a dot of blood and flesh, which is stained and examined for any of those diseases which plague the living world. He had seen cancer in them all. At a cocktail party his wife, Ann, had once dragged him to (their friends, as everyone's now, were divided into stand-up drinkers and lying-down dopers; he felt uneasy with both), he had tried to tell some woman about his depression when, for two or three weeks, almost every slide he looked at had shown malignancy. Her face had gone blank with sympathy; then she remembered: "Well, they're only dogs and cats!"

He was thinking about cancer as he drove home. There were theories that not only was it a virus but that you were born with it walled up in secret cells. As you grew older and more tired, the walls crumbled; all it took was one crack in the millions and billions of cells and it escaped, beautiful and silent, the way fog sprinted silently and at tremendous speed under the Golden Gate Bridge into the harbor. The walls broke because of cigarette smoke, or smog, or the chemicals they put in restaurant pies. Maybe they broke because of fluorescent lights or synthetic fabrics, and cancer was only one thing. Mehlhoff had worked with germs so awful that they had no names, much less a cure. What man could do with them was little, little; put up some more clapboard walls, that's all, and make camp, however tentative, in the land of the living.

He lived in San Francisco, and crossed the Golden Gate Bridge every day to his work in San Rafael. If his life was satisfactory now, it had started off in much the same way: plain living and square-shooting family life in Thief River Falls, Minnesota. He worked his way through St. Olaf College, the most elegant private college around. It had left its strict Lutheran stamp on him. He'd worked his way through romance too, with a combination of idealism and drudgery. The very first day at St. Olaf he'd met a wholesome beauty and circled her name in the list of incoming freshmen. Two years later on their first date he was still secure enough in his beliefs to ask her to marry him. It took her months to make up her mind. And by that time she was as necessary to him as baskets of oranges and buckets of cream.

His gains by now were modest, but his own. A nice upstairs apartment (the downstairs neighbors never complained about the kids), his degree as a veterinarian from the University of Minnesota. He'd only recently set up his own small practice. After taxes he was making $700 a month. He and Ann had been married for seven years. You man the barricades with a wife who knows you, and the exemplary two children (he'd had a vasectomy right after the second; if everyone did that, and no one brought home vegetables from the market in plastic bags, the world might be saved; anything is possible, even something good).

And a best friend (Dave) is next to you, who looks like you and lives your life. You hire a glamorous secretary—although he shook his head when he thought of Peggy. She was pretty and plain and quizzical, and there were snags in her stockings. She'd been a nurse, but she couldn't stand watching people die. Now she held doped and stupid puppies while Mehlhoff probed in their throats for eternal lost foxtails. He could hold out, maybe, with his wife, his children, his friend, and his secretary.

One night a week he took care of the kids while Ann went out with her girl friends. It was a benign if distant gesture. He was still young; so was she.

He heard about the collision of the two Standard Oil of California tankers almost, he supposed, as it happened. January 18, 1971, was a terribly foggy morning, and he craned as he made his slow way across the Golden Gate to see the ships beneath the bridge. The two tankers had collided, spilling more than 800,000 gallons of bunker oil into San Francisco Bay. It was news, a real event, but this morning he couldn't even see the bright orange spokes of the bridge itself. Once at work he forgot it. He worked on a mountain lion that day, and an English sheep dog that had nervously bitten its paw to a bloody pulp. A colleague of his brought in a Weimaraner dead from an interesting form of distemper. Mehlhoff wanted to take a slide from its brain. He'd just ordered a new power saw for trepanning, which lay, still wrapped, on one of his stainless steel counters. He put the Weimaraner, patient beyond the grave, on clean newspaper in the last cage in the corner.

His secretary's girl friend came over for lunch. She was sexy, with false eyelashes and no bra. Mehlhoff laughed a lot. Later, as he washed up, he examined himself in the mirror above the basin. Affable as the deacon who passes the collection plate every Sunday. He spent the afternoon at work; a mutt with diseased pancreas, and countless calls from labs and colleagues: Was this leukemia? Was that worms? And in the corner, in the gray steel cage, the Weimaraner waiting.

Mehlhoff drove home about eight thirty or nine. The radio was full of news about the spill, but he couldn't see a thing. Ann had already eaten and fed the kids. He found some sausage and cheese, and looked out toward the ocean, but there was only fog. He spent the evening listening to music on his stereo. The set had earphones; he liked them. Carved wooden trolls marched across the mantel of his fireplace. He owned the Great Books of the Western World and a series on natural history for his children, and there were novels; books galore, he said to himself, and saw himself inside the walls.

The next morning, groping to work in the fog, he heard reports of the first dead birds. Well. There were bound to be dead and more dead . . . from the oil. And people were bound to make a big thing out of it. But seven thousand birds had died this year of fowl cholera up at Tulelake, and nobody had made a big thing out of that. And he knew the stupidity of birds, the profound mindlessness of, say, a chicken. Seeing animals all day, every day, didn't do much for his sentimentality.

That night there was the stereo and the books and in the next room posters on the wall—all the accouterments of San Francisco life, the tools of the striving middle class with a wistful wave at youth culture—crap! He tried to get Dave on the phone, and then, instead of helping to undress the boys for bed, he put the older one in his nylon snowsuit and walked with him down along the beach to see what was going on.

It was cold for San Francisco. From the Cliffhouse, when the fog parted, he could see down the long strand, which was the sad, romantic face that San Francisco presented to the sea itself. On one side of the Great Highway, arcades and concessions and hotels and shops; and across the street, just sidewalk, a low cement wall, and then black eternity of water. Tonight yellow beams of light jerked and lurched across the sand. Mehlhoff heard the cries of people, short and shrieking, like birds themselves.

He walked down the slope toward Poor Richard's Ballroom. Its doors were open. BRING YOUR SICK BIRDS HERE, a hastily scrawled sign said. Mehlhoff went in.

He'd seen *Gone With the Wind* as a boy, and this was like the field hospital where Scarlett O'Hara searched for whoever it was. This was every spectacle before or afterward: Florence Nightingale in trouble in the Crimea, John Wayne in Guadalcanal. Mehlhoff stood in a huge room, the paint peeling, the faraway ceiling held up by columns around three sides, forming a verandah above, arcades below. A few lights in the ceiling weakly gleamed down on a cast of thousands; the place crept and crawled with sick and dying birds. They lay gasping in makeshift beds of filthy rags, or fagged out on their sides in open cardboard boxes. They futilely preened themselves and filled their beaks and eyes and noses with the thick black stuff. They made their way cautiously across the length of the ballroom like ambulatory patients down hospital halls.

In gawky relationship to the birds, a set of humans worked—maybe two hundred, maybe more. There were (as the newspapers were to repeat with morose delight in the coming days) hippies, housewives, and hard hats. Mehlhoff smiled to see an occasional person holding a bird in close, unaccustomed embrace; the human face somehow in flight as it shied away from what it was holding, and next to the human ribs, in some improvised clump of black and odorous rags, a transcendently deranged bird face; beady eyes and insolent bill which from time to time emitted a sharp, disgusted yawp. "Poor bird, poor old bird," he heard one guy say, then saw the man, once finished staring at a newly dead grebe, whirl it toward a raffish, slithery pyramid that Mehlhoff had absentmindedly registered as some sort of supplies, perhaps a different kind of rag, but that was made up of corpses of birds.

Mehlhoff took his son home, picked up his equipment for performing postmortems, and returned. He went up to a girl who was handing out coffee.

"I'd like a table, if I may, and a strong light."

"What for?"

"I'm a veterinarian, and I thought by doing some postmortems to find out exactly how the birds are dying, we could find out the most appropriate treatment . . ."

"Thank God, you've come!" she shrieked, throwing her arms around his neck. "Here's a vet!" she announced in the ringing tones of street demonstrations and bullhorns, cattle prods and mace. "A vet's here! He'll tell all of us what to do."

In the next six or seven hours, Mehlhoff did postmortems on maybe twenty birds. The main thing, he decided, was to keep them warm and treat them for shock; it wasn't the oil itself necessarily that killed them, but the shock. He thought of birds, and their life on other nights. To feel the air, to dive down in the water, deep (he was in the middle of a series of scuba lessons right now and he felt the hindrance of equipment and had a thousand mental reservations about diving), to swallow food that was alive and glittered in your mouth. To have a beak, to breathe in and have the air go all through your body, to suck air literally into your bones, and fly. And then to die. He felt the oil, the *hardness* of it, its intractability, and knew what it would be to die of it, to feel it burning in your stomach, or searing your eyes, coating your skin so that air, water, the things of life would be cut off.

Well, he had to get the oil off. Since the oil was so thick, so much like tar, maybe mineral oil would do. His mother had used it on him when he'd gotten tar on his feet as a boy. And something then to soak up the oil. Not flour—it was too gummy—but a meal, cornmeal. And injections of steroids and antibiotics as a preventive measure, and he'd have to think of feeding them: would they eat dead fish? And ways to keep them warm.

He thought he would remember it all forever: the kids' faces screwed up into grimaces as they worked over the birds feather by feather, the foul smell of crude oil, which, like the smell of a skunk—if it was faint enough—made you ultimately like it. He had his first meeting with Kasarian, an enormous man, a hairy eminence saying, "You want something? I can get you anything you want." True to the movies, Mehlhoff asked for hot water, and Kasarian built two huge bonfires out in back, and found two vats, and assigned two crews who, for the next eleven days, ate and slept and joked and made love around those fires and never left; day and night the fires burned.

Toward the end of that first night, at four or five in the morning, as Mehlhoff leaned, stupid with exhaustion, against his table, someone patted his hand, as though he were a boy, then held his wrist, as though he were the patient. Someone said, "It was a godsend that you came here"; and where his body had shied like a scared horse from the first goofy girl, it vibrated now like a tuning fork. He looked up and saw a woman's face on a level with his own, with tired eyes and hair the color of dry grass. He looked past her around the enormous hall, trying to spot Kasarian before he went home, to tell him what supplies to ask for and how to set about arranging the hall into a regular hospital.

Going to work the next day, he listened to the news for the first time in his life as though it were his own. Standard Oil was going to pay for everything. There were dead birds. There was going to be an inquiry . . . He'd been on the bridge that morning; the fog was too thick to see an inch. Why did they let ships go out in it, pass each other in it? And people were working together to save the birds.

There were other bird centers springing up. There was a Dr. Naviaux up in Pleasant Hill; he'd worked in the Santa Barbara slick in 1969, and from what the radio said it sounded as if they'd worked out much the same treatment as Mehlhoff had.

But officials had designated the city-run San Francisco zoo and a nearby game farm as the offical caring places for the birds, and they had sent for an "expert" from the East Coast. Mehlhoff felt a twinge of personal jealousy—they didn't even mention the work at Poor Richard's Ballroom—and a larger, more respectable surge of professional indignation. The "expert," from what they were saying about him, wasn't even a veterinarian. He was advocating the use of some product—biodegradable they said, but what difference did that make? Some of the kids had suggested using Basic H—a biodegradable detergent—last night, but the trouble with Basic H was that it took off not only the thick bunker oil but the birds' natural oil too, right down to the thinnest pinfeathers and the skin. So that if a bird set sail after that, his feathers gradually filled up with water, and he sank and drowned.

The birds' normal temperature was generally 105 degrees. Could the zoo keep them warm? Perhaps in the snake cages. (But what would they do with the snakes?) They couldn't be planning on turning sick birds loose in the aviary, in the cold wind and fog. He thought of the birds' heartbeat, frail and terrifically fast, a vibration really, thinly humming along with the universe. The great thing was to keep them warm; he was sure of it, and not sure that the zoo had the facilities to do it.

Today at his office, there were three German shepherd pups sick, eating all right but vomiting. They were still living partly on mother's milk. Mehlhoff ran a series of tests but couldn't come up with anything. A trainer came in with a hysterial Doberman. "His owner worked him with a belt," the trainer said, "and now he wonders why the dog wants to kill him."

Mehlhoff kept wanting to phone Kasarian at Poor Richard's to see how things were going; the work that he had left behind stayed in his mind with total clarity. And yet here he was, in a layout of his own design: waiting room, private office, two consulting rooms, small surgery and large lab, a two-thousand-dollar microscope and a brand-new power saw, a stack of slides to read, and after the Doberman, a woman saying, while he gave her dog a shot, "It's a good thing I know how to hold a dog." People were proud of the most minuscule accomplishments.

He drove straight from work to Poor Richard's. From San Rafael to San Francisco he saw isolated crews along one shoreline or the other, pitching straw and drawing it out, soppy and sticky, onto the sand. He saw helicopters hovering; he listened to KSAN's continuing coverage of where the oil was, and where more afflicted birds were. He heard a description of the oil he already knew so well; it was thick, like tar, almost completely unrefined. It moved according to the temperature of the water. It wasn't as though all the straw and various attempts by boats which skimmed and sucked could get all the oil up and out. It would stay in the water for years. Just now it had made itself into enormous strings sometimes twenty or thirty feet long, catching in breakers and rolling up onto the beach.

At Bolinas Lagoon, which had such an abundance of wildlife, the oil was just offshore and about to come in with the tide. Volunteer crews were desperately building a makeshift breakwater. (The city had made contingency plans against the possibility of an oil spill in San Francisco Harbor but hadn't taken into consideration the action of the tides.) What else was there? Standard Oil was coming through admirably, offering to pay for the care of the birds, operating a fleet of boats.

When Mehlhoff got back to Poor Richard's, the kids, the street people, remembered him. "It's the doc," they said unbelievingly. They recognized him, said hello, as in "What's happening, man?" and came to him with questions: "Do you get their eyes with swabs?" What about the holes in their beaks?" Girls came up and hugged him. Mehlhoff looked for Kasarian hungrily, as an old friend. Kasarian came up, enormous, and Armenian or not, took him into a formalized Mexican *embraso*. Mehlhoff shrank at every touch, and winced at every piece of slang, and drew in a bit at every tie-dyed T-shirt, but less and less and less.

The kids had done a great job. The supply unit (which had found a tiny room off the dance floor and stayed in it and stuck with it and made it a command post) had persuaded the phone company to set up a battery of phones. They had scrounged a generator; the place was much better lighted. Next to an enormous stack of cotton swabs and mineral oil and boxes of cornmeal and rags, there were cans of beans and tomatoes and creamed corn, the flotsam and jetsam of probably every San Francisco supermarket. It was as though all the Digger cant and dogma had culminated in one intense, practical finale.

They had washed, swabbed, tagged, penned, injected, force-fed hundreds of birds. Now the birds lay somnolent in cages and pens and stacks of boxes. An area under a verandah had become sleeping quarters. Sheets hung from the balcony; and behind, in semidarkness, birds dozed, looked out of makeshift cages with beady eyes, and kids slept, exhausted, for a few hours.

They told him that the place already had its lovers, its new romances, and pointed out a couple—but the girl couldn't have been more than fifteen!—who were holding hands and talking, while little eddies of efficiency swirled around them. "They don't do much work," a woman said, "but they add a little color to the place." It was the one who had taken his arm last night. He was immensely glad to see her. She looked like the rest of them, dressed in old clothes, but was almost certainly older than most of these kids, older than he was, even, maybe. Her hair was that funny color of weeds; there were a few gray hairs.

"They're awfully young," he ventured, and his own voice had never sounded so callow, so Van Johnsonish. She shrugged.

So he went to work. He cleaned birds and examined each new one that came in and injected each one with cortisone and antibiotics. He worked all night, under a harsh single light, treating grebes and scotors and gulls and loons, some fighting, some too profoundly sick to fight. Some died on the table, as he held them.

At about five A.M. he went home. He would sleep for a couple of hours, have breakfast, and go to his office. He didn't mind the lack of sleep, he liked it; but maybe half of his patients on this case had died. Before he left he glanced around for the woman, and hated it when he couldn't find her, and hated himself more for his own dumb romanticism. It wasn't as though he would ever dare do anything!

The hospital stayed open for eleven days. Mehlhoff averaged maybe three hours of sleep a night. The time unrolled like a jerky but utterly engrossing movie. One or two nights his wife begged him to stay home and threatened—he was exhausted, he would ruin his health. He stayed home, but it pained him to do it. He was addicted to the lights, the total activity, the people, the birds. Things "settled down": fewer birds came in, but they kept on dying. By the end over half would die; to work was to work against—or with—continual defeat. It was no longer just the frail girls who wept. And Standard Oil of California appeared to be coming through so handsomely that it seemed pointless to blame them for what was, after all, somehow, an accident. When, a week or so after the disaster, a few protesters left dead birds on the steps of the company's offices, it just laid ugliness on ugliness.

But one day they caught a middle-aged man in a business suit who had slipped past security and was taking notes on the care and feeding of the birds. When he carried his tiny camera to the kids' sleeping quarters, Mehlhoff asked him to leave.

Two young kids found a packing case and set up housekeeping there. People joked that all anybody ever saw of them were two pairs of feet, one turned up, the other down. Mehlhoff worried about it.

Another couple met, fell in love, planned to marry.

At his office he discovered that the Shepherd pups had contracted DDT poisoning from their mother's milk. Two out of the three died.

The ballroom, being so old and near the water, was rat-infested. Rats carry fleas. Bubonic plague is endemic in California. Mehlhoff worried about it.

He worried about dope. There were hundreds of syringes in the ballroom. He tried to keep a close check on them, but with so many people working it was almost impossible. As far as he knew, the kids were phenomenally careful. But he couldn't help worrying.

He brought his son down to visit one day, and held the small hand while he chatted with the woman. He heard the old, cracked affability in his voice. He didn't know what else to do. It wasn't a realistic atmosphere they were living in.

Network television came down to Poor Richard's to do an interview with Mehlhoff; when they came in the front door, he went out the back.

At the end of the week, Standard Oil of California tentatively refused to pay some of their rent; Poor Richard's needed eight hundred by the next morning. Mehlhoff had someone call KSAN, and by morning $1100 had been pledged. And the company was persuaded to pay the rent anyway.

Rumors circulated that the zoo people shot the birds with Adrenalin. The birds would then fly up into the air and die. A zoo official held a news conference, at which he stated that they were "using mineral oil like everyone else." Still, the mortality rate at the zoo was 98 percent.

One afternoon Mehlhoff performed postmortems on twenty birds. He checked out their eyes, looked at the skin to see if they were burned by oil, or if there were sores or cuts, or if the bird had by chance been run over or crushed. He looked in their noses and mouths for oil, then opened them up. He looked in their lungs and air sacs, and in their spleen and liver and pancreas. He cut tissues on each one of them, made slides to save for further histopathological examination.

A trio of representatives came in from Standard Oil of California. They hadn't sneaked past security like the man with the camera. With three of them there they could act as witnesses for each other in a court of law.

"What are you doing there?" one of them asked with earnest interest.

"I'm performing postmortems on birds you killed!" Mehlhoff snarled.

Later, when the company showed signs of hesitation about paying up everywhere in full for all the expenses of the harbor cleaning and facilities for bird care, he and two other concerned citizens filed a twelve-and-a-half-million-dollar class action suit against them in Mehlhoff's name, but on behalf of the public. The company paid up, quickly and informally, without further prodding in or out of court.

On the thirteenth day, Mehlhoff closed the hospital at Poor Richard's. The birds were sent to the Richmond Bird Sanctuary in trucks (the nervous grebes with socks over their heads), each truck with an attendant who played the guitar or sang.

A lot of the kids had given up their rooms or dropped out of school to take care of the birds. They hated to leave. Mehlhoff managed it so they could spend the last weekend in a party. On the last day there was a wedding. Mehlhoff thought: Was it legal? Would they stay together? Did they know about life?

The bride was radiant, dressed in tattered lace. Mehlhoff stood and watched. He spied the woman he knew across the crowded room. "It's none of my business," she'd said to him once. "I don't mean it personally, but I don't think you can go on living the way you do. There's more than what you have. The kids have something, you know. Really." But he thought of the other side of the proposition: this country had got to the place it was because of people like him working; maybe it could only get out of that place if people worked just as "efficiently," just as hard.

That night, before he went home, he stopped off at the office. He phoned his wife to say he'd be late. "What else is new?" she asked, good-naturedly. Her middle name was Liv—a good word after all that death.

As he hung up, the phone rang. Mehlhoff sighed between sentences as he talked, but his voice was affable, unremittingly cheery. This was what he was paid for, after all. " Your dog's in heat? Of course, with two poodles trying to get to each other, I don't envy you. We can always tranquilize them, I guess, but really the best thing is separation!"

He hung up. The office was silent. Seven thirty at night. His secretary had gone home. Ann would wait dinner, Fluorescent lights, white walls, linoleum, Lysol, stainless steel, silence. He walked once through the office, stopping to touch his two-thousand-dollar microscope. It was a beauty. He opened the package with the power saw and turned to his gray friend in the cage.

FURTHER THOUGHTS

1. Would you call Mehlhoff's attempts to save the birds an example of a leisure activity? Were his efforts directed just toward the birds themselves?
2. What was the status of love and creativity in Mehlhoff's regular job? in his efforts for the birds?
3. Do you think his experience with the birds changed Mehlhoff in any radical, lasting way?

Traditionally the poet has been the person who uses leisure to search for the truth that can be found in beauty and the beauty that can be found in truth. For some poets—like Louis Simpson—this beauty and this truth are found in everyday life among ordinary people, and are waiting for someone to find the right words to express them.

I WRITE POEMS

Louis Simpson

I write poems, but I teach for a living. Some writers and teachers are only half-writers and half-teachers, but I think a man can be both a full-time writer and full-time teacher. It all depends on what you want to write. If you wish to make writing pay, then of course you must give all your time to it, like any business. But if you write only when you have something to say, then you will have a lot of time left over. During that time I teach. I certainly would not recommend teaching to everyone. In the first place you must enjoy it.

W. H. Auden once said that poets should not marry. But not every poet is able to resist the temptation. Certainly there are drawbacks to being a married writer, as there are to being a married anything. There's the house, the car, the kids shouting, "Gimme!" But the unmarried writer is in no better pickle. For one thing, he will always be fretting that he is not sufficiently loved. The unmarried writer travels more, but he knows less about the ordinary lives of men and women. However, when you get down to cases, being married or unmarried does not determine the quality of a man's work. Keats and Flaubert were not married, but Blake and Tolstoi were. What matters is the writer's intelligence.

If writers may be put in two categories, those who live in artistic circles and those who have ordinary lives, I belong in the second category. This does not mean that I agree with middle-class ideas; it is simply that I find it less distracting to live as others do than to spend my energy trying not to.

Also, in my experience, people who build their lives around art become ill-informed, arrogant, and stupid. On the other hand, if you move among ordinary people—and not as a stranger, but subject to the things they feel—you can learn much. Indeed, unless you do this your thoughts will have no importance. But you must also be able to detach yourself. It is necessary to have a little of the cunning that Joyce recommended, if you wish to "forge the uncreated consciousnes of the race."

There is material in everyday life for a poetry that will be neither esoteric nor banal. Except in Whitman and Hart Crane we have had very little of this poetry in America. We do not find in writing images that correspond to the lives we really have. Most poetry is mere fantasy; most prose is merely reporting the surface of things. We are still waiting for the poetry of feeling, words as common as a loaf of bread, which yet give off vibrations.

SUMMER MORNING

Louis Simpson

There are whole blocks in New York
Where no one lives—
A district of small factories.
And there's a hotel; one morning

When I was there with a girl
We saw in the window opposite
Men and women working at their machines.
Now and then one looked up.

Toys, hardware—whatever they made,
It's been worn out.
I'm fifteen years older myself—
Bad years and good.

So I have spoiled my chances.
For what? Sheer laziness,
The thrill of an assignation,
My life that I hold in secret.

FURTHER THOUGHTS

1. What does Simpson mean when he says, "I find it less distracting to live as others do than to spend my energy trying not to"? Do you agree with this idea? Think carefully about the word *distracting*.
2. Very often quite ordinary people seem to speak "words as common as a loaf of bread, which yet give off vibrations." Have you ever known such a person— perhaps someone in whom simple swearing had become a poetic art? Or have you known a person who writes such language? In either case, try to write down some examples—either as a collection of "one-liners," or a speech, or even a dialogue, perhaps like that between Bateson and his daughter on pages 237-241.
3. In "Summer Morning" Simpson says "I have spoiled my chances." How is this line like or different from Wright's "I have wasted my life"? How is it like or different from William Wordsworth's lines:

The world is too much with us; late and soon,
Getting and spending, we lay waste our powers:
Little we see in Nature that is ours;
We have given our hearts away, a sordid boon!

Of all the symbols we use to maintain our sense of self and of others, words are at once the most public and the most private. Words can be anybody's—but if I use them, they are mine. They are the most promiscuous of symbols. Always ready for loving, for hating. Quick to expose, they mask just as quickly. The strands of love are woven with them. And circles of hate. A common tongue makes communality. The web of friends, of strangers, of all others and so of our selves—are all held in their symbolic place by words—words in books, on signs, on badges; words spoken in the midst of gestures of fear and hope. We tire of them, worry about their apparent treachery, about the masks people can make with them; we can't leave them, and at times only a poet can love them.

POETICS

A. R. Ammons

I look for the way
things will turn
out spiralling from a center,
the shape
things will take to come forth in

so that the birch tree white
touched black at branches
will stand out
wind-glittering
totally its apparent self:

I look for the forms
things want to come as

from what black wells of possibility,
how a thing will
unfold:

not the shape on paper—though
that, too—but the
uninterfering means on paper:
not so much looking for the shape
as being available
to any shape that may be
summoning itself
through me
from the self not mine but ours.

FURTHER THOUGHTS

1. Ammons says that when he sets out to write a poem, he tries to keep himself
   open to whatever there is that wants to emerge in him and in the subject and
   the language. How does this apply to the business of living a life?
2. What might be your "Poetics" for writing a life, especially in terms of work,
   play, and leisure?

3. Answer the following questions—even if occasionally they seem a little strange. Don't be afraid to spend some time making up your mind. Be prepared to discuss your answers:

> Are you more like water or more like stone?
> Are you more yes or more no?
> Are you more here or there?
> Are you more now or then?
> Are you more summer or winter?
> Are you more potato or pomegranate?
> Are you more the past or the future?
> Are you more the tortoise or the hare?
> Are you more the hammer or the nail?
> Are you more a clothes line or a kite string?
> Are you more a fly swatter or fly paper?
> Are you more a mountain or a valley?
> Are you more a tool chest or a liquor cabinet?*

Eric Hoffer is a man who combines his job with constructive leisure in a way that is—but probably needn't and shouldn't be—unusual. As Calvin Tomkins says in his brief biography of Hoffer: "The individual longshoreman is free to work as many days a week as he pleases, and during the lulls in the work on the docks nobody tells him what to do with his time. At these moments Hoffer could usually be seen reading or writing in his pocket notebook. . . . It was while he was actually on the job that some of his best ideas came to him." A sense of this blend of working and thinking is conveyed by the selections from his diary, published as *Working and Thinking on the Waterfront*. Some sense of the product of this blend is conveyed by the following selection from his book *First Things, Last Things*.

MAN'S MOST USEFUL OCCUPATION

Eric Hoffer

Almost all the engravings, carvings and paintings of Paleolithic man were of animals. What was his attitude toward animals? He adored and worshiped them. They were his betters. Man among the animals is an amateur among superbly skilled and equipped specialists, each with a built-in tool kit. Man has neither claws nor fangs nor horns to fight with, neither scales nor hide to shield him, no

*Some of these questions are taken from Simon et al., Values Clarification, pp. 95-97.

special adaptations for burrowing, swimming, climbing or running. He craved the strength, speed and skill of the superior animals around him. When he boasted he likened himself unto an elephant, a bull, a deer. He watched the adored animals with the total absorption of a lover, and could paint them in vivid detail even on the ceiling of a dark cave.

Man's being an unfinished, defective animal has been the root of his uniqueness and creativeness. He is the only animal not satisfied with being what he is. His ideal was a combination of the perfections he saw in the animals around him. His art, dances, songs, rituals and inventions were born of his groping to compensate himself for what he lacked as an animal. His spirituality had its inception not in a craving to overcome his animality but in a striving to become a superior animal. In the cave of Trois Freres the sorcerer painted high on a ledge above the ground seems to rule over the world of animals depicted on the walls below, and this sorcerer, whose face is human, is a composite of animals: he has the antlers of a stag, the ears of a wolf, the eyes of an owl, the paws of a bear, the tail of a horse, and the genitalia of a wildcat.

The most crucial consequence of man's incurable unfinishedness is of course that he cannot truly grow up. Man is the only perpetually young thing in the world, and the playground is the ideal milieu for the unfolding of his capacities and talents. It is the child in man that is the source of his uniqueness and creativeness.

I have always felt that five is a golden age. We are all geniuses at the age of five. The trouble with the juvenile is not that he is not yet a man but that he is no longer a child. If maturing is to have meaning it must be a recapturing of the capacity for total absorption and the avidity to master skills characteristic of a five-year-old. But it needs leisure to be a child. When we grow up the world steals our hours and the most it gives us in return is a sense of usefulness. Should automation rob us of our sense of usefulness, the world will no longer be able to steal our hours. Banned from the marketplace we shall return to the playground and resume the task of learning and growing. Thus to me the coming of automation is the coming of a grand consummation, the completion of a magic circle. Man first became human in an Eden playground, and now we have a chance to attain our ultimate destiny, our fullest humanness, by returning to the playground.

FROM
WORKING AND THINKING ON THE WATERFRONT
Eric Hoffer

June 1, 1958

5 A.M. I am getting self-righteous. This usually happens after a long stretch of work. I remember Tolstoi saying somewhere that work makes not only ants but men, too, cruel.

4 P.M. Went to the dentist to have my teeth cleaned. Lili and the boy met me afterwards and we went to the beach. We had a good, plentiful meal at the Hitchrack. It is long since I tasted such good liver. The boy has learned several dirty words. Lili does not seem alarmed.

. . . .

October 16

Eight hours on a German ship (the *Bamberg*?) at Pier 26. I still wonder whether the German republican flag (black, red, and yellow) grates on the average German as it did after the First World War. Considering the present absorption of the Germans in private affairs and their determination to cultivate each his garden it probably matters little what the flag is. It will be a momentous turning point in the affairs of Europe if it be true that the Germans have wearied of their nationalism. Of course, the German tendency toward fanaticism may find a new dangerous outlet, though I cannot see what it could be.

All day long I mused vaguely and apprehensively about the coming vacation. I must guard myself against isolation. I shall be seeing Lili and the boy every Tuesday. I have just received two invitations for dinner, and I have to meet the editors and journalists from Southeast Asia. The main thing is not to take myself seriously.

October 17

Finished the German ship at Pier 26. Seven hours. On the way home I was overcome by a fit of drowsiness. This is surprising since I had a good night's sleep and the work during the day was fairly easy.

I just read several thoughts I had copied last night. It is surprising how many words I had missed. After a day's work I find that I can sketch a train of thought in bold strokes, but I can't copy faultlessly nor can I express myself with precision.

October 18

Eight hours at Pier 29 on a Luckenbach ship. I am replacing a regular dockman in Rekula's gang. Most of the gang are Finns, and when I am with them they stuff me full of Finnish words. Today I learned to count up to ten, and a dozen words or so concerning the weather, ships, and the work.

It occurred to me during the day that in my present state of weariness I ought not to make any plans. My mind is not in good shape. After catching my breath and spending some time with myself I may be able to gauge things and decide what to do. Tomorrow is my last day of work. Perhaps for the first time in my life I am looking forward to a vacation.

. . . .

November 18

Just as there isn't a human society without speech so there isn't a human society without art. The origins of art are far more mysterious than the origins of writing.

After breakfast I went to Macy's to buy glasses for Lili. I bought six each of wine, brandy, and cocktail glasses—for $11. Next time I shall get a tray.

I am intrigued by the fact that art is primordial, that its roots reach back to the earliest phases of humanization. It antedates toolmaking. Man used clay to mold figurines long before he made clay pots. When grubbing for necessities man is still an animal. He becomes uniquely human when he reaches out for the superfluous and extravagant.

. . . .

December 2

It is fantastic how much of a feeling of well-being I can derive from performing duties. Today I took care of the laundry; mailed figs, dates, and money to Sara; paid dues and signed up in the hall; drew a hundred dollars from the bank for Lili. By the time I got through I was so much at peace with myself that I went and bought half a dozen roses for the room.

. . . .

January 4

Eight hours on the *Java Mail* in Richmond Inner Harbor. Steady grind all day loading drums of DDT for India. My partner was a Negro. I have seen him on the docks before and the impression I had of him was of a labor faker. It turned out he was a fairly good worker, and a quiet, pleasant fellow. He looks sickly but did his share. We parted friends.

Marvin Kalb's book about Russia has set off several trains of thought. The great crimes of the twentieth century were committed not by money-grubbing capitalists but by dedicated idealists. Lenin, Stalin, and Hitler were contemptuous of money. The passage from the nineteenth to the twentieth century has been a passage from considerations of money to considerations of power. How naive the cliché that money is the root of evil!

This terrible century has seen more attempts to realize ideals, dreams, and visions than ever before. We have seen the dissolution of illusions and the dimming of dreams and visions. Just as the nineteenth century saw a paling of the faith in God and in the kingdom of heaven, so the twentieth is seeing the loss of faith in man and in a heaven on earth. We have found out that when dreams come true they may turn into a nightmare.

. . . .

February 22

Nine hours on a Luckenbach ship at Pier 29. I am taking the place of a steady hook-on man. All day I had the bay before my eyes. The water was light green speckled with white caps. The hills beyond were wrapped in a powder-blue veil through which shimmered the mass of white houses. In the afternoon, over Treasure Island, there was a massing of dark gray and smoky white clouds. One could trace the roots of the white clouds in the gray mass, and the whole thing gave the feeling of a violent reaction out of which something wholly new might emerge.

8:15 P.M. The question of the readiness to work keeps tugging at my mind. My explanation of freedom as an energizer of the masses, and of individual separateness as an irritant which keeps people on the go, is not wholly satisfactory. These are valid causes, but not the main ones. There is, for instance, the fact that there is a greater readiness to work in a society with a high standard of living than in one with a low standard. We are more ready to strive and work for superfluities than for necessities. People who are clear-sighted, undeluded, and sober-minded will not go on working once their reasonable needs are satisfied. A society that refuses to strive for superfluities is likely to end up lacking in necessities. The readiness to work springs from trivial, questionable motives. I can remember Paul Henri Spaak saying after the end of the Second World War that to energize the Belgian workers for the stupendous effort of rebuilding and recovery he had to fill the shops and tease the people with all the "luxuries and vices" they had been accustomed to. Attlee, a better socialist but a lesser statesman, instituted at that time in Britain a policy of "socialist austerity." A vigorous society is a society made up of people who set their hearts on toys, and who would work harder for superfluities than for necessities. The self-righteous moralists decry such a society, yet it is well to keep in mind that both children and artists need luxuries more than they need necessities.

· · · · · · · · · · · ·

April 16

Nine hours on the *C. E. Dant* at Pier 17. A weary day. Had Skeets for a partner—a poor worker with a bleating voice.

At intervals I peeked into an English translation of the *Lun Yu*. The aphorisms do not seem brilliant, yet you want to reread them. Perhaps it is because of the vagueness of some of the terms, the strangeness of the setting, and even the modernity of some of the sayings. "It is hard to find a man who will study for three years without thinking of a post in government." This is true even now in Asia, Africa, and Latin America. "To remain unconcerned though others do now know of us— that is to be a great man."

· · · · · · · · · · · ·

May 21

Eight hours on the Pope & Talbot *Voyager* at Pier 38. An easy and pleasant day. Indeed, I was in something like a festive mood all day long. It was partly due to the fact that I had on new working clothes. No one has fully investigated the effect of clothes on man's moods and behavior. Nietzsche said somewhere that a woman who feels well-dressed would not catch a cold even if she were half-naked. Emerson quotes a lady saying that when she is perfectly dressed she has a feeling of inner tranquillity which religion is powerless to bestow. I have never been well-dressed; never had on things of perfect fit and excellent material.

FURTHER THOUGHTS

1. In the first selection Hoffer says that "man first became human in an Eden playground" and that "the playground is the ideal milieu for the unfolding of his capacities and talents." What do these statements mean? Do they seem consistent with the selections from his diary? Do you think Hoffer is right? Would you say that the ideal milieu is the library? Or is it the workroom? In which milieu do you feel that you are—or would be—at your best? What does *best* mean here?
2. What does Hoffer have to say about the sources and function of creativity?
3. Hoffer has an aphoristic style, one that packs ideas into short, well-formed sentences and thus produces a number of maxims. From the two selections select maxims that seem especially significant to you and be prepared to explain your choices.
4. On the basis of your knowledge of the two men, what similarities do you notice between Hoffer and Thoreau? What differences?

Hoffer sounds nostalgic for the lost Eden playground when he says, "When we grow up the world steals our hours and the most it gives us in return is a sense of usefulness." Surely in a country where things are abundant, though not always well distributed, time should also be abundant, at least for those whose income is above the subsistence level. But things seem more attainable than time. Somehow the problem seems to involve the old notion of the work ethic—or maybe it is a matter of a consumer's ethic, with time becoming one more consumer item, like corn flakes. In his book *Of Time, Work and Leisure*, Sebastian de Grazia discusses some of the complexities of a culture that consumes time. Here is a section.

THE STORY OF TIME PIECES

Sebastian de Grazia

Most men today may not be aware that they are geared to machines—even while they are being awakened by the ringing of a bell and gulping down their coffee in a race with the clock. The clock, though, is a real machine, an automatic one, too. The monasteries did not invent the clock (rumor to the contrary), but they did discipline daily living within their walls to a routine of seven periods marked by bells. The thus-many-hours-for-sleep and thus-many-hours-for-prayer was one of the things Erasmus poked fun at. A routinized or ceremonial life for priests and kings and court too, as a matter of fact, appears in history at other times and places. The ancients, moreover, knew that time could be determined astronomically and did so determine it. But to ordinary people the day was divided into 12 hours from sunup to sundown—longer in summer, naturally, than in winter. Similarly, automatic machines had appeared long before among the Greeks and Moslems. The mechanical clock did not appear evidently until the thirteenth century. For a long time it made its way mostly to church towers and public buildings. In monasteries and churches it marked canonical hours or called the faithful to prayer. (*Clock* comes from an Italian word of Celtic origin, *clocca,* meaning bell tower; its historical relation to an auditory signal is significant.) Not until Cellini's time did it attain any reliability, and even then it had only an hour hand to worry about. The development . . . of mechanical time-pieces was carried on by groups of master artisans who were fascinated by this toy and in their fascination created a new metier—watchmaker.

In the beginning, the clock exerted a strange, almost morbid attraction as though it were ticking off life itself. Whereas the motto on a Roman solar quadrant might read *Lex mea sol,* many of the old public clocks in Europe carried sayings like *Mors certa, hora incerta* or *Toutes les heures vous blessent; la derniere vous tue.* But more and more they came to exercise the attraction of an ingenious mechanism. People felt as if they were carrying the brain of a genius in their pocket. Watches became the foibles of rich clients, kings and queens, and great ladies especially. Marie Antoinette received fifty-one watches as engagement gifts. The new watches, all of them encrusted with diamonds, pearls, gold, silver, enamel, and miniature portraits, were indeed remarkable. Centuries had been required to perfect them, but in each century master watchmakers created masterworks that inspired admiration and wonder. The clock, as the first fully automatic machine, remained the first in its perfection for so long because good artisans had spent so much effort and passion on it. It held up high its complicated meshing of gears as the exemplar for other machines.

Not until the nineteenth century did the clock begin to spread. The cheap watch appears in Switzerland in 1865 and in America a few years later, in 1880.

Within eight years the Waterbury factory in the United States was producing and selling half a million clocks and watches a year. Switzerland alone by now has exported between twenty and twenty-five millions. Why didn't the clock remain a toy? Why didn't it delight or fascinate a few people, and stop right there, to suffer the fate of the ingenious toys invented by the ancient Greeks and Moslems? Why were the nineteenth and twentieth centuries its day of diffusion? People don't buy a thing just because it is cheap, and in any case watches, though mass-produced, were not *that* cheap. Evidently they were needed.

Though its original contribution as a model was great, the clock's main function became to give frequent signals, auditory and visual, to enable men to start or stop an activity together. Before the clock there was the bell tower which from far off could not only be heard but also be seen for orientation. Then there was, and still is in some places, the factory whistle. But both these devices were limited for work in the big, noisy cities. The clock, first placed in a tower and later hung up wherever work was to be done, provided the means whereby large-scale industry could coordinate the movements of men and materials to the regularity of machines. Over the span of these several centuries, the seventeenth to the nineteenth, a new conception of time developed and spread over the industrial world, going hand in hand with the modern idea of work.

Time today is valuable. The clock's presence everywhere, and its tie to the factory with its relatively unskilled work, soon gave rise to the idea that one was selling time as well as, or rather than, skill. The lightening of toil and simplifying of tastes brought about by machines gave a related impression: that one was selling time rather than labor. The "hourly rate" and the "piece rate" express these notions. So time begins to be money, and, like money, a valuable, tangible commodity, to be saved, spent, earned, and counted. Clock time first governs work time (one sees the same happening today in countries moving toward industrialization), while social life holds to the old pattern. Later the clock's hands sweep over life outside of work too. . . . Hardly do you find manufacturers fixing hours of work, than you see workers mobilizing for a shorter working week. Free time takes its bow, like work decked out in clock time.

To be bought and sold in this way, time had to be neutralized. Customary ways of spending days had to be deprived of significance so that one day was much like another, and time could thus be spent in one activity as well as another. Days, hours, and minutes become interchangeable like standard parts. It was helpful that in countries that were to become industrial, Protestantism refused to recognize the saints, thus taking away the 100 days assigned to their celebration. Before this, one could not work on such days. Essentially, as the French Revolution made clear, the process was one of secularizing the calendar. When the year has its religious and other celebrations, certain activities are to be done at certain times and in a certain order. They take up time, but no matter how much they take, they must be done. And they are not interchangeable. At a given time one goes to market or to church, to work, to bed, to festivities, to the tavern or back home. One cannot work at a time for feasting or dancing, for church or the siesta. Something remains of this time in the notion of excusable absence from work—if a close member of the family dies, if a new one is born, or perhaps if one gets married—but the time allowed is cut to the bone, leaving nothing like the fat festivities that once were the rule on such occasions. The payment nowadays of time and a half for overtime or double time on Sunday indicates that one is dealing with a kind of time that bears the imprint of an earlier day. In European languages generally one still does not speak of "spending" time but of "passing" it, a usage reminiscent, too, of an earlier epoch.

With time well secularized, the possibilities of choice seem to increase. One has a whole 24 hours a day and can fill them as one pleases. The lone obligation is to give the first and best part of the day to work. After that—freedom. In this way free time came to be called what it is. The calendar has been secularized, however, but not really neutralized. By and large, work takes first place in time, while other activities partake of work's time characteristics. In olden days what one had was "spare" time, not free time, time unexpectedly left over, as might happen if one got help from a neighbor or found working materials unusually pliable, or if things just went right. If this happened one could properly engage in a pastime, perhaps play cards. But unless circumstances were particularly difficult—a storm having wrecked part of the house or the like—one was not supposed to work in this time, was not to engage in what we would call productive activities. In rural parts of the world today, in Burma, for example, one can see the pattern. After a man's tasks for the day are finished, he is not supposed to be busy. He goes to sit and smoke, gossip and drink "rough tea," or he visits. In Greek villages they say about work done after dark, "The day takes a look at it and laughs."

In the cities of the industrial world, once his debt to work is paid, a man is said to be off duty. He can fill his time as he chooses. He has a decision to make, though: which alternatives to choose for each hour or half or quarter thereof: play, work, chores, moonlighting?

He does have some rules as to how that time should be spent. A man should first of all spend it on things that give visible evidence of doing something. He should be busy at something. In some parts of the world, sitting or standing still, whether thinking or not, is considered an activity. In the United States it is not. Secondly he should do things to better himself. "To better" usually means to do something that will improve his own or his property's position, appearance, or money-making qualities. One should keep one's house in good condition (keep up the property) and should also try to increase its value by improvements. One should not just read (an activity still somewhat suspect because the only moving organs involved are the eyes) but should shun trash for books that are instructive, informative, useful. In short, a man off work should (1) do something and (2) do something productive. An American could not have

written the lines that follow, because only to him or to the egocentric species to
which he belongs could time be so busy and dear.

> Don't waste precious time
> Now, tagging along with me . . .
> Little butterfly.

The Haiku is one of Issa's (1763-1827).

So, all told, time is not neutralized but commercialized, or, better,
industrialized. Free time as we know it is a kind developed by the industrial
world's clock time. Here again it is clear that recreation is best understood as an
ally of work rather than as its opposite or as an activity independent in its own
right. Recreational activities are bound on all sides by work time. The activities
with which one fills free time cannot be such as to encroach on work time. The
worker on the assembly line, if he had a bad night of it, because of drink or wild
jazz or a drawnout battle with his wife, nevertheless has to be at the plant on
time. His alarm clock is not misnamed. It really is an alarm for a serious
danger—being late to work. If he gets there on time, he may be able to arrange
with co-workers, or even the foreman, to get someone to take his place for
fifteen minutes of shut-eye in the corner of a little-used stockroom, but barring
extraordinary traffic tie-ups or acts of God, should he appear late on more than
two or three occasions, well spread out and for only a few minutes apiece, he
can go draw his pay. It won't be long before he gets a pink slip.

Since clock time has precise units, it is measurable. Time-keepers measure the
ins and outs of employees; they also measure the time that operations and the
flow of materials take. There are always new processes being instituted in a large
plant, and one has to know how much time they need. References to time in
industrial areas are literal. "Be here in half an hour" means in 30 minutes.
Precision inside the plant has its effect outside. "Come here this second," says an
American mother to her child, using a word a Roman mother could not have,
because the word for "second" was not in everyday use. The ancient Egyptians
for common use had not even a minute of any measured duration, much less a
second.

The American office schedule is tight and sacred, too. "I'll see you at 4:10,
then," is a sentence that would have been comprehensible to no other
civilization this earth has seen. Violators of the schedule are punished. If you are
not on time for appointments you will come to be regarded as an irresponsible
person. If a man is kept waiting in the outer office for ten or fifteen minutes,
careful apologies are necessary. In some countries, in the Ottoman Empire
tradition, a man can be kept waiting without offense for an hour or an hour and
a half. Tacitus, in writing of the ancient Germans, said they never assembled at
the stated time, but lost two or three days in convening. When they all thought
fit they sat down. This still happens among some American Indians and among
literate peoples, too. The social schedule follows suit. In Greek villages no time is

set for dinner guests. You arrive and after a while dinner appears. Persons who are punctual are rarities, and sometimes dubbed "Englishmen." In parts of Latin America, if you are invited for dinner at 7:00 you can appear then, if you wish, but eat a snack first. Dinner may appear at ten or midnight. On the Continent still today, except for the clockmaking countries, if you arrive on time for social engagements, you're early. In the United States ten minutes late for a dinner begins to look serious.

The clock then with its precise units breaks the day into equal parts that by conscious decision are to be filled with worthy activities. A man may want to loaf his time away, yes, but loafing is wasted time, and time shouldn't be wasted. It is valuable and scarce. One has only 24 hours of it a day.

The scarcity of time may appear puzzling. One has always had 24 hours of it. They should not seem less now than before. Before, however, one did not have 24 hours. There was a sunrise and a sunset, a noon or a hottest part, and there was night. Above all one had a day, a day of a certain character according to the calendar. Then that great space was partitioned into 1,440 tiny cubicles. By our standards even those engineers, the ancient Romans, had vague time notions. The Egyptians divided the days and nights into 12 hours each (the Babylonians were the first to do this) but paid little attention to the hour of any event. One lady's baby was reported to be born in the fourth hour of the night, but she was the wife of a priest. The night was a constant unit, no matter how light some of its twelve hours were in summertime. A day of 24 hours or 1,440 minutes divided into 5- or 10- or 20-minute groups survives in popular custom only if the divisions prove useful. Today they apparently do, at least in the cities. A dermatologist can schedule patients in his office at 10-minute intervals. Many people in business and government schedule 10- or 15-minute, sometimes 5-minute, appointments. Trains and planes go by schedule in odd minutes—7:08, 10:43. All appointments must be kept by continual reference to the inexorable clock. If you miss a bus or train, or only fail to make a stop light when on a schedule, the result is fear and nervousness at being late, or the tension of not getting done all that you were supposed to. The cramming of hours and minutes takes place because of the belief that time's units are interchangeable and commercially valuable, but it is the clock itself that permits the constant checking and adjusting of one's actions.

Other commercial societies have had the feeling of urgency and of many things to do, similar to ours, but ours can be more tightly scheduled and made almost escapeproof by the ubiquitous clock and the machines geared to it. We have here, it may be, why our dreamers of free time foresaw the future badly and why, with abundant free time to dispose of today, there is everywhere the tenseness of haste. The poet Ciro di Pers in the seventeenth century, when clocks first began to make headway, already saw that they make time scarce and life short:

> Noble machine with toothed wheels
> Lacerates the day and divides it in hours . . .

Speeds on the course of the fleeing century.
And to make it open up,
Knocks every hour at the tomb.

No other nation by now is as precise in its time sense nor so time-conscious as the United States. Americans generally are aware that time runs by steadily and is being used up evenly, minute after minute, hour after hour, day after day—inexorable, impersonal, universal time. In countries without dependence on the clock, there is largely the sense of passage of biological time. In the seasonal rhythm is an age-consciousness: one notices oneself passing through youth, prime, and age, all the stages that Horace and Shakespeare marked with appropriate lines. There is nothing very precise about the units— one season comes late, one day is long, another night is longer, the heart beats faster one morning and respiration slows down the next.

We have almost lost this rhythmical sense of time. We can hardly believe that some not-so-primitive tribes have no word at all for time, or that if a native of a remote rural area is asked how long it takes by foot, mule, or car to get to a certain place, he cannot say, though he can describe every yard in the road all the way to the destination. Can you make it by noon? He doesn't know. You certainly can make it by noon, you would think? Yes, he says, of course. Is it really possible to go that far by noon? Oh no, says he.

It is not unusual for people living without clocks not to know the day of the week except Sunday and even on Sunday not to know the hour of mass. Until the Gregorian reform of the calendar, toward the end of the sixteenth century, Europeans seem to have been little interested to remember just how old they were, if they had ever known in the first place. Modern biographers of that century probably know more about their subjects' chronological age than the subjects cared to know themselves. We can usually distinguish a 5-minute from a 10-minute wait, without the clock, because we have been trained to do so.

The synchronizing of activities by the clock begins early. The child sees his father arise by the clock, treat its facial expression with great respect, come home by it, eat and sleep by it, and catch or miss his entertainment—the movies, a TV show—by it. Also the child at home is explicitly taught time—it is one of the few subjects nowadays in which parents feel fully competent to instruct their children—by example, precept, and books, and taught also in the classroom, where experience is as sharp as at the factory. Alas for the tardy scholar who comes not at 10:00 o'clock or at noon but at 8:40 instead of 8:30.

Getting first-graders to be regular as clockwork, to use a favorite Victorian expression, is not the easiest job in the world. For children of ten or twelve to master the elements of the American time system takes attention from all sides. This done, there is thenceforth less of the feeling of imposition that people have for the clock when introduced to it only at a later age. Many of the latter learn to like to wear watches or have clocks as baroque ornaments for the house.

Whether they are running or stopped makes little difference. They like them as a symbol of wealth and modernity, not as a despot to be obeyed.

In England during the early days of industrialism, workers turned from the straitening embrace of clocked machinery to gin and revivalism. Today, it is believed, time pressure is reflected in certain nervous disturbances, the claustrophobias in time. Cooped up in time a person still seeks, but finds harder to reach, the timeless worlds of gin-sodden slums and nineteenth-century Methodism. In Samuel Butler's *Erewhon* the workers destroyed all machines, as indeed the Luddites tried to do in the early machine age until shot, hanged, and deported into submission. They had acted like bulls, hypnotized not by the flashing red cape but by the whir of machinery. All the while the real enemy, the matador, was there behind, silent, imperturbable, the clock on the wall. Had they destroyed all clocks, the industrial world would have remained at most a lively commercial age.

There are other signs that the clock's imperiousness is resented still. The impersonality of its coordinating action, the fact that face-to-face synchronizing has largely been eliminated, that bigness is possible only at the cost of (as the phrase aggressively puts it) punching a time machine in and out and being clocked by stop watches—all this is one side of the story. The free professionals today are envied because their time is not clocked off like industry's. The newer, salaried professionals, who now outnumber the others by about six to one, are directly linked to the system.

Of its inhabitants clockland also requires regularity in habits. A person can resent regularity not alone in himself but in others too. In recent years concern has grown over the uniformity in American behavior. Writers usually contrast it with the Puritan individualist. Besides the Puritan as nonconformist, there have been other forces for variety in American history. The many breeds of immigrants and mixtures of races, for one, and their pushing into and taming the wilderness, for another. Each kind of people brought widely differing customs. The American Indian himself, obedient to the camp circle was to the whites a devil of nonconformism. They rarely approved of his bucking against slavery. With the closing of new lands, the shutting up of the Indians on reservations, and the feeding of immigrants to factories, mines, and sweatshops, these forces for variety had to turn back and cast their lot with the machine.

Once the buccaneering of the frontiers and that of industry were spiritually akin. The flare of energy that swept across the West turned back east and for a while made industry, both owners and workers, glow with a rude, ruddy industrialism. Before long, though, the clock had its way. Some of the old industrialism yet exists, chiefly as an ideal to which lip service is handsomely paid, but the verve has been flattened by standardization. When we speak of synchronizing the actions of men by clocks, we are not using a merely fanciful phraseology. The clock, to repeat, is an automatic machine whose product is regular auditory or visual signals. Who lives by it becomes an automaton, a creature of regularity.

FURTHER THOUGHTS

1. De Grazia points out that the clock started out as a toy. Why do you think it didn't stay that way? Can you think of other toys that became serious tools or instruments?

2. Consider some other toys and try to imagine what would happen if we were to begin to take them as seriously as we do the clock. What about Ouija boards, for instance? kaleidoscopes? Look up the word *fetish*; how does it tie in with this line of thought?

3. How often do you look at your watch? For one day try wearing it on the opposite hand so you will be more aware of how frequently you consult it.

4. The Latin and French maxims on page 312 can be translated as: "My law is the sun," "Certain death, uncertain hour," and "All hours wound, but the last kills." They contrast Roman and medieval European views on time and death. Try writing and collecting some maxims that express modern views.

5th Interlude

When this country was founded, Thomas Jefferson expressed one of the dreams of its founders, a dream in which people had land enough to live on. One of the things the Mexican basket-weaver in Traven's story knew he had, with his less than fifteen acres, was land enough to live on. That is one reason why he could reject Mr. Winthrop's promise of riches and glory in favor of the friends who helped him, his little crop of beans and the corn he could trust. One obvious characteristic of modern life is that most of us are landless. The old Jeffersonian dream still exists, in all the suburbs of all the cities of America, where all we have left is a small piece of land, which we mow with a lawnmower, and two cars but little corn we can trust. In the ghettoes, of course, there is less than that—no land but masses of poor people. Someone once said that if you could explain why people prefer to be poor in the city rather than poor on the land, you could solve the problems of modern urban America. Oddly enough, Saroyan's shaggy-dog story in Part 1 suggests a possible solution to the problems of the landless poor in American cities. There is a way we can "make" money, as Saroyan's class did. It has been suggested by someone as "liberal" as Robert Theobald and as "conservative" as President Nixon's advisor Milton Friedman. This shaggy-dog theory of economics, which may be the salvation of our urban poor, is outlined here by Mr. Theobald.

FROM
ALTERNATIVE FUTURE FOR AMERICA II

Robert Theobold

Society must now choose between two primary directions, both of which have fundamental implications but which move in diametrically opposed directions. We can try to ensure that everybody is able to find a job and therefore is able to earn an income, or we can set up a system in which every individual receives an income as a matter of right and is given the responsibility to develop himself and his society.

A recent Gallup poll makes it abundantly clear that the American people prefer the first alternative; that is, a very substantial number of people prefer the idea of guaranteed employment to the idea of guaranteed income. In fact, however, this choice would actually destroy the social and economic patterns of behavior which America most values.

Guaranteed employment represents a continuation of past traditions. It claims that human beings should hold a job if they are to be entitled to an income. Implicit in this proposal is a conviction of the dignity of work, the requirement that each individual contribute to the society, the unwillingness to provide resources to those who are merely parasitic on the society. It is not surprising that Americans, when they come to understand the reality of hunger and poverty, should opt for this approach.

Unfortunately, the guaranteed employment proposal is based, like the war on poverty, on an understanding of reality which is from the past rather than of the future. In the 1930's, people couldn't find jobs because there was no demand for the products they produced. Most of the unemployed had meaningful skills in terms of the technology of the period and could be absorbed as demand increased, a fact shown by the way unemployment melted as war needs increased. Today, however, there is no lack of demand in the overall job market for those with meaningful skills. It is those who have inadequate training, inadequate skills or problems such as bad health, alcoholism, etc., who cannot find jobs today.

Training programs, in so far as they are successful, remove people from the unemployable class. The proposal for government as the employer of last resort recognizes implicitly that not everybody can be retrained to be useful in the conventional job market, and that only specially created job opportunities will absorb such people.

But what activities are those unemployable in the normal job market going to be able to do? If they are unemployable in the normal job market, where will there be meaningful activity for them? Few activities today can be based on an unskilled, uneducated or unreliable work force, and yet this is what the government will have to provide as employer of last resort.

We must recognize the reality of the problem: there are a growing number of people who are not competitive with machines today. To take one example, it is not economical to employ people to dig ditches in competition with a ditch-digging machine. Even leaf raking requires intelligence and responsibility unless it is *pure* make-work.

What, then, of the dynamics of any program designed to ensure that anybody who cannot find an income through a conventional job should be able to go to the government in its capacity as employer of last resort? The government must inevitably find itself confronted with the most ill-trained, ill-educated, disinterested part of the population. The activity into which these people would have to be moved would always be boring and usually be meaningless. Those who wished to work meaningfully would rebel against the meaninglessness and the trouble would be encouraged by those who had been forced into the program against their will. Absenteeism would be high and work standards abysmally low, while heavy demands for changes in activity would endanger the efficiency of the program.

Congress would find the situation intolerable. It would be argued that advantage was being taken of the program, that administrative lines were inefficient, Assuming that the program continued, there would be pressure to tighten up and to introduce rules to prevent abuse. One might imagine proposals, for example, that nobody should be permitted to change his job more than once every six months and that those who had a consistent record of absenteeism should be fined part of their wage if they failed to turn up for their work.

This scenario for the future is shared by others, although it is not accepted by most economists. Almost all science fiction writers—the best futurists in our society—who have examined this issue have concluded that such an evolution is inevitable if we continue to develop technology and yet demand that everybody should hold a job. The science fiction novel most to this point is *Player Piano* by Kurt Vonnegut.

What then of the basic goals of those who propose "guaranteed employment?" Will they be fulfilled? We have seen that the work people carry out in this program will not add to their dignity, for it will be make-work which can better be carried out by machines. We have seen that these people will not contribute to society, for if they had the skills to do so—*or* could be trained to have the skills to do so—they would not need to apply to the government as an employer of last resort.

Finally, the attempt to keep these people in jobs would actually decrease the wealth available to the society rather than increase it. The scarcest commodity in this society is organizational skills. Running this program would be extremely difficult and would require very high levels of skills which would have to be diverted from other valuable uses while the production achieved by the employed labor force would not be significant. Thus the decision to employ the unemployables would actually decrease wealth.

Should we then abandon the goals of achieving dignity from work and requiring that each individual contribute to the society? Of course not. Man is a striving animal and the destruction of the opportunity for achieving meaning will inevitably destroy him. In addition, it is clear that the survival of any social system requires that all its members work toward the survival and development of the society. We do not need to abandon our fundamental goals; rather, we need to discover how they can be effectively fulfilled in present circumstances.

We do, however, need to make a distinction between our fundamental goals and those which have come to be seen as immediately necessary. We have developed a society in which efficiency and maximum consumption have become critical both to many individuals and to the functioning of society. If we are to consider the issues involved in the distribution of income we have to accept that the most important requirement is that each individual should be given the maximum opportunity for self-development in a social structure in which he can function effectively.

This approach is, in reality, the main point of disagreement between those who perceive the necessity for man to be employed and those who believe that man should be set free by being provided with his income as a right and by being encouraged to accept the responsibility for developing himself and his society. Those in favor of jobs accept a view of man which is derived from the work of Professor B. F. Skinner, who argues that men respond only to positive and negative sanctions—the carrot and the whip. They argue that if human beings are not afraid of losing their jobs and not enthusiastic about achieving higher standards of living they will sink back into apathy—or, in more colorful language, they will sit in front of the television set all day swilling beer.

A new school of psychologists has emerged to challenge the assumptions of Skinner and to argue that man is capable of self-development. Perhaps the most developed theoretical scheme stems from the work of Abraham Maslow, who argues that man's patterns of behavior change as his situation changes. So long as man does not possess the food, clothing and shelter he needs for survival he places his energy into creating the material necessities for life. But as soon as man moves beyond the necessity to strive for material goods he is driven by his own internal necessities to try to discover what will allow him to develop his own capabilities.

If Maslow is right, as I believe he is, his theory demonstrates the profound immorality of the present welfare system and all techniques which use the whip and the carrot. Individuals who are provided with insufficient money to feed, clothe and shelter themselves adequately are simply incapable of rising above their immediate material needs to consider the wider possibilities that face them. In the words of a welfare recipient, "If you're hungry it's very hard to think beyond where and when the next meal will come from."

If Skinner is right, the whip and carrot technique is necessary. While we may deplore it we dare not modify it for fear that the society will break down as more and more people fail to contribute to the necessities of the society. If, on the other hand, Maslow is right, the present welfare system is the very pattern which is preventing large numbers of individuals from contributing as they could to the development of the society.

One's view of the proper pattern for the future therefore depends on one's view of human nature. Such views cannot be proven correct on the basis of objective data, for the way that people behave depends very much on the attitudes toward them of the society and of the individual observing them. If the society treats a group of individuals as though they are lazy, irresponsible bums, it sets up patterns so that the only "sane" form of behavior is to *be* a lazy, irresponsible bum. This is like the case of the paranoid who, believing that all other people are threatening, acts in such a way that the reaction of others becomes threatening to him. If Maslow is right then the younger generation which has grown up in an abundance economy are looking for ways in which they can engage in self-development. Unfortunately, however, there are few routes by which they can contribute to the society. In their frustration, therefore, they are led to draw attention to their needs through protest, which sometimes becomes violent. I consider such violence unwise, but I consider the attempts to suppress and drive it underground even more dangerous. The young people in our society are warning us by their actions that there are serious problems and that we must pay attention to them. If we should continue our present pattern of repression we may succeed in "calming" the country, but we will do so at the cost of suppressing those very symptoms which might lead the country to re-examine itself. We will do it also at the cost of breaking the heart of the very generation which must save us, by instead driving them to drugs, drink, sexual excess and meaningless crime.

The unwisdom of our present patterns of activity can be seen most clearly if we consider a physical analogy. The body runs a high temperature in many diseases and this serves as a symptom to alert the doctor to the need for action. He would be considered stupid if he acted simply to reduce the temperature without consideration to the causes of the temperature. Similarly we show no intelligence if we try to reduce the temperature of the body politic without considering the reasons for that temperature.

Now let us turn to the method of introduction of the guaranteed income. I have become convinced that the means proposed in my 1963 book, *Free Men and Free Markets,* are no longer desirable. This book stated that we should provide additional resources to every individual if his income should fall below a certain level, but that we should recognize the need for a premium to those who worked at jobs seen as desirable by the society. Even at the time of writing *Free Men and Free Markets* I stated that this premium was largely necessary because of the present views of the society rather than in terms of the ethical or economical requirements of the situation. It now seems clear to me that we must eliminate the idea that income rights should be different if the individual holds a job or not.

There are two reasons for this. First, negative income tax schemes, based upon payment of the difference between a given income level set by the government and the individual's present (lower) income raise incredibly complex problems of calculation. They also provide major possibilities for cheating and it would be naive to assume that some cheating will not take place. Such schemes would also tend to encourage new patterns of disintegration in family life.

Guaranteed income should be administered in the following way. Every individual in the United States should receive a direct payment from the federal government which would not be affected by his present income. The level of this income would have to be set in the light of fiscal possibilities and the commitment of the American people to provide resources. The goal, however, should be $1,400 per adult and $900 per child.

All other income received from any source would be taxed. The individual exemptions and almost all tax deductions would be eliminated. The amount of tax paid would depend only on the amount of money received by the individual rather than the source of the income. The degree of progression in the tax rate and the overall pattern of income distribution would depend on the views of the public about the degree of inequality it felt was appropriate and justified.

In this context, I am convinced that we must be prepared not only to provide resources to those who are poor but also to deal with the other acute problem of income distribution—the problems which will confront those now in middle-income groups who will see their earning opportunities destroyed as the computer continues to develop. That is, not only will there be an increasingly inadequate number of market-supported jobs for those with lower levels of education and skills, but it can also be expected that many of those now engaged in middle management and similar occupations will lose their present jobs and be felt by prospective employers to have insufficient intellectual flexibility to take on new types of work. The drastic and abrupt drop in income which will follow will mean that members of this group will find themselves suddenly unable to meet the expenditure commitments already undertaken as part of their way of life, both on a day-to-day basis and incorporated in their long-term plans. In contemplating the possibility of hardship for the individuals in this group, we should not forget that their personal difficulties will have far wider implications for society as a whole. For just as individuals need the support of some form of basic economic security, society needs support for its standards and a source of initiatives and drive to move it toward its goals. It is this support, these initiatives and this drive which are supplied by this group. As an alternative to allowing the complete disruption of the way of life of this standard-supporting and societally useful group, it is necessary that a method be devised to maintain its level of incomes.

Therefore, in addition to *guaranteed income,* a second principle should be introduced, embodying the concept of the need to protect the existing middle-income group against abrupt major declines in their standard of living; this principle could be called *committed spending.* Together the principles of guaranteed income and committed spending could be called an Economic Security Plan, a plan designed to provide security for society as a whole and for each individual within it.

The payments to those receiving committed spending from the government would be related to their incomes before they became eligible for payments under committed spending. The continuance of higher levels of income for those entitled to committed spending, compared to those available under guaranteed income, would allow the middle-income group to continue the expenditures to which they had become committed and which are vital to the short-run stability of the country. However, to avoid major differentials in entitlements, no payment under committed spending would exceed a given multiple of the amount available to a family of the same size under guaranteed income. This multiple might possibly be three; thus, if a family receiving guaranteed income would be entitled, for example, to $3,700 then a family of comparable size would have an income ceiling of $11,100 from committed spending.

· · · · · · · · · · · · ·

We may not have reached a free goods situation by the end of the 1970's but we will certainly have moved a long way towards it.[1] This is inevitable because an increasing number of people will be living on Basic Economic Security (BES) and Committed Spending (CS). People who live on BES and CS are not going to use money for exchanging goods among themselves. They are going to swap human services without exchanging money.

The availability of free goods would lead to some very interesting developments. First, we could begin to eliminate the power which has been

[1] Theobald defines a free goods situation as "one where a person walks into a store and takes whatever he wishes off the shelves."

accorded by the community to certain groups in the society, which enables them to peg high prices, rates of interest, wages and salaries. In the future, prices, wages, rates of interest and salaries should fall because prices would be related to scarcity and we are moving into a position of abundance. Second, as people can choose to move out of jobs they dislike into areas of activity which seem good to them, because of their possession of BES and CS, wages and salaries available for pleasant jobs would start to decline. Because of this decline in wages and salaries, it would become less attractive to spend money inventing and installing machines to replace pleasant areas of work. At the other end of the spectrum, the first result of a guaranteed income would be to force people to pay an adequate wage for unpleasant jobs.

No one would do unpleasant jobs unless he got paid an adequate wage for it. The consequent rise in wages would make it attractive to automate and thus eliminate the jobs that people don't want to do.

This combination of forces would move us towards a system of free goods. A theoretical analysis of this necessity has been developed. It was created by a non-economist, which is perhaps not surprising. The argument is essentially very simple. It is first demonstrated that we are moving beyond the point where work is unwanted. If work is pleasant, why should we pay somebody to act in ways which are attractive to him. In addition, we are moving to the point where the overall supply of goods could be adequate if we were not bedazzled into buying things we don't need, thus increasing our sensory overload. In these circumstances, where work is attractive and consumption available, the old methods for distributing income are no longer valid: the only possible route is to provide each person with the option to work as much as he likes and to consume as much as he wishes.

FURTHER THOUGHTS

1. Theobald's reasoning is tight and stark. You may have to study it very carefully to get his argument clearly in your mind. In particular, watch for summary sentences. Copy out the six or seven crucial ones that seem to you to present the outline of his argument.
2. Do you agree with his analysis of the error in the concept of full employment? If not, where do you think his analysis goes wrong? Do you agree with his argument in favor of a guaranteed income? If not, what do you suggest as a workable alternative?
3. It is important to watch how Theobald works out the implications of his ideas. What do you think some of the long-term implications would be? What would happen, for instance, to ambition and personal enterprise, points on which critics often attack Mr. Theobald? What effect would his proposals have on the nature of the family? What expectations would be changed for

the roles of father, mother, children, grandparents? What would happen to schools? to leisure-time activities?

4. If this is the first time you've encountered the kinds of questions asked in this exercise, go back to page 65 and read the instructions there.

a. Which of the following do you most agree with?

_____ money is both necessary and evil

_____ money is necessary but not evil

_____ money is neither necessary nor evil

_____ money is evil but not necessary

b. If you were unexpectedly given $1,000,000.00, tax free, what would you do?

_____ continue living as you do now

_____ make some solid investments

_____ really live it up

_____ contribute a lot of money to charities

c. If you saw somebody like the character in Terry Southern's novel *The Magic Christian*, throwing $100 bills into a pond filled with excrement and foul garbage, what would you do?

_____ dive in and get some of that money for yourself

_____ call the police

_____ stop the man

_____ watch the other people diving in

_____ walk away

d. Why do you want more money (if you do)?

_____ to get better food and clothes and housing

_____ to get some luxuries

_____ to feel more secure

_____ to feel more independent

e. Write two questions like those above, dealing with money and economics.

Our Future Works

Many of the favorite stories in our culture concern an armed man on horseback. He is a loner, a victor. Even though the lone hero was joined by other warriors and arms were massed into larger and larger blocks of force, the image of the lone, victorious hero has remained a moral guide, a good mythic figure.

The Judaeo-Christian tradition gave the pagan hero, with his goals of honorable destruction and glorious victory, the weapon of righteousness. As a result of the Industrial Revolution the horse-powered, masked-man grew more powerful, and the enemy to be defeated was nature itself. The end of that story can be seen in the lakes he killed and the hills he stripped.

That myth goes back to the time of warrior-herdsmen. It never did express the needs of urban life. We are still seeking a hero for our times. The first of the urban heroes was the medical man, whose victories were always partial, for death is only delayed, never conquered. The ancient Greeks posed the man who made things, the makers, as the hero of some of their stories. Their name for him was *poet.* Our current archetypal craftsman is not the poet but the engineer Vulcan, who in Roman myths armed the hero. He has played an important subsidiary role in a contemporary myth about war that has grown too dangerous to believe anymore. We need a new hero.

ADVICE TO AN INTERPLANETARY VISITOR

Bruce Dawe

When you find him,
that last citizen,
hiding wherever there is left to hide,
too timid to surface,
living on nuts or whatever was at hand
when the flash came
—be kind to him, comfort him,
break the news to him gently
that he is the *sine qua non*, the ultimate reason
for everything.

Let him walk where he will,
let him reassure himself with trees, yes, and the light
walking between them, let him listen to waters
conversing like children, the rain
telling its secular tears, let him
lose himself in what *was,* roaming
the city streets where wires hang
like ganglia, let him touch things
and remember. Soon enough
logic may cross his brow
like an evil shadow.

When you find him
—give him your alien kindness,
stroke him with feelers of love.

OZYMANDIAS

Percy Bysshe Shelley

I met a traveller from an antique land
Who said: Two vast and trunkless legs of stone
Stand in the desert . . . Near them, on the sand,
Half sunk, a shattered visage lies, whose frown,
And wrinkled lip, and sneer of cold command,

Tell that its sculptor well those passions read
Which yet survive, stamped on these lifeless things,
The hand that mocked them, and the heart that fed:
And on the pedestal these words appear:
'My name is Ozymandias, king of kings:
Look on my works, ye Mighty, and despair!'
Nothing beside remains. Round the decay
Of that colossal wreck, boundless and bare
The lone and level sands stretch far away.

FURTHER THOUGHTS

1. Look hard at the following phrases in Dawe's poem: *"sine qua non,"* "telling its secular tears," "logic ... like an evil shadow," and "alien kindness." Explore some of the various meanings contained in each of these phrases as they are used in the poem.
2. At least part of the point that Shelley's poem makes is that things we say at one time (especially proud and boastful things) can come back to mean something quite different later on. Can you think of other examples of this—perhaps from your own experiences, perhaps from history, perhaps from fiction?
3. Imagine what things will be like five thousand years from now. What will be left in the sands of America that will be like Ozymandias' statue? Missile silos, perhaps? freeways? aluminum beer cans?

Once upon a time there were a scientist and a technician. More precisely, a physicist and his engineering aide were working together on an unlikely project spawned by the jet age. They were in charge of a machine that would track and photograph jet engines in the sky. And the machine kept breaking down. The technician would turn to his workbench and start making another machine to fit onto the old one, thinking that was the way to get the old machine to work. He always failed. The physicist, drafted rather hastily into the project, would watch and shake his head—"No, Carl, another machine won't do. We have to think our way out of this."

This seems to us to be the message of R. Buckminister Fuller. The power of thought can weigh the scales in favor of survival. There is, he insists, an unacknowledged form of wealth that is as powerful as grain or minerals: man thinking, the power of thought.

TOWARDS A FULLER FUTURE*

R. Buckminster Fuller

Long ago, now, scientists had discovered from their studies of steam etc. what they called thermodynamics. There they found that every system always tends to lose energy. This is called entropy: systems run down. Thus when I went to Harvard as a student, that intellectual community was assuming that we all live in an "instant universe," just as Newton had. The stars were simply there—they always had been—and Newton's gravity operated instantly everywhere in the universe. If you have an instant universe, then this universe is a system and as such it must be losing energy and is, then, "running down." This was the way men were explaining things as recently as my student days. There had been some sun disturbance eons ago and the sun had thrown off light all right but ultimately we—the earth—would stop spinning for, as Newton said in his first law of motion: "A body persists in a state of rest, or in a line of motion except as affected by other bodies." His first statement, the "at rest," is the norm, and things are going to come to rest in the universe—eventually. If the universe is running down and energies are involved, then anybody who goes in for something new and uses up energies is anathema. This was when the great pirates were saying they didn't want any new inventions, because they had invested quite a lot to get those factories and they didn't want any change in their monopoly. As you can imagine, it was very easy to get scholarly support because they said: "Anybody who's using up that energy is 'spending' and helping the universe to 'run down' and die."

But then there had already been some experiments concerning speed-of-light measurements, around the turn of the century, and soon we have Einstein and Planck going even further and saying that the speed of light is 186,000 miles a second. They said it would take about eight minutes for the light to come to us from the sun, the nearest star to earth, and four years from the next nearest. As we now know, as we look around the sky we're seeing a live show taking place thirty thousand years ago, if we just shift the eye a little we see another live

---

*The first prose selection, on pages 332-334, is by R. Buckminster Fuller, from his "Education for Comprehensivity" in *Approaching the Benign Environment,* The Franklin Lectures in the Sciences and Humanities, First Series (University, Ala.: University of Alabama Press, 1970), pages 46-51. The second prose selection, on pages 334-335, is from the same source, pages 59-60. And the third prose selection, on page 335, is also from the same source, pages 67-68. The short passage at the bottom of page 335 is from William Marlin's article about Fuller, "The Evolution and Impact of a Teacher," from *Architectural Forum* (January/February, 1972), page 65. The selection at the top of page 336 is also from Fuller's "Education for Comprehensivity," pages 72-73. The passage on pages 336-337 is again by Fuller, this time from his *Operating Manual for Spaceship Earth* (Carbondale: Southern Illinois University Press, 1969), page 79 of Marlin's article. The middle selection on page 338 is from pages 76 and 81 of Marlin's article. The bottom selection on page 338 is from Fuller's "Education for Comprehensivity," pages 66-67. The selections by Marlin are in italic.

show taking place 150,000 years ago, and so forth. Therefore, Einstein and Planck said: "Well, the universe must be an aggregate of nonsimultaneous and only partially overlapping events."

This is still the best description we have of the "universe." We see a little child growing bigger but certainly not running down and it's clear that a child is not entropic right from the time of birth. Thus, there are apparently areas where energies are accumulated. Einstein said that in this nonsimultaneous aggregate of events, when energy is disassociated from one local system, it had to be associating into another. Exhaustive experiments, review of all experiments, and careful accounting of all further experiments made it perfectly clear that this was exactly what was going on—that when energy disassociated here it always associated there and was always a hundred percent accounted for. When there was any amount that wasn't readily accounted for, scientists began to discover that nature has some kinds of behavior that they hadn't experienced as yet, and that a lot of these kinds of energy behavior occur relatively seldom—hence man's not having run into them before. The scientist learned, then, to respect that fraction of the total that he didn't know about, and if he made further experiments and the same fraction was there, then he had to say: "Well, we don't know exactly what the behavior is but this is about the energy it takes, and we'll give it a name; we'll call it a meson." Still later, the scientists were actually able to isolate the meson and begin to find out what that behavior is. Even so, the experiment has disclosed neither the creation of new energy nor the loss of any of the existing. Energies, apparently, are finite and accountable. This law, the law of conservation of energy, states that energy cannot be lost, created, or destroyed. Which is simply to say that the working assumption of the best minds up to the time of the turn of the century, that the universe was running down, is no longer tenable.

This fact, that energy is not lost, has not yet found its way into our books on economics. In them we still find the word "spending"—a word referring to that now outdated thinking before man knew that there was a speed of light.

What, then, do we know about our wealth—about what we can "afford?" I think it is very important to ask this because you are quite a large audience. I've tried what I'm going to do with you now with several large audiences, the first time with fourteen hundred people at Stanford University, and later with fifteen hundred people at the Congress of American Planners, in Washington, D.C. According to a count I was given earlier, there are more than a thousand of you here tonight. Now I am going to propose several things to you and, if any one disagrees with me, please put up your hand. I'm going to say to you, first, that no matter what you think wealth is, would you agree with me that no matter how much you have of it, you can't alter one iota of yesterday? No hands. Did you all hear it right? There are still no hands, and I assume everyone agrees that no matter how much wealth you have, no matter what you think wealth is, you can't change yesterday in any way. So we don't have to give any thought to yesterday as we try to think about what wealth is. Whatever wealth may be, it has to do with our now and our tomorrows but not our yesterdays. Consider now a man who has plenty of all the items we now say certify great wealth. This man has all his checkbooks, and all his stock certificates, and all his bonds, and all his deeds with him. He has a big stack of gold bars and a number of bags of diamonds with him. He's a certified billionaire—a billionaire on board a ship in the middle of the ocean. Suddenly the ship catches fire and all the life boats are burned and there this man is. If he hangs on to his gold he'll just sink a little faster than the others. They may be poorer in gold, but his kind of wealth isn't very powerful. If he could have gotten to the shore, he might have had some tomorrows, but he didn't have any way of doing that.

I would say, then, that what we probably mean by "wealth," really, has something to do with how many forward days we have arranged for our environment to take care of us and regenerate us in life and give us increased degrees of freedom.

Now, regeneration of life is produced first with energy, which we have in two fundamental conditions: energy associative as radiation that can be focused on the ends of levers etc.; and energy as radiation that can be converted into energy as mass or matter, and vice versa. Now we find that the energy part of the universe is conserved—that it cannot be created or destroyed—and we use the energy as matter for levers and energy as radiation to impinge on the ends of levers. This is really the fundamental great general scheme. Energy is conserved and there's plenty of it. Every time we rearrange our environment, we can get more energy and more levers to do more work to take care of the regeneration of more and more of our forward days. These energies are there, and they cannot be spent.

The other element of wealth to be defined is by far the more important. It is our intellectual capacity to recognize generalized principles that seem to be operative in the universe and to employ these principles. This is man's metaphysical capability, which we use to make an experiment to find out how the lever works and to discover generalized principles. There are a number of very important irreversibles to be discovered in our universe. One of them is that *every* time you make an experiment you learn more; quite literally, *you can not learn less*. That's a pretty interesting fact, isn't it, because it means that the metaphysical factor in wealth is one that is *always* gaining.

So we find the physical, or energy, component of wealth is being conserved and never will be lost, we find the metaphysical component to be gaining always—and wealth consists of these two. The weightless metaphysical and the physical—that's everything of the universe. I've left nothing out. That's all there is.

We find Einstein's mind taking the measure of the physical, writing those beautiful, economical equations such as $E = MC^2$. Saying that the physical universe is energy and you have to have one differentiation of energy on one side and another on the other side of the equation in order to understand it. And one is energy as associative matter, and the other is energy as disassociative radiation.

And the rate of the radiation is to the second power or the rate of growth of a wave of 186,000 miles a second, to the second power. This tells us how much energy there was in that mass.

Here we have, then, intellect taking the measure of energy. We have nothing in our experience to suggest that this is reversible. Nothing suggests that energy will ever write the equation of intellect. I simply say to you that we have the metaphysical apprehending, comprehending, and ordering the physical. The physical tending to be disorderly and the metaphysical apprehending, comprehending, and putting together. Man, therefore, represents the very clearly demonstrated function in the universe that is essential to the regeneration of universe. Also we discover that the universe is a perpetual motion machine because its energy is never lost. So the minimum number of transformations is universe. It is the minimum and only perpetual motion machine, and perpetual conservation requires this metaphysical functioning of order and collection inherent to man.

It became perfectly clear to me long ago that in our land economics, we could make fantastic strides; and that realization brought me into trying geodesic domes. I now have five thousand of them in fifty countries. Thousands of these domes are light enough, strong enough, sufficient enough to be delivered by air. They weigh only about three percent of the weight of a traditional building of equal span. They are also proof against earthquake and relatively fireproof (for a given amount of time, code determined). They bear up under arctic snowloads and hurricanes. They are doing these things at only three percent of the weight of the best known alternate conventional solutions for buildings. So I discovered there was fantastic room for improvement to be made for the living arts on dry land. My investigations made perfectly clear what upping performance per pound of employed resources can mean in economics. Incidentally, during the time between 1900 and today, in two-thirds of a century we have gone from less than 1 percent to more than 40 percent of humanity living at a high standard. In the same period the amount of resources per man has been continually decreasing, so we obviously did not accomplish that high standard of living as a result of our having more resources to exploit. It came only as fallout of the doing-more-with-less design philosophy.

The big message here is that Malthus was wrong. If man's resources are properly managed, if his technology is applied in the direction of conscience, there can be enough for everybody. "Bare maximums," as Fuller puts it, of energy, food, shelter, medical care, education. In a world where scarcity has been sanctioned and abundance abused, a new day is dawning. There is no longer any excuse for scarcity. No longer any excuse for the fear, want and ignorance which have persisted in man's competition for what there was not enough of. The new day, in Fuller's vision of the global village, is one of cooperative enterprise by which mankind will break down the barriers dividing them in order to build the Earth.

Students can *learn* the following: that technical evolution has this fundamental behavior pattern. First, as I have explained to you, there is a scientific discovery of a generalized principle, which occurs as a subjective realization by experimentally probing man. Next comes objective employment of that principle in a special-case invention. Next, the invention is reduced to practice. This gives man an increased technical advantage over his physical environment. If successful as a tool of society, it is used in ever bigger, swifter, and everyday ways. For instance, it goes progressively from a little steel steamship to ever bigger fleets of constantly swifter, high-powered ocean giants.

There comes a time, however, when we discover other ways of doing the same task more economically. For instance, we discover that a 200-ton transoceanic jet airplane, considered on an annual round-trip frequency basis, can outperform the passenger-carrying capability of the 85,000 ton *Queen Elizabeth* or that a quarter-ton transoceanic communications relay satellite outperforms 150,000 tons of transoceanic cables. All the technical curves rise in tonnage and volumetric size to reach a giant peak, after which progressive minaturization sets in. After that, a new and more economical art takes over which also goes through the same cycle of doing progressively more with less. First, by getting bigger and taking advantage, for instance, of the fact that doubling the length of a ship increases its wetted surface fourfold while increasing its payload volume eightfold. Inasmuch as the cost of driving progressively bigger ships through the water at a given speed increases in direct proportion to the increase in friction of the wetted surface, the eightfolding of payload volume gained with each fourfolding of wetted surface means twice as much profit for less effort each time the ship's length is doubled. This principle of advantage gain through geometrical-size increase holds true for ships of both air and water. Then doubling of length of sea-going ships finally runs into trouble; for instance, the ocean liner made more than a thousand feet long would have to span between two giant waves and would have to be doubled in size to do so. However, if doubled in size once more, she could no longer be accomodated by the great world canals, dry docks, and harbors.

At this point the miniaturization of doing more with less first ensues through substitution of an entirely new art. David's slingstone over Goliath's club operated from beyond reach of the giant. This overall and inexorable trending to do more with less is known sum totally as progressive ephemeralization. Ephemeralization trends toward an ultimate doing of everything with nothing at all—which is a trend of the omniweighable physical to be mastered by the omniweightless metaphysics of intellect.

As we study industrialization, we see that we cannot have mass production unless we have mass consumption. This was effected evolutionarily by the great social struggles of labor to increase wages and spread the benefits and prevent the reduction of the numbers of workers employed. The labor movement made possible mass purchasing; ergo, mass production; ergo, low prices on vastly improved products and services, which have altogether established entirely new and higher standards of humanity's living.

Our labor world and all salaried workers, including school teachers and college professors, are now at least subconsciously if not consciously, afraid that automation will take away their jobs. They are afraid they won't be able to do what is called "earning a living," which is short for earning the right to live. This term implies that normally we are supposed to die prematurely and that it is abnormal to be able to earn a living. It is paradoxical that only the abnormal and exceptional are entitled to prosper. Yesterday the term even inferred that success was so very abnormal that only divinely ordained kings and nobles were entitled to eat fairly regularly.

It is easy to demonstrate to those who will take the time and the trouble to unbias their thoughts that automation swiftly can multiply the physical energy part of wealth much more rapidly and profusely than one man's muscle and brain-reflexed, manually-controlled production. On the other hand humans alone can foresee, integrate, and anticipate the new tasks to be done by progressively automated wealth-producing machinery. To take advantage of the fabulous magnitudes of real wealth waiting to be employed intelligently by humans and unblock automation's postponement by organized labor we must give each human who is or becomes unemployed a life fellowship in research and development or in just simple thinking. Man must be able to dare to think truthfully and to act accordingly without fear of losing his franchise to live. The use of mind fellowships will permit humans comprehensively to expand and accelerate scientific exploration and experimental prototype development. For every 100,000 employed in research and development, or just plain thinking, one probably will make a breakthrough that will more than pay for the other 99,999 fellowships. Thus, production will no longer be impeded by humans trying to do what machines can do better. Contrariwise, omni-automated and inanimately powered production will unleash humanity's unique capability—its metaphysical capability. Historically speaking, these steps will be taken within the next decade. There is no doubt about it. But not without much social crisis and consequent educational experience and discovery concerning the nature of our unlimited wealth.

The social implications of Fuller's discoveries take on tremendous importance, for the gap between science and society has been one of the most grievous aspects of 20th century life. Science is held responsible for wars, pollution—even our crisis of the spirit. Cities are said to be dying because billions are spent on killing people instead of improving their environment.

Technicians are condemned for moral neutrality as they piece together the engines of war and pollution, rarely measuring the social impact of the projects they are part of.

Reading all the articles announcing Armageddon, you would think we are approaching Samuel Butler's Erewhon, *that "idyllic" society which, hating machines, put them all in museums and went back to farming. But technology is not the outlaw. Mankind must assess and act on the trends which lead to crisis—preventing, not just managing, the results of what Fuller calls our "cosmic nearsightedness." He insists that Universe is the ultimate technology, that man must discern and employ its principles, that our acquisitive society, confusing expediency with progress, is the* real *outlaw.*

Certainly, technology has been much abused. And much maligned. But it has also been the basis of man's increased economic success. A century ago, over one quarter of all farm land was given over to raising feed for plow horses. Technology replaced the plow horse and, since then, more and more people are eating. The so-called Green Revolution did not sprout from somebody's thumb. It too is a product of technology. As a result, even such underdeveloped countries in India are becoming self-sufficient in the staple grains.

Such "bumper crops" are dividends of doing more with less. When copper is scrapped, it is recycled at a higher level of efficiency. The first telephone wires carried one message; later on, thousands. Now microwave replays arc information from point to point in seconds. Computers and satellites are becoming more compact even as work loads increase. Technology is trending toward the miniature, and Fuller is quite convinced that as it reaches its true fulfillment, it will completely disappear. Automation would free us to think, trout fish, or travel. Spare time would be productively used. Abundance would assure altruism. The meek wouldn't have to worry about inheriting the earth. Everyone would be eating.

Mankind is imperiled as never before, not by inadequate resources but by inadequate attitudes. Common world problems have generated the need for a world language which will transcend the biases and fears of yesterday. A language, not of words, but of approach. In the exploration of space, in the stewardship of the oceans, in the distribution of food, in the exchange of information, nations must converge in a common effort. There can be no other way in a world where technology has stretched the spectrum of human experience, where technology has taken the telephone poles and village back fences into the sky and launched mankind into a new era of mobility and freedom.

The increased awareness of these social synergies is one of the most exciting and reassuring aspects of life in our times. Despite political inertia, despite still-prevalent ignorance, want and fear, there is a healthy option for man in the coordinated management of his resources.

We've all been working under the assumption that man is destined to be a failure. I say man is quite clearly like the hydrogen atom: designed to be a success. He is a fantastic piece of design; it is completely wrong to think he is meant to be a failure. I assume he is supposed to use his mind to make himself a success; and to understand things like wealth, as I gave it to you a few minutes ago—to understand those generalized principles and to realize that when you employ them you aren't "spending" anything of the universe. You are simply employing what the universe is—turning the universe to your account. And that is what you are meant to do in order to demonstrate man's success.

*Two years ago, Fuller returned to the same Chicago slum where he had
cloistered himself in 1927. The "Young Lords," a militant gang of Puerto
Ricans, had invited him to speak about the problems of renewing their
deteriorated neighborhood. Typically, however, he soon had them thinking
about renewing themselves. Something he had gone through a good deal of pain
to do years before.*

*"Society is full of this horrible thing, fear," he told them. "And when society
is fearful, it gets panicky and does stupid things. So don't do things just to defy
or make people fearful. Do things to give them confidence. Don't do things
which invite opposition. Do things which invite support. Try to think clearly,
and you will find answers for your problems. Very shortly, society will be in
enough trouble to want them."*

FURTHER THOUGHTS

1. Fuller says that the notion of "spending" found in our economics books is
   wrong. Look at what de Grazia says on page 313 about spending time. What
   other words do we have to label what we do with money or time, rather than
   spending?
2. What do you think of Fuller's description of wealth as having "something to
   do with how many forward days we have arranged for our environment to
   take care of us and regenerate us in life and give us increased degrees of
   freedom"? Check carefully the meanings and etymology of *regenerate*. Then
   do the same for *energy, synergy* (or *synergism*), and *cooperation*. How do
   these words seem to be related?
3. Fuller's language tends to be a bit difficult at times, especially when he is
   talking about the creativity of the human mind at work—for instance, "we have
   the metaphysical apprehending, comprehending, and ordering the physical.
   The physical tending to be disorderly and the metaphysical apprehending,
   comprehending, and putting together." You might find it useful here to
   notice the larger outlines of his statement: First, he opposes the physical and
   the metaphysical; the first leading to disorder, the second to order:

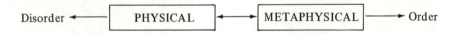

Disorder ◄——— PHYSICAL ◄——► METAPHYSICAL ———► Order

Second, there is the suggestion that the metaphysical orders things in three
ways: by apprehending, by comprehending, and by putting together. How can
these three processes be fitted into the diagram? What would be the parallel
process for the physical side in the opposition?

4. One of the main points in Fuller's "economics" (you might check the etymology of *economics* while you're at it) is the idea of "doing more with less." What examples of this can you find in our country today? How does this idea compare with, say, Thoreau's idea of getting by with less?

5. Do you agree with Fuller's optimism?

Photo Credits

Title page photo by Bill Finch

page   2 Mark Silber

page 25 Bill Binzen

page 55 Magnum Photos, Danny Lyon

page 84 Ken Kobré

page 93 Magnum Photos, Paul Fusco

page 125 EPA Documerica, Bill Gillette

page 181 Frank Siteman

page 198 top, **MANPOWER** Magazine, U.S. Dept. of Labor

page 198 bottom, Elizabeth Hamlin

page 199 top, right and left, **MANPOWER** Magazine, U.S. Dept. of Labor

page 199 bottom, Editorial Photocolor Archives, Inc., Andrew Sacks

page 245 Stock, Boston/Donald Wright Patterson, Jr.

page 266 Hope Finney

page 272 Bill Binzen

page 286 Frank Siteman

page 289 Lee Friedlander

page 308 George Knight, San Francisco

page 339 Stock, Boston/Harry Wilks